FATEFUL TIES

FATEFUL TIES

A HISTORY OF AMERICA'S
PREOCCUPATION WITH CHINA

Gordon H. Chang

HARVARD UNIVERSITY PRESS

Cambridge, Massachusetts, and London, England

2015

Cataloging-in-Publication Data available from the Library of Congress

ISBN: 978-0-674-05039-6

For Vicki, Chloe, and Maya

Contents

Note on Romanization   *ix*

Introduction   *1*

1 Ties of Opportunity   *9*

2 Physical and Spiritual Connections   *49*

3 Grand Politics and High Culture   *90*

4 Revolutions and War   *130*

5 Allies and Enemies   *168*

6 Transformations   *203*

7 Old/New Visions   *237*

Afterword   *263*

Notes   *269*

Acknowledgments   *305*

Index   *307*

Note on Romanization

Chinese proper names and terms will usually be rendered using the Pinyin romanization system and will be followed by the name or term rendered in Wade-Giles or another system when such renderings are more familiar to present-day Americans. Thus, the last dynasty in China was known as the Qing (Ch'ing). The leader of the Republic of China in the 1940s was Jiang Jieshi (Chiang Kaishek). Chinese terms rendered in Pinyin that are not commonly known in the United States today will be rendered in italics followed by a translation or a more familiar transliteration in English. Thus, for example, *gonghang* will be followed by (cohong). In some instances, Chinese names that are very familiar today, such as Sun Yatsen, will be used instead of the Pinyin rendering.

FATEFUL TIES

Introduction

China has long been one of the richest, that is, one of the most fertile, best cultivated, most industrious, and most populous countries in the world

Adam Smith, 1776

There was China before there was an America, and it is because of China that America came to be.[1] Even before it was found, America was joined at the hip with China, as paradoxical as that may sound. The European discovery of America was one of history's most profound unintended consequences, a colossal mistake arising from Columbus's underestimation of the circumference of the globe in his search for a new water route to China that would enable European merchants to avoid traveling through the Muslim world. Columbus thought the world was smaller than it actually is. He never succeeded in delivering the letter of introduction that he carried from his Spanish sovereigns for the "Great Khan," the presumed ruler of China, and went to his grave convinced that his several voyages to what became known as the New World had actually taken him to Asia. On his first voyage of discovery, Columbus carried a Latin translation of Marco Polo's *Travels* and used its description of people and places to support his conviction that he had charted a western route from Europe to Asia. His was a grand misreading of a text. What Columbus did discover, though, was a whole new world for other Europeans. As an American Presbyterian minister and returned missionary from China reminded Americans 400 years later, "We people of America may be said, in some sense, to owe to China the discovery of our continent."[2]

The lure of Asia, China in particular, had drawn Europeans from the most ancient times. Columbus, from reading the accounts of Marco Polo and other European accounts of Asia, believed he would find temples with roofs of gold, citizenry draped in the richest of silks, and inestimable opportunities for commerce. In his copy of Marco Polo's book, Columbus penned *"mercacciones innumeras"* (incalculable amount of trade) next to a reference to Peking. His simple notation expresses the enormity of his dream. Columbus's patrons also hoped that direct contact with Asia might provide a strategic advantage in Christendom's war with Islam. One hundred and fifty years after Columbus's voyages, the English were still seeking western routes to the riches of the East. Their quest led them to found their first settlements in the territory that would become the United States of America. Roanoke and then the colony of Jamestown, which was founded in 1607, were business ventures of English financiers who hoped the colonists would find gold or a water route through North America to the Pacific and win them the coveted advantage of a new route to the Far East, as they called it.[3]

The Virginia Company's first instruction to the colonists was that they should look for a water route to the "Other Sea." James Smith, the leader of Jamestown, was convinced that such a route existed, and he shared his assumption with the English explorer Henry Hudson, who sought a northwest passage through the continent. In the course of his efforts, Hudson encountered what became known as Manhattan Island, the great river and bay that bear his name, and other points north all the way to the Arctic. Europeans and Americans, inspired by the riches of Asia, continued to search for that elusive passage. Though a northwest route was never found, Westerners never abandoned their dreams of the East with its presumed importance to their national wealth and greatness. China, indeed, possessed the most productive economy in the world from roughly the sixth to the nineteenth centuries. It is estimated that in 1800, China alone accounted for a third of the total economic production of the world, with all of Europe, including Russia, counting for perhaps 28 percent. There was very good reason for China to be the object of quest and desire.[4]

At the same time, China was considered to be the farthest away from Europe not just in distance but also in culture. It was the epitome of the mysterious, unfathomable East. China came to be seen as the antipode to Europe and all that Europe believed it embodied: rationality, reason, modernity, progress. China became the "eastern extremity," as it was said, of the East. It was the site of both fantastic material opportunities and perplexing and dangerous ways. Its way of life, language, spiritual beliefs, philosophies, arts, and political order were not just different but monumentally alien. Europeans, of course, encountered many peoples who were very different than themselves, but the Chinese seemed to pose a complex, almost incomprehensible, alternative to the West that defied mastery, either intellectually or geopolitically.[5]

Americans inherited this "China mystique" from Europe, but China became more than a beguiling destination or an immense trading entrepôt, as it had for Europeans. In the minds of many leading Americans, it became essential for America's fate. The idea of "China" became an ingredient within the developing identity of America itself, and America's national destiny, which preoccupied (and continues to preoccupy) Americans, became ineffably linked to that of China in the great national enterprises and the expansive ventures of the eighteenth and nineteenth centuries. The Far East was the reason to reach the far west: the search for a northwest passage, the Lewis and Clark expedition, the coveting of the Oregon territory, the waging of the Mexican-American War, the construction of the transcontinental railroad, the purchase of Alaska, the conquest of an insular empire in the Pacific, the Panama Canal, among other imperial projects and ambitions, were all inspired in various degrees by the lure of China and Asia.[6]

In the twentieth century, China, in this way of thinking, remained pivotal to national well-being and security, a conviction that helped lead America into violent conflict in the Philippines, in the Pacific, in Southeast Asia, and on the East Asia mainland in the late nineteenth and twentieth centuries. Sometimes made explicit and at other times simply assumed, the imagined future of America came to be inseparable from that distant land across the Pacific, on the other side of the globe. America's unique *destiny,* the proposition that America possessed a singular fate, an exalted condition it was to realize and a grandeur it was to assume, could not be realized without the proper China connection. As John K. Fairbank, the great dean of Chinese studies in the United States, once observed, many Americans came to see lucrative trade with China in the nineteenth century as "our manifest destiny under the invisible hand of divine providence."[7]

The word destiny, or fate, suggests many things and has been used in different ways. For the early Puritans, destiny, or, more precisely, "predestination," expressed God's omnipotence and purpose. The notion meant inevitability, a future that human action could not alter. More commonly in American history, however, the idea of destiny was used paradoxically to *inspire* human action. America, it was said, had a providentially ordained mission, but Americans also had to work to realize that glorious national future. "Manifest destiny," the term first coined in 1845, called on Americans to rally behind the flag against Mexico, seize Texas, and expand the nation across the entire continent. "Destiny" was the reason to decide to go to war. The idea of America's national destiny also was sometimes conjured after the fact to justify an action that had already been done: the colonization of the Philippines, it was argued, had been necessary to advance American power over the Pacific and gain closer access to China. President William McKinley maintained that his order to take the islands was done according to God's will for America's destiny. Whether it was used to inspire or to rationalize, destiny pointed to a future where a greatness and promise would be fulfilled if only contemporary Americans accurately discerned what were claimed to be inexorable historical currents and acted accordingly. The notion of destiny, in other words, usually referred to history in order to call on the present to reach a grand future. The notion seemed to point to what was to come, but its purpose was to legitimate an ambition or justify a fait accompli. Destiny, as paradoxical as it sounds, had to be pursued.[8]

In the seventeenth, eighteenth, and nineteenth centuries, social and political leaders often conjured America's destiny, but in the twentieth century and beyond, the word dropped out of fashion, seemingly out of step with a secular, willful world. But the notion that life is somehow determined by a greater force than ourselves is still very much with us: we speak of a romance that is "meant to be" or someone's demise as "a time that had come." Campaigning politicians stir the blood of audiences by expounding about how their agenda coheres with God's exalted purposes for the nation. Here in this book the focus is on destinarian attitudes and how Americans have perceived China as a critical element in their fate and thus in their history over the centuries, from the country's earliest moments to today. The concept of destiny and the presumed importance of America and China to each other's pasts and futures run as central elements in the long and complex historical relationship between the two countries and, indeed, in America's own conception of its very identity as a promised nation in the world.

One person's vision of destiny can certainly be another's prescription of folly. Americans understood their fateful ties with China in many different ways and with different implications. Although few Americans were ever well informed about China, that did not stop them from having strong opinions and feelings about the country and its people. China and the proper relationship America should have with it eluded clear and unanimously accepted definition.

China long loomed larger in the American mind than material circumstances alone would have seemed to warrant. The meaning of China for America was grander than the bottom line in ledger books, in geopolitical calculations, or security, as important as these were at various times in the story. For Americans, China until quite recently was, according to Fairbank, a matter of "mind and spirit more than of the pocketbook." Mentalities— that is, images and perceptions that Americans hold in their minds—have occupied a remarkably important place in relations between America and China. It is clear that Americans and Chinese have often had powerful assumptions and feelings about each another that have affected their behaviors. Much in the history of the relationship between the two countries has been attributed to misperception and misunderstanding.[9]

So much about the history of U.S.-China relations has been about the intangible, feelings, and will, as well as the promise or potential of the relationship instead of the tangible present. Histories that focus on material interests alone in international relations are often stumped, as they alone don't seem to explain much in the tangled history between the two countries. Not until quite recently did the two countries have extensive and weighty economic relations, and China did not have the military might that would make it a major security concern for the United States. Nonetheless, many Americans through the centuries thought otherwise. China loomed large in their thinking, out of proportion with any actual role it could play or gain it could secure. China was more a matter of an imagined future, of what it could become and what it might mean for America. China has long occupied a place in the American mind similar to the place it occupied in Napoleon Bonaparte's, who said in 1807, "Let China sleep, for when it wakes, it will shake the world." China was perceived as a powerhouse that was unaware of its own potential for the moment but not likely to remain so. China's future would certainly bring incalculable change, it was assumed.

In a contrary way, other Americans, especially in the late nineteenth through the mid-twentieth centuries, believed that China's destiny lay very much in the hands of America. It was America's fate, many believed, to be China's friend, protector, benefactor, and savior. This self-flattering myth, so fondly held by many Americans, inspired periodic warm expressions of friendship such as the statement uttered by Secretary of State Dean Acheson in the spring of 1950, just before the outbreak of the Korean War: "The American people will remain in the future, as we have been in the past, the friends of the Chinese people." Within a few months, Chinese and Americans were fighting each other in the rugged hills of Korea. The belief that China's fate was in America's hands also inspired the famous outcry of "Who lost China?" that helped ignite the witch-hunting expedition known as McCarthyism after the Communist triumph on the mainland. China had been in America's hands, so who or what was responsible for robbing America of its China connection?[10]

Seeking to understand patterns in American sentiments toward China leads one to consider ways of thinking, values and attitudes, and cultural assumptions rather than the particulars of diplomacy and the politics of policy. A long view of the relationship over four centuries affords perspectives that can be missed in a preoccupation with short-term decision making, be it business calculation or diplomacy rooted in the myopia and self-centeredness of the present. Reflecting on our historical experience might help us see continuities and contrasts with the past and provide ways to help us navigate the challenges of our rapidly developing relationship with China today. We might be able to see what is genuinely new in the relationship and which elements from the past are unnecessary today.

The focus of this book is on those Americans whose creative imaginations considered what China meant or, more precisely, might mean for the United States. Most Americans who thought about China's past or present really had their attention fixed on what was to be, on what China could be, might be, for America's future. Unlike formal documents and diplomatic archives, the creative imaginings of China by entrepreneurs, political commentators, missionaries, academics, artists, and political activists (right and left) reveal far more of the rich texture and mental underpinnings of relations. They tell us the different ways Americans understood their future as being inextricably tied to China and help explain why Americans have long had a special place for China in their global visions. These are issues that have absorbed Americans in the past, as they continue to do in the present. The views ranged widely and were often contradictory, but important patterns emerge from taking a long-term view of the conversation about the meaning of China to America.

Today Americans are fixated on China more than ever. They assume that the future of their nation lies in the evolving relationship with China. The fates of the two have become so intertwined in popular thinking that the historian Niall Ferguson coined the term Chimerica to describe a future mega-entity where the two countries are fully and mutually interdependent. Ferguson even has China preceding America in the neologism. Chimerica recalls the chimera, the dreaded mythical beast within which two or more different animals reside in an uncomfortable but symbiotic relationship. Another China-watcher has called on China's leaders to forge a "United States of China" and emulate American federalism, thus making the political structures of the two countries mirror images of each other.

Reportage on China fills our daily papers, detailing China's growing influence over the world of golf, the consumption of fine wine, and the performance of European classical music. Americans are interested in its burgeoning economy and the opportunities presented for business. *The Atlantic* declared that "if you plan on having a career in the 21st century" you had to study James Fallows's DVD on "doing business in China." Fallows, the respected periodical claims, is the "preeminent U.S. journalist in China."[11] Such boasts reflect genuine and widespread interest in the country. Americans wonder about the dramatic transformation of its once closed and rigid society and about the values, lifestyles, and aspirations of its peoples. At the same time, China's human rights record and politics dismay many, and security conflicts, even the threat of war, preoccupy some American observers. China simultaneously fascinates and repels; it intrigues and infuriates. Americans across the country from preschool to universities are studying the Chinese language, convinced that it is the global language of the future.

China has changed dramatically in recent years. Compared to the years under Mao Zedong or even Chiang Kaishek, China has undergone a social and economic revolution that appears to finally confirm Napoleon Bonaparte's prediction of 200 years ago. Indeed, China presents challenges to America and to the rest of the world that were once unimaginable. Yet if one takes a step back and examines American responses to the dramatic rise of China in recent years, one sees pronounced continuities and legacies from the past. The strong feelings many Americans have about China today are just the latest in a long and turbulent engagement of Chinese and Americans. Americans' curiosity about China and involvement in its life are, in fact, even older than the United States itself. From the earliest days of colonial America, China, with its promise, exoticism, and dangers, occupied a special place in American thinking and imagination. For more than 400 years, China has played an important and oftentimes central role in the lives of American businessmen, missionaries, educators, travelers, military leaders, and political figures.

When seen over the span of several centuries, it is evident that China and America developed a particularly unique relationship of a sort that neither of the two countries has constructed with any other nation. Through historical experience, America came to have a special place in Chinese foreign relations and China has come to have a special place in American foreign relations. America was a special land of hope, opportunity, friendship, and sometimes danger for many Chinese over the years. But though the Chinese have their notion of destiny or fate—*mingyun*—rarely did the Chinese link their own country's destiny with that of America. China occupied a different position for Americans. Many Americans in the past have seen China as an extraordinary place of ambitions, dreams, threat, and inspiration, as many do today.

Today Americans from all walks of life are concerned about China. They study, wonder, and speculate as to what might happen with that geographically distant yet closely proximate nation. This book speaks to those beyond China specialists to encourage reflection on the American past as the country navigates into an uncertain future with a country that is in the midst of unprecedented and monumental transformation. China has been a central ingredient in America's self-identity from its very beginning and in the American preoccupation with national fate. This cultural and intellectual study considers that long, troubled history.

Though Americans had nothing to do with the ancient Silk Road that linked the West with China, it does today. The Silk Road was the conduit along which a vast quantity of the world's wealth traveled from the second century BCE to about the fifteenth century. It fell into disuse six centuries ago with the rise of the maritime world. It inspired countless stories of the fabulous treasures of the East in Europe and then in America. Today, the American hi-tech giant Hewlett-Packard is helping revive the 7,000-mile trade route, as it ships hundreds of millions of dollars of its electronic products made in western China to markets in Europe. This Silk Road carrying goods made in China for an American company inspires new visions of wealth and the exotic. Is our twenty-first-century obsession with China something really new or are we just returning to the ancient norm?[12]

1

Ties of Opportunity

The Chinese are "the wisest of nations."

Benjamin Franklin, 1785

The twenty-first century, it is often heard today, will be China's century, a time when China will ascend to become the world's dominant nation in economic and, possibly, political influence. Whether that will come about remains to be seen, but it might be more correct, from a historical perspective, to say that China could *resume* the top position it once held in the world's economy, a position it had relinquished for 200 years. In the sweep of history, at least Chinese history, two centuries is the short term.

This perspective may help contemporary readers appreciate the place China occupied in the world at the time Europeans first came to America and the subsequent rise of the colonies to nationhood from the late fifteenth to the early nineteenth centuries. It provides a broad context within which to appreciate the importance of China to America in its formative years and beyond and challenges us to step back and consider the long view in America-China relations. Examining 300 years of these relations provides us with perspectives on trends and patterns beyond what we gain from focusing on the cacophony and overload of the here and now.

For the millennium before the early 1800s, China likely possessed the most productive economy in the world. From the 1500 to the 1800s, the period usually considered the to be the rise of the Atlantic world and the ascendancy of Europe over the rest of the world, the Chinese empire produced up to one-third of the world's annual domestic product, a far greater share than any Western nation. China per capita was not wealthy, but as a collective, China wielded immense productive power and remained the object of European desire for hundreds of years.[1]

At the start of the eighteenth century, few could have predicted the spectacular rise of Europe over the rest of the world during the next 150 years. From all appearances, it was China that would remain the great economic center of the world. It possessed an ancient, influential civilization; dominated the vast area of East Asia; and was poised to expand its imperial boundaries. During the eighteenth century, the Chinese empire would double its territory through the incorporation of lands we now call Mongolia, Xinjiang, and Tibet. Its population would almost treble in size, from an estimated 150 million in 1700 to an enormous 400 million in 1842, making it by far the most populous country in the world, a status it may never relinquish. The population increase was founded on a highly productive agricultural economy, remarkable domestic order, internal and external stability, and effective governance.[2]

The seat of power was the Imperial Palace in Beijing, the capital of the Qing (Ch'ing) dynasty, so named by the Manchus, a Tungusic semi-nomadic people who had conquered China in 1644. They all but assumed the existing system of government and Chinese cultural and social institutions that had developed over the centuries, even as they attempted to maintain their distinct ethnic identity in the grasslands north of China proper. The emperor, the Son of Heaven, ruled over the empire, having absolute though elaborately prescribed and delineated powers, duties, and responsibilities. He governed through a sophisticated, though relatively small, administrative bureaucracy that reached down through the provinces and then loosely into localities. Actual state power from the center was often more nominal than actual, especially over everyday life. Late imperial China was more a highly developed "cultural entity," or civilization-state than a well-organized bureaucratic structure, as we now think of the modern nation-state. A formalized body of classical literatures that Europeans called Confucianism comprised the moral and ideological foundations of official behavior and thinking. It was in many ways the actual glue that held together the empire, with its enormous population, ethnic diversity, and land reach.

The Manchus tried to maintain their distinctive language and social customs in their isolated Manchuria homeland. Though they became increasingly Sinicized over time, they never lost their separate identity, which became a source of tension with the majority Han people whom they had conquered. Under Manchu rule, China largely assumed its present borders.

The Qing expanded the boundaries of the empire into central Asia to incorporate Tibet, Turkestan, and Mongolia, in addition to Manchuria. Taiwan became part of the empire, and neighboring countries from Nepal to the Ryukyus became tributary states. The empire became vastly multi-ethnic and diverse in culture, religion, and ways of life. In the seventeenth and eighteenth centuries, Chinese culture and learning also reached grand heights under the Manchus, who vigorously cultivated Confucian scholarship and traditional Han painting and ceramics. The population almost trebled in size from the sixteenth century to the early nineteenth century, making China by far the most populous country on earth.

The United States at this time could hardly offer a greater contrast to China. In 1790, the first official census counted a population of less than 4 million people, a mere 1 percent of China's population. The newborn country was weak politically and poor economically, though it had great natural riches and the potential for expansion. The Euro-American population was spread out thinly along the eastern seaboard, with few venturing into the extensive lands beyond the Appalachians. The U.S. population was a social polyglot of Europeans and Africans (mostly slaves) and their descendants born in the New World. Native peoples continued to control broad stretches of the territory but were not considered part of the American family. American political identity was counted in single years, not millennia. Its central government was immature, experimental, and untested. Its military was barely able to meet its security needs or support the activities of its merchant vessels on the high seas. Trade is what made a few Americans wealthy, but the country produced very little that others wanted to purchase, other than some rough foodstuffs, furs, timber, and other raw materials. Yet the country's elite possessed an extraordinarily high level of confidence and energy. Their ambition far exceeded what their material circumstances should have justified, allowed, or predicted. But their hunger was great and their visions grand. They were poised to lead one of the most dramatic national transformations in modern times. The territorial, economic, and social growth of the United States in the first half of the nineteenth century would be astonishing. And it was the desire to engage the trade of the Pacific, especially that of China, that helped stimulate the voracious appetites and fill the burgeoning coffers of the New England elite.

China, in contrast to America, was fundamentally self-sufficient in food production, handicrafts, and luxury goods. Trade with others constituted a very small portion of the economy, which meant that aside from a few merchants in certain localities, imports or exports meant little for most Chinese, peasant and official alike. In China's long historical experience, the desire of outsiders for what China had to offer was always greater than what the Chinese hoped to receive from others. Trade and international commerce, which became central to the modern European and other imperial powers, was usually of negligible interest to the Chinese elite. If anything, foreign trade was usually considered a minor irritant to state authorities, one that required means to control bothersome outsiders. Traditionally, the Chinese court tightly regulated foreign intercourse, both commercial and social. At times, the court tried to ban trade altogether in order to minimize undesirable influences. The idea of extensive free trade between Chinese and others, conducted by relatively autonomous individuals or firms, was virtually unknown and certainly not considered a positive good. Under the Ming and early Qing, however, the combination of a virtual commercial revolution from below and the challenge from abroad would profoundly alter the landscape.

In contrast, Europeans, from the Venetians and Iberians to the Dutch, were keenly interested in trade, which for centuries was seen as the key to power and wealth. Europeans vigorously traded among themselves, throughout the Mediterranean and beyond to the "Orient." In 1511, the Portuguese, the first Europeans to arrive by sea, established an outpost in China for trade when they received a permanent lease of Macao in 1557 in exchange for their help in suppressing irksome pirates. The British took a more aggressive stance in trying to open China to Western commerce. Five English ships arrived in 1637, and more began to appear regularly in China's ports in the mid-seventeenth century. The British East India Company came to dominate trade with China for 100 years, during which time the Chinese court permitted trading ships to enter China's ports with little restriction. In 1757, however, Beijing reversed the policy after British activity, including unruly port behavior, angered the Chinese authorities. The court established what became known as the Canton system to regulate and limit seafaring trade along China's long coast. In that year, the court closed all Chinese ports to Western traders except for the one southern port at Guangzhou (Canton). For the next eighty years, until China's defeat in the First Anglo-Chinese War, known popularly as the Opium War, European traders and Westerners generally were confined to a single walled compound in Guangzhou. There, European traders were subject to strict, though at times only laxly enforced, Chinese controls. Trade could be conducted only during certain times of the year and foreigners were confined to a prescribed area of just several blocks from which they could not freely leave. Foreign women were completely forbidden to reside in the quarter. The traders were subject to Chinese taxes and could conduct business only with a small number of officially designated Chinese merchants, the *gonghang* (cohong), a court-designated monopoly. The Chinese recognized no political representation from European governments. The so-called hong merchants were responsible for handling the foreign traders and supervising the quarter where they resided.

This is the system Americans encountered as they began their own China trade. Though irritating to the acquisitive Westerners, who had long traded largely unencumbered among themselves elsewhere, the restrictions were tolerated because the profits of the China trade far outweighed the inconveniences and control. The Canton system aimed to regulate foreign commerce, but it was also a way of controlling foreigners, especially those who came by sea from across the great oceans. Westerners were hugely distant in linguistic, moral, cultural, and social ways from the Chinese and from the other peoples from Eurasia and East Asia, such as Persians, Arabs, Turkic peoples, and South and Southeast Asians, with whom the Chinese had interacted through the centuries. Chinese cultural and commercial interaction with others beyond their borders had often been extensive and mutually beneficial.

Formal political relations were a different matter, and by the eighteenth century, the Chinese court had developed a sophisticated and effective system for organizing interstate relations with its neighbors in Asia. The Chinese developed what we would now call an international system, or at least a regional system, a way of regularizing foreign relations with explicit and implicit rules, norms, procedures, expectations, and etiquette. Unlike the system that developed in Europe with many competing, small states of relatively equal power, China's overwhelmingly dominant economic, military, and territorial position in Asia grounded and defined the East Asia system. It was a system that explicitly accepted inequality in status, the supremacy of the Chinese emperor in all affairs, and the authority of the Confucian moral and philosophical world view as interpreted by the imperial court. This system functioned well, at least from the perspective of the Chinese court and the so-called tributary states, for hundreds of years. At its height, the system included some 100 tributaries. By the early nineteenth century, the main tributary states were Korea, the Ryukyus, Annam, Siam, and

Burma. By the end of the century, other powers would remove these states from the Chinese sphere and incorporate all of them into their own empires.

For Beijing, the traditional political order embodied the moral universe of civilization. Those outside this order were considered uncultured peoples who were lacking in propriety, morality, and proper knowledge. Europeans accepted the outsider status accorded them by the Chinese interstate system when they visited. Seventeen European missions traveled to Beijing from 1655 to 1795, and all but the last, under Lord Macartney in 1795, performed the required kowtow (*koutou*) before the emperor, a ritual prostration of emissaries that acknowledged his supremacy. Macartney considered it a humiliation of his sovereign and refused to do it. He agreed only to lower himself to one knee, as he said he could do as a sign of respect to his own king. Fifty years later the British invaded China and humiliated the Chinese in the first Opium War, fought to open the door to British opium and goods.[3]

Before the American Revolution, fewer than a dozen Anglo-Americans had been to China, and an undetermined number of Chinese, South Asians, and other deckhands lived in ports such as Philadelphia after sailing to and from Asia. The British had controlled the international China trade through the East India Company and prevented subject Americans from directly engaging in the very profitable business. London's restrictions became a major irritant in the colonial relationship, because China and its imported products had become an integral part of the everyday lives of many early Americans.[4] Their homes, both grand and modest, contained a wide array of Chinese crafts, silk, textiles, silverware, furniture, decorative wares, ceramics, and fine porcelains. Chinese craftsmen could produce items of elegance and rarity, signs of sumptuary wealth. Wealthy Americans would custom design wallpaper and dinnerware and Chinese artisans on the other side of the globe would embellish porcelain with the ordered family regalia or scenes of American homes and towns. George Washington, Thomas Jefferson, and other American gentry held Chinese wares in the highest esteem. The Chinese also could produce modest objects for the homes of the less privileged, such as everyday home decorations and eating utensils. China had developed the most sophisticated and productive system for export trade in the world. As much as a fifth of the contents of an early-nineteenth-century home in Salem, Boston, or Philadelphia came from China. The China trade was a major source of wealth for many of

America's leading import merchants, and they were not happy with London's enforced role of intermediary between its colonies and China.[5]

This was because London ensured that British homeland merchants and the Crown would principally benefit from the trade between America and Asia. London's control particularly hampered the efforts of merchants in the colonies. The 1651 Navigation Act and subsequent legislation prohibited direct trade between North America and Asia. The British East India Company, the only enterprise the Crown authorized to conduct trade with Asia, brought items from China to London, where they were offloaded and taxed. These goods, in turn, could then be redirected to the American colonies, but with prices substantially higher than if the goods had come directly from the original sources. The system ensured that the British Crown, concerned about the cost of maintaining its growing empire, directly benefited from all the trade between China and the colonies.

As this trade grew in importance and value, London's control became an increasingly serious irritant for the colonies. Restrictions on the conduct of American trade became closely associated with the problem of taxation and political representation in London. The Townshend Acts of 1767, especially those that affected the burgeoning trade in tea, especially aggravated already tense relations. Chinese tea had been an important commodity for English and Americans since the early eighteenth century, and by the 1760s colonists were consuming large quantities of the beverage, some 1.2 million pounds a year, or about three-quarters of a pound per capita. Most were black and green teas from southern China. India and others did not yet produce significant qualities of tea for export. Many of the most prominent and wealthiest colonial merchants included the lucrative China tea trade as part of their businesses.[6]

Americans consumed tea as a regular staple in their daily diet and the duties on tea imports became the single most important source of revenue from commodities for the Crown. To evade these burdensome levies, American colonists, among them the leading merchants of the day, trafficked with smugglers, who brought hundreds of thousands of pounds of tea to the Atlantic coast. With the Tea Act of 1773, London hoped frictions would decrease. It allowed the East India Company to import tea directly to the colonies, thereby reducing its price, eliminating the London middlemen, and undercutting the smugglers. However the tea was still taxed, though at a reduced rate, and only a handful of American merchants the company selected were permitted to market it. The act infuriated Americans, who linked the duties on tea and the restrictions on their commercial activities with the general principle of taxation and representation. Boycotts of the imported tea, threats against ships arriving with the tea, and then the incendiary Boston Tea Party of December 16, 1773, inflamed relations to a breaking point. To prevent thousands of pounds of tea from landing, a hundred or so men stormed three tea ships and dumped the China cargo into Boston Harbor. News of the action spread and inspired further anti-tea actions throughout the colonies, but the flagrant destruction of private property sent London over the edge. It retaliated by imposing draconian measures on Boston. The American colonies then rose in rage against London and its attack on their liberty. Americans boycotted tea and all imported goods from England. Tea became a symbol of the tyranny of the Crown and London's commercial monopoly. Masses of Americans joined the protest against London by publicly burning their tea stashes. Within a month, the American colonies were in open rebellion and the War of Independence had begun.[7]

Chinese tea and the China trade more generally were thus deeply implicated in the causes of the American Revolution and the formative events of defining American political identity. However, the China connection increased in importance after the winning of independence. Beyond the material dimensions of actual commerce, the China trade assumed symbolic importance. China, the freedom to trade, and political independence became intertwined. These associations surrounded the 1784 voyage of the *Empress of China,* the first American ship to sail directly to China, and in some accounts the first ship to fly the new American flag of stars and stripes and sail to a foreign port. This most significant voyage initiated the U.S.-China trade.

This direct trade between the United States and China began auspiciously. Coincidentally, the newly constructed 360-ton sailing vessel named the *Empress of China* set out from New York Harbor on George Washington's fifty-second birthday, February 22, 1784. Preparations for the voyage had actually begun almost a year earlier, when eager financiers, merchants, and ship owners, encouraged by American military successes against the British and a preliminary settlement granting independence to the colonies, started to raise capital, locate a suitable vessel to refit, and organize a crew. Wealthy Philadelphians were the main backers of the enterprise. The main investor was Robert Morris, the "financier of the American Revolution" and himself a former tea smuggler. Morris was also then the richest man in America and the superintendent of finance of the United States, the earliest version of the secretary of the treasury. Excited rumors about the ambitious plan had spread months before—the *Salem Gazette* reported in August 1783 that "many eminent merchants in different parts of the Continent are said to be interested in this first venture from the new world to the old." John Ledyard, the famous early American explorer and entrepreneur in the China fur trade, called it the "greatest commercial enterprise" that the young country had undertaken.[8]

Ice floes from a particularly cold winter blocked the ship from leaving New York Harbor for weeks, but a warming trend opened the channel and the ship finally set sail early in the morning. The *Edward*, another American ship that left New York Harbor the same morning, carried the newly ratified Treaty of Paris, which formally ended the hostilities with London and recognized American independence. That the *Edward* and the *Empress of China* sailed on the same day was unplanned, but their simultaneous departures had great symbolic importance. One ship represented the passing of dependence and war and made for Europe; the other symbolized independence and enterprise and headed for Asia, where many believed the future of the fledgling republic lay. Recognizing the importance of the venture for the new country, Congress gave the voyage its blessing and provided the captain of the *Empress* with an official letter of passage. Gathered multitudes along the way out of New York Harbor cheered the ship as it sailed past. At Fort George on Manhattan Island, the *Empress of China* boomed a thirteen-cannon salute, which was replied to in kind from the fort. The festivities signaled what all believed was a most propitious beginning.[9]

Philip Freneau, called the "poet of the American revolution," captured the unique interplay of the voyage's grand political symbolism and practical enterprise in verse. Freneau, who wrote prolifically and regularly commented on the political and social matters of the day in his poetry, composed a verse dedicated to the voyage of the *Empress of China* in which he captured the excitement and promise that attended the voyage. Freneau's poem inspired the imagination of his readers with imagery of the high seas and travel to a distant, largely unknown land. But his was not mainly a simple tale aimed at conjuring visions of adventure or good wishes for safe travels. It hailed the beginning of the opportunity for the new American nation to pursue its ambition to pursue the China trade unencumbered by London's restrictions. In Freneau's mind, political independence and the chance for national wealth in the China trade were indelibly linked. One of the last stanzas reads,

> From thence their fragrant TEAS to bring
> Without the leave of Britain's king;
> And PORCELAIN WARE, enchas'd in gold,
> The product of that finer mould.[10]

In 1797, Freneau published a series of his poems under the title *The Book of Odes,* honoring the *Shijing* of Confucius and the new U.S.-China connection.[11]

The *Empress of China,* with a crew of just thirty-four sailors, crossed the Atlantic and rounded the Cape of Good Hope and a long six months later arrived at Guangzhou. The ship carried 2,600 furs and some raw cotton and lead. But its main cargo was thirty tons of ginseng harvested in the mountains of the eastern seaboard, where it grew abundantly. It was the largest importation of ginseng into China ever. North American Indians, who used the root as a medicinal agent, had collected the herb for European merchants, who sent it to China during the early colonial days. The Chinese valued ginseng, especially the varieties that grew throughout northeast Asia, for male potency and vitalization. Now the acquisitive Americans hoped to capture the ginseng import market to pay for the Chinese exports they would bring back to the United States. They also knew they had precious little else that the Chinese would want in trade for their goods. Chinese consumers, however, found the American ginseng to be much inferior in potency to the varieties they found in northern China and Korea, and the American ginseng trade never amounted to a substantial American export. It was the fabulously lucrative fur and opium trade with China that would later realize American dreams of profits.[12]

The crew of the *Empress* were the first bona fide Americans to visit China. "The Chinese had never heard of us," wrote John White Swift, the purser of the *Empress,* "but we introduced ourselves as a new Nation, gave them our history, with a description of our Country, the importance and necessity of a trade here to the advantage of both, which they appear perfectly to understand and wish."[13] As required, Swift and the rest of the crew of the *Empress of China* stayed in the foreign quarters of the trading entrepôt of the Huangpu (Whampoa) anchorage, located twelve miles below Guangzhou, for four months. The ship returned to America loaded with expensive teas, cloth, silk, and porcelains. The ship also returned with Samuel Shaw, the lead business agent on board and his travel journal, one of the earliest American accounts of China. Shaw kept detailed records of the journey, including his observations of Chinese life, business ways, personalities, and society generally. Much piqued his curiosity, and his descriptions of Chinese food, customs, etiquette, and daily life are colorful and engaging. But they also were devoid of the kind of romanticism other travelers to the East had previously offered and would continue to be presented to American readers through the coming years. He explicitly wanted to avoid the sort of tales that he said were spread by missionaries, accounts that bordered on the "marvelous," he claimed, and enveloped the country in much "mystery." His account is also devoid of information about life outside the walled compound where the Americans and Europeans were required to stay. Shaw, who later became the first American consul in Guangzhou, also wrote about matters that perplexed, even disgusted, him, such as the despotism of the throne and his inability to have direct contact with the people. These negatives grew larger in American minds in the coming decades, even as commercial interests continued to attract Americans to China. But other aspects of China primarily impressed Shaw: he found the Chinese merchants with whom he dealt to be scrupulous in detail and honest in manner. He praised their ethics. They were good businessmen. Though he dismissed petty traders as knaves and "rogues," the designated cohong merchants were "intelligent, exact accountants, punctual to their engagements, and, though not the worse for being looked after, value themselves much upon maintaining a fair character The concurrent testimony of all the Europeans justifies this remark." Overall, China fascinated him, and he concluded the account of his journey on a note confessing ignorance as well as respect, "All we know with certainty respecting the empire of China," Shaw wrote, "is that it has long existed[,] a striking evidence of the wisdom of its government, and still continues the admiration of the world."[14]

The voyage of the *Empress of China* brought Robert Morris and the other investors a handsome profit of 25 percent, though it was far less than the 600 percent they had hoped for. News of the success of the voyage spread widely, and excited Americans concluded that the China trade would be of unprecedented economic importance for the new nation. Indeed, a booming China trade did become one of the mainstays of the early American economy. Within a year of the ship's return, five other American vessels sailed for Guangzhou, and by 1789 there were fifteen American vessels traveling back and forth to China. By the mid-1790s, seventy ships were engaged in the trade, comprising the second-largest contingent of Western traders in Chinese waters. Only the English had more. By the turn of the nineteenth century, American trade with Asia surpassed that of all other Western nations except Great Britain. Between 1784 and 1814, some 618 American vessels reached Guangzhou or Macao. The profit for the Americans has been described as "immense"; 300 to 400 percent returns on investments were commonplace. Imports from China expanded beyond tea to include finished products for the home, decorative items, furniture, foodstuffs, various forms of cloth, and luxury items. The port cities of New York, Philadelphia, Baltimore, Boston, and Salem thrived with the so-called Canton trade. American vessels left East Coast ports, rounded Cape Horn, stopped along the western coast of South America, ventured up the eastern Pacific Rim, and then sailed across the Pacific, to Hawaii, the South Seas, the Philippines, and then China. Other ships took the Atlantic route along the coast of Africa, around the Cape of Good Hope, and then into the Indian Ocean and the East Indies, to China. In the early 1800s, American companies began stationing their representatives in Guangzhou on a long-term basis.[15]

The voyage of the *Empress of China* initiated what is known as the Old China Trade, to distinguish the period of 1784 to the mid-nineteenth century from subsequent crests in the economic relationship between America and China. This period captured the American imagination and has been romanticized by Americans ever since, not without good reason. The Old China Trade is associated with the rise of the great New England and mid-Atlantic port cities, with the glory days of the Yankee clipper ships, the appearance of the first great American fortunes and blueblood families (Forbes, Astor, Cushing, Whitney, Cabot, Lowell, Russell, Peabody, Girard, and others), and the irrepressible urge of Americans to go west to the Pacific. The vast profits associated with the China trade and the Atlantic slave trade were the principal stimuli to American commercial expansion and even the beginnings of American capital accumulation and industry. The legendary Lowell, Massachusetts, textile mills, celebrated as the start of America's factory system, were financed and managed to a large degree by investors who had been enriched by the China trade.[16]

In the late 1780s, luxuriant sea otter pelts from American waters became one of the most important American exports to China. American traders exploited the bountiful numbers of animals along the northwestern Pacific Coast to supply the Chinese market and became middlemen between Indian trappers and the Chinese, who valued the fur for winter coats. Sea otter fur is exceptionally dense, dark, and lustrous, and it became the most expensive pelt on the world market. Although the trade was once dominated by Russian traders, Americans became increasingly active, and from 1790 to 1818, more than 100 American vessels visited the waters of the northwest to collect otter pelts. The China market made huge profits for the merchants, especially John Jacob Astor, who became the richest man in America and its first multimillionaire. Astor gave his name to the first American settlement on the Pacific Coast when Astoria was established in 1811 at the mouth of the mighty Columbia River. Thomas Jefferson personally supported Astor's efforts, believing that a formal American presence was an important strategic claim to the Pacific Northwest and a boost to the China trade. Jefferson was one of the earliest prominent Americans to make the connection between continental expansion and the coveted trade in the Pacific. Astor's fur trade proved immensely profitable and helped provide him the capital to engage in his later New York real estate investments, for which he is best known. The slaughter of the sea otter, however, almost caused its extinction and made the trade short lived. By the 1830s it had ended almost entirely.[17]

The heart of the Old China Trade remained the importation of tea. From the vantage point of the twenty-first century, some might dismiss the simple agricultural product as being of dubious importance. But in the early nineteenth century, tea was one of the world's most important commodities, spurring economies from southwest China to Western Europe, where it had become an everyday staple in diets, especially in Britain. The tea trade played a critical role in the accumulation of capital, the development of modern banking, shipbuilding, taxation (it accounted for 10 percent of Britain's revenues in 1784), and the trade of other products including sugar (for taste) and later opium (to help the British balance their trade deficit). In America, tea had also grown in importance as a consumer staple since the colonial days, playing a role akin to coffee in today's American diet. After the *Empress of China* brought back tea from its maiden voyage, tea imports rose steadily. Imports from Guangdong rose from 880,000 pounds in 1785 to over 3 million pounds in 1790. By 1850, Americans were importing some 30 million pounds of Chinese tea each year. Tariffs and competition with India and Japan subsequently cut the China trade, but in its heyday, the tea trade accrued handsome profits for tea merchants, both American and Chinese. The size and nature of the trade was such that huge fortunes could be made quickly. Astor boasted about the enormous amount of money he had made from tea. Traders such as John P. Cushing returned rich to New England from Guangdong and then invested their capital in real estate, railroads, and other domestic enterprises. It also helped make a Chinese tea merchant named Houqua (Wu Bingjian, 1769–1843) perhaps the richest man in the world in the 1830s. In 1834, he estimated his personal wealth at 26 million U.S. dollars. In an early reversal of the investment pattern, Houqua partnered with American friends to invest some of his capital in railroad construction in the United States.[18]

To pay for the tons of tea Americans consumed, American traders tried to use ginseng, sandalwood from Hawaii, and then furs to balance their payments. But even at the height of the fur trade in the early nineteenth century, Americans had to pay vast sums of silver specie to purchase the Chinese products they brought home. In 1810, 75 percent of the value of American imports at Guangzhou was in silver specie. From 1805 through 1812, the United States exported $22,000,000 worth of specie and only $9,000,000 in goods to China.[19]

The tea trade created a troublesome problem for American merchants, but it stimulated the development of another, more romantic, dimension of the early American economy, shipbuilding. The hallmark of American shipbuilding became the tall-masted, sleek sailing ships that were known variously as the China or Yankee clippers. First developed as fighting vessels or as smuggling ships, Americans modified the design to make them capable for long-distance sailing. The Yankee clipper ships became the fastest trading ships in the world, eclipsing their British competition. They cut weeks, even months off travel time. In the 1820s, an American ship could make three voyages to China in a year, compared to two voyages for a British ship using the same route. By 1849, when the British Navigation Laws were repealed, Americans could even bring Chinese tea directly to the huge market in London. The clipper ship design exchanged cargo capacity for speed, for it was speed that the traders wanted. Still, a Yankee clipper could store over a million and a quarter pounds of tea in its hold. Getting the newly harvested tea to market quickly was a coveted advantage, as the most delicate and complex tea taste, especially from green teas, came from the most freshly picked leaves.[20]

Beyond this limited commercial interaction, Americans and Chinese had little contact and even less substantive knowledge of one another. Chinese elites in the late eighteenth and early nineteenth centuries knew virtually nothing about the United States. They also seemed not to care very much about who these English-speaking, non-British people were. Need fuels curiosity, and the Chinese elite, believing they already had everything important, were uninterested in the foreigners from far across the Pacific. *Hailu,* now described as the most complete Chinese geographical work of its day, for example, says virtually nothing about the United States. Based on an account of a Chinese sailor's travels on the seas from 1782 to 1795, the 1820 book could say of America only that it was an "isolated island in the middle of the ocean, its territory rather constricted. Originally a fiefdom of England, it now has become a nation." Twenty-five years later, in 1844, the high Chinese official who negotiated the first diplomatic treaty between the United States and China reported to the emperor that

> the location of the United States is in the Far West. It is the most uncivilized and remote of all countries. Now Your Majesty has granted them the Imperial Favor of a special Edict which they can observe forever. You have rewarded the sincerity of their admiration for our righteousness and are encouraging their determination to turn toward culture. The different races of the world are all grateful for your Imperial charity. But the said country is in an isolated place outside the pale, solitary and ignorant. Not only are the people entirely unversed in the forms of edicts and laws, but if the meaning be rather deep, they would probably not even be able to comprehend. It would seem that we must make our words somewhat simple.[21]

The American attitude could not have offered a sharper contrast to the haughty and officious attitude that surrounded the emperor. Americans were extremely curious about other lands, and one of the countries outside of Europe that most commanded their attention was China. Americans inherited Europe's lively interest in China that became a passion, a Sinophilia, in the mid-eighteenth century. European thinkers such as Voltaire in France and Leibniz in Germany praised China for the quality of its rule, its moral philosophy, and its agricultural productivity. They believed China could serve as a model for their own visions of an enlightened society ruled by reason. Leading Americans believed China held promise for them not just for material enrichment but for ideas and social practices that Americans might adopt. Benjamin Franklin, one of the most educated and learned of early Americans, took an unusually active interest in China because it offered, he believed, a positive cultural model for Americans. As early as the mid-eighteenth century, Franklin was avidly studying books on Chinese civilization and publishing an English translation of *The Morals of Confucius,* a French study about Confucius's writing. In the 1750s he partnered with William Allen, one of Philadelphia's wealthiest citizens, to support a multiyear effort to locate a northwest passage to China. Franklin expressed interest in traveling to China himself. In 1771, as the intellectual leader of the American Philosophical Society, Franklin endorsed this high praise of China that appeared in the society's newsletter: "Could we be so fortunate as to introduce the industry of the *Chinese,* their arts of living and improvements in husbandry, as well as their native plants, *America* might in time become as populous as *China,* which is allowed to contain more inhabitants than any other country, of the same extent, in the world."[22]

Franklin studied Chinese science and technology and of course used the kite, a Chinese invention, to discover electricity. "The Chinese are an enlightened people," Franklin wrote in 1789, they are "the most anciently civilized of any existing, and their arts are ancient, a presumption in their favour." His view of the Chinese emperor was that he was a benevolent, moderate, and sage leader guided by moral philosophy. America, he once argued, would be better modeling itself less on Europe and more on China, "the wisest of Nations." In 1786, he helped gather funds to support stranded Chinese sailors in America. Franklin even thought that the English language would evolve in the future to be more like Chinese script, with written words becoming symbols of things, not an indication of sounds! Franklin was the first, but not the last, of America's Sinophiles. The early American elites' veneration of Confucius, like Franklin's, is permanently embodied in the building housing the U.S. Supreme Court, where an image of Confucius appears next to Moses in its eastern facade.[23]

Thomas Paine, the great pamphleteer of the American Revolution, also greatly admired the Chinese and, unlike others interested purely in an economic relationship, praised their cultural superiority over the West and criticized the negative effect of trade on their country. The Chinese, he wrote, were a "people of mild manners and of good morals, except where they have been corrupted by European commerce." He positively compared Jesus and Confucius as great moral teachers. As a young man, Thomas Jefferson took an active interest in Chinese literature and drama, recommending several translated Chinese works to his brother-in-law in 1771. He believed they favorably compared to Western classical work that encouraged virtue. China's deliberate distancing from Europeans so intrigued Thomas Jefferson that he even suggested that America would be wise to emulate the Chinese court's policy of limited contact with foreigners. China's difference from the West appealed to Americans seeking to break from familiar European models of social organization. Old China could offer something new to Americans. Writing in October 1785 when he was in Paris as the American ambassador to France, Jefferson advanced the idea that Americans should "practice neither commerce or navigation, but to stand with Europe precisely on the footing of China." Jefferson's vision of a relatively autarkic continental republic based on the independent farmer seemed to find precedence in China's imperial experience based on domestic agriculture. He, with Franklin and Paine, also continued to have a keen interest in the commercial possibilities of the lucrative China trade after the Revolution.[24]

Another avid early student of China was Ezra Stiles, president of Yale College from 1778 to 1795 and one of the country's leading intellectuals, clergy, and political figures. Stiles perhaps exceeded all other Americans in the extent of study of China, a country he described in a 1783 sermon as "the wisest empire the sun hath ever shined upon." On another occasion, he called China "the greatest, the richest & most populous Kingdom now known in the World." Clearly a Sinophile, Stiles carefully studied China's agricultural production, Confucianism and other philosophies, silk production, geography, politics, history, and social customs to see what might benefit America. In his eyes, Chinese civilization embodied a benevolent humanism. His papers at Yale University's archives contain hundreds of pages of his China research.[25]

Not all Americans, however, had such a positive view of China and the Chinese. Some rejected "Chinomania," the term one jaundiced observer coined to describe the eighteenth-century idealized rage about things Chinese. Others expressed contempt for the Chinese, especially for their non-Christian beliefs, strange customs, and physical difference. Critical attitudes toward the Chinese would steadily grow in the nineteenth century, but in the early republic, Americans generally held China in high regard. Even China's Grand Canal, which was constructed in the sixth century, helped inspire the imagination of New Yorkers about their own "grand canal," as it was originally called (when it opened in 1825 it was better known as the Erie Canal). In 1834, the leaders of Canton, Georgia, hoped their town would become the center of an American silk industry. Americans in Maryland,

Michigan, Illinois, Ohio, South Dakota, and a dozen other states honored China by naming their towns and city districts Canton or Pekin, as Peking was often known at the time. A good name would help bring an auspicious future.[26]

Though most educated Americans knew China about as well as their counterparts in Europe, their knowledge was still rudimentary and often insubstantial. A most telling example of this is George Washington's confusion about the "racial" character of the Chinese. For years, Washington had taken an active interest in the China trade, and he and his wife Martha collected luxury goods from Asia for their homes. They owned hundreds of pieces of Chinaware. In the fall of 1785, Washington received a letter from a merchant friend telling him of the return of an American trading ship that had followed the *Empress of China* and was full of Chinaware. Washington's correspondent described the crew as being all "natives of India" and "of the countenance and complexion of your old groom"—most certainly one of Washington's African slaves—and "four Chinese" "who are exactly the Indians of North America, in color, texture of hair, and every external mark." Washington wrote back to his merchant friend to order goods and thanked him for the description of the crew. "Before your letter was received," George Washington wrote, "from my reading, or rather from an imperfect recollection of what I had read, I had conceived an idea that the Chinese, tho' droll in shape and appearance, were yet white."[27] The American construction of a defined Oriental or Asian "racial" type would develop later in the nineteenth century as American contact with Chinese increased, including on American soil.

In the early nineteenth century, American traders returning from China wrote extensive reports on their experiences and observations. The reports and tales whetted the appetites of Americans for more information and contact with China. No longer did Americans have to rely on British and translated European accounts for information about China. These early American accounts remain fascinating even for twenty-first-century readers, for they are filled with colorful anecdotes and candid personal reflections. Seeking to dispel early and unconfirmed tales of the exotic, these first-person efforts offered what their authors hoped were dispassionate, unbiased, and intelligent descriptions of a land far removed from the daily experiences of all but a small handful of Americans in the early nineteenth century.

Amasa Delano's *Narrative of Voyages and Travels in the Northern and Southern Hemispheres,* published in 1817, addressed an audience eager to learn of life on the high seas and in foreign lands. Delano was one of the most widely traveled Americans in the early republic, and his 600-page book offered an extended travelogue documenting his rich experiences in the Pacific, South America, the Caribbean, Africa, and Asia. He was born in 1763 in Massachusetts, fought in the Revolution, and at an early age went to sea, where he stayed most of his life. His engagingly written *Narrative* tells of his many travels as a ship captain around the globe and of life in distant lands, especially in the China trade. He was one of the first Americans to visit the country, and his repeated visits to China made him one of the earliest "China hands," those Americans who came to know China well. Today, his *Narrative* is more well known as the source for Herman Melville's famous novella *Benito Cereno*, one of the classic American stories of deception, slavery, and cruelty. Melville based his story on an actual incident Delano experienced off the coast of Chile during his return trip from China.

The China Amasa Delano describes is grand and exotic and commands immense respect. It is the most populous country in the world, he wrote, and has a long history of generosity toward foreigners, including Europeans, until their wanton misbehavior forced the court to restrict them to a quarter in Guangzhou. In "modern times," Delano informed his readers, China is the "foremost in the arts and sciences and in agriculture. It is one of the best regulated governments in the world. The laws are just and maintained with such strict impartiality, that the guilty seldom escape punishment, or the injured fail to obtain prompt justice." Meritorious individuals are commonly rewarded "very liberally" by the emperor. All in all, Delano was generous in his praise of China, a country that he clearly believed was essential for America's future. China, he told his readers, "is one of the most fertile and beautiful countries on the globe." Its fruits, vegetables, and made goods were abundant. China "is the first for greatness, riches, and grandeur, of any country ever known."[28] He could not know that his words would be read by his famous twentieth-century relative, President Franklin Delano Roosevelt, who would have his own long engagement with China.

In 1844, Robert Bennet Forbes, who had first sailed to China in 1817 when he was just 13 years old and later headed Russell & Company, the largest American trading firm in China, published the earliest study of American interaction with China. Forbes recounted activities between the two countries from 1784 until the Opium War of 1840, focusing almost exclusively on commercial activities. His *Remarks on China and the China Trade* carefully recounted the nature of the trade, the commodities involved, and the intricacies of the Canton system under which the American merchants operated. He argued that the British government clearly and openly encouraged its merchants to engage in opium smuggling, an activity London knew full well was an illicit activity in China. Forbes, as did many Americans, sympathized with the Chinese side in the dispute with the British, even though he himself was also involved in the opium trade. Although much about the imperial control of trade irked him, including the machinations of local officials, he had kind words for the Chinese merchants with whom he worked, especially the famous head of the merchant consortium, Houqua. Forbes described Houqua as hard-working, upright, and a "warm friend to the Americans" and as a man with "a most comprehensive mind . . . [who] united the qualities of an enterprising merchant and a sagacious politician." Other leading American merchants developed similar affection for the man; the leading American trading firm, Low and Company, even named one of its commissioned ships the *Houqua* to honor him. In the ensuing years, many other Americans who went to China developed similar close and respectful ties with other individual Chinese, so much so that a notion developed that Americans and Chinese had a special affinity for one another.[29]

Certainly not all Americans wrote so admiringly of China and Chinese as did Delano and Forbes. Samuel Shaw, on board the *Empress of China* in its maiden voyage and on several subsequent trips, was much less taken with the country, though his views were not made public generally until fifty years after his death in 1794. By the late 1840s, his unfavorable views of China were commonplace and they found a hearing audience. Shaw had found the confinement imposed on the foreign traders and the petty corruption of Chinese officials distasteful and he also thought that the government, despite the praise it received from others, was arbitrary and oppressive, perhaps the most "oppressive" in any "civilized nation upon earth." The common people, he found, were full of idolatry and superstition. And yet much in China attracted Shaw, especially its commercial opportunities, which brought him back repeatedly to the country as a trader and as the first official of the United States in China. A young Ralph Waldo Emerson once called China a "booby nation," "reverend dullness! Hoary idiot!, all she can say at the convocation of nations must be—'I made the tea.'" (Later in life, though, he had a complete change of opinion and came to regard Chinese philology and classical philosophy highly.) Still, the initial respect for China that was widely expressed by many of the early American China traders formed a reservoir of positive feelings that long endured in American life and legend.[30]

The conflict between Britain and China in the late 1830s and early 1840s over the importation of opium from India dramatically transformed China's existence and its relationship with America. In the late eighteenth century, the British had turned to selling opium to balance its highly unfavorable trade relationship with the Chinese, who had much to sell to the British but bought little. Opium, grown in British India and carried on British ships, could bring famous profits. The infamous international trade that began in the late eighteenth century and rose rapidly through the nineteenth century marked a turning point not just for China but also for the world economy and global politics. It created incalculable suffering for Chinese, who became addicted to the drug in the tens of millions, the largest episode of drug addiction in human history. It was a direct cause of the dramatic decline in China's power and stature, a historic humiliation that continues to shadow the modern Chinese nation.

Opium was used in limited and sporadic ways in Chinese history, but in 1729, the Qing government, concerned about the spread of serious addiction, banned opium smoking. Dozens of prohibiting edicts followed. The trade was sufficiently odious that the London-charted East India Company even forbade the shipping of opium to China on its vessels in 1733. But the Chinese coast was long and porous, addiction was on the rise in southern China, bribery and corruption of local officials became endemic, and profits were enormous. British traders not associated with "the Company" brought the opium to islands along the China coast near Guangzhou and sold it to Chinese smugglers, who paid in hard silver, the basis of the Chinese monetary system. The British shippers insisted that they were not actually smuggling or doing anything that violated Chinese law; they claimed that they offloaded the opium, cultivated in their India colony, outside the limits of Chinese authority. The British traders would then bring their loot from the opium sales to Guangzhou, where the East India Company arranged the purchase of Chinese goods for export back to England. It was a perfect setup for the aggressive and arrogant British merchants, who claimed the moral high ground of upholding the civilized principle of "free trade" while engaging in the drug trade. Opium helped the British pay for their endless purchases of Chinese goods, including tea. Moreover, opium smuggling and the attendant erosion of local authority opened the southern China coast to a wide variety of other illicit traffic in goods. Millions of pounds of opium flooded into China, where it fed the habit of an estimated 10 million addicts in 1839 and an astronomical 40 million by 1900. The horrible physical toll that opium addiction took was widely known at the time. A popular periodical in America published long, detailed descriptions of the degraded addict, concluding that opium addiction produced the "most fruitful images of human suffering." And yet the trade flourished: in the 1830s it was more valuable than any other commodity in the entire world and, in the estimate of some historians, helped fuel Britain's own nineteenth-century industrial revolution and the rise of the modern global economy.[31]

Although it was the British who dominated opium smuggling, the Americans were second in line. They entered the trade in 1806, when the *Eutaw*, a Baltimore ship, took "twenty-five chests, fifty-three boxes" of opium grown in Turkey to China. By 1817, Americans were responsible for 10 percent of the opium brought into the Guangdong region and their participation in the trade grew steadily, especially after 1838, when the British allowed them to enter the India opium market and purchase the product. Philadelphia merchants dominated the trade, though many others among the eastern elite also enriched themselves through the illicit activity. Opium fattened the coffers of the Boston Brahmins. In 1837, opium comprised 57 percent of the value of all imports into China, which bled silver to pay for its habit. From 1828 to 1836, $38 million in silver left China to pay for the addiction. The silver hemorrhage worsened over the following decades and continued well into the twentieth century.[32]

In 1839, Chinese official Lin Zexu, on direct authority from the emperor, seized and then destroyed 3 million pounds of British opium and refused to compensate the merchants for the destruction of the property. In reaction, London declared war against the Qing. This was the beginning of the first Anglo-Chinese War, or the First Opium War (to distinguish it from a second war in the 1850s). It lasted for two years, during which British war ships, which commanded the seas in the absence of any effective Chinese navy, destroyed Chinese coastal settlements and fortifications with impunity. The Chinese conducted a sort of war of attrition, dragging out a conflict that became increasingly unpopular in Britain, itself already beset with a demoralizing effort to subdue Afghanistan and make it London's colony. Parliament came close to pulling the country out of the Opium War. The British did not easily win the victory, but eventually win they did with their strategy of devastating China's southern coast with their dominant sea power and threatening to destroy Nanjing with its ships in the Yangzi River. Britain forced China to "open" itself to contemporary commercial and diplomatic practices. China ceded Hong Kong to Britain in perpetuity, opened five new ports to foreigners, ended the state-sanctioned monopoly on foreign commerce, and agreed to begin regularizing diplomatic interactions along European lines.

Though America was officially neutral during the conflict, Washington quietly sympathized with the Chinese and the American public initially strongly favored the Chinese position. Antipathy against the British, the former colonial master and the recent enemy in the war of 1812, ran high, and few could see any righteousness in the side that went to war to sell opium. *Hunt's Merchants' Magazine,* a New York periodical and one of the leading public voices in its day, was unrestrained in its condemnation: Britain, the so-called "Christian, slavery-hating nation" inflicts "manifold outrages upon the liberties of men—these barbarous impositions and cruelties—these palpable, repeated, and continued violations of morality, religion, and common justice." Britain held India in bondage and chained millions of its people "to the cultivation of a drug, the consequences of which are misery, disease, and death." China was "perfectly right" in trying to stop the trade. "And should Great Britain invade the Chinese empire, blockade its ports, and expel from its waters the commerce of other lands," *Hunt's* concluded, "the whole enlightened and Christian world ought solemnly to protest against it, as an unwarranted act of arbitrary power, committed in violation of the broad principles of eternal justice."[33]

But not all Americans agreed. One of the most prominent and influential Americans to take exception to the anti-British view was the pious and thoughtful John Quincy Adams, son of the second president of the United States and himself the sixth. As secretary of state under President James Monroe, Adams distinguished himself in establishing the foundations of American foreign policy. He is seen as perhaps America's most important secretary of state, and in 1840, when he was in his early 70s, he was an elder statesmen, serving as one of Massachusetts' representatives in Congress, where he was the chair of the House Committee on Foreign Relations. Adams had long been interested in China and was close friends with many of the old New England traders from Boston, Salem, and Newport. Adams was an ardent expansionist and at the same time deeply opposed to human slavery as a great moral evil. Both views were rooted in his religious beliefs, which included the opinions that America was blessed by God and that its people were "chosen" to build a model society. America, he believed was destined to transform and enlighten the world.[34]

Adams took a keen interest in the outbreak of the Anglo-Chinese war and read everything he could find about the developing situation in China. He repeatedly pressed Secretary of State Daniel Webster and President John Tyler to provide studies on the history of U.S. contact with China and used this research material to compose a long-winded lecture on the war, the issues at hand, and what America's attitude should be toward the belligerents. What he said in the lecture marked a turning point in the American attitude toward China. His talk, which also circulated as an essay (it was published in full in Boston and then in Macao), widely influenced public opinion. His erudite and extended discussion helped sway many Americans against the Chinese and toward support of the British position. Until then, Americans, with the exception of the missionary community, believed that commercial opportunity formed the core of American interest in China, an interest that was believed to be essential to the current and future prosperity of the United States. After Adams's talk, however, increasing numbers of Americans concluded that America's purposes in China were not only commercial but were also moral and political. It was America's duty and destiny to help transform a backward civilization by requiring it to accept Western Christian norms and practices.[35]

Prompted by the editor of the *North American Review,* the leading journal of informed opinion in the country at the time, Adams worked on his lecture for nearly a year before its delivery. He crafted it even as he was embroiled in the infamous *Amistad* case that he was arguing before the Supreme Court. Adams represented Africans who had been enslaved by Spanish traders but whose ship had run aground off the coast of Connecticut. He based his antislavery position on his devotion to the natural rights of humankind and argued that the Africans should be freed, in contrast to those who considered them Spanish property to be returned to their owners. Paradoxically, Adams's defense of the freedom of the Africans was based on the same beliefs that led him to support the British and their right to import opium into China, namely, that God-given natural law held human enslavement an abomination just as it did the regulated trading and closed political system of the Chinese that prevented the free pursuit of property. He opposed the slavery imposed on the Africans, just as the British opposed the constraints imposed by the Chinese on countries who wanted to interact with them. He believed that in China, the British were fighting "against Slavery" and for the "cause of human freedom, a glorious and a blessed cause."[36]

On November 22, 1841, Adams delivered his remarks to an overflow crowd at the Massachusetts Historical Society. For hours, he carefully explored the evolution of European thinking about international relations and the nascent idea of international law, a notion that was still novel in theory and inconsistent in practice. He identified a central dilemma, the difficulty in determining the moral and political basis for "civilized" conduct among nations, given the absence of a supreme human authority ruling over the various, independent states. Upon what ethical or legal foundation would Christian interstate conduct be based? Adams argued that the answer could be found in natural law, the state of independence, liberty, reciprocity, and the equality of people and countries that God provided for all to enjoy. Those who were moral and Christian did not always respect God's commands, but Adams believed they should. They, as Christians, he believed, were obligated to support and advance natural law and the European-based "family of nations," or what we today would call the international system, as the embodiment of that natural law. But what of non-Christians? Adams argued that different systems of law and prescribed conduct obtained in those cases, such as with the Muslim world and American native peoples, the objective in these cases being to subdue them and induce them to accept the proper Christian view. His conception of the universality and equality of international law was in fact limited to the Christian nations of Europe and explicitly accepted the righteousness even of going to war to bring other nations to accept his law of nations.

Having established fundamental philosophical and moral principles, Adams then came to the crux of the matter, which was what to do about China and Britain in the current conflict. For Adams, the issue was clear. It was Britain that had righteousness on its side: it stood for unfettered trade, the foundation of the Christian notion of reciprocity, or loving thy neighbor as thyself, as he put it. The principle of the pursuit of happiness, written into the Declaration of Independence, required this reciprocity, which was understood to be attained through the buying and selling of goods by unencumbered individuals pursuing their own interests. China, a "heathen Nation," on the other hand, stood for despotism, selfishness, and arrogance in its unilateral control of trade. It did not believe in reciprocity and equality and held itself above all other nations. "The fundamental principle of the

Chinese empire is anti-commercial," Adams asserted, and commerce in his view was a natural right and duty. China's view was "selfish," an attitude that for Adams was an outrage against "human nature" and the fundamental principles of natural law. Adams invoked the epic moment in the birth of the United States to press his case: opium, he said was "but no more the cause of war than the throwing overboard of the tea in Boston harbor was the cause of the North American Revolution." In the instance at hand, it was Britain that stood for "the natural equality of mankind." "Britain has the righteous cause," Adams declared. Opium was incidental to the war; the issue at hand was the "Ko-tow! The arrogant and insupportable pretension of China, that she will hold commercial intercourse with the rest of mankind, not upon terms of equal reciprocity, but upon the insulting and degrading forms of the relation between lord and vassal." Adams claimed that the United States was on the verge of being drawn into the conflict, and he wanted to make clear whose side the country should join.[37]

Although Adams's argument focused on the immediate conflict between China and Britain, his lecture raised fundamental issues about the ends of American foreign relations. This was a test case for Adams as to whether Americans could understand the greater purposes of the nation to which he was so devoted. Liberal, international commerce was essential, not just as the way a people's well-being could be advanced but as the practice of a nation's fundamental moral beliefs. For Adams, America was given a providential mission to redeem and perfect the world. Trade would be an essential element in its effort to bring the world together and extend human freedom. Ending China's exclusivity and opening it to Western trade would be a central element in this mission, which was now being carried forward by the British. But it would clearly be America's moral obligation to do the same in the future in China and other areas of the world.[38]

Adams's view outraged many of his fellow Americans, and some, such as leading China trader Russell Sturgis, chastised him for sacrificing morality for the crass pursuit of profit. Why should China be required to accept a commodity and a trading system it did not want? What kind of civilization went to war to impose its will on those deemed heathen and barbarous? Didn't China, like any other nation, have the right to regulate its commerce with other nations? China just wanted to be left alone, and the actions it took to suppress the opium trade were completely reasonable. Sturgis condemned the British for conducting a venal war under the banner of a "civilizing mission." For Sturgis, the view of the British and of Adams was unsupportable. He expressed an alternative American attitude toward China that would resonate throughout the long history of U.S.-China relations, an attitude of respect for the Chinese wish *not* to be reformed or remade by foreigners. Other American merchants in China joined Sturgis and watched the British brutal conduct of the war in horror. British slaughter, looting, and rapine repelled many Americans.[39]

Even though many Americans disliked the aggressive and arrogant British, Adams's philosophical support for the British and the perceived importance of opening China to an increasingly significant world commerce gradually gained support. Washington also had little compunction about benefiting from the spoils of the British war. London forced major concessions from the defeated Chinese, including a huge indemnity (one-third of which Houqua paid from his own coffers), the cession of Hong Kong in perpetuity to the Crown, the opening of five Chinese ports (Guangzhou, Shanghai, Xiamen, Fuzhou, and Ningbo) to trade and foreigner residence, and a treaty mandating diplomatic and commercial relations between the two countries on the basis of Western norms. The treaty marked the beginning of China's entry into the evolving Europe-based "family of nations."

When the war ended, Washington did not want to let an opportunity to expand American trade pass and feared that the British would seek exclusive access to the China market. Before the hostilities were concluded and the British had obtained the treaty with China, American officials, even though most had not supported the British, considered how to exploit the development for America's benefit. In early 1843, President John Tyler appointed Caleb Cushing to be envoy extraordinary and minister plenipotentiary to the court of China. He was to travel to China and conclude a formal treaty along the lines of what the British had extracted from the Chinese by force. Secretary of State Daniel Webster crafted the careful, studied directive that guided Cushing's mission. The principal interest of Washington was commercial, to obtain rights and privileges for American traders equal to those of the British. Unlike the British, the United States eschewed interest in acquiring Chinese territory, but in other respects the United States went further than the British in what they obtained from the Chinese. Cushing came from a family long associated with the Pacific maritime trade—his father was a shipbuilder and his cousin was John Perkins Cushing, head of Perkins & Company, one of the largest American trading firms in China—and he himself had thought much about how to advance American interests in

China. He was politically ambitious and actively committed to westward expansion. In his mind, the Oregon territory, the Pacific, and China were all intimately linked and access, if not domination, of them was necessary to America's well-being and greatness. He had served as a member of Congress from Massachusetts for eight years and recently as chair of the House Committee on Foreign Affairs. He did not speak Chinese (he did learn some Manchu during his journey) but had made himself an expert on China by reading all he could about the country before leaving on his mission.[40]

Cushing was thrilled with his appointment to China, which he believed would have historic consequences for the country and for the entire world. Many shared his enthusiasm, and when he spoke at the dedication ceremony of the newly constructed Bunker Hill memorial in Boston, his words reached back to the ideals of the past Revolution but he mainly spoke of grand visions for America's future and his own mission. In June 1843, before the assembled crowd, which included President John Tyler, Cushing described his impending journey to China in momentous terms, portraying his endeavor as virtually embodying America's providential mission. "I have myself been honored with a commission of peace," he declared, "and am entrusted with the duty of bringing nearer together, if possible, the civilization of the Old and New Worlds—the Asiatic, European, and American continents." It was from the "East" that civilization and learning first came, he declared, but the tide had turned and Westerners were now the "teachers of our teachers." "I go to China . . . in behalf of civilization," he said, but he quickly added a reminder of the commercial dimension. He was also going "to open the doors of the hundreds of millions of Chinese to America."[41]

In July 1844, Cushing left the country with an impressive squadron of four warships, including the *Missouri,* along with its sister ship, the largest steam frigate then afloat, and a letter from the president to the emperor. As Catholic missionaries had done centuries before him, Cushing also brought mechanical devices meant to display the genius of Western civilization and impress the Chinese. These objects included a pair of six-shooters, models of a steam excavator, some sort of daguerreotype, a telescope, a barometer, and the thirteen-volume first edition of *Encyclopedia Americana: A Popular Dictionary of Arts, Sciences, Literature, History, Politics and Biography, Brought Down to the Present Time.* It is not clear which items made the strongest impression on the Chinese, the bang or the book.[42]

After months of travel, Cushing arrived in Wangxia, a small village in the Portuguese colony of Macao, where he met with imperial commissioner

Qiying. The two quickly concluded the first American treaty with China, signing it on July 3, 1844, one day short of American Independence Day. There was little deliberation about the terms. The high point of Cushing's time in China, as the story has come down through the years, was the unfamiliar etiquette and strange foodstuffs presented in a sumptuous four-hour Chinese banquet. Unknown to Cushing, the Chinese had decided even before his arrival that they would extend the privileges extracted by the British to the Americans in the hope of using the Americans against the British. Cushing did press the Chinese further and added terms to the final treaty that placed Americans on an even more advantageous position in China than other foreigners. The treaty with the United States not only granted Americans most-favored-nation rights but also provided living accommodations that met the specifications of the Americans, rights of study and learning, and the free practice of religious belief for the Americans in China. (The latter item grew in importance in the coming years.) It confirmed the privilege of extraterritoriality to Americans (the British had included it in their demands from their victory in the Opium War), meaning that Americans in China were under the jurisdiction and privileges of American, not Chinese, law and courts. The treaty ensured that the United States would remain in a competitive position with the European powers who sought to dominate the China trade and would enjoy the same economic and political privileges as they did.

Despite the fact that Cushing never made it to the imperial court in Beijing to deliver the presidential missive, word of the concluded China treaty absolutely thrilled John Tyler, a dour man not easily aroused. "The Chinese Treaty is accomplished,—Hurrah!" Tyler's young wife Julia wrote to an intimate friend. "The documents came in to-day . . . I thought the President would go off in an ecstasy a minute ago with the pleasant news."[43]

The Treaty of Wangxia marked the beginning of formal relations between the United States and China that continued for more than the next 100 years, through war and revolution, until Cold War animosities ruptured the relationship. The treaty set the pattern for other European treaties with China over the next decade. *DeBow's Review,* a leading periodical in the south, celebrated the treaty as opening virtually limitless commercial possibilities. "We expect," the journal's editor declared, "an extension of trade of the world in an inconceivable degree." *Hunt's Merchants' Magazine* declared that Cushing's treaty would usher in a new, glorious future and that the United States was "destined ultimately to command all the trade in the Indian and China seas." *Hunt's* proclaimed the treaty the greatest event since the discovery of the New World. This was clearly hyperbole, but it was still indicative of the widely held extravagant hopes of Americans about the implications of the political and economic breakthrough with China. Their predictions would not be realized, of course, but it is what they hoped for. In fact, only a modest expansion in trade actually resulted.[44]

After Cushing's triumphant return to the United States in January 1845, he was in popular demand and spoke widely about his journey. He received dozens of invitations to speak to civic groups throughout the east and the south and planned to write a three-volume study on China. The few Americans who had been in China previously had interacted mainly with a handful of Chinese merchants and had had little exposure to everyday life, sequestered as they were in the foreigners' compound in Guangzhou. Cushing officially represented the United States and had engaged with a high emissary from the emperor. Back in America he addressed the widespread curiosity about the nature of Chinese personality and life.

Cushing's shallow observations described a foreign people who were not just exotically different but were in some ways antithetical to the Westerner, a trope that long endured in the popular imagination. Lecturing before a gathering of fellow Bostonians in late October 1845, Cushing expressed a befuddlement about and wonder of China that was common among visitors from the West. Arriving in China, he found himself, he said, at an "antipode," geographically and psychologically. The Western visitor to China, he informed his audience, would see "countless myriads of men in a strange garb, and with a general appearance unlike to all that to which he has heretofore been accustomed. . . . A thousand things admonish him that he is in a strange land." Cushing offered a real-life Alice in Wonderland story: the Chinese read their compass to locate the south, not the north, and they wrote from top to bottom, right to left, with the date at the bottom of the letter. They wore white, not black, in mourning and placed their saucer on top of the teacup instead of placing the cup on top of the saucer. They played shuttlecocks with their feet instead of their hands and "compressed" women's feet instead of their waists. A Chinese swam striking his "hands vertically and not horizontally," they shaved "the top of the head" (presumably instead of the front of the face), and when one Chinese meets another on the street, "he does not shake your hands, but shakes his hands at you." The infantryman carried a matchlock but the cavalry rode with bow and arrow. And so on.

Cushing did not mean to mock but rather spoke in wonder that such an ancient and accomplished people could be so radically different from Europeans, usually assumed to be the standard of civilization and reason. Cushing even suggested that "unfortunately too many of our ideas" came from Europe. China "had for ages cultivated the arts, literature, and the sciences." They had Confucius, "the contemporary of Herodotus," gunpowder, the compass, silk, porcelain, the printing press, and paper currency "centuries ago." The Chinese had everything before Europe except the steam engine. Their form of government, which emphasized benevolence and paternalism, was not a reality, but it was still a "beautiful" fiction. He expressed admiration for the scholars who staffed government positions based on a system that selected them through examinations, the great respect for public opinion (it was "as much regarded in China as in Great Britain or the United States"), the high moral level of the population, and their high level of intellectual attainment ("the country abounds in books, public libraries, and shops for the sale of books"). Ending his remarks to pique the interest of the many businessmen in his audience, Cushing indicated that commercially, "China is complete in herself." But that was changing with the Chinese importation of American raw cotton and British textiles that used American cotton. This Chinese trade "greatly benefits us." Cushing's global vision neatly articulated the linked interests of acquisitive New England Yankee traders, aggressive southern cotton plantation owners, and boisterous continental expansionists.[45]

Cushing's treaty together with China's defeat in the Opium War and the subordinate status the British imposed on it marked a historic turning point for the Chinese. The events around the Opium War initiated what Chinese today call the century of humiliation, 100 years of a downward spiral in the condition of the Chinese people and nation, which only the Chinese Communist Revolution of 1949 finally ended. The downward trajectory of China that began in the 1840s is matched in drama only by the upward trajectory of the United States as a continental and then a world power from the early nineteenth century onward. America's rapid growth in population was evidence of the young country's vigor. From just four million in 1790, the population grew fourfold, to sixteen million in 1835. Cushing's treaty, significantly, led to greatly expanded social contact between the two countries. From the early 1850s, thousands of Chinese and Americans began traveling to each other's lands, many staying indefinitely. Americans settled in China as educators and missionaries and tens of thousands of Chinese migrated and then stayed permanently in America. The ties between the two countries grew beyond economics and commodities to include extensive human dimensions. Few appreciated the implications of these at the time, but in historical perspective, the presence of Americans in China and Chinese in America left a vast historical inheritance, positive and negative, for each people.

America's early contact with China is a grand story, but it is intimately linked to a chapter of American history that has occupied an even grander place in the American pageant: the story of discovery and westward expansion.

Leading figures in the early republic had audacious, bold visions about an immense continental empire that spanned North America. From the beginning of the republic, Americans understood that the defense of their political independence required economic well-being. Their vision of national greatness required economic self-sufficiency, and they pursued every possible opportunity for territorial and commercial expansion. The rapid and seemingly irresistible westward expansion of the United States from east to west, past the Alleghenies, then the Missouri and Mississippi Valleys, across the Great Plains and Rocky Mountains and to the Pacific, became the great national epic immortalized in countless cultural forms, from music, drama, and literature to the textbooks every school student read. Plentiful land, adventure and discovery, and boundless resources are said to have been the attractions for the restless and ambitious Americans. However, what is often overlooked today is China, the lure that lay beyond the Pacific Coast.

For many Americans, China and the Far East was the reason to go to the far west. Seeking a waterway through the continent was a prime reason the English first settled in America. The task of the Jamestown colonists, who settled in Virginia in 1607, was to enrich their London backers and satisfy their desire to locate a passage that would link the Atlantic to the Pacific and thus to the markets of the East. Early Americans and Europeans took the existence of such a route as a matter of literal faith. None believed that God would have created the New World as a land barrier to their ambitions. English, Spanish, and French explorers all were convinced that such a route existed, and they repeatedly sought to locate it. After independence, the dream of the passage to the East though the west continued to inspire Americans to explore the continent, to covet the Oregon Country, to justify the war with Mexico, and then to annex the ports of California. Spanning the continent was America's irrefutable destiny. Controlling the west would bring America closer to the riches and resources of the East. The eminent late-nineteenth-century American historian of American nationalism, Frederick Jackson Turner, declared that the westward movement had been the "fundamental process" in American life, and Americans, as people of the Pacific, he once observed, shared a "mysterious and unfathomable" "common destiny" with those across the great ocean.[46] He, as did other Americans, believed that the Pacific was not a barrier or an obstacle to contact but rather a conduit for intimate and mutually beneficial exchange.

The acquisition of the Louisiana Territory from France in 1803 was inspired in part by the lure of the Pacific, and in turn it further encouraged Americans to think about their future as irresistibly linked to Asia and China. Early Americans, among them Thomas Jefferson, had dreamed about a continental empire, a country that would span the entire northern American continent. Such an immense territory would not only embrace vast lands and natural wealth but would physically, territorially, link the world's great oceans, the Atlantic and the Pacific, giving America an unsurpassed advantage over others. The idea of finding a waterway along which one could go from one ocean to the other, a northwest passage, had been a longtime dream of Europeans and then of Americans. Jefferson's purchase of the Louisiana Territory was the single most important advance in furthering American continental ambitions. Within weeks after finalizing the purchase, Jefferson received congressional support for what became known as the Lewis and Clark Expedition, whose primary objective was to locate a water route across the continent to the Pacific Ocean. "The object of your mission," Jefferson instructed Lewis, "is to explore the Missouri River and such principal streams of it as by its course and communication with the waters of the Pacific Ocean may offer the most direct and practical water communication across the continent for the purpose of commerce."[47]

Having acquired much of the central territory of the continent, American leaders turned to the far west and argued for the necessity of controlling the West Coast. They repeatedly invoked the importance of Asia, and China in particular, to America in the public debates and discussions about the occupation of Oregon and California as early as the 1820s. One of the most vocal was Congressman John Floyd of Virginia, whose cousin had been with Lewis and Clark. Floyd would become Virginia's governor and a presidential contender later in his career, but in the 1820s he distinguished himself as the first in Congress to urge the United States to occupy the Oregon Country, an enormous reach of land that stretched from California to southern Alaska and east into Wyoming. Europeans and Americans disputed its ownership. America's control of the northwest, he declared, would enable it to command the great trading potential of Asia, a goal "which the West has been seeking ever since Solomon sent out his ships in search of the gold of Ophir." He envisioned an American Tyre, the fabled Phoenician trading city that commanded the wealth of the ancient world, at the mouth of the Columbia River that would supply China's millions with American flour, cotton, and tobacco. His biblical and Old World references emphasized the monumentality of the possibility.[48] In the antebellum years, political figures from the southerner John C. Calhoun to New Englander Daniel Webster loudly trumpeted the importance of the China trade for America. Ardent expansionist Senator Thomas Hart Benton of Missouri envisioned the Columbia River Valley becoming the granary of Asia. Others envisioned American tobacco replacing British opium and American wheat replacing Chinese rice. The possibilities were limitless in the imagination. Asa Whitney, the first booster of the construction of the transcontinental railway, saw the future of America as residing in the commercial potential of the inviting Pacific. Others who looked to the Far East dismissed the Atlantic as relatively unimportant, calling it a "petty and petulant sea."[49] In 1848, Congress organized the Oregon Territory as part of the United States.

The idea that America had a transcendent future, a providential national greatness, had several origins. From the founding of the colonies, many devout Americans believed that America, because of the virtue of its citizens, was destined to realize God's will on earth. It was to be a "city upon the hill" for the rest of the world, in the words of Puritan leader John Winthrop. Political leaders also believed its experiment in liberty and equality would show the way forward away from the inherited privileges and class structure of the Old World. Explorers and entrepreneurs believed America occupied a singular geographic position; the country was bound to span the continent, in their view, because no great European power stood in its way. The continent was to be the nation and it would achieve what Europeans had long wanted, the linking of the Atlantic and Pacific Oceans. A continental America would territorially embody that longtime ambition. These strands of thought all came together to produce the widely popular urge to push the country to expand westward, to take Texas, Oregon, and then the northern half of Mexico, in the Mexican-American War of 1846–1848. "Manifest destiny" rallied the country to advance and conquer, claiming that it was evident that America was meant to inhabit the entire land mass from the Atlantic to the Pacific Ocean. Such a destiny was perceived to be divine and irresistible. Americans were to acknowledge their fate and act in accordance with providential design to achieve greatness. They were to be self-conscious agents of their own destiny.[50]

The idea of China intruded in multiple ways in American thinking about destiny and expansionism. China could be a motive, a reason for continental expansion. Expansion was necessary to obtain the necessary connection with China, with its products and millions of people. Expansion across the continent and capture of the ports on the Pacific Coast was a means to this distant end. Hawaii and the islands of the Pacific all were convenient steps to China. Then, when expansion was within reach, other Americans who had not thought much about the country's international connections began to see the possibilities that Asia presented for achieving greatness. Asia was the place that could receive America's agricultural bounty. China and Asia more generally, with their boundless markets, were hungry for American products.

The desire to acquire the port of San Francisco and the West Coast inspired expansionists such as President James K. Polk to wage a predatory war on Mexico and seize its northern territories. Midway through the Mexican-American War, Polk spoke to Congress to rally support for the plan to annex what is now called California. The region, said the president, would soon be settled by Americans; San Francisco Bay and other ports along the coast would harbor an American navy, whalers, and other "merchant vessels"; and these ports would soon "become the marts of an extensive and profitable commerce with China and other countries of the East." In other addresses, Polk repeatedly spoke about the importance of California and the China trade for the future.[51]

These ideas linking continental expansion, Manifest Destiny, and the China trade came together in the fertile and ambitious imagination of Asa Whitney, who is credited as the first person to advance the audacious idea of constructing a transcontinental railroad. Whitney came from a comfortable New England family (he was distantly related to the inventor of the cotton gin) and had made a fortune in the China trade around the time of the Opium War. During his two years of living in China, he had closely studied the economies and societies of China, the rest of Asia, and the Pacific Islands and had concluded that America was singularly positioned geographically between "Europe, with a starving, destitute population of 250,000,000" and Asia with a population of "700,000,000 of souls still more destitute." This position placed an immense responsibility upon America, a responsibility that required the construction of the transcontinental link. Convinced that the project could bring "vast commercial, moral, and political results," he returned to America resolved to "devote my life to the work which I believed promised so much good to all mankind." As he immodestly but piously claimed, "nature's God" had made absolutely clear that the route he proposed across the continent was "the grand highway, to civilize and Christianize all mankind." Whitney eschewed any thought of possible personal gain from the proposal and declared that he was willing to risk his very life and fortune for his vision. As with many other Americans as they thought about their country's purposes, Whitney presented arguments of commercial advantage, control of the continent and seas, and divine moral purpose that seamlessly reinforced one another.[52]

For much of the rest of his life, Whitney lobbied for government support for his vision, repeatedly asking Congress and the president to support his idea. Whitney's plan combined exacting detail with epic vision. He calculated ocean and land distances, defined the best overland routes, consulted business and political leaders around the country, and presented proposals for Congress and the president that argued that a rail link from the shores of Lake Michigan to the Pacific Northwest or San Francisco was more than feasible, it was essential for advancing the transcendent goal of bringing the East and the West together. The rail line would open "an unlimited market for our cotton, rice, tobacco, hemp, corn, flour, beef, pork, manufactured goods, and all our various and vast products." But more important, it was America's own singular, providential purpose to construct this link that would bring together human history, natural geography, practical economics, military security, and God's design.

Whitney anticipated challenges to his grand proposal. What of a canal through the Panama isthmus, another approach to linking the two great oceans that some favored? Whitney argued that a canal had huge logistical and political problems and would require a much longer ocean run, from the north Atlantic and then through the Pacific to China, than transporting goods and people from the East Coast ports along a rail line to the West Coast ports. Who would populate the great reaches of the western United States and the Pacific? Whitney believed the poor masses of Europe would flock to America once its plentiful land was within reach. And as for the peopling of the Pacific? Why, "millions of Chinese would emigrate" and it would be American ships that would move them. "What a field, then, would there not be here opened for industry and enterprise—for the humane, for the missionary, and for the philanthropist!" Whitney could not foresee the intense anti-Chinese hostility that would erupt in the United States in just a few years.

Whitney's most powerful argument drew not from economics but from a dramatic historical imagination that bordered on the millenarian. He declared,

> The change of the route for the commerce with Asia has, since before the time of Solomon even, changed the destinies of Empires and States. It has, and does to this day control the world. Its march has always been westward, and can never go back to its old routes. . . . Through us must be the route to Asia, and the change to our continent will be the last, the final change.
>
> We see the commerce of Asia, with civilization, has marched west. Each nation, from the Phoenicians to proud England, when supplanted, or forced to relinquish it, has declined, and dwindled into almost nothingness, and a new nation, west, risen up, with vigor and life, to control all. When this road shall have been completed, that commerce, with civilization, will have encircled the globe. It can go no further. Here, then[,] would be the consummation of all things; and here it would be as fixed, as fast as time and earth itself. Here we should stand forever, reaching out one hand to all Asia and the other to all Europe . . . seeking not to subjugate any; but all, the entire, the whole, tributary, and at our will, subject to us.

Whitney received wide support for his lobbying efforts. State legislatures and many in Congress endorsed his grand proposal, but he never obtained full federal backing. That went, ultimately, to another, much more powerful and better positioned group more than a decade later, the so-called Big Four, led by Leland Stanford. Whitney, though, had succeeded not only in popularizing the idea of joining America's newly acquired lands but also of linking continental expansion with the vision of American domination of the Pacific and Asia beyond. America's "manifest destiny" was not limited to a contiguous land mass but was linked to an even grander destinarian imagination. As *DeBow's Review* declared in a long, elaborate article not long after the United States had realized its North American *continental* expansion, China and the Indies were "Our 'Manifest Destiny' in the East." China had special significance for America, the journal pointed out. It was "more important to us than to Europe; and more important to Europe than all Southern Asia besides." As many believed at the time, *DeBow's* suggested that geography was predestination, but territorial contiguity no longer demanded expansion. Now it was the Pacific that called. America must control the ocean and Asia for its commercial advantage, its security, and its general well-being. The far west had moved to the Far East.[53]

Actual trade between China and the United States in the early republic was in fact surprisingly limited. Up until 1840, U.S. commerce with China never amounted to more than 6 percent of all U.S. foreign trade in any single year, and then it fell to less than 2 percent later in the nineteenth century. While the rate of profit at times soared to unheard-of heights early in the trade, it had stabilized to earth-bound levels by the time of the Opium War. Certainly individual enterprises profited immensely from the China trade, but the overall modest amount might prompt some to wonder why China had so captured the American entrepreneurial imagination. Trade figures alone belie the perceived importance of the commerce with Asia to Americans, who, acquisitive and audacious as they were, had their eyes on the future. They were inspired by the promise, more than the actual reality, of the relationship with China. In that sense, they continued in the tradition of Europeans before them whose dreams were filled with the possible splendor of Asian riches. The riches of China Americans had so far obtained were just a taste of things to come. With more work and good fortune, the limitless China market could be America's—the profits already made were just the beginning. The lure, the mystique of China beckoned them to push on. As one distinguished historian of the American west observed early in the twentieth century, the American push west and across the continent should be seen as a "chapter in the oldest movement in our history—a movement that reaches back . . . to the far voyages of Columbus, of Magellan, of Henry Hudson, of La Salle . . . of English colonists on the Atlantic coast. . . . At the same time, it becomes a part of the great world-struggle for the control of the rich and varied Eastern trade—a trade which has been one of the powerful forces of the world's past, as it is of its present, and bids fair to be through the unknown years of the future." The link between the American far west and control of the Asia trade was "of transcendent interest."[54]

From the time of the American Revolution to the conclusion of the Opium War, U.S.-China relations underwent a dramatic change. China, for many early Americans, was a storied source of wealth and wisdom and a country from whom the young republic might learn. There was an enthusiasm, a romantic idealization even, of what the putative oldest civilization could teach the fledgling nation. But by the 1840s, flush with the energy of expansion and filled with the newfound faith in continental destiny and American power, many Americans concluded that there was little to emulate in China. The effusive praise of China that had once been heard from persons such as Benjamin Franklin and Amasa Delano was heard much less. Culturally, it now appeared backward, idolatrous, and resistant to change. China was in need of change. It seemed to have little to offer the rapidly rising Western world, which would transform the globe with the Industrial Revolution.

In retrospect, much of America's early-nineteenth-century Chinomania was overblown. At the time, some, such as Robert Bennet Forbes, himself an old China hand, cautioned that American exuberance was excessive. He thought much more time would need to pass before fabulous profits could be made. Projects did turn out to be wild flights of the imagination. One dreamer, a man named Benjamin Morrell, predicted that the trade of the United States would all pass along the Colorado River, into the Gulf of California, and then across the Pacific. Others, such as Senator Thomas Hart Benton most prominently, thought the Missouri River could be linked to the Columbia to form a waterway across the continent. The Rockies proved to be a much more stubborn obstacle than he had assumed. Even the *New York Times* shared the exuberance about the possibilities of securing a China connection. With the advent of steam navigation, the newspaper predicted that "we may reckon on having Cathay for a next door neighbor. Then we may snap our fingers at the competition of the world, and bear away the productions of that immense empire to enrich our earth-wide shores." These schemes and dreams bear testimony to the power that China had over the American imagination.[55]

Perhaps Commodore Matthew Perry, who led the expedition to open Japan in 1852–1853, best captured the unique association of the identities of China and America. The goal of Perry's mission to Japan was to advance the American presence in Asia and was motivated largely by the grand promise of China. After his triumphant adventure and the apotheosis of his expedition, Perry wrote a long "narrative" of his journey to address the American public's fascination with his experiences in the formerly closed and mysterious country of Japan. Perry, though, began his story by providing broad geohistorical context and historical vision. America had changed with its occupation of the whole continent, he wrote. America now constituted the "shortest route" between East Asia and Western Europe, and therefore, Perry declared, America was "in truth" "the Middle Kingdom," the label that China had long applied to itself.[56]

The conviction that China, with its immense resources and population, remained central to America's economic well-being and future greatness continued into the nineteenth century. In some ways, the conviction grew as Americans populated the continent. There was money to be made and souls to save. China was a market land of opportunity and a place that needed salvation. For tens of thousands of Americans, China became the place where they would find their own salvation.

2

Physical and Spiritual Connections

You brag of your East! *You* do?
Why, *I* bring the East to *you*!
All the Orient, all Cathay,
Find through me the shortest way.

Bret Harte on the completion of the transcontinental rail line, ca. 1870

China's defeat in the Opium War did more than humiliate the imperial court and demonstrate its vulnerability. The treaties that concluded the war had far-ranging consequences for the Chinese, for their contact with the Western world, and for China's future as a nation. It began the sorry era of the treaty system, or more accurately, the era of the *unequal* treaty system, in which China was steadily reduced to a subjugated, abject nation that barely survived intact into the twentieth century. Though the United States did not play a leading role in the humiliation of China, it supported the European effort and partook of the spoils. Because the United States did not wage full war against China and covet territory, however, some Chinese and many Americans believed that America was unlike other foreign powers and more supportive of Chinese interests than those who came on warships and carved up China's land. America could be a friend to China. It was a fond, if faulty, notion that many held sincerely and persistently.

The unequal treaty system was constructed piecemeal over the decades as foreign powers imposed arrangements on China, usually at the point of a gun, that formalized foreign privilege, exploitation, and authority in the country. At first, Europeans justified their actions along the high-sounding lines that John Quincy Adams had articulated in his support for the British in the Opium War. China's arrogance and exclusivity was backward, unnatural, and contrary to the global system of commerce, political relationships, and social interaction that was emerging. China's Great Wall became the symbol not of power and security, which it once suggested, but of isolation and insolence. The bourgeoisie "draws all, even the most barbarian, nations into civilization," Karl Marx wrote in his 1848 *Communist Manifesto*. Commodity production "batters down all Chinese walls."[1] But as time went on, the foreign predation of China became undisguised and brutal. By 1900, foreign powers had colonized or occupied large areas of China, including Hong Kong (Britain); Taiwan (Japan); Macao (Portugal); Guangzhouwan (France); the Shandong Peninsula (Germany); and Dalian, or Port Arthur (Russia); thirty-two treaty ports; and dozens of concessions and foreign settlements, all along the China coast where foreigners were, to lesser or greater degrees, virtual sovereigns within a nominally sovereign country.

The imposed treaties that followed the Opium War first breached the wall but it was the Second Opium War, otherwise known as the Anglo-French War or Arrow War, against China from 1856 to 1860 that tore it asunder. Unlike the first conflict, during which the fighting occurred mainly in the southern part of the country, the British and the French took the battle to the seat of power, the dramatic high point being their utter destruction of the protective fortresses at Tianjin and Beijing and the military occupation of Beijing itself in 1860. While the emperor fled the city, the British and French looted his treasured Summer Palace, the Yuanmingyuan, or Gardens of Perfect Brightness. (The palace was the actual residence of the imperial family on the outskirts of the city. At 850 acres, it was almost eight times the size of Vatican City and five times the size of the Forbidden City, which was largely a ceremonial site.) They carted off countless valuables and intellectual and art treasures of inestimable value that are now scattered in imperial museums around the world. They burned down scores of elegant buildings and pavilions that formed the palace. All that survived was some stonework that Jesuit missionaries had designed in the early eighteenth century. The ruins still stand today as a reminder of the savagery of the past. The aggressors, in their wisdom, decided to spare the Forbidden City.

The treaties France and Britain extracted from China further "opened" China to the West. The notion that China needed to be opened, in physical, political, and mental dimensions, was the popular trope used to justify aggression at the time and continues to suggest China's difference from the West. "Open" implied civilized intercourse, liberality, progress, and mutual benefit. China, though, was deemed "closed," removed behind its walls, mysterious, conservative, exclusive, and arrogant. In actual practice, opening China to the West meant that China lost sovereignty and became subordinate to those who had the power to set the rules, define the terms, and dominate it politically and militarily. The experience made the Chinese acutely skeptical of their relationships with foreign powers and sensitive to the issues of sovereignty, control, and national strength.

The treaties required that China open ten additional ports to foreign commerce, allow foreigners to trade on the entire Changjiang (Yangzi River), the geographic aorta of China, and confirm the privileged legal status of Westerners in China, such as extraterritoriality. They established the right of foreigners to maintain a diplomatic presence in Beijing, permission for foreigners to travel to all parts of China, and the right of missionaries to reside and proselytize anywhere in China. The treaties conceded further territory to the British and French and, most odiously, legalized in practice the trade in opium, the issue that had ignited the first Opium War. After 1860, the British, Americans, and others openly imported the drug into the country, just like any other commodity. Opium flowed into China at triple the rate it had at the start of the first Opium War. Only after the Communist Revolution in 1949 did the flow of opium cease and widespread addiction to it in China end.

As it had during the first Opium War, the United States declared its formal neutrality during the conflict, though its military forces were drawn into battle against the Chinese on several occasions. In one instance, an American commander reminded Washington that he had come to help beleaguered British troops because "blood is thicker than water." And in ending the conflict, the United States (and Russia) carefully exercised most-favored-nation status and concluded treaties with China that ensured they would also enjoy all the commercial and political rights and privileges the British and French had obtained through war. Washington and Moscow received the benefits without the bloody costs. President Abraham Lincoln appointed Anson Burlingame, a leading antislavery member of the House of Representatives from Massachusetts, to be the first resident U.S. minister to China. He arrived in Beijing in 1862. However, it was not until 1878 that Chen Lanbin presented his credentials as China's first ambassador to the United States to President Rutherford B. Hayes.[2]

The American occupation of the West Coast, especially the port of San Francisco after the Mexican-American War of 1846–1848, boosted the American presence in the Pacific, but because of the sectional crisis and then the Civil War, the numbers of Americans and interests in China grew more slowly than many had envisioned earlier in the century. By the early 1850s, after decades of missionary activity, the 150 Protestant missionaries of all denominations and nationalities in China claimed just 350 conversions among the hundreds of millions of Chinese. Many of the American missionaries believed that the Chinese were eager to receive Christ, but the reality was quite different. The missionaries found indifference at best and violent hostility at worst. Many of the targeted Chinese found the Christian message inaccessible. It was conveyed through an indecipherable mix of missionaries who used different foreign languages and spoke only crude Chinese in the early years. They argued among themselves over a variety of arcane theological differences that appeared irrelevant to the everyday lives of Chinese. There were more than thirty different groupings just among the Protestants in 1865. Traditionally, many Chinese had no problem accepting a variety of spiritual beliefs, be they Buddhist, Taoist, or other. They found evangelical sectarianism and the demand for exclusive fidelity to Christianity above other faiths to be alien to their sensibilities. Others simply found the missionary association with opium and gunboats outrageous and actively, sometimes violently, resisted the Christian message.[3]

But over time, Americans of the Book did influence the course of China's history. As the shorthand goes, Americans came to China as the three M's, merchants, missionaries, and military, but it was the missionaries who had the most enduring effect on China and on Americans back home. The first contact many Chinese had with Americans was with the missionaries and it was through these same missionaries upon their return that millions of Americans formed their opinions about the Chinese for the next 100 years.

Jesuit missionaries from Europe had visited and stayed in Beijing from the sixteenth century. (Nestorian Christians from Persia had arrived even earlier, but their presence was largely gone by the fourteenth century.) The most famous of these Catholic missionaries was Mateo Ricci, who came from Italy and lived in China from 1582 to 1610, when he died in Beijing, where he is buried. Ricci was the first Westerner to enter the emperor's palace, *Zijin cheng,* or the Forbidden City. Ricci and the others were learned and used their knowledge of science and technology to impress the court in the hope of influencing China's elite to convert and bring the country to Christianity.

Though Ricci became an important advisor to the court, few officials accepted his Catholicism. But over time, the court feared that the spread of Catholicism would undermine its authority, so Christianity was banned outright in China in the mid-eighteenth century. Preaching Christianity was punishable by the penalty of death. Even so, it is estimated that there may have been as many as 200,000 Chinese Catholics in the general population of several hundred million by the early nineteenth century, though this is probably an exaggeration.

As the power of Britain and the United States grew in China, the number of Protestant missionaries increased and they became more important in China. Unlike their Catholic predecessors, who focused on the elite, the Protestants focused on individual conversion among the everyday people of China. Though their efforts won them few converts relative to China's vast population, they profoundly influenced important sectors of Chinese society and those back home who received their reports about Chinese life, events, and the progress of propagating Christianity among the heathens. An elder American statesman of foreign relations in the twentieth century, Henry L. Stimson, observed that America's interest in China was primarily because of the missionaries. They were the first to study the Chinese language and society seriously and systematically and served as critical cultural interpreters and mediators. In widely circulated books, reports, and periodicals, they wrote for eager American audiences and personally testified before large audiences when they returned home, describing the enormity of their job in China and the importance of their spiritual endeavor. They pioneered American Sinology, becoming the country's earliest "China watchers." Americans in the nineteenth century came to know China, it was said, "through the eyes of missionaries."[4]

By the mid-1930s, when the foreign missionary movement peaked in China, Americans comprised almost half of the 6,000 Protestant missionaries in China. More than half of the American missionaries were women. Many thousands more Americans went to China under church auspices as lay workers to do good deeds and teach. The thirteen Christian colleges were among the best in the country and served almost 6,000 students, and the 255 Christian middle schools served 44,000 students. Some 250 mission hospitals treated more than a million patients each year. Today's Beijing University, Peking Union Medical College, and Qinghua, Nanjing, Zhongshan, and Zhejiang Universities substantially trace their origins to the Protestant colleges established in the nineteenth century. The American missionary movement in China, with its extensive education, medical, and social improvement efforts, was the unique form of the American presence in China. This contrasted with the practices of Europeans and Japanese, who largely pursued old-style territorial colonialism. The American missionary effort in China exemplified one of the earliest examples of the social dimension of the nation-building approach to foreign relations the United States favored as the method for spreading its influence overseas. The missionaries were the principal agents in creating a westernized, liberal, professional elite in China that would play an increasingly important role in China through ensuing decades.[5]

The first Protestant missionary to go to China was Robert Morrison from England. Because of the British East India Company's hostility toward missionaries, he actually traveled to China via the United States in 1807 and worked closely with the American Board of Commissioners for Foreign Missions after its founding in 1810. Morrison enjoyed generous support from American merchants in China, especially from D. W. C. Olyphant, one of the most prominent American businessmen in China. For both faith and business reasons, merchants saw the missionaries as invaluable help in breaking down the doors of China. Morrison stayed in China for most of the rest of his life, dying in the foreign district in Guangzhou in 1834. During his time there, Morrison devoted himself to the translation of the Bible and compiled a dictionary for English speakers so he and other missionaries could reach the Chinese masses directly. Among the first Americans to go to China as missionaries were New Englanders Elijah Coleman Bridgman and Samuel Wells Williams, who together edited and published the *China Repository,* one of the most important sources of information about China for Americans in the antebellum period, and Peter Parker, a medical doctor. All were extraordinarily dedicated to their calling and personally influenced U.S.-China relations in the mid-nineteenth century. Bridgman is accorded the honor of being the first American to learn the Chinese language, reportedly in 1833.[6]

They were inspired to proselytize during the Second Great Awakening, a broadly popular Protestant revival movement that swept across the United States in the early nineteenth century. The movement promoted evangelical work among those at home who had not yet been touched by the Gospel, including among Native peoples and slaves, but foreign missionary work soon followed. Americans began to go out into the broader world to propagate their faith and organize Protestant missions. They went to Latin

America, Africa, Hawaii, the Near East, South Asia, and China. Their crusades overseas drew on domestic support, and in turn churches sought to use missionary zeal to rejuvenate churches at home. Congregations were tutored about their responsibility to the heathen masses overseas and vicariously experienced missionary adventures and sacrifices. China's millions desperately needed help from the devout in a restless America. In the era of Manifest Destiny, missionaries' appeal drew from the expansive westward mood of the country and its growing interest in Asia. Americans saw themselves as a people chosen to expand across the continent and beyond. Many Americans came to believe they had a unique obligation to spread the Gospel to the world's peoples.[7]

What inspired them to face a life of hardship, even possible mortal sacrifice, in a faraway land? For Peter Parker, the attraction of China ran parallel to that which it held for merchants: the belief that China would play an especially important role in the future of the world. For Parker, though, it would be China's salvation through Christianity, not in commerce, that would help global transformation. In 1832, just before he made his way to China, Parker confided in his private diary,

> But O Lord by what process have I come to the preference of China as the destined field of my labor? Is it not because there are these millions on millions who are perishing for want of the Gospel and the faithful heralds of salvation, forerunners of the Holy Spirit, which other fields have but thousands or perhaps hundreds? [If] the Celestial Empire shall become Christian, will not her influence on the civilization of the remainder of the Earth be greater?[8]

But missionary work was slow going because of the imperial government's prohibitions against proselytizing. As late as 1840, there were fewer than 100 converts to Protestantism in China. (The Protestants did not include Catholics in the convert numbers, as they considered them to be virtual idolaters.) The dozen or so Protestant missionaries, restricted to the same district as merchants in Guangzhou, toiled away to master the Chinese language and translate works into Chinese. They were not permitted to go among the people, though they violated the imperial edicts by distributing their tracts secretly and on occasion even evading local authorities and traveling inland. Still, they made very little headway in their work in China. They had greater success in promoting their cause among the Chinese communities in Southeast Asia and, paradoxically, with audiences back home in the United States who regularly received their commentaries about events in Asia. The ambition of reaching the Chinese multitude inspired the missionaries, but the immensity of the job and the slow progress also overwhelmed them. "Were it not for the exceeding great and precious promises, my heart would fail me," wrote E. C. Bridgman soon after he arrived in China. "We are as nothing. I am not discouraged . . . but I am often, as now, *sad*."[9]

These missionaries occupied a conflicted position with regard to the Chinese people and their religious mission. They often suffered physically, endured privation, and sincerely believed in their mission to save the heathen. These attitudes encouraged them to sympathize with the masses of the downtrodden Chinese as the objects of their efforts to save and uplift. They strongly condemned the odious opium trade as an unmitigated evil. Yet at the same time, they were absolutely convinced of their moral and cultural superiority and were determined to bring the heathen Chinese to Jesus. They held themselves apart from, and above, the Chinese. Official policy of course tried to keep them away from the masses as much as possible, but the missionaries, imbued with an absolute sense of their spiritual superiority, believed they were to achieve nothing less than the overturning of fundamental features of Chinese life and belief, and they went inexorably forward. In this way, much more than the merchants who came before them, they sought to transform the very nature of China. As a matter of practicality, the missionaries easily attached themselves to the general Western task of breaking down China's exclusivity and expanding the foreign presence in the country. Thus, the missionaries could easily be said to be "imperialists of righteousness," or as historian Arthur Schlesinger Jr. once put it, missionaries were "cultural imperialist[s]."[10]

One who fit this description is David Abeel, another of the early American missionaries in China. After returning from two years in China, Abeel wrote about his experiences in order to enlighten fellow Americans about the monumentality of the task of missionaries in China. The conversion of China, he wrote, was of a historic immensity that could hardly be fathomed: "How infinitely vast, how worthy of all sacrifice—all hazard, all experiment— does the moral elevation of this nation appear, when viewed in its connection with the Redeemer's glory. Here is a triumph and a trophy for His victorious grace, a gem, the purest and brightest which earth can offer, to deck His mediatorial crown!" Abeel called on missionaries to go to every possible place in China: "The coasts should be invaded, and the sea-ports entered. . . . Every opening should be searched out, every tenable post occupied." "Look where we may, beneath the wide expanse of the heavens, we can find no distinct enterprise so laudable, so imperious, so inconceivable in its results, as the conversion of China."[11] Pious churchgoers at home could not but be inspired by the glorious task that lay before the self-sacrificing and visionary missionary.

Although the strength of the spiritual conviction of the missionaries fueled their efforts, it also set them apart from those they were ostensibly to save. In E. C. Bridgman's words, "Darkness covers the land, and gross darkness the people. Idolatry, superstition, fraud, falsehood, cruelty, and oppression everywhere predominate, and iniquity, like a mighty flood, is extending far and wide its desolation." China, as did other countries of the East, existed "without hope, without God, the willing slaves of Sin and Satan." The strength of the piety of the early missionaries rivaled their cultural arrogance. They saw licentiousness, depravity, and wretchedness everywhere in China. Merchants had wanted something from China and often found much to admire. They could overlook or ignore the problematic. Missionaries, in contrast, needed nothing from China but eternal souls and ardently believed that China desperately needed what they had to offer—salvation and transformation. Missionaries wanted to remake the country in their own image.[12]

During the opium trade and the subsequent Opium War, American Christians expressed these strongly held and at times contradictory beliefs, revealing as much about their feelings toward the Chinese as they did about themselves and their religious objectives. Back home, Christian publications universally condemned the British as predatory, the opium trade as evil, and the British position as immoral and unchristian. The *Christian Examiner,* a leading religious periodical edited by Nathan Everett Hale, nephew of revolutionary war martyr Nathan Hale, was typical in its attitude: the war was "a sin against God and a curse to man." But as the conflict developed, growing numbers of religious figures, including missionaries in China, came to believe that the war would help break down China's stubborn resistance to their work and thus further their evangelicalism. Bridgman closely read the British parliamentary debates over the war and concluded that he found not a trace of "Christian spirit" in them, and yet his frustration over the lack of progress in his work eventually led him to see that the war might do good in breaking down China's exclusion. Medical missionary Peter Parker went further; he thought the war was a blessing in disguise.

He saw the conflict as not a matter of opium or British commerce but rather as a "great design of Providence to make the wickedness of man subserve his purpose of mercy towards China." The American missionaries wound up welcoming the British victory as the beginning of a new millennial order in China.[13]

The life story of the first American female missionary to China provides other insights into the personality of the missionaries, their experiences, and the impact they had on those back in America. The life of Henrietta Hall Shuck is still told today in the Southern Baptist church, which reveres her as one of their greatest figures. Her plentiful writings and biographies continue to be circulated to inspire today's Baptists, who are offered her life as the story of a Christian martyr. Hall was born in Virginia in 1817 to evangelical parents who were also farmers and slave-owners. As devout Baptists, they raised their children in a protective family environment. Prayer and religious devotion were a part of daily life and the children were instilled with a sense that what lay beyond the home (slave-owning notwithstanding) was a deeply sinful and dangerous place. In her early teens, Hall accepted Jesus as her savior as a result of her attendance at a revivalist camp full of exhortation and emotion and soon decided she had to give herself to mission work. At age 18, with faith in "millennial destiny" firmly in her heart, Hall decided she should leave the safety of home and America for China to evangelize. She and her missionary husband J. Lewis Shuck soon left, Hall never to return. They lived for the next eight years in Hong Kong and Guangzhou, where they attempted to learn Chinese, teach school, and spread the Gospel, all with little success. Hall focused her efforts on young Chinese women, her "sisters," as she called them, whom she saw as especially degraded, but she died in 1844 at the age of just 27, from complications during the delivery of her fifth child. She was buried in Hong Kong. Rev. Shuck returned to America and worked among Chinese immigrants in Sacramento, California.

Hall sacrificed herself to her faith, but even at this early time of the American presence in China she lived a privileged life and maintained a superior position over the Chinese. She had servants. She was regularly transported in a sedan chair carried by them. She and her husband disliked the Chinese environment for raising their children and considered sending them back to the United States for their education and upbringing. She was horrified that her son spoke more Chinese than English and she complained that her servants "lie, cheat, and steal, and try us in a thousand ways." She knew that if her children were with them, they had to be "learning something sinful." And though she condemned the British for spreading opium among the Chinese, she rejoiced in the march toward war. "God," she believed, "in His power may break down the barriers which prevent the gospel of Christ from entering China."[14]

Other missionaries in China assumed similar militant positions when it came to the practical problem of breaking down China's resistance to their evangelism. With the confidence born of self-righteousness, they supported whatever measures were needed to open China's doors. Empathy and humanitarian concern only went so far for many a missionary in the effort to bring the heathen to salvation. For the rest of the century, many American missionaries understood every Western invasion of China as an act of Providence, the gun making the way for the Bible.[15]

The missionaries' spiritual zeal and support for imperialism can be explained by their identification of their own salvation and the moral regeneration of America itself with the effort to win China (and other heathen lands) to Christianity. They understood their sacrifice in China as God's calling and as an integral part of the recovery of a genuinely moral America. Even more, many American evangelicals embraced the millenarian thought that resurged toward the end of the nineteenth century and through the early twentieth century. They concluded that the second advent of Jesus Christ on earth was imminent, but only on the condition that the Gospel was spread through all the lands of the world. Christ's appearance would inaugurate a 1,000-year reign of His peace on earth and the fulfillment of biblical prophecies. This belief emphasized the foreign missionary enterprise as an urgent, if not the foremost, duty of the church and spreading the Word to the vast masses of China became one of the central concerns of American Christians for decades. Many believed that the spiritual revival at home in a real sense became dependent on the propagation of the Word abroad and would help realize transcendent American purposes. As Rev. J. H. Barlow, secretary of the American Board of Foreign Missions, pungently declared in an effort to gain support for American missionaries in China later in the century, "Wherever on pagan shores the voice of the American missionary and teacher is heard, there is fulfilled the manifest destiny of the Christian Republic." Thousands of ministers and their families and many more volunteer church workers and lay evangelicals made their way to China through the nineteenth and well into the twentieth centuries; it was the largest American missionary effort in the world at that time. Sherwood Eddy, the commanding leader of the YMCA in the early part of the twentieth century, saw China as "the goal, the lodestar, the great magnet that drew us all."[16] The mystery of China certainly beckoned, but even more compelling was the grandeur of the challenge. As Rev. Charles Ernest Scott, an American missionary in Qingtao who was filled with "apostolic enthusiasm," declared in his lecture at Princeton Theological Seminary in 1914:

> Verily the vastest prize on this planet for continued mastery over which Satan contends is China. And verily the most stupendous single task that faces the Christian Church till Christ shall come again is the bringing of the knowledge of the True and Living God to China.

And politically, Scott wrote, China was "the burning question of current history—irrepressible, fascinating and mysterious."[17]

Evangelizing in China was a deeply personal experience for missionaries, especially for female missionaries and church workers. Life for them in that distant and difficult country meant privation and sacrifice, but it also offered them opportunities for new experiences, autonomy, and social relationships they could never have back home. They sensed the power of cultural and spiritual superiority over the Chinese, but they also often developed sincere, intimate ties with Chinese that went beyond condescension. In the March 1914 issue of *Woman's Missionary Friend*, Alice Brethorst wrote of the Chinese, "Oh, they are a wonderful race! One just can't help loving them." Christian teacher Ellen Lyon confessed that she "loved the Chinese next to God." These and other similar effusions could betray infatuation with the exotic or the affection a superior develops for an inferior, but they also came from a genuine attachment that many everyday Americans developed with a people whose eternal souls they dedicated themselves to saving in their service to God.[18]

Though they would have vehemently objected to being characterized as cultural imperialists, many missionaries in fact worked hand in glove with American business and political forces to advance their righteous cause in China. And merchants in turn supported the missionaries because they had the energy and contacts to advance into areas where merchants could not go. The colorful and influential missionary Karl Gutzlaff, who lived in China for most of his life from the 1830s to the 1850s, translated for opium smugglers and used them to help him enter the interior to spread Christian tracts. Parker and Bridgman served as secretaries and as translators for

Cushing in the negotiation of the Treaty of Wangxia, the first U.S. treaty with China. They and other missionaries served as the main translators for the United States for forty years. Washington made Parker the commissioner of the new U.S. mission in Guangzhou in 1855–1857, making him the top U.S. representative in China. In one of his last messages as commissioner, Parker urged Washington to seize the entirety of the island of Taiwan and have it serve as the outpost of U.S. power in the Far East, much as Gibraltar, Aden, Singapore, and Hong Kong did for Britain in its various areas of interest. Washington declined to pursue the idea. It is easy to see why, from the viewpoint of the Chinese, missionaries were often indistinguishable from their aggressive secular counterparts: merchants, opium smugglers, military personnel, and officials.[19]

One of the strangest episodes of the dissemination of Christianity in China is its association with the devastating upheaval that swept through China in the 1850s and 1860s. The Taiping Rebellion, which eventually claimed an estimated 20 million lives, is the largest civil conflict in history. It began in villages in southern China that were far from Beijing but close to the area most influenced by Western opium trading and evangelism. The founder and leader of the rebel movement was Hong Xiuquan, who had read simple Christian missionary tracts as a young man in the late 1830s and even briefly attended a missionary school in Guangzhou in 1847 run by Rev. Issachar J. Roberts, an American Southern Baptist. These cursory introductions to the Bible apparently left a deep impression on Hong, who developed a bizarre syncretic creed that combined aspects of Christian thought and indigenous Chinese peasant millennialism. He attacked Confucianism and declared himself a follower of Christ. He and his followers propagated translations of the Bible, promised radical land reform, and suppressed evils such as opium smoking. Hong enforced strict moral codes for his male and female followers. He even declared himself the younger brother of Jesus Christ and sought to realize a new paradise on earth, the Heavenly Kingdom of Great Peace, commonly called the Taiping (*Taiping tianguo*). Astonished American missionaries who heard murky rumors about this uprising wondered if the movement was genuinely Christian and if so whether China would be won to Christ sooner than they had expected.

In 1853, the Taiping army defeated imperial forces throughout southern China and entered the great city of Nanjing, the former capital of the Ming dynasty. One American missionary, William Speer, who later worked among Chinese immigrants in San Francisco, recalled that "the Christian world was thrilled" when missionaries learned the news that the Taiping had captured Nanjing and established a rival capital. "It seemed as if a nation had been born in a day," Rev. William Speer wrote. "The prophecies of Isaiah as to the mighty victories of the gospel were indeed about to be realized." Even President Franklin Pierce, eager to divert American attention away from the growing sectional crisis in the country, optimistically predicted in his annual message to Congress in 1853 that the rebellion would soon improve commercial relations between China and America.[20]

At the moment of their greatest victory, however, the Taiping also began to lose the support of erstwhile Western supporters. Rev. Roberts and several other American missionaries who had accepted invitations to visit the Taiping capital found, to their profound disappointment, that the Taiping were not what the missionaries had hoped they would be. They concluded that Hong Xiuquan was delusional and his so-called Christianity heretical. Rev. J. L. Holmes, a colleague of Roberts who also visited the Taiping capital, reported, "I found to my sorrow, nothing of Christianity" but rather a "system of revolting idolatry." Holmes was later killed at the hands of Taiping. Catholic missionaries, who had never liked the iconoclasm of the Taiping, encouraged their suppression. Foreign governments also soon concluded that the Taiping were more anti-foreign and threatening to their interests, including the lucrative opium trade, than the conservative Manchu court, and they aided the Manchus in suppressing the Taiping movement. Their combined forces included a few Americans, such as the flamboyant soldier of fortune Frederick Townshend Ward, from Salem, Massachusetts, who commanded the so-called Ever Victorious Army before being killed in battle. Ward organized Chinese soldiers into a fighting force modeled on Western military concepts and weaponry. Its battlefield successes so inspired Chinese authorities that they bestowed the vainglorious name on it. Chinese imperial and foreign forces retook Nanjing in 1864 and "mercilessly slaughtered" the Taiping leadership and its followers. Imperial efforts to eliminate the Taiping in the rest of southern China continued into the 1870s.[21]

The American experience with the Taiping was the first, though far from the last, dramatic example of what might be called American wishful thinking about China. The missionaries and their supporters back home at first thought the Taiping were the revolutionary force for which they had prayed. They saw what they wanted to see in the Taiping, even when there was ample evidence to the contrary. When they eventually concluded that the Taiping were not God's instrument, they reversed themselves and welcomed the bloody suppression of the rebels, convinced that the end of the Taiping was actually God's will. "It was a mercy of Heaven that this revolution was brought to naught," Rev. William Speer eventually concluded.[22]

The end of the Taiping reign, the Treaty of Tianjin of 1858, and the Treaty of Beijing of 1860, which ended the Second Opium War, made it possible for missionaries to go inland to do their work and required the Chinese government to allow Chinese to convert to Christianity without negative repercussions. Proselytizing was now protected by international treaty. Missionaries began to expand their work and went widely into the inland areas. Because of increased contact with the Chinese people and, after the end of the American Civil War, greater financial and organizational support from home, the Protestant missionary effort began to see increased success. In 1870, missionaries claimed almost 8,000 converts, twenty-two times the number in 1853. By the end of the century, there were as many as 100,000 converts and in the 1920s there were reportedly more than 800,000 converts, Protestant and Catholic, in China.[23]

Although access to the population certainly facilitated the work of missionaries, so had a change in approach. Missionaries had long argued among themselves about the correct way, practically and theologically, to bring Christianity to China. In the early years, missionaries largely worked as evangelical ministers did in America; that is, by preaching the Gospel to the masses and bringing them to salvation one by one. Proponents of this model believed that exposure to the true Word alone would bring the Chinese to Jesus. Other missionaries, though, combined their evangelism with good deeds, or what today would be called humanitarian work, such as attending to the enormous health, educational, and social welfare needs of the Chinese masses. Over time, this latter approach brought truly significant results in establishing Christianity in China and embedding it within the social fabric of the country. The missionary enterprise became an influential constituency within China. By the 1920s, American Protestant churches supported a force of some 5,000 workers, including spouses, in China, 13 Christian colleges, over 200 middle schools, some 200 hospitals, scores of YMCA and YWCA centers, and a wide variety of charitable endeavors, such as orphanages and rural reconstruction projects. Churches owned prominent sites of land in cities and in the countryside and employed thousands of native Chinese workers. Missionaries often provided food, housing, and even stipends for their students, workers, and converts. Protestant churches and stations spread throughout the country. Through these avenues and sites and through the famine relief efforts missionaries regularly conducted in rural China, the missionary project directly touched tens of millions of Chinese.[24] Graduates from missionary colleges and schools, who numbered in the tens of thousands, filled positions in the realms of business, education, and government. Christians appeared in greater numbers among China's leaders, including revolutionaries, and Chinese converts and pastors began to bear greater portions of the work of conversion.

Despite the undeniable contributions missionaries made to improving the lives of many individual Chinese, the missionary project as a whole operated to subvert the traditional order. "Christianity was, in a measure, like opium," wrote Tyler Dennett, one of the early scholars of U.S.-East Asian relations, "being imposed upon China without the consent of the people."[25] Dennett may have gone too far in his negative opinion, but it is undeniable that missionaries made a lasting impression on China that continues to this day. Many missionaries developed a genuine fondness of China and its people. At a time when many Americans held the Chinese in the lowest contempt, missionaries spoke against such prejudices and encouraged Americans to appreciate the importance of China and its potential for social, political, and of course spiritual transformation. And many missionaries spoke of the particularly close and peculiar association of America and China.

William Speer, among American missionaries one of the most hopeful about U.S.-China relations, predicted a future China virtually remade in the image of Christian America. "China shall be all and completely Christian," Speer announced in 1870. The pagan temples and altars will come down. The inscriptions, banners, flags that littered the streets will disappear, he predicted, as will the "long-robed priests" with their incense and idols. China will even sound different: "the din of gongs, the scream of wind instruments, the roar of gunpowder in crackers, guns and cannon, the clamor of the intoxicated crowds of worshipers, all the discordant and painful noises of idolatry and superstition and folly and vice, are silent." "Light prevails instead of darkness." And what will replace heathen life? Speer declared that Americans will "see the white spires of Christian churches and schools" throughout the land. "Factories and mills" will produce "all the products of Christian civilization. Steamers and railroads will take the goods throughout the land, now linked by telegraphic wires." "You survey," Speer prompted, "the same loveliness, the same peace, the same prosperity, which charm and satisfy the mind and heart in a summer landscape of favored America or Britain." "How complete, how wonderful, how delightful the transformation," Speer enthused, and "simply the faithful and unwearied preaching of the gospel of the Lord Jesus Christ has done it all."[26]

As importantly, missionaries and their supporters back home significantly contributed to the popular conviction that a close association with China played an important, perhaps even central, role in realizing America's future of greatness and its unique destiny as a nation. Their view emphasized national exceptionalism, the idea that America was fated for glory in the world, above and beyond other nations. As for China, America, not just the Christian world in general, bore a special responsibility for bringing the great heathen country to Jesus and was providentially positioned to play that historic role. In 1867, the American Board of Commissioners for Foreign Missions, for example, identified the singular qualities of America that suited it for evangelism in China: America had special "physical characteristics," such as resources and an expanding population, that "fit us for great missionary undertakings"; the Republic and the modern missionary movement shared a "common origin in time"; China and America were Pacific neighbors; and China was "destined to enrich us by her commerce." Thus, "it becomes us, as a Christian people, to enrich her with words of eternal life"; and, perhaps most importantly for the devout, America itself would be raised to the "proper level of a Christian state" through its China missionary work.[27]

For these American missionaries, China was a source of both physical and spiritual wealth. They widely disseminated a message among Americans back home that reinforced the sense of national superiority but also of obligation, a dual theme that runs consistently through America's long engagement with Asia. America would uplift China and remake it in its own spiritual and worldly image but, paradoxically, would also become dependent upon the outcome of its own mission to transform.

China sent no one like the missionaries to America, though the importance of the early Chinese who came here was as great and perhaps even more enduring in the history of America-China relations. Chinese students and intellectuals came to learn. Many more Chinese came to work and seek economic opportunity. Neither group came to transform or proselytize, but they left permanent marks on the social landscape of both China and America. Many of their descendants are now part of the American family. The story of the Chinese arrival in America offers another way to understand a deeply personal dimension of the relationship.

American missionaries were very much involved with many of these stories. As early as 1818, the Cornwall Foreign Mission School in Connecticut enrolled young Cantonese, hoping to shape them into good Christians who would return to evangelize in China. How they all arrived in the country is not clear and none seem to have made much of an impact, but over the years other Chinese would come for school in America and many of them would make their mark on history.[28] The most prominent of these was Yung Wing (Rong Hong, 1828–1912), the first of a number of remarkable individuals who developed a special attachment and affection for America and worked to advance friendly and mutually constructive relations between the two countries they loved.

Yung Wing was born to a poor farming family in the Pearl River Delta in Guangdong Province. When he was just 7 years old, in an unusual move, his father sent him to an American missionary school in Macao to study English, possibly in the hope of making him an interpreter. After receiving further education in mission and Chinese schools, the adventuresome Yung Wing accepted the invitation of Rev. Samuel Robbins Brown to travel to America for higher education. American and British merchants in China funded his journey and he arrived in New York in April 1847. After a stay at the Monson Academy in Massachusetts, Yung Wing entered Yale College and graduated four years later in 1854, the first Chinese to graduate from an American university. His patrons hoped he would become a missionary in China. Yung Wing, however, accepted Christianity but declined to help spread the Word. He believed such a status would limit his ability to contribute to China's own reform efforts. After he returned to China with his language abilities and knowledge of America, he eventually came to the notice of high officials, who asked him to help with the urgent task of strengthening the country. One of these officials, Zeng Guofan, selected Yung, then just 35 years old, to travel back to the West to purchase machine tools for China's first modern munitions factory.[29]

After traveling through the Middle East and Europe, he arrived in the United States in the spring of 1864 in the midst of the Civil War. He attended his college class's tenth reunion, arranged the purchase of machinery for the Chinese arsenal, and then went to Washington, D.C., to volunteer for the Union Army, a duty he felt compelled to fulfill for his "adopted country," as he put it. (He had become a naturalized U.S. citizen in 1852 when he was at Yale.)[30] His offer of service was graciously declined and Yung returned to China. Twenty years later he was back in America as the deputy head of the Chinese Education Commission, a bold Chinese government initiative to send students overseas for education, especially technical training. The commission was headquartered in Hartford, Connecticut. Over 100 participated, and although the mission ended abruptly in 1881 and few of the students ever completed college, many of the returned students subsequently became prominent in China. Yung Wing himself became China's associate minister to the United States in 1878. He married an American white woman, Mary Kellogg, and had two sons, whom were named for missionaries in China. For the next thirty years, Yung Wing traveled back and forth between China and America, where his family stayed, and eventually settled in exile in America because of his association with liberal reform in China. He had to enter the United States illegally because the American citizenship that he had held for fifty years was stripped from him because of the Chinese Exclusion acts. Yung Wing died alone in poverty in 1912 and was buried in Hartford. Yung was never fully accepted in either China or America because of his personal and professional iconoclasm. A few years before he died, he narrated a touching memoir of his life, aptly entitled *My Life in China and America,* in which he conveyed a clear sense of his abiding affection for America, despite the shallow treatment he had received from its government.[31]

Americans going to trade, settle, and evangelize in China was one thing, but the movement of Chinese coming to America's homeland was another. In the minds of leading American traders and missionaries, opening China to American contact required a reciprocal opening of America to Chinese. Other Americans, however, held different points of view. America was to be a white, Christian country and the arrival of nonbelievers and other nonwhites in this land was anathema to their cultural sensibilities and racial convictions. They agitated to close America's doors to the Chinese, who were so unfamiliar in manner, language, and belief. The experiences in America of Yung Wing the intellectual were sorry. The experiences of many other Chinese who came to America were brutal and tragic.

The story of Chinese immigration to America usually focuses on the violent mistreatment they endured when Chinese began to appear in large numbers on the Pacific Coast in the early 1850s. They suffered physical violence, exploitation, rampant prejudice, and legislation that eventually resulted in their almost total exclusion from the United States and denial of naturalization privileges for the period 1882–1943. The 1882 Chinese

Exclusion Act ended the long-standing American policy of open immigration and imposed an unprecedented racial/ethnic disqualification. The Chinese were commonly seen as racial and cultural inferiors who threatened American material well-being and virtue. America's determined effort to open China occurred at the same time as it just as persistently tried to close its door to Chinese until well into the twentieth century. America had passed a law "to keep the Chinamen out, violating all the traditions of the country," lamented a Christian minister opponent of the 1882 bill, "and to import *the Chinese wall!*"[32]

The influence of Chinese immigration on Sino-American interaction was profound and compares with that of the American missionary in China in many ways. Immigrants and missionaries played unique roles in the relationship: they were both external forces from without that became "internal" within each country. They, with their detractors and supporters, provoked powerful reactions in the host country, decisively influencing the course of their countries' respective histories. They left deep, abiding marks on each society that remain today in the forms of beliefs, physical structure, and human population. The Chinese immigration question in America, as it was called in the nineteenth and twentieth centuries, formed one of the most fraught dimensions in modern China's experience with the great powers. The Chinese had plenty of rapacious colonialists and invaders, but with no other imperial country did Chinese authorities have to expend as much energy in handling the problems of its overseas subjects as they did in the Americas. And the United States had to grapple with the issues raised by the presence of large numbers of Chinese on its home soil; the presence of the alien Chinese provoked raging controversies about what it meant to be an American and about the purposes and principles of the country. The United States wound up with more than 100,000 Chinese in its population by the latter nineteenth century, far more than any other metropole. No other power had such numbers within its national boundaries at the time. (Japan annexed and occupied huge areas of China, but Chinese immigration to the Japanese home islands never approached the numbers that came to the United States.) Immigration both bound together and deeply divided China and America.

The story of Chinese immigration to America from the nineteenth to the mid-twentieth centuries is a complex one with two sharply clashing elements. American hostility toward Chinese immigration linked to domestic racism is a central part of the story, but there was another attitude that was curious but not marginal by any means. This held that the mingling of Chinese with others on North American soil was a historic inevitability. In the minds of some, it was the culmination of an epic human drama that began in the earliest moments of human civilization. That idea was not about actual immigrants so much as it was about an idealized vision of migration and the intermingling of the white and yellow "races" that had been separated in the distant past but were destined to meet again and amalgamate in America. In more prosaic terms, from America's very early days, voices have accepted, even welcomed, the presence of those from China on American soil.

The idea that the native people of North America originated in Asia was already popular among the first English settlers in North America. Columbus, of course, never surrendered his belief that he had successfully navigated to Asia and that the people he encountered in the Caribbean were Asian. They were misnamed "Indians," and the name continued to link New World native peoples to Asia, at least etymologically. English settlers in Jamestown in the early seventeenth century believed that the "Indians" they met were descendants from ancient migrants who had come from Asia or were somehow recently closely connected to traders from China.[33]

The Spanish and British brought small numbers of people from China as they colonized North America. Chinese settlements even appeared in Mexico in the late sixteenth century. American explorers to the Pacific Northwest in the late eighteenth century found Chinese carpenters brought by the British. Other Chinese arrived in America as deckhands on ships and were seen in port cities along the Atlantic. Some stayed and formed unions with white women and had families as early as the 1820s. Merchants who returned from China sometimes brought their servants with them to New York or Philadelphia, and missionaries facilitated the travel of several dozen young Chinese to America for education as early as 1818. Chinese resided in North America long before Americans began living in China, and in the early nineteenth century, their numbers far exceeded the number of American residents in China.[34]

In their exhortations to Americans to move across the continent, expansionists in the early nineteenth century often argued that settlers from China could help populate the regions of the Far West. John Floyd, the Virginia congressman who was the first to campaign for the American seizure of the Oregon Country, predicted that Chinese would immigrate to the region and would help settle the wild land there. The Chinese, he maintained in an 1821 report to Congress, "would willingly, nay, gladly, embrace the opportunity of a home in America, where they have no prejudice, no fears, no restraint in opinion, labor, or religion." Floyd may have been misinformed or simply naïve, but he clearly believed that the prospect of Chinese immigration was a positive one and would help win public support for his visionary proposal.[35]

Missouri senator Thomas Hart Benton, one of the country's most ardent expansionists in the 1820s, also welcomed, at least rhetorically, the possibility of large-scale Asian immigration to the western part of the country. Anticipating doubters who thought the idea of taking distant Oregon was an expensive and unrealistic ambition, Benton argued that Americans could transform the Columbia Valley into a great granary and sell the bounty, with good profit, to the vast markets of Asia. The Oregon Country, Benton forecast, would also become an outlet for Asia's "imprisoned and exuberant population," presumably providing the agricultural labor needed for the granary.[36]

Benton's expansionism was intimately linked to his version of grand history, in which race determined and explained all great human developments. He anticipated the white supremacist arguments of the race theorists of the end of the nineteenth century by many decades. (He himself was a slave-owner.) In Benton's version, in the ancient, dimly seen human past, the "Caucasian race (the Celtic-Anglo-Saxon division) . . . alone received the divine command, to subdue and replenish the earth." This "race" began in western Asia (presumably the Caucasus), followed the sun and went west, left "the Mongolians" behind, and eventually inhabited the shores of the Atlantic, where it lit the lights of science, religion, and arts. In time, "in obedience to the great command" the white race "arrived in the New World, and found new lands to subdue and replenish." It then arrived on the edge of the Pacific, "the sea which washes the shore of eastern Asia." On the other side of the ocean was "the Mongolian or yellow race," "once the foremost of the human family in the arts of civilization, but torpid and stationary for thousands of years." Though "far below the white," the yellow race was "far above" "the black," "the Malay, or Brown," and "red," and inevitably the white race would influence eastern Asia. "The sun of civilization," Benton pronounced, "must shine across the sea" and the white and yellow "must intermix." The two races would once again unite. And he must have shocked his fellow senators when he declared, "They must talk together, and trade together and marry together. Commerce is a great civilizer—social intercourse as great—and marriage greater. The white and yellow races can marry together, as well as eat and trade together." There was no doubt in Benton's mind that the result would be salutary for the world: the advanced white race would help rejuvenate the stagnant yellow. "The moral and intellectual superiority of the white race will do the rest: and thus the youngest people, and the newest land, will become the reviver and the regenerator of the oldest." Benton's vision and support for miscegenation conjured an epic human drama, if not a divine plan.[37] Since 1868, a massive grand statue honoring Benton has stood in St. Louis. He faces and points west, exhorting Americans to go to Asia where the future lay.

Benton was not alone in his vision of the west as the meeting ground of grand history. William Henry Seward, U.S. senator from New York in the 1840s and 1850s and later secretary of state for Abraham Lincoln, was also an ardent expansionist and saw the Pacific as the natural center of American interests. Controlling the China trade was essential for America's future, as would be the acquisition of islands and strategic points all along the Pacific. As secretary of state, Seward pressed for telegraph connections with Asia and regularized steamship traffic. He was behind the acquisition of Alaska in 1867. All of these were efforts to bring the United States closer to Asia. And he too believed that like the conflict over slavery—he famously called the impending Civil War the "irrepressible conflict"—America faced another historical inevitability. The shift of power and world attention to the Pacific would produce grand, inevitable human intermingling. In 1852, he declared from the floor of the Senate that "the commercial, social, political movements of the world, are now in the direction of California" and in turn California was the gateway to the grand Pacific. Da Gama, Columbus, Americus, Cabot, Hudson, and even the discovery of the entire New World and its settlement, he believed, "were but conditional, preliminary, and ancillary to the more sublime result, now in the act of consummation—the reunion of the two civilizations, which, having parted on the plains of Asia four thousand years ago, and having travelled ever afterward in opposite directions around the world, now meet again on the coasts and islands of the Pacific Ocean. Certainly, no mere human event of equal dignity and importance has ever occurred upon the earth."[38]

Benton's and Seward's largely secular visions of the mission of America complemented those of missionaries. In a curious twist, religious figures presented views similar to Benton's but drew from the secular to support the biblical. The most prominent of these was William Speer (1822–1904), who lived from 1846 to 1851 in Guangzhou, China, as a medical missionary. He was one of the leading evangelicals in America in the nineteenth century and remained deeply connected to China and the Chinese for much of his long life. He lost his young wife and his child to illness while the family was living in China, and he himself had to return to America to recover his strength. He then spent six years among the Chinese migrants in San Francisco and founded what is now known as the Chinatown Presbyterian Church, which claims to be the oldest Asian Christian church in North America. In San Francisco, he also founded the first Chinese-language newspaper in the country, *The Oriental,* and a school and dispensary for the local Chinese. He devoted himself to evangelical work throughout the United States afterward and served as an officer for the Presbyterian Board of Education. He wrote several books, the most important of which was the highly regarded and influential *The Oldest and the Newest Empire: China and the United States.*

Unlike fellow missionaries who disdained the heathen Chinese, Speer was an unabashed Sinophile. He admired China's long civilization and culture, praising China the way Voltaire and other Enlightenment figures did in the eighteenth century. He devoted much of his life to what he called the regeneration of the great Chinese people, who had slipped into backwardness, through Christianity and modern knowledge. He felt that although it was clear that the Chinese needed Jesus, they deserved none of the prejudice heaped upon them. The Romans, he argued, were a "far more depraved and cruel people than the Chinese" and yet they were routinely praised. According to Speer, there was no more urgent task before the Christian church and the American nation than the rejuvenation of "the Oldest Empire" by the new, as such "consummating work" had to be performed "to prepare the earth for the Kingdom of the Messiah." For Speer, the millennium, America, and China were all intimately linked in providential fate.[39]

Much like Benton, Speer believed that Americans, as representatives of the great white race, and the Chinese were destined to be reunited after many centuries of separation. Speer drew on his study of scriptures and ancient history to argue that the Chinese may very well have been one of the tribes that survived the Great Flood. Historical evidence and sacred literature suggest that it was actually Noah, wrote Speer, who founded the colony along the Yellow River that became China. Speer was convinced that the contact of Americans and Chinese on the shores of the Pacific was bringing history full cycle; it was the "termination of that westward course of empire which began in the first period of the history of man." It was nothing less than "the completion of one great cycle of the Divine government on earth" and the commencement of another—the glorious and golden age of mankind." Speer concluded that "the coming of the Chinese to America is excelled in importance by no other event since the discovery of the New World."[40]

Beyond the metahistorical, Speer highlighted other evidence to support his conviction: the Americans and Chinese, though very different in some respects, were much alike, which suggested something more than mere accident. Each country resembled the other much more than any other on earth. They inhabited great stretches of land of similar size, geographies, and climate and their national personalities had much in common (each people was "naturally thoughtful, earnest, acquisitive and enterprising"). They were even analogous politically; neither was ruled by a nobility (Speer must have been thinking of the Chinese administration staffed by those who advanced through the examination system) and each country was "now in the travail of a change from old bondage and feebleness to new power, light and influence" (Speer might have been thinking about the aftermaths of the Civil War and Taiping Rebellion). All in all, Speer foresaw, the wonderful day was soon coming "when many millions of Chinese will be dispersed over the Pacific coast, the Mississippi Valley," Mexico, Central America, South America, and all the islands of the Pacific. Americans needed to learn from the tragic experience with Africans, which eventuated in a "stupendous and calamitous civil war," and appreciate "the race whom He is now bringing to our shores." The Chinese, Speer warned, are "so incomparably greater than the negro in numbers, in civilization, in capacity to bestow immense benefits on our land or to inflict upon it evils which may end in its ruin." He hoped his book would help prepare the American audience for this new racial group God was bringing in his Divine plan, for the coming days would bring profound changes to America, the rest of Asia, the islands of the Pacific, and the peoples of the whole New World. Their "destiny," he wrote "is to be decided by the influences that shall proceed from the United States and China."[41]

Speer devoted most of his book to recounting China's long history and its arts, habits, and ways, drawing from existing scholarship and his own ethnographic investigation and personal experiences. But the emotional and intellectual heart of his work was a sympathetic discussion of the arrival of the Chinese in America. Much was unfortunate and tragic in that history and he maintained that the Chinese, for whom he clearly had affection and respect, deserved none of the brutal mistreatment and political approbation heaped upon them by his fellow white Americans. Their behavior was unchristian, un-American, and, in Speer's view, likely ultimately to be harmful to America. The Chinese would accept only so much abuse before they would rise to correct the injustice. Speer reminded his readers that Napoleon Bonaparte himself had warned of such an eventuality if the West continued to mistreat the Chinese. "In the course of time," Napoleon declared, the Chinese will take up the battle and "defeat you." But the heart of Speer's effort to win favor for the Chinese immigrant was his view that the arrival of the Chinese to America must be seen as nothing less than the working of God's will. The appearance of the Chinese was actually their *return* to the North American continent, which their ancestors, in God's plan, had settled in the distant eons, he claimed. They had been sent "to occupy the New World until the appointed time," when "the Protestant Christian nations" came to transform the continent. Now the Chinese immigrant signaled the great reunion of the "two great streams of civilization" that had separated long ago when one went west and the other east. The "peculiar glory" that "the great Ruler of nations" has given to America is to be the place where the unification of humankind will occur.[42]

Speer's support of the Chinese immigrant had the backing of many church leaders who wanted as much access as possible to the Chinese, in both China and America, in order to further their evangelical mission. They had the confidence that came from their belief that the Chinese could be as Christian and as elevated as other Americans as long as they had access to the Word. It seemed that God was physically bringing Chinese to Christian America for their conversion, and through them He would effect the transformation of their homeland.

The Chinese arrival in North America was not a matter between China and the United States alone but was part of an immense Chinese outmigration to faraway lands that began as early as the seventeenth century, when those who were loyal to the overthrown Ming dynasty and those who opposed the Manchus fled to Taiwan and Southeast Asia. Later, many Chinese from the southern part of the country moved into Southeast Asia because of social and economic deterioration. The Qing government saw these emigrants as possible troublemakers and malcontents and tried to control their numbers by forbidding emigration for long periods of time. However, the migrants could not be contained, and their numbers reached into the hundreds of thousands by the early nineteenth century. Their descendants form large populations throughout the region today. The encroachments of the West and the effects of opium, war, and peasant uprisings that marked southern China through the first half of the nineteenth century stimulated further waves of emigration to Southeast Asia and to other regions under Western colonialism, including Hawaii and other islands of the Pacific, the Caribbean, South America, and North America. Approximately 1 million Chinese left Guangdong and Fujian Provinces for overseas countries from 1840 to 1875.

The most notorious and tragic aspect of this mid-nineteenth century Chinese out-migration was the infamous "coolie" trade, a brutal system of forced labor that provided Chinese workers for mines, plantations, and large-scale construction projects around the world. (South Asians were subjected to a similar experience.) For several decades, Chinese criminals and foreign procurers and traders preyed upon unfortunate young Chinese men, many of them debtors, prisoners, and other captives from the region around Guangzhou, and forced them into a system that many contemporaries saw as replacing the African slave trade. American traders actively participated in the trade by transporting coolies to destinations around the globe, and their reports of the mistreatment of the coolies outraged many Americans. Thousands died in transit, including on American ships, and thousands more perished from disease or from abuse in mine or plantation work, especially in Cuba and Peru, the two areas where the treatment was the worst. Roughly 250,000 Chinese were delivered to these two sites. In 1856, Peter Parker, the medical missionary-cum-American minister to China, condemned the coolie trade as "replete with illegalities, immoralities, and revolting and inhuman atrocities, strongly resembling those of the African slave trade in former years, some of them exceeding the horrors of the 'middle passage.'"[43]

> His miseries are not ended by death;
> His charred bones are ground to powder
> To whiten the sugar "of Havana."

So wrote the first resident Chinese minister to the United States, Chen Lanbin, after investigating the desperate plight of Chinese laborers in Cuba in the 1870s.[44]

"Coolie" labor originally referred to forced, involuntary labor of the meanest sort but over time the term was used loosely to refer to all

Chinese workers, both unfree and free. At the time, it was not always easy to distinguish those who were forced into servitude from voluntary "adventurers," as Parker called them. The case of the *Robert Bowne* is a case in point. The American ship, under Captain Lesley Bryson of Connecticut, left Xiamen, a port in southern Fujian Province, on March 21, 1852, with more than 400 "coolies" on board, ostensibly bound for California. After nine days at sea, the Chinese revolted, killing Bryson, the ship's first and second mates, and four crew members and took control of the ship. They threatened to kill the rest of the crew if they were not returned to China. But after running aground on a small island in the Ryukyus, most of the Chinese abandoned the vessel and fled, leaving it to the crew, who took the remaining twenty-three Chinese prisoner. A British naval force came to the aid of the Americans and rounded up several dozen more of the escaped laborers, killing several in the process. They were returned to Xiamen for trial, accused of piracy on the high seas. The Americans concluded that seventeen were guilty. Parker thought the Chinese authorities should punish the prisoners under the terms of the Treaty of Wangxia, and he soberly declared that they should all be tried "fairly and justly" and then beheaded. Parker exhibited no sense of irony or contradiction in his words.[45]

After a lengthy investigation, the Chinese authorities acquitted all but one of the accused and released them. No executions occurred. The Chinese report on the incident said that the Chinese laborers had been deceived by the captain, who actually intended to take them to Peru and not California, as he had claimed. The Chinese knew that a future of toiling in Peru's guano beds and mines would be deadly and very different from a future in California. The captain and the crew had cruelly abused the Chinese, including throwing the ill into the sea, administering beatings, and meting out other physical mistreatment. The Chinese court concluded that the *Robert Bowne* had engaged in the "buying and selling of pigs," the Chinese term for the coolie trade, which violated Chinese law. Far from mollified, Parker was furious and wanted to call in a U.S. navy force to compel the Chinese authorities to reverse themselves. The local Chinese officials continued to investigate the case over the next two years, but they never reopened it. We are left with competing versions of the events that will never be fully resolved. Did Parker, even though he believed the coolie trade was an abomination against humanity, not see indentured servitude right before his eyes? Did the Chinese authorities not understand the seriousness of alleged mutiny on the high seas or did they simply favor their countrymen? We will never know.[46]

The *Robert Bowne* mutiny was just one of many incidents in the mid-nineteenth century that revealed the ignominy of the coolie trade and provoked the conscience of the public. A scandalized international society called for its suppression, and the United States was the first to finally take vigorous steps to prevent its nationals from involvement in the trade in 1862, when Congress forbade American ships from carrying any Chinese who were not determined to be free and voluntary migrants.[47]

Existing evidence today strongly argues that the great majority of Chinese males who came to North America were voluntary migrants who arrived under a variety of arrangements, including as contracted labor for a specified period of time. (Early Chinese females who came to America are a different story; many were clearly brought into the country as captive prostitutes and were virtual chattel.) Males worked in the mines, railroads, mills, and fields of the growing west and sent remittances home. Some of them eventually returned to their villages as successful "Gold Mountain Men." British, French, and Dutch colonizers organized similar streams of Chinese workers for projects in Canada, Australia, Indonesia, the Pacific Islands, and Southeast Asia. Other Chinese migrants settled in America permanently, becoming the ancestors of some of today's Chinese Americans, including the author of this book. From 1852, the first year of significant immigration of Chinese into America, until 1882, when Congress passed the first of discriminatory immigration legislation, some 300,000 Chinese, almost all of them from the Pearl River Delta near Guangzhou, entered the United States. The majority did not stay. By 1882, there were barely 100,000.[48] Chinese first worked in the California mother lode and the Sierra foothills, then spread throughout the west and Rocky Mountain states to work for wages in a variety of occupations. Some opened small stores. Their single largest employer was the Central Pacific Railroad, which required their labor to complete the western portion of the first North American transcontinental rail line. It is clear from business records and public statements that the company considered the Chinese to be free, not coerced or unfree, labor. Hundreds and then thousands began working on the line in 1865. Their accomplishments were nothing short of heroic; they dug tunnels through mountains of granite, constructed trestles across steep ravines, endured killing winters, and lay hundreds of miles of iron rails in record time. Perhaps up to 20,000 Chinese worked on the line, and a select team laid the last rail at

Promontory Summit, Utah, in May 1869. The *Scientific American* declared that the Chinese worker "commenced" the great project in the west, and "he it was who finished the great work." "But for his skill and industry," the journal concluded, "the Central Pacific Railroad might not now have been carried eastward of the Sierras." "The Chinaman is a born railroad builder," the periodical claimed, "and as such he is destined to be most useful to California, and, indeed, to the whole Pacific slope."[49] Engraved on the ceremonial "golden spike" that symbolizing the completion of the historic line are these words: "The Railroad unites the two great Oceans of the world." Chinese went on to labor on other railway lines throughout the United States, Canada, Mexico, and China.

In 1882, when President Chester A. Arthur vetoed a bill sent from Congress to exclude Chinese from the United States, he defended the Chinese and praised them for being "largely instrumental in constructing the railways which connect the Atlantic with the Pacific." He cited the tremendous growth of the states on the Pacific Slope as further evidence of the importance of the Chinese to the American domestic economy. Trade with China, and Asia generally, he declared, "is the key to national wealth and influence."[50]

Though Arthur and many others honored the Chinese for having contributed mightily to the completion of the physical unification of the country, which was subsequently celebrated as an iconic national accomplishment, others reviled them as inferior racial competitors. In the minds of many white workers, the Chinese were servile semi-slaves and threatened so-called free labor. The Chinese were accused of taking jobs away from deserving whites and of threatening Anglo-American mores, civilization, and the republic itself with their alien and pagan ways. Arriving at a time of heightened tension over issues of race and labor, Chinese found themselves the target of racial hatred and objects of ridicule and violent attack. Denis Kearney, the leading anti-Chinese agitator, declared, "The Chinese Must Go!" The worst violence occurred in Los Angeles in 1871, when more than twenty Chinese were killed, including eighteen who were lynched in the streets, and in Rock Springs, Wyoming, in 1885, when twenty-eight Chinese were murdered during a day of rioting.[51] The inability of the Chinese government to protect its nationals from bodily harm and political discrimination in the United States and elsewhere became further evidence of its abjection. Chinese, it seemed, could be humiliated anywhere with impunity and the Chinese government could do little about it. The saying went, "Find a crime, hang a Chinaman." For Washington, the animosity directed against the Chinese became a potent domestic political and social force that influenced American politics, including its diplomacy, for decades. The mistreatment of Chinese in America and the mountain of federal and local legal discrimination was a bleeding blister in the relationship between the Chinese and U.S. governments until World War II when Washington began to reverse its attitude.

American merchants interested in trade and capitalists concerned about labor supply, such as Leland Stanford, one of the magnates of the Central Pacific Railway, felt that the hostility toward the Chinese was misplaced and even threatening to their business and political ambitions. But many other Americans wanted nothing to do with the Chinese in America and fomented a national campaign to rid the country of their presence. The Chinese were thought to be ineffably foreign and not the material from which true Americans were made. This violence and political discrimination were the visible manifestations of an animus that had its roots in the earliest contact between Americans and Chinese.

Opinions that were much less positive toward the Chinese were common. American merchants, missionaries, and travelers had criticized the Chinese for their backwardness and non-Western ways. In America, such opinions came to the fore with a vengeance, for now Chinese were on American soil. Opening China to America for trade, missionizing, and U.S. political influence was one thing; opening America to the Chinese was another. Those who were hostile to the Chinese required a distancing from the Chinese or even their complete removal in order to realizing the destiny of America as they defined it. While many Americans passionately believed that the fate of America lay in the China connection, other Americans just as passionately concluded that the future of America required close attention to the danger China posed to the American heartland.[52]

For many white Americans, the Chinese were a debased race whose mental, moral, and physical qualities were inferior to those of Anglo-Saxons. Their bodies and their cultural differences were often targets of ridicule and racist caricature that reduced them to subhuman beings who deserved whatever scorn or violence came their way. Historians have seen this prejudice as a manifestation of white supremacist thinking similar to that directed against other nonwhites. The Chinese, whether in China or in America, were disrespected just as the African or the subjected American Indian; they were all a lower order of human.[53] There were common elements in American racial stereotyping, to be sure, but the hostility directed against the Chinese included a particular element that elevated the sentiment above the level of disdain. If inferiority implied diminished ability, why should the superior white fear the inferior yellow? The reason was that white superiority, it seemed, was not assured. It was vulnerable. Anti-Chinese sentiment was an emotional mixture of disdain toward a presumed inferior and deep fear. The title of an 1871 tract said it all: *The Chinese Invasion: They Are Coming, 900,000 More. The Twenty-Three Years' Invasion of the Chinese in California and the Establishment of a Heathen Despotism in San Francisco. Nations of the Earth Take Warning!* In the U.S. Senate, John P. Jones of Nevada alerted his colleagues during an 1879 debate on Chinese exclusion that "our sturdy Aryan tree will wither in root, trunk, and branch if this noxious vine be permitted to entwine itself around it."[54]

The cultural expression of this attitude was the phantom of the "yellow peril," as it came to be called, and examples of it filled the press, literature, and cultural production in America. Though the idea of the yellow peril did not originate in the United States, the idea found fertile ground here. From the mid-nineteenth century, anti-Chinese antipathy grew from local expressions of prejudice to a general national feeling by the end of the century. While it was first directed primarily against Chinese, the term "yellow peril" came to refer to all of the peoples of Asia as a profound, mortal menace to the West. Europe had long harbored a deep fear of the East. It was associated with barbarian invasions as early as ancient Greece and later with Genghis Khan and the Mongols. But it was the growing Western presence in Asia that stimulated the modern version of this fear, as the Western advance meant increased connection with the East and the arrival of Asians on American soil.[55]

Within America, mid-nineteenth-century anti-Chinese sentiment was at first closely associated with class sentiment in the west: many white workers, including European immigrants, concluded that the inferior Chinese were threats to their welfare. Labor saw Chinese as docile tools who enriched the coffers of bloated, selfish capitalists, such as Leland Stanford, at the expense of white workers. But over time, anti-Chinese sentiment widened to include other Americans who believed that the Chinese were corrupting the moral fabric of the nation with their heathen and alien ways. And other Americans went even further, concluding that Chinese actually coveted America itself and imperiled republicanism. It was a fantastical nightmare, of course, but one that was widely shared among Americans who were convinced that humanity was locked into a clash of racial civilizations.

One of the most elaborate and provocative of these expressions was the 1880 novel by San Franciscan Pierton W. Dooner. *The Last Days of the Republic* was a call to action, to awaken a slumbering American public to the designs of China on the country. The story looks back from the imagined vantage point of the early twentieth century and recounts how the United States disappeared from the family of nations because it did not take the Chinese threat seriously. Chinese immigrants, according to Dooner, flooded the country in the late nineteenth century and gradually assumed greater and greater economic and political power, first in the west and then the south, where they displaced blacks, who disappeared into the mist of history. At an arranged moment, the unassuming and hardworking Chinese laborers arose as one and with armies of soldiers from China defeated the republic's forces. The book ends with the Chinese seizing Washington, D.C., and Chinese mandarins occupying the seats of power. The book was richly illustrated with depictions of the imagined scenes.[56]

Dooner, who was a serious writer, hoped his book would help rally support for the exclusion of Chinese from America, which in fact did begin to happen after the passage of the 1882 Chinese Restriction Act. Though Dooner's story seemed wildly farfetched, his book was not unusual or especially extreme at the time. Scores of other books and articles during the late nineteenth and early twentieth centuries similarly predicted race war between yellows and whites and the danger yellows posed to America unless white America defended itself from the invasion. Prominent themes in Dooner and other yellow peril literature were racial competition—yellows vied with whites for control of the world; deception—Chinese were not who they appeared to be; power—the Chinese, through their numbers and intelligence, would overwhelm the west; and cataclysm—the most extreme measures had to be considered to protect the supremacy of the west.

Perhaps the most respected contributor to this peril literature was Jack London, the celebrated writer and journalist of the early twentieth century who glorified the muscular way of life of the far west. His 1910 short story "The Unparalleled Invasion" resembles Dooner's novel in the way it looks back from a future point in time to highlight a contemporary problem, though London's story ends in American triumph. In London's account, the future was the 1990s. He described how an imperiled West responded slowly and foolishly to the rise of China in the early part of the century. Through military conquest and mass human migrations, China threatened the rest of the world. Ultimately, the West turned to war to eliminate the danger and used biological weapons of mass destruction. An airship dropped glass vials containing horrible pathogens that had been "cultured in the laboratories of the West" on China in order to achieve the complete "sanitation of China." Every last Chinese is killed, the country is occupied by a consortium of Western nations, and an unprecedented era of Western peace, prosperity, and multinational cooperation arise from the soil of the former Middle Kingdom, now perished forever.[57]

A wide spectrum of important Americans contributed to this yellow peril literature. They included Edward Alsworth Ross, one of the founders of American sociology; publisher William Randolph Hearst; U.S. senator from California James Phelan; Brooks Adams, brother of Henry Adams and descendant of two American presidents; T. Lothrop Stoddard, a eugenicist and a theorist of white supremacy; and Josiah Strong, a national religious leader and one of the founders of the Social Gospel movement. Celebrated labor leader Samuel Gompers published a vicious diatribe against the Chinese under the incendiary title, "Meat versus Rice: American Manhood Against Asiatic Coolieism, Which Shall Survive?" Even President Theodore Roosevelt's views often had much in common with the yellow peril literature. The twenty-first-century alarm heard in America about a China threat builds on a long historical undercurrent in American political and social thought.

The yellow peril perspective in many ways was a mirror image, the flip side, of the view that held the Chinese in esteem, a view that merchants, missionaries, and scholars had commonly propagated to encourage closer ties between Americans and Chinese. The Chinese, such advocates said, were a highly intelligent people, but those who feared the Chinese saw them as "wily" and devious. Advocates characterized them as hardworking and industrious, but those who saw a yellow peril saw them as machine-like workers who competed unfairly against whites. Advocates noted that they had a long, rich, complex history, but those who feared Chinese portrayed them as inscrutable. Advocates saw their numbers as evidence of their success as a race and their desirability as customers or converts, but those who saw them as a "yellow peril" believed that they threatened to overtake the rest of the world. The turn-of-the-century view of the Chinese as friends or enemies, in other words, actually shared many assumptions about their supposedly innate qualities. Even Americans who considered themselves educated and sober-minded believed that the Chinese were a race apart from Americans and behaved in ways that were unfathomable and challenging.

In 1912, Harvard president Charles W. Eliot described the Chinese as an "Oriental race," quite distinct from the Occidental, that had a "purity" that Europeans did not. "It is the Oriental that has demonstrated the advantages of race purity," he observed with evident envy. The Chinese, he said, were "unknown hundreds of millions, tough, industrious, frugal, honest, and fecund." He meant to compliment them, but his image could also disturb. As Arthur H. Smith, a missionary who had lived in China for more than two decades and considered himself friendly to the Chinese people, pungently observed in 1894, for many around the world, the Chinese "is seen to be irrepressible; is felt to be incomprehensible." His book, *Chinese Characteristics*, assessed what he saw as the everyday features of the common Chinese, and while he found the people deeply wanting and in need of Christian uplift, he also revealed a deep anxiety about what China's future could mean for the West. The book, which was alternately dismissive and alarmist about the Chinese, was the most widely read nonfiction book on China in America from the 1890s until the mid-twentieth century.[58]

The danger the Chinese supposedly posed to America was far out of proportion to the actual numbers of immigrants who arrived. A few thousand landed in America at a time when tens of millions of poor Europeans were streaming into the country. It is difficult to explain the fear of total war with China or even a Chinese invasion of America at a time when China itself was on the verge of being dismembered by foreign powers and had no military power to speak of, unless one considers the wider context of racial thinking and empire in these years.

From the latter nineteenth century into the first decades of the twentieth, many educated Americans believed that humanity was locked into a social Darwinist "survival of the fittest," in which the various so-called races of humankind were engaged in mortal competition for supremacy, if not for their very existence. Many in the West considered the Chinese and the Japanese, especially after Japan's victory in the Russo-Japanese War of 1905, the only other "races" that might rival the West for domination. Whites were intellectually, physically, and morally superior, it went without saying, but the yellows, though fundamentally inferior, could still undermine the superior race through their guile, numbers, and depravity. (As one California senator put it, the Chinese had some advantages "over our own race in the battle for the 'survival of the fittest.'" The Chinese "can subsist on anything, and almost upon nothing." The Chinese, he claimed, had evolved over so many hundreds of years "to train their bodies down to their present state, in which they possess the capacity for labor and the power of endurance equal to that of the most stalwart races, at the same time possessing such a marvelous vital organism and digestive machinery that they are able to subsist on less than half the food necessary to sustain life in other men.") These convictions were founded on the assumptions, of course, that identifiable races of humans actually existed; that distinct behaviors, traits, and personalities marked each of these races; and that all races possessed, to greater or lesser degrees, a collective will to power. Chinese, the Orientals, the "yellows," with their limitless numbers, human and material productivity, tenacity, and perceived mental abilities were the most threatening to the continued preservation of white world supremacy and civilization itself. "One cannot help forecasting a time," wrote Arthur Smith, "when the white and the yellow races will come into a keener competition than any yet known. When that inevitable day shall have arrived, which of them will have to go to the wall?" Smith was uncertain which it would be. It was the future clash of racial civilizations that troubled many Americans.[59]

It is difficult to develop a nuanced sense of Chinese thinking in these years, given the less extensive archive that has survived, but it is evident that the attitude of at least elite Chinese toward the United States ranged widely. Many Chinese viewed Americans, along with any other Westerners, as invaders of their land, as barbarians who lived in privilege and mistreated Chinese on their own soil. The open hostility of Chinese in the Guangzhou area toward any foreigners was well known. Unsurprisingly, there was a direct relationship between the extent of the impact of foreigners on China and popular Chinese antipathy: the areas of greatest foreign impact on the country were also the areas where the strongest anti-foreign sentiment emerged. Chinese diplomats and elite travelers who visited the United States, however, sometimes returned to describe a country of wealth, beauty, and developed technology. These visitors often conveyed a sense of admiration for, even awe of, the material abundance of America and its social freedom. They also brought back reports of its odd customs, including the relatively common presence of women in public life. "Of all nations in the world, America is the most interesting to the Chinese," wrote Wu Tingfang, one of China's eminent diplomats and minister to the United States in the early twentieth century.[60]

One of the earliest writers about his observations of America was a man named Zhang Deyi, one of the first Chinese interpreters of English and a member of the inaugural Chinese diplomatic mission to the United States in 1868. Zhang published excerpts from his diary after he returned to China, and although he included nothing about private meetings and interactions, he made many exuberant comments about everyday life in America. His travels took him from San Francisco to the East Coast. He found New York City "vying with Paris for broad avenues and elegant architecture and with London for residential and commercial density and concentration"; its streets were "in a perpetual state of round-the-clock carnival and loud with carriage traffic with clashing speed." Zhang commented on the racial makeup of Americans, especially the presence of African Americans. "The Americans are now a tripartite people," he observed in Washington, D.C., "and differ in colour as they have parents of mixed native, white and black stock, producing brown, black, red and maroon offspring." He described the history of slavery in America and its war for independence from Britain. He wrote positively of the meetings with President Andrew Johnson, Secretary of State William Seward, and other leading Americans and the warm welcome he and his delegation received around the country from common citizens. Their down-to-earth demeanor and apparent openness impressed him. He quoted Johnson as saying during a banquet at the White House that "the long contact between China and the West presages firm friendship between the United States and the Qing Dynasty, which are true neighbors for all the ocean that lies between them. You have farming skills to teach us, and we have labour-saving agricultural machinery to show you. Let us select each other's best and we need never look back!" He took special note of the workings of American democracy and the strength of the American economy. Favorably comparing the United States to European powers, but not without some hesitation, Zhang noted that America "relies less on military than on financial might, of which it has no lack."[61]

Other visiting Chinese were more troubled by what they encountered in America. The crime, violence, and social inequality of late-nineteenth-century American cities, as in New York for example, shocked them. They found the treatment of African Americans appalling. And though impressed by the material wealth of America, they found the manners and habits of the people uncivilized. What they perceived to be callousness toward the elderly disturbed them. They also feared the growing might of the United States in the Pacific.[62]

One aspect of American life that especially upset Chinese visiting America was the mistreatment of their compatriots because they interpreted such mistreatment as an expression of an arrogant and menacing attitude toward China generally. Huang Zunxian, the Chinese consul general stationed in San Francisco from 1882 to 1885, had once admired America's political ideals and advanced educational system, but he became disillusioned with the country during his stay. America, he believed, had abandoned the ideals of equality once espoused by George Washington. In a long and bitter poem, Huang decried the plight of Chinese in America,

> Our country today is exceedingly weak.
> Demons and ghouls are hard to fathom; Even worse than the
>   woodland and monsters.
> Who can say our fellow men have not met an inhuman fate,
> In the end oppressed by another race?

Toward the end of his epic poem, Huang lamented,

> Heaven and earth are suddenly narrow, confining;
> Men and demons chew and devour each other.
> Great China and the race of Han
> Have now become a joke to other races.[63]

One of the most influential Chinese writers on America was the brilliant journalist Liang Qichao, who visited the United States for five months in 1903, during which he traveled far and wide in the country and met Americans from many walks of life, including President Theodore Roosevelt. Liang is considered to be China's first modern intellectual and one of its most influential social commentators in the early twentieth century. The information about America and his acute observations about its culture and ways influenced many other Chinese, including Mao Zedong. In his extended commentary, Liang devoted most of his attention to American politics, history, and ways of life. He was less interested in factories and technology. And though much impressed him about the pace of life and the prosperity of the country, much also disturbed him, including the power of the trusts, the appalling gap between rich and poor, and the mixed record of the practice of democracy. Perhaps most alarming to Liang was the expression of what he saw as open imperialist sentiment, especially directed toward the

Pacific. The United States had just won the Spanish-American War, taking Guam, the Philippines, and Puerto Rico as possessions and was then engaged in a brutal war against Filipino independence forces. In 1900, the United States had also sent marines to join seven other imperial countries to suppress the Boxer uprising in northern China. Liang was sensitive to this growing military might of the United States, a country that had been a negligible military power in the world up to that moment.

Liang took special note of President Theodore Roosevelt's open promotion of American imperialism, as expressed in what is now known as the Roosevelt Corollary to the Monroe Doctrine, which he advanced in his 1904 address to Congress. Asserting the right and responsibility of the United States to intervene in the affairs of other nations in the Americas, Roosevelt declared that the country would act as an "international police power" in the Western hemisphere to preserve peace and order. "What was his point," Liang asked, "in talking about 'role' and 'purpose' when he said, 'playing a great role on the world's stage' and 'carrying out our great purpose'? I hope my countrymen will ponder this." Liang continued, "The original meaning of the Monroe Doctrine was 'the Americas belong to the people of the Americas,' but this has become transformed into 'the Americas belong to the people of the United States.' And who knows if this will not continue to change, day after day from now on, into 'the world belongs to the United States'?"[64]

Sentiment toward Americans, and foreigners more generally, could be even more hostile among the Chinese masses than it was among the cultural and political elite. The most dramatic example of such sentiment was the outbreak of mass violence in north China in 1900 that targeted foreign residents, especially missionaries and their Chinese Christian converts. The Boxer Rebellion, as it is commonly known in the West, exploded in June and lasted until August. The so-called Boxers, Yihetuan, the Society of Righteousness and Harmony, believed that their martial arts abilities gave them superhuman powers.

The tens of thousands of men and women who filled the ranks of the Boxers largely came from the laboring poor in the Shandong Peninsula, where the Germans and British had recently expanded their control, but their message soon appealed to others throughout northern China. Japan's defeat of China in war in 1895 and its seizure of Taiwan, French aggressiveness in southern China, and Russian predation in the north further contributed to the sense that China faced imminent dismemberment. The disaffected began to form motley gangs in the late 1890s and began to attack local symbols of the foreign presence found throughout the region: missionaries and their churches, railroads and foreign government personnel, and businesses. The bands armed themselves with modern weapons and formed armies. The court at first opposed the Boxers but then changed its mind as the uprising grew in strength. "The foreigners have been aggressive towards us," the Empress Dowager Cixi, the effective leader of the country, declared in her new support of the Boxers. She noted that the foreigners had "infringed upon our territorial integrity, trampled our people under their feet.... They oppress our people and blaspheme our gods. The common people suffer greatly at their hands, and each one of them is vengeful. Thus it is that the brave followers of the Boxers have been burning churches and killing Christians."[65] Monuments to the martyred Americans at Oberlin College memorialize Oberlin missionaries who were killed in China during the uprising.

During the summer months, the Boxers killed hundreds of foreigners and thousands of Christian converts throughout the countryside in northern China and surrounded the barracks of the Legation Quarter of Beijing, the location of foreign embassies and the residences of ambassadors. The West, appalled by the reported atrocities committed by the Boxers, watched as it appeared that China was taking on the entire Western world. The *New York Times* asked in its headline, "How Great Is This 'Yellow Peril'?," wondering whether the rebellion was truly an awakened *monstrum horrendum* or just a "little Chinese devil." The uprising finally ended when the largest multilateral force assembled to date of 60,000 foreign troops, including 6,300 American soldiers and marines, landed in Tianjin and fought their way into Beijing and lifted the siege of the legations. The brutality of the foreign troops and their pillage and rape of the Chinese civilian population shocked even those who had first supported the foreign invasion. From then until 1949, thousands of foreign soldiers, Americans and others, continued to occupy Chinese territory. Among those who were rescued in China was a recent Stanford graduate named Herbert Hoover, future president of the United States. Hoover and his wife, Lou Henry Hoover, had traveled to China to manage the operations of a coal mine. Hoover vividly recalled the terror of the Boxer siege many years later, and he continued to have a deep interest in China for the rest of his life. Over forty years, Lou Henry Hoover and he assembled one of the major collections of Chinese porcelains in the West. The Chinese people, he said, were a "great race," one for which he had an "abiding admiration."[66]

In the nineteenth century, the tens of thousands of Americans who went to China as merchants, missionaries, soldiers and the tens of thousands of Chinese who came to America as students, workers, and seekers of fortune bound the countries together in deeply spiritual and material ways. Their presence on each other's soil provoked strong reactions, from the positive to the hostile, and left tangible legacies that remain with us still. Chinese and Americans are buried in each other's countries. Monuments and markers give evidence of their historical presences: in the United States, plaques show where Chinese railroad workers helped complete the transcontinental line, in China, tombstones mark the final resting places of American missionaries. The descendants of these Chinese and Americans continue the connections today.

America and China reversed positions in the nineteenth century. At its start, Americans from the young nation traveled to the putative oldest nation, China, seeking fortune. At home, many leading Americans held China in high regard as a place of wise and ancient civilization and an indispensable source of wealth. It was a place that was deemed to be essential for America's very future. Though its ways of life and governance were far removed from the American experience, the very longevity of its existence was ample evidence of its importance and worthiness of respect. Mighty China, for its part, tolerated the ambitious American traders and eager missionaries who sought to proselytize. By the end of the century, humiliating defeats in wars had humbled the Chinese empire. Internal rebellion threatened to end 2,000 years of imperial rule. Chinese at home and abroad received no respect, instead suffering insults and violence. Americans, coming now from a country that had become a great power itself, enjoyed the spoils of war at China's expense. The shameful widespread looting of China's great cultural heritage by the invading powers marked the depth to which China had fallen. America still wanted Chinese wealth, but not the Chinese people themselves. They became the first (though not the last) to be excluded from America's shores and denied citizenship privileges because of their ethnicity. America's destiny, many Americans were convinced, must not include the Chinese.

3

Grand Politics and High Culture

The day will soon come when we shall be the east and China the west . . .
and the western passage—the long-lost hope and desire
of the ancient navigators—shall be accomplished.

Boston mayor Nathaniel B. Shurtleff, 1868

Commerce, immigration, and religion dominated the relationship between the United States and China through most of the eighteenth and nineteenth centuries. The political relationship developed more slowly. Washington was primarily interested in supporting the activities of its merchants and traders, and secondarily, its missionaries, and saw little need to complicate matters. Unlike the European powers who made China a target of their imperial ambitions, Washington largely remained aloof from China's internal affairs. Washington leaders actually tried, albeit unsuccessfully, to keep American politics out of the relationship by quieting the domestic rage over Chinese immigration. For its part, Beijing only slowly responded to the unprecedented crisis to its existence that was brought on by the advance of the great powers, and it responded in desultory ways. Still, early U.S.-China political interactions exhibited certain features that in time would develop into a "special relationship" between the two countries, a complicated but singular relationship that endured through time.[1]

In contrast to the great enthusiasm in America for the China trade and evangelism, the formal relationship between the Chinese and American governments developed quite slowly for the twenty years after the initial fanfare over Caleb Cushing's conclusion of the Treaty of Wangxia in 1844. A string of U.S. representatives came and went, but they stayed only briefly and sought mainly to facilitate commerce and ensure that the United States received the same business privileges as the other foreign powers. Though Americans interested in China were not happy with their inability to develop direct relations with the Qing court, there was little they could do about the situation. They occasionally urged Washington to join with the European powers to press for greater advantages in China, but Washington maintained a firm policy of neutrality in conflicts between the Chinese and European nations. Relations between the United States and China were characterized by friendship (other than on the immigration question) and peace through most of the nineteenth century. Quite unlike the other Western powers (and later Japan), the United States from its earliest contacts with China declared its respect for China's territorial integrity and avoided interference in its internal affairs. Washington believed that the United States was best served by maintaining a discrete distance from the aggressive Europeans and encouraging the Chinese to see Americans as a different sort of foreigner. Even during the great Taiping Rebellion that so threatened and weakened the Qing, Washington eschewed the temptation to exploit the situation for its own gain; the United States declared its neutrality in the civil conflict. Commodore Matthew Perry, commander of the Pacific forces and leader of the famous naval expedition that went to "open" Japan in 1853, described American policy toward China as one of "masterly inactivity."[2] Indeed, the United States commanded few resources in that distant part of the world and politically was absorbed by the sectional crisis at home.

Washington understood the limits of its overseas power at the time, but it still had an important presence in China and, in the eyes of the Chinese elite, Washington's policy elevated its reputation above that of the predatory Europeans. Lewis Cass, the secretary of state from 1857 to 1860 in the administration of President James Buchanan, clearly summarized the established American policy in his 1857 instructions to William Reed, the first U.S. minister to go to Beijing. America, wrote Cass, "is not at war with the government of China, nor does it seek to enter that empire for any other purposes than those of lawful commerce, and for the protection of the lives and property of its citizens. The whole nature and policy of our government must necessarily confine our action within these limits, and deprive us of all motives either for territorial aggrandizement or the acquisition of political power in that distant region. . . . With the domestic institutions of China we have no political concern, and to attempt a forcible interference with them would not only be unjust in itself, but might defeat the very object [commerce] desired."[3]

In contrast to Western states that had long experience in regularized multistate diplomacy, in China, foreign relations were handled largely through an antiquated apparatus at the imperial court and through provincial authorities until the debacle of the Second Opium War of 1860. The Qing's humiliation on the battlefield made it clear that it had to change its ways. The court established the *Zongli Yamen* (the full name was *Zongli Geguo Shiwu Yamen,* the Office for the Management of the Affairs concerning Various Countries or, roughly, the Foreign Affairs Office) to handle foreign relations. Under the terms that ended the war, foreign powers could establish permanent missions in the Legations Quarter in Beijing to represent their governments to the top authorities. The Manchus had seriously underestimated the challenge of the West after the first Opium War and had barely survived the Taiping Rebellion, but the court had finally realized that it had to respond seriously to the dire crisis before it if China, and the rule of the Qing, was to survive. Its reform efforts reflected the Qing assumption that the United States was a different sort of foreign power and could be used to the court's advantage.

What is known as the Tongzhi Restoration, so named for the emperor's reign period, was a series of top-down reforms the court made from 1860 to 1874 that aimed at strengthening the country militarily and developing the technical and political knowledge necessary to defend it. The Qing sponsored railway and factory construction projects, developed military forces equipped with modern weapons, and built arsenals and weapons plants. Americans figured prominently in many of these efforts. When the court decided to study and distribute Henry Wheaton's *Elements of International Law,* then widely consulted in the West as the authority on modern diplomacy, it selected a translation by an American missionary, W. A. P. Martin. The court later appointed him to organize an interpreters' school in Beijing that later expanded to offer other subjects, including mathematics, physical sciences, and international law specialists. The *Tongwen Guan* was the forerunner of the Imperial University. And in 1864 the court sent the American-educated Yung Wing to obtain machine tools in America for China's first modern arsenal. It was at this time that China had its most positive experience with a foreign emissary, the American Anson Burlingame, and entrusted him with the responsibilities of its first diplomatic mission to the West.

Burlingame arrived in Beijing in the summer of 1862 as the American minister to the Qing. A leading Republican who was favored by Abraham Lincoln, he played an important and most curious role in U.S.-China relations. He was a prominent member of Congress from Massachusetts with close ties to the Radical Republicans, including William Sumner, whose strong support for the abolition of slavery he shared. He watched the American Civil War from Beijing, where he resided until he took a six-month leave of absence in the spring of 1865 to return to Washington. During these months, he and Secretary of State William Seward developed what has been called a "cooperative policy" toward China that was intended to replace the aggressive and belligerent approach European powers had followed. Burlingame and Seward hoped that their policy, which was influenced by the British approach emphasizing the commercial value of Chinese integrity, would reduce competitive friction among the foreign powers, promote peace and cooperation with China, and help China maintain at least a semblance of territorial control and sovereignty. Their strategy was to encourage trade and commerce; cultural exchange, including religious rights; regular diplomatic interaction; and free immigration, with the protection of immigrants' rights. Together, these elements formed an enlightened package that Seward and Burlingame argued would well serve the interests of all parties involved. Theirs was an ambitious and audacious plan.[4]

Burlingame returned to Beijing in December 1865 but was unable to present the cooperative policy to the court until 1867. At that time, he resigned his post as the American minister to China and offered his services to the Chinese to become *their* envoy to the West! China had never sent an emissary to Europe or America. The court, with confidence in and affection for Burlingame, accepted his offer and in November 1867 appointed him envoy extraordinary and minister plenipotentiary to lead a mission to the United States and major European powers. Inadvertently because of a translation miscue, he was given the power to negotiate treaties.

With two other ministers, translators, and dozens of assistants, bodyguards, and attendants, the Burlingame mission arrived in San Francisco in the spring of 1868 and made its way across the country. Burlingame, an accomplished and gifted orator, made few public appearances because of the controversial nature of his position as an agent of a foreign power and the turmoil surrounding the impeachment proceedings against President Andrew Johnson. But his arrival still drew much attention. China had "converted a citizen of the youngest nation of the world into the Ambassador of the oldest," wrote the *Daily Alta California,* the leading Republican paper in San Francisco. In June, when he arrived in Washington, D.C., Burlingame immediately went to see Seward, who then drafted a revised agreement between China and the United States embodying all the elements of the cooperative policy the two had formulated a few years earlier, including the promise that Chinese immigrants would be protected and enjoy the same rights as others in America. Burlingame and his entourage met President Johnson, his cabinet, and leading members of Congress to garner support for his treaty. The work went quickly and on July 24, 1868, the Senate unanimously ratified it. Word of the document circulated immediately, exciting American elites. When the draft was sent to Beijing, the Zongli Yamen closely studied it and concluded that it was "thoroughly advantageous to China" and "in no way prejudicial to her." The Chinese court accepted the treaty in November 1869, with not one change.

Indications of the tremendous excitement Burlingame's mission generated were the warm receptions he and his entourage received in New York and Boston, even before the treaty was finalized. New York City's financial and political elite hosted a grand banquet for Burlingame and his colleagues on June 23, 1868. The organizing committee consisted of some of the most powerful men of the city, including a young Theodore Roosevelt, China trader William H. Fogg (for whom the famous Harvard Art Museum is named), and mining and railroad magnate William E. Dodge. Delmonico's, on 14th Street and Fifth Avenue, was festooned with Chinese and American flags, and honored guests made speech after speech lauding Burlingame's work. History hung in the air as orators repeatedly invoked "destiny" to emphasize the importance of the moment. Governor of New York Reuben E. Fenton declared, referring to the Burlingame mission, that "no event in modern diplomacy or intercourse has equal significance, or promises so much of benefit to the human race." It fell to America to help bring this momentous event about, as it was its "destiny, under Providence," to link Europe and the West to China in the East. Respected jurist Edwards Pierrepont observed that "the completion of the Pacific road, the opening trade with the East, and the vast emigration from China, are the grand events which follow our terrible war, and reveal something of our great destiny."[5]

Two months later, Boston, not to be outdone in honoring Burlingame, a native son, honored him with a celebratory parade and reception. Organized and hosted by the city's financial, political, and intellectual elite, the event, like the one in New York, offered an opportunity for a visible and aural ex-

pression of the importance of U.S.-China relations. After Burlingame's entourage arrived from Washington, D.C., they were conducted on an elegant
procession that wound its way throughout the city and included gun sa-
lutes at Boston Common. On August 21, the city hosted a banquet for the
mission and 225 of the city's most important citizens at the posh St. James
Hotel. Among them were Massachusetts political leaders, including Caleb
Cushing, who had negotiated the first American treaty with China in 1844
and was then a prominent Washington statesman; Senator Charles Sumner;
and distinguished military figures. Luminaries from the arts and sciences
included Oliver Wendell Holmes, Ralph Waldo Emerson, and Louis Agassiz.
In his welcoming remarks, Boston mayor Nathaniel B. Shurtleff waxed eloquent about the magnificence of China, speaking of its refinement, ancient
culture, and material accomplishments. He reminded his guests that Boston
was the American city that had initiated the China trade that had generated "much of the wealth of the old families of Boston." The future, he predicted, would bring even grander commercial benefit and, in an imaginative reversal of the traditional trope of the vigorous, outgoing West going
East for riches, he declared that one day soon America "shall be the east
and China the west" and the "western passage—the long-lost hope and desire of the ancient navigators—shall be accomplished." Shurtleff's somewhat
confusing play on words nevertheless emphasized his estimate of the historic dimensions of the mission.[6]

A high point of the evening's event was the presentation of a heroic poem
composed especially for the occasion by Oliver Wendell Holmes Sr., one of
the leading intellectuals of mid-nineteenth-century America. "Brothers,"
Holmes's poem, begins by addressing the visitors from afar: "we, the new
creation's birth, greet the lords of ancient earth." Holmes hails "fair Cathay"
and its wisdom, power, and glory and calls on China to merge with America:
"May the girdle of the sun / Bind the East and West in one." He ends with
a transhistoric vision of the great winds of Mount Shasta mixing with those
of China's Daxue Mountains, of the blue waters of Lake Erie blending with
those of Dongding Lake, and of the water of the "deep Missouri" flowing
together with the "rushing Hoang-Ho."[7]

In his own public comments in Boston about his mission, Burlingame
also explicitly linked his own life, the fate of America, and the future of
China. In his "dear Boston," he said, "I learned to denounce that pride of
race which denies the brotherhood of man," recalling his early opposition
to slavery in America. "I learned to plead for four millions of human

beings as I now speak for four hundred millions of human beings. . . . I speak today as in the old time for the equality of men—for the equality of nations." Few other Americans at this time would be so forthright in proclaiming respect for the national equality of a non-Western country. Tragically, Burlingame died from illness just four months later in St. Petersburg, Russia, while still on his mission in the service of the Qing. He never got to enjoy his retirement ranch along the San Francisco Bay, now the location of a town that bears his name. His good friend, the usually sharp-tongued and unsentimental Mark Twain, sincerely eulogized him as a "very, very great man. America lost a son, and all the world a servant, when he died."[8]

The Burlingame Treaty has the distinction of being the most equitable treaty China entered into with a Western power in the nineteenth century. It expressed an attitude of reciprocity, mutual respect, and desire for peace that no other agreement concluded between China and other countries after the Opium War did. Though Washington later abrogated the most important features of the treaty, including the provisions about the protection of Chinese immigrant rights in America, the treaty was still a bright moment in the relationship. It guided the nation's relationship for more than a decade and helped establish the idea—cynics would say myth—that the United States stood for equality in its relations with China.

The symbolic high point in nineteenth-century U.S.-China relations may well be the triumphant visit of former U.S. president Ulysses S. Grant to Beijing in 1879, when the Burlingame Treaty was still largely in effect. The Chinese received Grant with great respect and spectacular celebration, and the future political relationship between the two countries still looked bright from both sides. Grant, military commander of the Union forces in the Civil War and president of the country from 1869 to 1877, became the first former head of state of a Western country to visit China when he arrived in the country's southern region in 1879 on the last leg of his journey around the globe. Grant shared Seward and Burlingame's sympathetic attitude toward China, as evidenced by his personal meeting with the students in Yung Wing's China Educational Mission at the 1876 Philadelphia Exposition, where he went out of his way to shake the hand of each of the 113 boys. The former president spent two months in China and was accorded a grand welcome everywhere. He arrived in Hong Kong in April and toured the Guangdong region, and then his flotilla traveled up the coast, stopping at ports along the way, including Shanghai. At each stop, he, Mrs. Grant, and his companions received tributes and attentive, gracious care. The former president and his wife had long been enthusiasts of Chinese products. Among their personal possessions was a 315-piece dinner service they had obtained from Canton in 1868. The well-documented record of his trip to China offers fascinating looks at China through the experiences of one of the most distinguished Americans of his day. The meticulous chronicler of the journey was John Russell Young, later American minister to China and then librarian of Congress.[9]

Young recorded the profound differences between Chinese and Americans in everyday life, in the organization of cities, and in behavior and thinking. The Grant party found the street life of China to be raucous and colorful (though often dirty and unhealthful), and they were impressed by the grand architecture of houses. The ceremonies were endless and at times tedious. The potential of the country was obvious to Grant, but so too were its many problems, especially its political conservatism and resistance to change. For Young, the visit to China was the event of a lifetime. "I have seen some extraordinary sights," he reflected, which included the celebration of the end of the Confederacy and the funeral of President Lincoln. "Among these I place the spectacle of General Grant's entrance into Guangzhou. The color, the surroundings, the barbaric pomp, the phases of an ancient civilization—so new, so strange, so interesting." It was one of the "most wonderful sights I have ever seen," he wrote. The event included, as a compliment to America, a full 21-gun salute, the first ever accorded to a foreigner by the Chinese. Local Chinese hosts repeatedly praised the friendship between China and America.[10]

At one dinner, Grant and his entourage arrived at the local viceroy's spacious manor, carried in sedan chairs by silk-robed attendants. The manor was resplendent with banners and gongs. After a formal greeting, the party moved to another pavilion and the dining hall. Chimes filled the air, and the gardens "dazzling with light." The hall was open on three sides, and for the next three hours, Grant enjoyed what surely was the meal of a lifetime. "In splendor and suggestions to the appetite, and appeals to a luxurious taste," Young noted, "the Chinese have surpassed us. I can imagine how a Chinaman might well call us barbarians as he passes from our heaped and incongruous tables to his own, where every course seems to have been marked out minutely with a purpose, and the dinner is a work of art as ingenious as the porcelain and bronze ware, over which you marvel as monuments of patience and skill." Here is Young's description of the elaborate meal:

The dinner began with sweetmeats of mountain-cakes and fruit-rolls. Apricot kernels and melon-seeds were served in small dishes. Then came eight courses, each served separately as follows: Ham with bamboo sprouts, smoked duck and cucumbers, pickled chicken and beans, red shrimps with leeks, spiced sausage with celery, fried fish with flour sauce, chops with vegetables, and fish with fir-tree cones and sweet pickle. This course of meat was followed by one of peaches preserved in honey, after which there were fresh fruits, pears, pomegranates, coolie oranges, and mandarin oranges. Then came fruits dried in honey, chestnuts, oranges, and crab-apples, with honey gold-cake. There were side dishes of water chestnuts and fresh thorn-apples, when the dinner took a serious turn, and we had bird's-nest soup and roast duck. This was followed by mushrooms and pigeons' eggs, after which we had sharks' fins and sea-crabs. Then, in order as I write them, the following dishes were served: Steamed cakes, ham pie, vermicelli, stewed sharks' fins, baked white pigeons, stewed chicken, lotus seeds, pea-soup, ham in honey, radish-cakes, date-cakes, a sucking pig served whole, a fat duck, ham, perch, meat pies, confectionery, the bellies of fat fish, roast mutton, pears in honey, soles of pigeons' feet, wild ducks, thorn-apple jelly, egg-balls, steamed white rolls, lotus-seed soup, fruit with vegetables, roast chicken, Mongolian mushrooms, sliced flag bulbs, fried egg-plant, salted shrimps, orange tarts, crystal-cakes, prune juice, *bich de mer,* fresh ham with white sauce, fresh ham with red sauce, ham with squash, and almonds with bean curd. In all there were seventy courses.

Between each course, Young said, there were cigars and pipes. It is a wonder anyone survived the repast.

In Beijing, Grant met the highest leaders of the land, including Prince Kong, the prince regent of the empire, and Viceroy Li Hongzhang, the so-called Bismarck of Asia, but he had no audience with the emperor, then just a child of 7 years old. He saw the wonders around Beijing: the Ming Tombs, the Temple of Heaven (he was the first non-Chinese to enter the sacred site), and the Great Wall where it met the ocean. China and the Chinese deeply impressed Grant. He commended their commercial abilities and their potential to make China into a great military power. The leaders he met understood the need for change, he believed, and they were proceeding to reform. But he thought the Chinese state was incapable of defending the country. It is as weak, he noted, as the U.S. federal government would be "if States rights, as interpreted by Southern Democrats, prevailed." But he saw positive change coming to China and predicted that within the next two decades the world would not complain about China's backwardness but would worry about its "absorption of the trade and commerce of the world." Grant was more than a century off with his prediction.[11]

Grant's expectation that China would quickly rise were misplaced indeed. The Tongzhi Restoration failed to strengthen the country sufficiently to withstand the continuing demands of the foreign powers or appreciably improve the circumstances of the population. During the 1880s and 1890s, the ability of the Qing to govern declined further, and by the end of the century China faced virtual dismemberment and extinction. Its geopolitical position was bleak: in 1874, China lost control of the Liuqiu Kingdom (later known as the Ryukyus, of which the largest island is Okinawa) to Japan, which annexed the islands in 1879. The Sino-French War of 1884–1885 ended with France establishing its dominance over northern Vietnam and part of southern China. During the conflict, French forces destroyed much of China's fledging modern navy, ending its effort to develop any serious naval strength. In the mid-1880s, the British assumed control over the former Chinese tributary states of Burma and Sikkim. In China's northwest, Russia took vast stretches of territory. In the Sino-Japanese War of 1895, the Japanese crushed Chinese forces in northern China, established their influence over Korea, and annexed Taiwan and the Penghu Islands (Pescadores). A few years later, Germany occupied Qingdao, the key port on the Shandong Peninsula, and the Russians took control of Dalian and Shenyang (Mukden) in Manchuria. The United States, in contrast, was only marginally involved in these depredations.

In the 1890s, however, the U.S.-China relationship began to sour. The positive feelings, exemplified by the Burlingame Treaty and Grant's visit to China, fell into the shadows of history, replaced by a more difficult relationship as the United States became increasingly involved in determining the political fate of China. In a major change, the internal affairs of China and its politics began to absorb the attention of American policy makers. This shift in the U.S. attitude accompanied the dramatic industrial changes in America in the 1880s and 1890s that propelled it to the top of the world's economic powers. As China's circumstances continued to deteriorate and approached national extinction, America's resources and powers boomed. The contrast between the national trajectories of the two countries could not have been starker. In the post–Civil War years, America's expansive industrial economy became the wonder of the world. In 1893, the United States became the world's second larger exporter, after Britain. Its railroad, steel, coal, banking, and food processing industries created an economic powerhouse second to none.

America had entered the "gilded age," the term Mark Twain coined to characterize the era's unprecedented wealth and excess. Leading figures spoke openly about the need for America to assume its position among the ranks of the great European powers and take up the noble torch of imperialism. Among the most vocal of the imperialists were Albert J. Beveridge, Theodore Roosevelt, and Henry Cabot Lodge. Joining them were intellectuals and writers such as Brooks Adams, Hubert Howe Bancroft, and Josiah Strong. A wide range of other influential turn-of-the-century Americans encouraged the vigorous promotion of American interests, specifically in China. Among these were James Burrill Angell, president of the University of Michigan and former U.S. minister to China; Bishop James Whitfield Bashford of the Methodist Episcopal Church; Seth Low, mayor of New York and later president of the American Asiatic Federation; and railroad mogul Edward Henry Harriman. These voices from different social positions formed a loud chorus supporting American overseas expansion, especially in China, which seemed to be more important than ever as a site for American products, capital, and imagination. It would be the vast market that would help industrial America avoid the economic problems caused by industrial surpluses.[12]

In the late nineteenth century, the United States brought island group after island group throughout the Pacific under its control, and then, in 1898, it annexed Hawaii, the crown of an insular empire that included Midway, Guam, and Samoa. Then came the 1898 Spanish-American War, the turning point in America's ascension as a global power. Though the war started because of American outrage over the Spanish mistreatment of Cubans, who rebelled against colonial rule, the war's focus quickly shifted from the Caribbean to the Pacific. After a brief conflict with Spain, the United States, which had been born of anticolonial rebellion, found itself a colonial power, a committed military force in the Caribbean and the Pacific that was at war with Filipinos who were fighting for their own independence.

"For the people of the United States," wrote William Elliot Griffis, one of America's leading experts on Asia at the time, "the oceanic event of May 1, 1898, changed their view of the world." On that day, American commodore George Dewey utterly destroyed the Spanish fleet in Manila Harbor and ended Spanish control of the Philippines, which had been its colony since the mid-sixteenth century. The American victory "made the Far East a Near West," declared Griffis. China and Asia were no longer "perspective" but "prospect." Americans would now "see the whole Pacific through their western windows and at their own doors," and like the shots fired at Lexington, the roar of the naval guns at Manila "foreshadows change." Griffis, writing just months after the events in Manila, was confident that his fellow Americans would rise to the demanding occasion, take the Philippines, "yield to the necessity of national expansion," and "share with the Anglo-Saxon peoples the supremacy of the Pacific." The daunting possibilities seemed to impress even the expansionist-minded Griffis: "How strange does the very suggestion (as if it were a novelty) of our being a World-Power seem!"[13]

The Philippines formed the commercial gateway to China, Griffis noted, as did many other important American leaders, including President William McKinley, who saw the importance of the islands in much the same way. McKinley decided that the United States had to retain the Philippines and soon declared that they should be annexed and placed on the map of the United States. As the imperialist Beveridge famously declared, "The Philippines not contiguous! The oceans make them contiguous. And our navy will make them contiguous."[14] This acquisition of the Philippines immediately made the United States a rival of and perceived threat to the other great powers in Asia, especially Japan, a development that would have great and tragic consequences in the mid-twentieth century. The empire in the Pacific, with China as the lodestone, would bring opportunity but also great cost. The United States would not end its claim on the Philippines until 1946.

In the 1890s, geopolitical thinkers had prepared the ideological way for America's Pacific empire and, by extension, a more energetic China policy. The most prominent of these was Alfred Thayer Mahan, the most famous military strategist in nineteenth-century America. Mahan is best known for his work on the importance of naval power, but his development of what is now called "grand strategy" also had an enormous influence on American political leaders. Mahan studied the interconnections between economics, politics, military power, and geography and their implications for national policy. Mahan assumed that America was, and should be, a great world power: its particular location in world geography, its size and economic heft, and its history determined its great responsibilities and its expansive interests. For Mahan, empire was a given destiny, not a choice.

Mahan published *The Problem of Asia* a few years after his classic work on the influence of naval power in history and virtually in the midst of the Spanish-American War. It included several articles that had first appeared in *Harper's* and the *North American Review*. In this effort, Mahan considered the rise of the importance of Asia in contemporary American and world politics and the implications for America's geopolitical interests. As with Griffis and many others in these years, Mahan expressed a heightened appreciation for Pacific politics and the importance of Asia, especially China, for the United States. No longer was China a parochial matter for merchants, traders, or missionaries. It was, according to Mahan, a basic geopolitical concern for the nation. "The problem of Asia," declared Mahan, "is a world problem," and within Asia, China was "the central issue."[15]

Mahan was among the first to grapple with the strategic challenge of America's ascendancy as a world power, one that possessed, in his view, vital Atlantic, Caribbean, and Pacific interests. Along with economic activity, political and military concerns were shifting into the Pacific. As early as 1897, he had written Theodore Roosevelt, an admirer of his writings, that turmoil in Asia, not in Europe, represented the greatest danger to American interests and that the importance of Asia would continue to rise. Senator Albert J. Beveridge likewise argued that America must be a Pacific power and have access to "China's illimitable markets." "China is our natural customer," he declared. "She is nearer to us than England, Germany or Russia, the commercial powers of the present and future." At the height of his presidency, Theodore Roosevelt predicted that America's "future history" "will be more determined by our position on the Pacific facing China than by our position on the Atlantic facing Europe." In 1907, he wrote that "the Atlantic era is now at the height of its development and must soon exhaust the resources at its command. The Pacific era, destined to be the greatest of all, and to bring the whole human race at last into one great comity of nations, is just at the dawn." Roosevelt, who actually had no love of the personal qualities of the Chinese, nevertheless shared this estimate of the long-term geopolitical and economic significance of China to America. The "fate" of the American people was to lead this new association of peoples of the West and East. "We cannot escape our destiny," Roosevelt trumpeted.[16]

The rise of Asia had two major implications for America, in Mahan's view in 1900. For one, he emphasized the realization of an isthmian canal. The canal certainly was not a new idea for Americans, but it now assumed even greater importance, not so much because of its regional significance alone but because of its global significance for trade and the projection of American military might. The canal would allow American naval power to travel from one great ocean to another, playing a strategic role similar to that of the Suez Canal for the British. Mahan considered America's interests in the two great oceans that were contingent with America as an integrated issue that required new visions and political commitments. The American line of communications to China, Mahan declared, lay through the Isthmus of Panama. Within a few years, the United States began construction of the Panama Canal.[17]

The second major implication of Asia's rise, according to Mahan, was that Americans needed to elevate their appreciation of events in China and affirm a muscular policy toward the protection of American interests there, the most important being open and equal commercial and intellectual access to the country. China, he colorfully wrote, "may not—cannot—be forced to drink, but she must at least allow the water to be brought to her people's doors"—by force of arms against an obstructionist Chinese government if necessary. Concomitantly, it also meant that the United States had to prevent any other external power or group of powers from assuming "preponderant political control" over a China that would "exclude our commerce and neutralize our influence." The American people, Mahan warned, had to be "ready to throw not only our moral force, but, if necessity arise, our physical weight into the conflict to resist an expropriation" of power by another force in China. Mahan's talk was vague, and he must have wondered what kind of "physical weight" the United States could actually deploy in a country as far away from its shores as China. And as farsighted as Mahan could often be, he did not foresee the full implications of his words for Japan; it rose in the coming decades to seek the exact sort of "preponderant political control" over China that he so adamantly opposed.[18]

Mahan helped give popular voice and backing to an emergent China policy that would occupy an increasingly prominent place in American foreign affairs. The articulation of this policy, now famously known as the Open Door Policy, is seen as a milestone in American diplomacy. In it, the United States declared that it had a vital interest in seeing that China should be open to all. No one power or group of powers should dominate that vast country's resources and markets. In declaration after declaration through the years, Washington committed itself to guaranteeing equal access to

China and to guaranteeing China's territorial integrity and national independence. Its aim was to keep China from partition and dismemberment. The Open Door Policy ranked second only to the Monroe Doctrine in the history of American foreign affairs, according to the estimation later of Walter Lippmann, the eminent political journalist, and was propagated by the United States with nothing less than "missionary zeal," in his words. George F. Kennan, known as the architect of the Cold War policy of containment and the dean of American diplomatic historians, wondered whether the Open Door Policy substantially provoked America's interwar antagonism with Japan.

From the time it was advanced, the Open Door Policy inspired admiration, scorn, and controversy. Its principles have come to be seen as forming a central element of American diplomacy more generally, at least in the first half of the twentieth century. In this expanded sense, the Open Door Policy has been taken variously as representing the nobility of American political ideals in international affairs—Walter Lippmann characterized it as the "expression of the American political religion"—or the cynical expression of a unique form of American nonterritorial imperialism. To some, it symbolized a naïve, fuzzy sentimentality toward others based on good intentions but an unclear identification of real interests and capabilities; to others, the Open Door was about advancing American commercial interests at the expense of its avowed support for national self-determination. That this controversy emerged first over America's China policy indicates the looming significance of China to American foreign policy makers. Everyday Americans endorsed the Open Door Policy for a variety of reasons: perceived economic advantage, morality and international law and order, sentimentality toward China, and even greed. China should be held open for all, it was said, but especially for the United States. For its part, the Chinese government warmly welcomed America's defense of the open door and its declared opposition to exclusive foreign privilege in China as helpful to its own efforts to avoid imperialist domination.[19]

The Open Door Policy was presented through a series of pronouncements about the American attitude toward the possibility that China would be dismembered by foreign powers, first made by President William McKinley's secretary of state, John Hay, beginning in September 1899. As a young man, Hay had been a close White House aide to Abraham Lincoln and then spent much of his life as a diplomat in subsequent Republican administrations. Consistent with the views of other leading Republicans before him, Hay held an abiding interest in China and its importance to America, notwithstanding his own strong racial prejudices against Chinese people. In a statement that has repeatedly been reproduced over the years, Hay once declared, "The storm-center of the world has gradually shifted to China. Whoever understands that mighty empire—socially, politically, economically, religiously, —has the key to world politics for the next five centuries." As secretary of state, he responded to the real danger of great-power dismemberment of China in 1897–1900 and issued several "notes" to the other great powers expressing the views and interests of the United States. The key elements of these were America's interest in enjoying equal access to Chinese markets and its opposition to exclusive privileges enjoyed by any other power, including within their own spheres of influence. The opportunity to exploit China equally was the essence of the Open Door Policy. But the other important element in Hay's notes was the insistence on recognizing and upholding China's territorial integrity. The United States did not want to see the division of China into zones under the exclusive control of any foreign power, as such control would upset a balance of power in Asia and jeopardize American access to the country. Though the notes expressed respect for the Chinese people's interest in self-rule, their purpose was much more about limiting possible foreign control of China to the disadvantage of the United States. American commerce with China was seen as dependent upon maintaining its territorial integrity and preventing the country's dismemberment. Even though actual American commerce with China never amounted to anything substantial, it was always the bright, seemingly limitless prospects of the future that beguiled American businessmen and political leaders. Though Hay had not consulted with the Chinese government before he issued his notes, Beijing came to embrace the principles of the Open Door Policy as part of its long-standing effort to play the foreign powers against one another.[20]

In formal substance, the notes did not represent a major shift in the American attitude toward China. The ideas of equal access to China and most-favored-nation status were as old as the 1844 Treaty of Wangxia. The Burlingame Treaty of 1868 explicitly recognized the principle of respect for China's territorial integrity. What was new in the issuance of the notes was the vague suggestion that the United States would enforce the principles of the Open Door Policy, even though the notes never explicitly stated what Washington would do if other powers did not respect them. The notes expressed a new self-consciousness of national power and will that a wide range of Americans expressed in the late 1890s and that they identified with the American presence in China.[21]

The Open Door Policy notes elicited the popular expression of moral regard for the welfare of the oppressed Chinese masses, a sentiment that would become an integral part of America's relationship with China and an active ingredient in Washington's subsequent policy formulations. This professed paternalism tapped into the long-held idea in America that the two peoples had a special bond, with America acting as a unique friend and presumed protector of China. From the earliest contact, Americans tried to distinguish themselves from the avaricious Europeans and Japanese. As The Nation had proudly declared in 1868, "America stands alone as their constant friend and advisor, without territorial aspirations, without schemes of self-aggrandizement—the unpretending but firm advocate of peace and justice."[22] The Open Door Policy notes of 1899 were thus seen not as a defense of American commercial or even strategic interests alone; they were also perceived to be a noble expression of the American values of fair play and respect for others. The missionary and church press in particular praised the Open Door Policy notes for these reasons, but so did the public generally. In its editorial entitled "A Victory for Civilization," the New York Times welcomed the news that foreign powers had reluctantly acknowledged the American position. The Nation, which had attacked McKinley's imperialism, hailed Hay's work as a "noble work of peace." The Open Door Policy brought profit, geopolitical calculations, and righteousness together in a way that won the endorsement of the American people. Even the hard-nosed military strategist Mahan reflected this confidence that America had right and not just might on its side in the Open Door Policy notes. America, Mahan observed, "is for good," and its efforts were that "of a nation which respects the right of peoples to shape their own destinies, pushing even to exaggeration its belief in their ability to do so." America's purposes, he claimed, were not for our own immediate interests alone but were "to the general interest of the world."[23]

Events in China quickly tested the principles espoused in the Open Door Policy notes. In the summer of 1900, the Boxer Rebellion erupted and the West declared that China was at war with civilization itself. The Great Powers, including the United States, formed a combined expeditionary force to invade the country to rescue the surrounded foreign community in Beijing from the upsurge against foreigners in north China. The United States, Britain, France, Germany, Russia, Japan, Italy, and other foreign powers united to force the Chinese government to accept truly humiliating terms, including erecting monuments in China to the foreigners killed by the Boxers, imposing staggering indemnities amounting to hundreds of millions of dollars, and permanently installing foreign military personnel in Beijing to protect resident foreigners. Some called on the United States to join the other great powers in the actual partition of China. America should do so, wrote the English China scholar Demetrius C. Boulger in the *North American Review*, "to prevent the Yellow Peril from becoming a menace." In contrast, Mark Twain denounced the invasion of the country (he sympathetically called the Boxers "traduced patriots") and declared the settlement the foreign powers demanded outrageous. Twain found the Christian missionary calls for vengeance against the Chinese especially shameful, and in response he wrote a bitter, sarcastic essay, "To the Person Sitting in Darkness," that condemned American behavior in China and the Philippines as just as cynically imperialist as European colonialism.[24]

But behavior of American forces during and after the suppression of the Boxers again set it apart from the other invaders. The U.S. military maintained discipline and did not engage in the atrocious behavior of the Germans and Russians, who wantonly raped and pillaged. The United States coordinated its command with the other powers but maintained its mission of relief and rescue, not punishment. After the expeditionary force lifted the siege of the foreign legations in Beijing, the United States quickly withdrew most of its personnel from China, leaving behind a small token force of a few hundred soldiers to protect its legation. Secretary Hay again reiterated the American position against the partition of China and worked to restrain the Europeans and Japanese. Chinese officials took notice and praised the Americans for their restraint.

China barely escaped dismemberment and extinction. In the settlement of the conflict, Hay tried, without success, to decrease the amount of the indemnity foreign powers demanded. He believed it was excessive and would weaken China, only increasing its vulnerability. Several years later, the United States used its indemnity money to support the education of Chinese students in the United States. Though not entirely altruistic—the effort aimed to enhance American cultural influence in China—the Boxer Indemnity Scholarship Program helped sustain the popular impression in America that the country was a friend and supporter of the Chinese people.[25]

Many Americans sincerely believed the United States' relationship with China had ethical and practical benefits for their own country. "America holds in China today a position of unprecedented strength and significance," John Barrett, a leading diplomat and political observer, declared in November 1902 after visiting China. This was because "America is implicitly trusted by China. . . . In commerce America is everywhere welcomed in China, because her commerce involves no territorial aggression." Immigration exclusion was a major sore point, but it was just an "incident" compared to the loss of territory. Americans, declared Barrett, could be "honestly proud, and her material and moral opportunity is one that is tempting in its possibilities."[26]

Barrett was overly optimistic about America's future in China and underestimated the sting of American immigration restriction. In 1904–1905, Chinese consumers and merchants in the Shanghai area, prompted by Chinese residents in Hawaii, boycotted American goods for months to protest yet another discriminatory act against Chinese immigration to the United States. Though the boycott failed to move Congress to amend the legislation, the mass protest sufficiently worried American businessmen and officials that they sought to soften the implementation of the new exclusion orders. But many Americans had a blind spot about racial discrimination and failed to appreciate the depth of Chinese anger against American immigration restriction. Wu Tingfang, one of the most astute early-twentieth-century Chinese diplomats and a believer in the transmigration of souls, said that he hoped that American exclusionists would be reborn in their next worldly lives "in Asia or Africa, and that the injury that they are now inflicting on the yellow people they may themselves have to suffer in another life."[27]

In his famous assessment of the history of American diplomacy, George F. Kennan observed that the Open Door Policy declarations resonated with the American public. "Its imagination was fired," Kennan wrote, "its admiration won." The Open Door Policy, Kennan concluded, produced a "myth" that America was a protector of the Chinese nation, a myth that was not founded on clear interests and could not be enforced. The American people developed "sentimentality" toward the Chinese people that profoundly affected subsequent U.S. policy and the course of history in Asia. This sentiment disturbed some, like Kennan, who believed it was misplaced, but it gratified others who saw a special American connection with China. As Jacob Gould Schurman, American minister to China, former president of Cornell University, and U.S. commissioner in the Philippines, proudly reported to Secretary of State Charles Evans Hughes in 1921, "We are universally regarded by the Chinese people as their special friend." Schurman was endorsing the Open Door Policy, but his comment says more about Americans' self-perceptions as democratic good Samaritans than about actual Chinese opinion. Schurman's fond hope was taken as reality.[28]

The ambiguities of the Open Door Policy, the peculiar mix of idealism and political calculation that characterized the American attitude toward China, and the complexities of internal Chinese politics all manifested themselves in the American response to the 1911 Republican Revolution in China and to Sun Yatsen (*Sun Zhongshan*), whom some Americans fondly claimed as one of their own. They liked to call him the "George Washington of China," a characterization that was offered as praise but was another example of Americans using their own history to misinterpret China's experience. The 1911 Revolution and Sun are icons to Chinese of all political persuasions: Chinese Nationalists and Communists both see themselves as their legitimate inheritors. Their historical realities, in fact, are murky, which helps explain the subsequent ubiquity of their appeal and the ease with which they were appropriated for very different purposes by opposing political forces.

Xinhai Geming, or the Republican Revolution of 1911, was unlike revolutions as they are commonly understood: there was no effective leading organization, no guiding ideology, no charismatic leadership, no coherent program, and no mass uprising, and the eventual result was national disunity and betrayal. The Revolution dates from the outbreak of a military revolt against the Qing government on October 10, 1911, in Wuhan, central China, that soon spread to other regions. There were several motivating sentiments: the anti-Manchu anger that the dominant Han population had long harbored; revulsion against the venality and ineffectiveness of the court; army discontent; and anti-imperialism. But there was little else that the array of revolutionaries—constitutional monarchists, socialists, liberal democrats, warlords—could agree upon. The emperor and his court, which represented 2,000 years of imperial rule in China, became the one target of all the revolutionaries. They found common ground in the demand that the Qing Xuantong emperor, five-year-old Puyi, abdicate. After he did so in early 1912, military leaders organized a vague form of republican government that drew upon representatives from throughout society. Real power, though, continued to be wielded by tough regional military commanders who had abandoned the Qing and had little patience with republicanism.

The revolutionaries turned to the one individual around whom they could unite, Sun Yatsen, a man honored because of his years of dedicated anti-Manchu effort. Sun had much prestige but little real power. He had actually been in Denver, Colorado, when he read about the military revolt in China, but unlike Lenin, who rushed back to Russia in 1917 from exile, Sun took his time before returning to appeal for foreign support. He landed back in Shanghai on Christmas Day, when the Revolution was largely over. The various revolutionary factions turned to him as the new republic's provisional president and Sun declared the founding of the Republic of China on January 1, 1912.

Sun was a determined revolutionary and an uncommon Chinese. He was born in the Guangzhou region in 1866 in the aftermath of the Taiping Rebellion but moved to Honolulu at age thirteen to live with his elder brother, who had emigrated some years before. Sun received his education at the Iolani School, a missionary institution, where he learned English, American history, and science. He graduated in 1882. He moved to Hong Kong in 1884, where he studied medicine at the Hong Kong College of Medicine, founded by the London Missionary Society. He also became a Christian and was baptized by an American Congregational minister, Dr. Charles Hager. In the early 1890s, Sun, increasingly disturbed by China's abysmal condition, turned from the pursuit of medicine to the practice of rebellion, and for the rest of his life he dedicated himself to realizing a strong, modern country. In 1895, he organized the first of many abortive anti-Manchu uprisings and became a man with a price on his head. For the next sixteen years, Sun lived largely in exile in Southeast Asia, Hawaii, Japan, and Europe, where he gained the political and financial support of many Chinese compatriots overseas. He made the first of several visits to the United States in 1904, when he stayed a year, making contact with Chinese Americans, 90 percent of whom were Cantonese like himself. The Chinese communities in Honolulu, Oakland, San Francisco, and New York became safe havens for him. On one trip to the United States, he established a still-mysterious and bizarre network of American backers that included retired army officers; Charles Boothe, a wealthy Los Angeles retired banker; Harrison Gray Otis, the conservative publisher of the *Los Angeles Times*; and Homer Lea, a self-styled military strategist who had studied Chinese at Stanford University, all of whom it seems were promised leading or profitable roles in a new Chinese republic. Lea, a colorful adventurer who actually suffered from kyphosis, a degenerative condition of the spine, was in fact Sun's close advisor when he returned to China in 1911. Sun also developed a loyal and enthusiastic popular following in the United States. One leading American businessman and author long associated with Asia wanted to anoint him "Sunyacius," an awkward title mimicking "Confucius" and Roman luminaries. American author John Stuart Thomson declared that "Sun Yat Sen will go down to history as the greatest dreamer, prophet, organizer, altruist and political philosopher, the modern world has known."[29]

Sun served as China's provisional president for just forty-five days before he handed over the office to General Yuan Shikai, former commander of the Qing's northern army, in order to win him over to the Revolution. But soon afterward Yuan began to thwart republican aims. He even tried to proclaim himself emperor. By 1913, Sun was in exile and once again was organizing rebellion, now against Yuan and the parade of warlord strongmen who took power in Beijing after Yuan's death in 1916.

Sun's politics were an amalgam of ideas gathered from his study of democratic and radical philosophies that ranged from American liberalism to European socialism, though he never displayed anything approaching a distinguished intellect or consistent political philosophy. He was, however, an indefatigable organizer and talented communicator to the overseas Chinese who commanded vital resources and connections. He was also an unusual and strange mix: a sincere Christian, a determined Chinese nationalist, and a pan-Asianist who admired Japan's modernization and strength. He appealed to the common Chinese but also married into the wealthiest of families. In 1915, he married Song Qingling, a woman twenty-two years his junior who had been educated in Macon, Georgia. She was a member of the famous Song (Soong) family and an associate of China's left wing throughout her life. Charles Song, Qingling's father, was a prominent Christian who had helped bankroll Sun's early political efforts but disapproved of the marriage. In 1917, Sun hailed Lenin and the Bolshevik Revolution and gratefully received advisors and aid from Soviet Russia to further his revolutionary efforts toward the end of his life. But he also befriended the militarist Chiang Kaishek (Jiang Jieshi), who became his brother-in-law when Chiang married his wife's sister, Song Meiling (Soong Mayling), better known later in life as Madame Chiang Kaishek. Chiang commanded the military wing of Sun's political party, the Guomindang (Kuomintang), and claimed Sun's mantle when he took over the leadership of the Guomindang after Sun died in 1925. Chiang was then a nationalist revolutionary who was still out of power, and China itself was a unified republic in name only. A patchwork of brutal regional warlords actually controlled the sorry country.[30]

Contrary to the later common assumption that the United States quickly welcomed the Chinese republic, most political leaders and the American public generally warmed slowly to the 1911 Revolution, assuming that it would destabilize the country and questioning the ability of the Chinese to rule themselves. Some in America, especially those connected to the missionary effort, proudly claimed the Chinese revolution as their own, as did the New York City journal the *Independent.* "America is responsible for the revolution," it wrote; "its leaders are largely young men educated in the United States or in the American mission schools. They have imbibed from us the spirit of freedom." One prominent international relations specialist even declared that the end of imperial rule should be called "The American Revolution in China." But President William Howard Taft joined the other great powers in delaying recognition of the republic. Japan, Russia, and others wanted the republic to acknowledge certain foreign privileges before granting recognition. Incoming president Woodrow Wilson, who had close friends and relatives who had been Christian missionaries to China, was more favorable to the Revolution and had even sent a personal message of congratulations to Provisional President Sun. Earlier in his career, Wilson, who was deeply racially prejudiced, had endorsed the exclusion of Chinese workers from the United States,[31] but in international relations he appreciated the importance of China to America. President Wilson took the controversial step of removing the United States from an international consortium of Western powers that sought to extend control over China's finances through foreign loans. Despite his predecessor's support for and the interest of American bankers in the consortium, Wilson feared it would undermine the young republic, and in March 1913, he withdrew support for the loan program. Wilson released a statement to the press that sharply criticized the consortium and stated that the United States was "earnestly desirous . . . of aiding the great Chinese people in every way that is consistent with their untrammeled development and its own immemorial principles." And then, in ringing language, Wilson made a statement that embodied the altruistic and commercial ideals of the Open Door Policy:

> The awakening of the people of China to a consciousness of their responsibilities under free government is the most significant, if not the

most momentous, event of our generation. With this movement and aspiration the American people are in profound sympathy. They certainly wish to participate, and participate very generously, in the opening to the Chinese and to the use of the world the almost untouched and perhaps unrivaled resources of China.[32]

Wilson's public sympathy for China helped make him immensely popular among the Chinese, and his translated speeches became best sellers in China.

Shortly afterward, in April 1913, the Beijing bureau chief of the Associated Press wired news back home reporting that Yuan Shikai, who was then leading China, had asked Christians to pray for him and the new republic. Yuan was not a Christian and though some thought his call was simply a political ploy, the news electrified many in America. The *New York Times* and other newspapers ran the report on their front pages. The news inspired the pious Wilson, and he gathered his Cabinet to discuss the development. Wilson, as reported by the secretary of the navy, who was at the meeting, confessed that he did not know when "he had been so stirred and cheered" as when he had read Yuan's statement in the morning paper. Wilson considered asking American churches to respond to the request from Beijing. Though considerations of separation of church and state led the president to change his mind, Secretary of State William Jennings Bryan circulated Yuan's message to mission boards throughout the country. In turn, the Federal Council of Churches forwarded the message to 150,000 Protestant churches and asked them to pray for China on a designated day. On April 27, millions of Americans in every part of the country offered sincere prayers for China. In the following decades, millions of churchgoing Americans continued to do so. They also raised money, volunteered to serve in China, and campaigned for China's Christian future.[33]

Under Wilson, the United States broke with the other great powers and formally recognized the Republic of China in May 1913, the first of the major powers to do so. Chinese enthusiastically celebrated the news and flew American flags throughout the country. Americans also warmly welcomed Wilson's decision and hailed it as an example of America's embrace of a democratic diplomacy. However, American unilateralism displeased the other powers entangled in China's affairs.

The importance of China for Wilson is seen in who he considered appointing as his ambassador to China. William Jennings Bryan, the charismatic and influential former populist and presidential aspirant, was high on the list before he accepted the post of secretary of state. Wilson then offered the position to the eminent former president of Harvard, Charles W. Eliot, but his family had other opinions about the educator's future and he declined. Wilson asked the leader of the powerful YMCA, John R. Mott, to take the position, but Mott also begged off. Wilson eventually succeeded in appointing Paul S. Reinsch, a Wisconsin progressive and prominent political scientist, Asia specialist, and friend of many Chinese students and intellectuals. In his 1900 textbook *World Politics*, he had predicted that China, with its vast resources and capable and huge population, was destined to become "the industrial centre of the world."[34]

Though Wilson believed in the invigorating power of democracy and anti-imperialism and spoke loudly about self-determination, events in China overwhelmed his high hopes for the Chinese republic, and by the end of his presidency, many of China's liberals, intellectuals, and students had become deeply disillusioned with Wilson and the United States. The disaffection with America began almost immediately after the warm celebration of Wilson's recognition of the republic. Wilson, believing that the autocratic Yuan Shikai could stabilize the country and maintain the Open Door Policy, threw his support to Yuan and distanced the United States from the radical Sun Yatsen and his followers. Washington opposed Sun's new revolutionary efforts and even accepted Yuan's efforts to restore himself as emperor. Wilson personally attended a memorial service held by the Chinese legation in Washington, D.C., for Yuan after his death.

World politics would further complicate Wilson's efforts to befriend China. In 1919, in order to keep Japan at the Versailles Peace Conference that concluded World War I, Wilson reluctantly acceded to its demands that it retain control of Chinese territory in Shandong that had formerly been held by the defeated Germany. When the shocking news arrived in Beijing, thousands of students protested in Tian'anmen Square on May 4, 1919, the highlight of the famous May Fourth Movement and the birth of China's modern radicalism. China had entered the war on the side of the Allies with the promise that Germany's possessions, especially the Shandong Peninsula, would return to Chinese sovereignty at war's end. China had sent some 150,000 laborers to Western Europe to build fortifications for the Allied effort and believed its contribution would result in the recovery of Shandong. (After crossing the Pacific, the Chinese had been transported in sealed trains that they could not step out of even for a moment because of the severity of the immigration laws. Among the translators sent to help the workers in France were future Communist leaders Deng Xiaoping and Zhou Enlai.)[35]

Versailles terribly disillusioned many young Chinese. Thousands of students and intellectuals, feeling betrayed by the Western democracies led by the United States, began to turn to radical politics and cultural rebellion, rejecting Wilson and his ilk as hypocrites. Wilson's own secretary of state, Robert Lansing, was despondent over the president's decision. "China has been abandoned to Japanese rapacity," he wrote in his diary. "I am heartsick over it," because Wilson will lose much goodwill with his "great wrong." Minister Paul Reinsch, Wilson's erstwhile friend, was so upset about the Versailles settlement that he resigned his post in Beijing. Reinsch returned to the United States vowing to devote the rest of his life to developing the relationship between America and China and correcting his government's betrayal of China. Wilson's refusal to support China's claim to Shandong helped sink the Versailles Treaty in the Senate, and in China the Communist Party soon emerged among those who were disenchanted with Wilson and the West.[36]

In the 1920s, toward the end of his life, the missionary-schooled, Western-oriented, and Christian Sun Yatsen turned to the Soviet Union for help. On his deathbed, Sun instructed his followers to ally with the Soviet Union and cooperate with the fledging Chinese Communist Party to conduct a new Chinese revolution. He sent his top military commander, Chiang Kaishek, to military school in Moscow and reorganized his Nationalist Party, the Guomindang, along Leninist lines.

American leaders, with moral gravity and idealistic vision, had declared their support for an "open door" policy for China. Wilson had believed that replacing imperial China with a republic offered great promise for the regeneration of the country and the strengthening of the historic ties between America and China. But the idealist Wilson surrendered to Japan's aggressive demands about China despite its betrayal of both China's territorial integrity and the open door. Washington continued to give verbal and diplomatic support for China's claims to national sovereignty, for example at the nine-power Washington Naval Conference (1921–1922) that addressed armament and Pacific issues, but the contradiction between American declarations and actions, on the one hand, and the challenges of China's domestic revolution and Japanese predation, on the other, produced one great dilemma after another for U.S. diplomacy for the next thirty years. The conflict between the practical realities of dealing with Japan's great-power

ambitions in Asia and U.S. verbal commitments to China's sovereignty and
territorial integrity continued to sharpen.

Individuals such as ex-ambassador Paul Reinsch insisted that the future
of America lay in a supportive relationship with China for obvious business, geopolitical, and moral reasons. Yet words of friendship and respect
were insufficient for him. "We are indeed blind if we do not realize that the
fate and future of China are inextricably bound with our own," he said. He
was convinced that Japan's ambitions in China directly threatened America.
"China," he declared in 1922 on the eve of the Washington conference, "will
soon be called the Asiatic United States." It had the "same continental outlook. She is new in resources, though old in civilization; young in politics,
though mature in social experience. She comes from a different stock but
she seeks the same aims as we have." Reinsch did not use the word "destiny" but it was his clear meaning: the grand interests of China and America
coincided and complemented each other. Reinsch was dedicated to, even
obsessed with, advancing the relationship for the "true liberation of the Chinese people," as he wrote in his memoirs in 1922.[37]

The story of Reinsch's tragic last days serves as a metaphor for the tensions between America's idealist hopes for China and the realities of power
politics. After an unsuccessful run from Wisconsin for the Senate, Reinsch
returned to China in the fall of 1922 to advise the Chinese government about
financial matters and arrange helpful loans from American banks. During
a tour of the country, however, Reinsch suffered what appeared to be a severe mental breakdown: he hallucinated that Japanese assassins were after
him, much as Japan was after China, and he became violent and irrational.
He was diagnosed with "delusional dementia" but later was found to have
a brain tumor. His health quickly declined and Reinsch died in Shanghai
in early 1923, among the Chinese, a "vast and lovable people," as he had
described them in his memoir.[38]

American leaders and diplomats struggled to respond to the unsettled, even
chaotic, political situation in China. Some advocated massive loans to assist with China's reconstruction efforts; others cautioned about being drawn
into what seemed to be an increasingly dangerous and unpredictable country.
At the same time, the American public continued to be drawn to China's
rich material, aesthetic, and philosophical traditions. This fascination
through the years deeply influenced the cultural lives of both countries.

Chinese arts and crafts had come to the attention of early Americans. In the eighteenth and nineteenth centuries, many Americans, both elite and non-elite, filled their homes with Chinese ceramics and porcelains, home decorative wares, furniture, and the like. This chinoiserie was widely appreciated and admired. American ships brought Chinese handicraft and art ware back by the tons, wonderful examples of which are now on display at the Peabody Essex Museum in Salem, Massachusetts, and at the Boston Museum of Fine Arts.[39] In the eighteenth and early nineteenth centuries, Chinese craftspeople and artists were the most adept producers in the world of items for international consumption. One shrewd entrepreneur even produced dozens of knockoffs of Gilbert Stuart's famous portrait of George Washington. (The U.S. $1 bill still displays this image.)

Chinese silk held a special attraction for American women. In the eighteenth and nineteenth centuries, embroidered Chinese shawls became prized possessions in America, and as the China trade boomed, the display of Chinese silks became a marker of sumptuary elegance for wealthy women. They decorated their homes with Chinese hand-painted wallpaper and silk window coverings and cooled themselves with carved ivory fans. Toward the end of the nineteenth century, American women's fashions began to be influenced by Chinese and Japanese designs. The looser fit of Chinese jackets and Japanese kimonos appealed to American women seeking bodily freedom. First Ladies Julia Grant and Helen Taft proudly wore elegant gowns made with Chinese silk for their husbands' presidential inaugural balls. Taft's fashionable Manchu style tunic was especially striking.[40]

Beyond the world of the elite, the domestic sphere of everyday Americans in the late nineteenth and early twentieth centuries was filled with a wide variety of items from China. Kitchen and dinner ware, clothes, decorative items, and interior design all showed the presence of China in the American home. Even the diet of Americans was changing. Chinese restaurants, recipes, and foodstuffs became commonplace in even the smallest American towns. The Chinese game of mahjong swept the country in the 1920s in a craze.[41]

As for art, the general American public first viewed Chinese paintings in 1838. In that year, Nathan Dunn, a Philadelphia merchant who had been enriched by the early China trade, opened what became known as the Chinese Museum to the American public. According to one estimate, more than 100,000 people viewed 1,200 objects Dunn had collected when he lived in

China. These items ranged from natural history specimens to garments, tools, housewares, and fine paintings. The crowds who visited were much impressed by paintings that were as large as nine feet wide by five feet high. The artwork, though, left even the Sinophile Dunn ambivalent. He wrote in the museum catalogue that the several hundred paintings in the show provided clear evidence of Chinese artistic ability. Chinese painters, he observed, could render images with "great correctness and beauty." However, he concluded that "shading," a staple in western realism, was something "they do not well understand." Nevertheless, Dunn appreciated aspects of Chinese aesthetics, or at least its exotic appeal to Americans, and incorporated elements of Chinese architecture in his New Jersey estate. Other elite Americans also did so in the eighteenth and nineteenth centuries.[42]

Dunn's museum generated great curiosity, and an effusive review of the show reveals not only the high esteem in which Dunn was held but also the admiration, even reverence, many in America had for Chinese civilization. Brantz Mayer, an author, traveler, and public official, praised Dunn's museum as one of the greatest collections about a people that had ever been assembled. The Chinese, Mayer observed, had attained a height of material and artistic development long ago, before civilization had even dawned in Western Europe. Though they were now languishing because of their disinterest in "novelty and change," this was something to be admired rather than "scorned as illiberal and barbarous." Mayer believed the Chinese were "the wisest people on the earth" because they were not swept up in the Western mania of the constantly new.[43]

Dunn's museum remained open for three years in Philadelphia before he moved it to London. A few years later, in 1844, John R. Peters, who had been a member of the first official American delegation to China, displayed his own Chinese art collection to the American public in Boston. It was even larger than Dunn's, with 500 paintings, including some in oils depicting everyday life in China. Other paintings presented birds and flowers "exquisitely done." Overall, Peters was more diplomatic than Dunn in his catalogue's evaluation of the artwork. "All the paintings in the Museum," he wrote, "are the work of Chinese artists, and for execution and finish speak for themselves." During its run, tens of thousands toured the show, making it one of the most popular exhibitions in Boston's history at that time. One of the visitors was a young Emily Dickinson, whose experience with it remained vivid through her entire life. References to it appeared even in her mature poetry.[44]

In the 1860s, important figures in the American art world developed a critical appreciation of Chinese painting and arts on its own terms. This began an important current in American arts and culture that found inspiration in East Asian arts. This inspiration and historical engagement is still in its early stages, as twenty-first-century interest grows unabated.[45] Among the first important American artists to incorporate considerations of East Asian art was the Bostonian John LaFarge. After Perry's 1853 expedition to Japan, LaFarge began to collect Japanese decorative and religious art. His own painting later displayed explicit Japanese subjects and Chinese and Japanese brush techniques. Ernest Fenollosa, another New Englander, lived in Japan in the 1880s and 1890s and became one of America's first experts on East Asian art history. He pioneered the appreciation of Chinese and Japanese painting and literature in the United States. His posthumous two-volume study, *Epochs of Chinese and Japanese Art,* and the immense collection of Asian art he bequeathed to the Boston Museum of Fine Arts enormously influenced American artistic production. Among Fenollosa's circle of friends were Lafcadio Hearn, William Butler Yeats, Percival Lowell, Sturgis Bigelow, and Henry Adams, all of whom shared his love of Asian art. A young Ezra Pound continued Fenollosa's study of Asian art and produced his own epic work, *Cathay* (1915), highly original verse inspired by Fenollosa's translations of Chinese and Japanese poetry. More than understanding the history of Japanese and Chinese arts on their own terms, Fenollosa and his associates thought deeply about the implications of Japanese art, Chinese poetry, and Chinese calligraphy for the Western arts and Western life. They saw Asian art and thought as alternative inspirations for their creative impulses and individual lives. Fenollosa became a Buddhist and publicly encouraged a literal and spiritual merging of the East and the West, a synthesis of two halves of the world that would be what he called "the final creation of man," echoing the metahistorical imaginations of nineteenth-century destinarians. He presented his vision in a 53-page-long epic poem, "East and West," delivered at Harvard in 1892, and in his widely read 1898 essay, "The Coming Fusion of East and West." In the latter work, Fenollosa went far beyond a discussion of art to advocate a new world outlook for the West, one that was self-conscious about a grand inevitability, the unity of Asia and the West in every sphere of life. Fenollosa, linking cosmic vision with world politics, prophesied that Japan would help reinvigorate China politically and that the two united together would then join the West in a fusion of civilizations that would be "man's final experiment," a meeting of "soul to soul," of "two brothers parted since childhood." It was humanity's destiny: "Columbus and his discovery," Fenollosa declared, were but a "four-century-old stepping stone" to this grand merger.[46]

The most famous of the nineteenth-century American artists to engage Asian culture was the American expatriate James McNeill Whistler. While living in London in the 1860s, Whistler joined European artists who were fascinated with Japanese and Chinese arts and began collecting Chinese porcelain and Japanese ceramics. He collected 300 Chinese blue-and-white pieces, some 200 years old, that he used to adorn his residence. He also obtained a Chinese robe that he wore as an exotic touch for a portrait. In 1864, Whistler's mother, the iconic figure in his most famous composition, reported to a friend that her son found the painting on the Chinese blue-and-white ware to be nothing less than "the finest specimens of art." Whistler played a large role in stimulating a rage for Chinese porcelain, a "chinamania," it was called, that swept Europe and America in the late nineteenth century. The wealthy, including the financier J. P. Morgan, poured out staggering amounts of money to build huge personal collections of Chinese art. In 1904, Detroit industrialist and art collector Charles Lang Freer purchased the entire dining room of one of Whistler's English patrons and brought it to America. Whistler, who had painted on the walls and attended to all the design details, had created his famed "Peacock Room" to display his interest in East Asian painting and ceramics. It has been on permanent view for the American public in the Freer Gallery in Washington, D.C., since 1923.[47]

Many other wealthy collectors and connoisseurs across the country acquired a fascination with Chinese and Japanese art in the first decades of the twentieth century. These years saw an extraordinary burst of collecting that required intense study of the art and its history. Major museums across the country gathered great collections of East Asian art through purchase and donation. The Boston Museum of Fine Arts; the Freer Gallery in Washington, D.C.; and the New York Metropolitan Museum all assembled world-class collections, the best that money could buy. They vied with European institutions to gather the most important classical art they could from Asia. Public and university museums in Chicago, Cleveland, Kansas City, St. Louis, Minneapolis, Philadelphia, and Portland amassed their own superb collections of Chinese painting, ceramics, jade, and other artwork. Major collections appeared on the West Coast after World War II. Across the country, possession of East Asian art became a requirement for a city's claim to sophistication and cosmopolitanism, and scholarly and popular appreciation of such arts were seen to advance civilized international relations.[48]

By the 1930s, a wide range of prominent American artists had engaged themselves with East Asian aesthetics. These included the famed American impressionist Mary Cassatt, architect Frank Lloyd Wright, pioneering print makers Bertha Lum and Helen Hyde, New York painter and art educator Arthur Wesley Dow, cubist artist Max Weber, modernists Alfred Stieglitz and Georgia O'Keeffe (she had 100 volumes on Asian art and culture in her home in Ghost Ranch, New Mexico), and Northwest artists Morris Graves and Mark Tobey. The artists were inspired by the color, perspective, technique, composition, and philosophy of East Asian art. Tobey, after taking a lesson from Chinese artist Teng Baiye, who visited Seattle in the 1920s, exclaimed, "I came out and I saw a tree and the tree was no longer a solid." Chinese ink painting and Buddhist and Taoist thinking deeply influenced his efforts.[49] Chinese and Japanese aesthetics gave American artists the freedom to break from long-standing Western realism and artistic conventions. It was a source of new ways of seeing and new ways of doing. Life, nature, reality, the cosmos, spirit, energy—all appeared afresh to the artists and inspired their creativity.

Benjamin Franklin and other American thinkers as early as the colonial days had wondered about the usefulness of China's agricultural practices, governance, and moral philosophy for the young country's own purposes. However it was the American transcendentalists of Massachusetts in the mid-nineteenth century who seriously engaged with East Asian, Indian, and Persian thought and developed unique ways of thinking about human spirit, nature, and the cosmic. The Orient, as it was called then, attracted the serious attention of Walt Whitman, Ralph Waldo Emerson, Henry David Thoreau, Emily Dickinson, Herman Melville, and other writers and philosophers who wanted to break with established rationalist thought and embrace forms of thinking that better appreciated intuition and introspection. They studied Confucian thinking about the human moral order and innate goodness and helped disseminate his philosophy and that of other Asian thinkers to American audiences. For them, Confucius's ideas offered a way of life that was fully human, spiritual, and moral, independent of organized religion and formal theology. The views of Confucius, Mencius, and other Eastern thinkers, they believed, saw humanity, nature, and spirit in universalist and unitary ways. Their vision assumed oneness. It was a way forward out of dogma, chauvinism, and narrow materialism.[50]

China continued to captivate the imagination of many American intellectuals and artists in the late nineteenth century as a place of mystery, wonder, and wisdom, among them an individual honored today as the author of one of the most influential expressions of American life and culture. Henry Adams, a blueblood who was the descendant of two presidents, an accomplished Harvard historian, and the author of *The Education of Henry Adams,* would seem an unlikely person to be captivated by China and Japan, but he was. From an early age, Henry Adams was fascinated by Chinese arts and history. He collected Chinese art and studied the histories, cultures, and governments of China and Japan. In 1886, after his wife Clover committed suicide, Adams wondered if he could escape his terrible grief by fleeing to the elusive East. He wrote to his close friend diplomat John Hay (the author later of the Open Door Policy notes), "China is the only mystery left to penetrate. I have henceforward a future. As soon as I can get rid of history, and the present, I mean to start for China, and stay there." Adams tried to get to China but got no further than Japan and returned to America, where he experienced China vicariously—he consumed the romantic travelogue *Diary of a Journey through Mongolia and Tibet,* written by his good friend and China scholar William Woodville Rockhill (later an American minister to China). This inspired visions of Marco Polo and Genghis Khan for Adams, who was taken with the alterity of China for the rest of his life, though he never actually visited. The otherness that was China was an exit from a West that he saw as troubled and uninspiring. He wanted to retrace the steps of Marco Polo and spoke about his pursuit of China as "after the manner of Ulysses, in search of that new world which is the old." He even took up the serious study of the Chinese language and directed the sculptor Augustus Saint-Gaudens to fashion a memorial to his departed wife inspired by the image of Guan Yin, the Buddhist goddess of mercy. The result was the famous Adams Memorial in Rock Creek Cemetery in Washington, D.C.[51]

The wider American intellectual establishment caught a China fever in the early twentieth century. Leading American universities vigorously competed with one another to establish an intellectual presence in China. Major university programs included Princeton in Beijing (established in 1898), Yale in China (1901), Harvard-Yenching (1928), and Wisconsin in China (ca. 1920). Prominent scholars actively involved themselves in China studies and

American policy discussions and even advised the Chinese government. After the 1911 Revolution, the government of China hired a number of Americans to advise the young republic as it wrote its constitution and established policy. Among these were Richard T. Ely, University of Wisconsin economist and founder of the American Economic Association; economist Jeremiah W. Jenks of Cornell; and Frank J. Goodnow, founder of the American Political Science Association and president of Johns Hopkins University. In China, they had the opportunity to take their social science theories beyond book learning. For others, China served as an immense field for social investigation. Thorstein Veblen, Willard Straight, Edward A. Ross, Charles Beard, and Herbert Croly wrote extensively about social conditions in China. Woodrow Wilson, former president of Princeton; Nicholas Murray Butler of Columbia; A. Whitney Griswold, future president of Yale; Ray Lyman Wilbur of Stanford; Henry Churchill King of Oberlin; and Benjamin Ide Wheeler of the University of California at Berkeley all took active interest in China and Asia matters. As educators, they viewed the rise of China and Asia as offering critical opportunities for American universities: Asia was a place that needed to be understood and tutored in modern learning. American universities wanted to open themselves to students from Asia, who would be the future leaders of their nations. Some American intellectuals developed a particular fondness for China that went far beyond the academic as a result of their personal contact. After serving as Harvard's president for forty years, Charles W. Eliot visited China for ten weeks in 1912 on behalf of the Carnegie Endowment for International Peace. During his stay, the educator met with people from all walks of life, including Sun Yatsen, Yuan Shih-k'ai, and other leaders of the revolution that overthrew Manchu rule. The country was then still in "prodigious confusion," he said, with barely any governmental authority in place. The immense political, economic, social, and moral tasks of constructing a new republic in a poor country animated and overawed the cosmopolitan Eliot. After he returned home, he declared with genuine excitement, "My journey gave me the most interesting stay in a foreign country that I ever had, or indeed ever expect to have." It was impossible, he said, not to "sympathize profoundly" with the Chinese people in their effort to establish a "free government." Beyond its own national fate, though, China had transcendent importance. "An intellectual interest in the affairs of China," Eliot observed, "will add not only to the breadth of our sympathies but to the enlargement of our hopes and expectations for mankind." Such engagements with China helped form a deep reservoir of personal connection and support among America's cultural leaders for China's effort to enter the modern age.[52]

At the same time that American students and intellectuals were traveling to China, hundreds of elite Chinese students were coming to the United States for study. They were not the first of their kind to do so: missionaries had brought a small number of Chinese for education in America throughout the nineteenth century and Yung Wing led a short-lived effort that brought more than 100 Chinese students to the United States in the 1870s. In the first decades of the twentieth century, many more Chinese traveled to America for education. The numbers grew steadily, from a few hundred in 1906 to 1,600 in 1926; many studied on Boxer Indemnity Scholarships. Most went to colleges and universities in the east and midwest and tended to study the physical and applied sciences, "practical" forms of knowledge they believed China needed. Most returned to China, and from among them came some of the most important scholars, educators, and leaders in Chinese society. They remained an important and direct connection with American society long after their return. They were the forerunners of the tens of thousands of Chinese students who have come as international students to America since the 1980s.[53]

The most well-known American scholars who engaged with China in the early twentieth century were the famous philosopher and Columbia University professor John Dewey and his wife Alice. The Deweys, among the most important and senior Progressive-era intellectuals, had never been to Asia before 1919, when they left for what they expected would be a pleasant holiday in Japan followed by a short visit to China. Instead, what they encountered in China so captivated and intrigued them that they stayed for more than two years, mostly at Peking University. The political and social turmoil, the energy of its young people, and the opportunity to participate in transformative events of historic proportions all appealed to the activist hearts of the Deweys. John Dewey spoke to eager academic and official audiences throughout the country about pragmatism, American political and civic life, modern education, and social reform, and as the first foreign scholar formally invited to lecture in China he enjoyed instant fame. Hundreds, even thousands of earnest listeners attended his lectures. They hoped to learn what would help elevate China into a modern, strong country, the most vital and pressing concern of the generation. The warm reception the Deweys received went far beyond their expectations.[54]

"Simply as an intellectual spectacle, a scene for study and surmise," Dewey wrote, "nothing in the world today, not even Europe in the throes of reconstruction, equals China." Among China's university students and professors, Dewey found unbridled energy and curiosity. Dewey saw exciting opportunities for cosmopolitan dialogue and urged Americans to work hard for an intellectual "open door" with China "of open diplomacy, of continuous and intelligent inquiry, of discussion free from propaganda." During his stay, Dewey engaged many of China's leading and future intellectuals. Among the students in his audiences was a young Mao Zedong, who for a short while was won over to Dewey's philosophy of pragmatism before giving it up as "impractical" for his country's abject condition. Mao turned to Marxism-Leninism as more relevant to China. Traditionalists and young leftist radicals alike challenged Dewey's evolutionary, experimentalist approach to social change. But Dewey's connection with others, especially Hu Shi, a Boxer Indemnity student who had been his philosophy student at Columbia and became China's leading liberal intellectual, were more profound and long lasting. Hu Shi advocated the use of the vernacular in Chinese writing, revolutionizing Chinese literature. In the late 1930s and early 1940s, he was China's ambassador to the United States. Dewey and many other American intellectuals of the Progressive era found China an inviting canvas for their ideas of social reform, as the country was embroiled in cultural and political ferment of staggering dimensions. Along with a long line of missionaries, philanthropists, and social reformers, these American intellectuals often saw China as a testing ground for their ideas on how to achieve progress and modernity. Dewey developed a relatively sophisticated understanding of China, and the possibilities for social transformation in the country continued to intrigue him for the rest of his life.[55]

Beyond intellectual and political engagement, however, the Deweys developed a close personal affinity with the Chinese people that bound them to the country. They were not the only American visitors to China who developed strong attachments to the Chinese people. A great many Americans over the years found themselves similarly connected, a phenomenon that is unique in the history of international relations in its depth, persistence, and implications. Why Americans and Chinese developed these intense personal connections has long fascinated observers. Some suggest that it is evidence that complementary cultural and social-psychological elements, above and beyond politics or economic benefit, linked the two peoples. Some Americans, not without some self-flattery, suggest that Americans and Chinese shared traits such as an earthiness of manner, practicality, humility, a strong work and family ethic, and a lack of pretension that drew them together.

The Deweys' personal reaction to China offers insight into one important couple's response to China, but it also suggests broader implications. The Deweys' extensive writings about their experiences widely influenced American public opinion. Even their daughter, Evelyn, contributed to the dissemination of Dewey's knowledge about China: while her parents were still in China, she published a collection of the many letters they sent to the family during their long Asian sojourn. They were apparently not intended for publication and thus convey a special intimacy and candor.[56]

The China the Deweys encountered in the spring of 1919 immediately appealed to their reform imaginations and impulses. It was a country in tremendous ferment, with students boisterously protesting the big power machinations at Versailles and Japan's imperialism in China. China's students and intelligentsia were also in the throes of a modern cultural revolution known as the May Fourth Movement that questioned all of China's intellectual inheritances, including its philosophy, language, arts, and social traditions. China was also a country of tremendous contrasts, something that fascinated the curious Deweys. They found the Chinese people alternately culturally hidebound and socially conservative and wonderfully flexible, energetic, and eager to learn. It was a country of miserable poverty and terrible housing but also of elegance, good food, and an appreciation of learning. "For a country that is regarded at home as stagnant and unchanging," they wrote their children, "there is certainly something doing. This is the world's greatest kaleidoscope." China seemed to be an immense experiment in social change and an arena for considering the possibilities of civic and political reform on a massive scale. They praised their reformer counterparts: the educated Chinese were better on the "woman question" than even the Japanese, and the students were courageous and bold in their protests. "To think of kids in our country from fourteen on, taking the lead in starting a big cleanup reform politics movement and shaming merchants and professional men into joining them," they wrote. "This is sure some country."[57]

Their letters tell of the friendly contact they frequently made with Chinese in all walks of life and the casual hospitality of the people, including during the many meals they enjoyed. Alice Dewey wrote about a fine banquet that ended with a Chinese rice pudding (it was probably what is called *babaofan*): it was the "most delicious sort imaginable" and something she declared she would have to learn how to make. On a more serious note, the Deweys liked to comment on the personalities of the Chinese they met. They found the Chinese physically attractive and often charming, both female and male. They appreciated the candor and openness of the Chinese. The Deweys believed that the Chinese made "wonderful companions" and could be almost American. "The Chinese," the Deweys once observed, "are socially a very democratic people" and it was easy to see why "everybody who stays here gets more or less Chinafied."[58]

The Deweys often compared the Japanese and Chinese. They found the Japanese admirable in many respects: they were orderly, polite, and nicely respectful of foreigners. But they also encountered anti-Americanism in Japan, whereas in China, they found many Chinese fond of Americans, even idealizing the United States as a benevolent friend to China. "Japan was rather baffling and tantalizing," Dewey wrote. "China is overpowering." As soon as they arrived in China after their long stay in Japan, the Deweys could not help but contrast the two peoples. The Japanese supposedly "cared everything for what people thought of them, and the Chinese cared nothing.... The Chinese are noisy, not to say boisterous, easy-going and dirty—and quite human in general effect." The qualities the Deweys admired about the Japanese were also the ones that came to irritate them: their construction of a modern nation was a wonder, "but everything in themselves is a little over-made, there seems to be a rule for everything, and admiring their artistic effects one also sees how near art and the artificial are together." In contrast, the Deweys found themselves attracted to the "easy-going" Chinese and their "slouchiness," a virtue of sorts after experiencing the self-regulating Japanese. The Deweys found themselves especially sympathetic to the underdog Chinese, whom the Deweys regularly characterized as the "prey" of the aggressive Japanese. "It is sickening," the Deweys wrote, that Japan kept America on the "defensive" in talking about the "open door," when in fact "Japan has locked most of the doors in China already and got the keys in her pocket." More seriously, the Deweys expressed trust in the Chinese and a desire for their improvement, even a "new revolution" against their thoroughly corrupt government, whereas the Japanese made them uneasy. "It's a wonder we were ever let out of Japan," they wrote. "You have to hand it to the Japanese. Their country is beautiful, their treatment of visitors is beautiful, and they have the most artistic knack of making the visible side of everything beautiful. . . . Deliberate deceit couldn't be one-tenth as effective; it's a real gift of art. They are the greatest manipulators of the outside of things that ever lived." Dewey warned his fellow Americans to beware of Japan's imperialist ambitions and urged support for China's self-determination and social transformation. They were, as were most other Americans, already sympathetic to the victimized Chinese and feared that friction between Japan and the United States over China could even lead to war between the two great powers.[59]

In 1946, when he was 86, Dewey accepted an invitation to visit China once again. His family, worried for his health and safety, failed to dissuade him from going, but because of unsettled conditions in China, the journey never materialized. The country had remained a deep concern for him ever since his historic trip in the 1920s. Indeed, his daughter-biographer wrote that China was the country "nearest to his heart after his own." His China trip had produced nothing less than "a rebirth of intellectual enthusiasms" in him. Today, more than sixty years after John Dewey's death, his work, which continues to inspire vigorous discussion in China, serves as one of the most important, enduring intellectual bonds between Americans and Chinese.[60]

The American writers, scholars, and art collectors who were fascinated by China were unique in their passion about a culture that was far removed from the lives of most Americans. They were also exceptional in their own professional circles, which were still largely oriented toward Europe and comfortable with the celebration of Western civilization. Their excitement about Asia can be seen as an expression of their cultural iconoclasm—they wanted to speak out against the dominant and stifling sense of European cultural superiority and discover something quite new and stimulating. They were among the most important intellectuals of their day and were highly influential, as the broader American intelligentsia was especially receptive to their ideas and experiences. As Michael Sullivan, the eminent art historian of Chinese painting, once observed, modern America found it easier to accept new cultural influences than did Europe, as Americans have constantly searched for ways to break from the European past and forge something novel and fresh. Becoming uniquely American has meant rejecting Europe (up to a point) and looking to the East (and North and South) for inspirations, Sullivan observed. Such aspirations led these artists and intellectuals to form a deep and enduring bond between China and America.[61]

To be sure, these individuals turned toward China and Asia for diverse reasons. Adams sought escape from personal unhappiness and relief from intellectual alienation; Fenollosa, a kindred spirit with missionaries, saw a cultural new millennium on the horizon; Whistler found new ways of seeing and doing art; Dewey found China a vast laboratory for his philosophy of education and political liberalism. After World War II, an even wider collection of writers and artists devoted serious attention to Asian cultures and philosophies as sources of their own creativity. Franz Kline, Robert Motherwell, Jackson Pollack, Jasper Johns, Philip Guston, Isamu Noguchi, John Cage, Yoko Ono, and Naim June Paik were all influenced by Zen, Taoism, and other East Asian ways of thinking.[62] The vital postwar bohemian and avant-garde artistic movements in the arts found much to gain from Asia as testified to by Alan Watts, Jack Kerouac, Gary Snyder, and many other creative figures who openly acknowledged their engagement with Asia. In 1954, the Beat poet Alan Ginsberg informed his friend Kerouac, "Of course I am a *Taoist.*"[63]

The cultural turn toward Asia in the first decades of the twentieth century was pronounced and formed an important part of America's abiding interest in China, and Asia more generally, that had steadily grown through the decades and would grow even stronger in the years ahead. China had captured the imaginations of a wide variety of Americans: those pursuing money, trade, souls, ideas, or aesthetics. China appeared to be a land of promise in many different ways and vital for America's own intellectual and cultural life. Europe may have been the source and foundation for American aesthetics, but Asia inspired visions of the new, authentic, or innovative and helped iconoclastic intellectuals self-affirm as they searched for identity and new ways to express. "Study any poet who infused American literature with new life," the acclaimed writer Maxine Hong Kingston observed, "and you will find Asian roots."[64] Ancient Asia continuously offered Americans a path to the fresh and the new.

Revolutions and War

It looks like China had the original idea of about everything that we had ever done and thought it was new.

Will Rogers, 1931

Today, it is known as Xintiandi, New Heaven on Earth, a district in central Shanghai that is now a site of conspicuous consumption. Young urban Chinese professionals and expatriates frequent the trendy restaurants and shops. A hundred years ago, it was where Chinese Communists held their first party congress. On July 1, 1921, thirteen delegates, all intellectuals of various sorts, secretly founded the Communist Party of China (CPC) in an upstairs hall of a girls' school in the French Concession of the city. Representing a few dozen members scattered in cells around the world, the delegates, even with the revolutionary enthusiasm and optimism that burned inside them, could not have imagined what the future would very soon bring to them. In six short years, the party grew to almost 60,000 dedicated members and, in close alliance with the much larger and more powerful Chinese Nationalist Party, Guomindang, appeared to be on the verge of triumphing in a new national revolution that would end the rule of warlords and challenge the foreign domination of the country.

The establishment of a Communist movement in China was a result of the profound disillusionment with the Western democracies brought about by the Great War and the simultaneous birth of Soviet Russia, which offered itself as a radical alternative to the bankrupt, bourgeois world. Communism now meant Marxism as interpreted by Lenin, who emphasized the revolutionary significance of the colonial and semi-colonial world suffering under imperialism. In addition, the industrial working class in the advanced capitalist countries had flocked en masse to die for flag and country in World War I, itself a product of interimperialist competition, according to Lenin. Leninism gave the Chinese and other Communists who emerged in the 1920s an explanation for their national oppression and a meaningful target: imperialism. It provided inspiration: the center of the world revolution was shifting to them, the colonial world in revolt. And it provided a way forward: they would advance with the support of the revolutionary Soviet Russia and the Communist parties representing the proletariat in the capitalist countries. No longer "backward" because of its weak proletariat, China could enter the vanguard of world transformation. The turn to communism was a result of a combination of betrayal by the West and hope for a new, rejuvenated nation.

Communism, with its appearance of scientism and modernity, attracted the attention of groups of young Chinese radicals across the globe. Some, including Zhou Enlai and Deng Xiaoping, were in France for study. Others were in Germany, Japan, or the Soviet Union. A young Mao Zedong organized an important group in Hunan Province. Though he was from a peasant background and did not have a college education, Mao was an intellectual like most of his young fellow radicals. He studied Western thought and politics for solutions to China's plight. In his teenage years, Mao had read about the histories of America and Europe and in 1919 had briefly served as the editor of the Yale in China review, *The New Hunan*, which was published in his home city of Changsha. He admired George Washington, and for a moment, the evolutionary approach to social change John Dewey espoused had attracted him. In far-off Moscow, Lenin and other leaders of the Communist International took a keen interest in the possibilities for communism in China and sent secret agents to lend organizational and ideological help to the fledging movement. The agents helped win one of the most famous intellectuals of China and a leader of the May Fourth Movement to communism. Scholar and author Chen Duxiu became the CPC's first chairman.[1]

The young party members came from a wide variety of intellectual and political backgrounds. Some had followed anarchism, others social democracy or western liberalism, but they found all of them lacking in their applicability to China. Their understanding of Marxism and Leninism was rudimentary at best, but the doctrine appeared to provide the most persuasive answers to their questions about finding a way forward out of China's misery. Communism, as they understood it, would attack both domestic reactionary forces and foreign imperialism and lay the foundation for a socialism that could rejuvenate the nation. They would ally with Soviet Russia, the only foreign power that opposed imperialism and promised its support for the oppressed masses of the world. China's Communists and masses would be on the side of the inexorable march of history. Communism, to them, was as much a call to action as it was an assured historical eventuality.

The most important decision the young CPC made was to ally itself with the political party of Sun Yatsen, the Guomindang (GMD), or Nationalist Party, as it became known in the West, which had also received substantial help from Moscow in its early years. Ever since the 1911 Republican Revolution had failed to realize his program of national construction and unity, Sun had worked to reestablish a new revolutionary movement, and by the early 1920s, it had become a force in the Guangzhou region of southern China under the protection of the local warlord. Sun and other leaders of the GMD eschewed communism, believing the conditions were not right for a class revolution in China, but they nevertheless welcomed Moscow's material and ideological support. Comintern agents even helped reshape the GMD along Leninist lines into an effective political instrument and helped it develop its military wing. In 1923, the GMD decided to allow CPC members into its ranks. Dual membership permitted dedicated Communist organizers, who had already begun to develop ties with China's working class, to help build the GMD. In turn, membership in the GMD made it possible for the Communists to gain much greater exposure in the country. Sun himself backed the idea and in his deathbed testament explicitly called on his party to continue to ally with Moscow.

The GMD-CPC alliance enabled the two parties to take advantage of an upsurge in popular anger against the foreign powers. In the spring and summer of 1925, Japanese and British troops fired on unarmed demonstrating workers in Shanghai and Hong Kong, killing dozens of workers and supporters, including students. Other deadly encounters occurred across the country, provoking outrage and a militant patriotic sentiment. Protracted labor strikes and boycotts of foreign goods paralyzed cities for months. Nationalists and Communists played leading roles in these events, and thousands flocked to their ranks in return. In June 1926, they began the Northern Expedition, a military/political campaign to end warlord rule and replace the ineffectual government in Beijing with a new republican government.

The campaign, under the leadership of Chiang Kaishek, advanced quickly and in the spring of 1927 was poised to take control of Shanghai, China's most vital city.

Then, early on the morning of April 12, 1927, Chiang unleashed a brutal coup against the unprepared left. Using the Shanghai underworld, with which he had extensive connections, Chiang sent hundreds of gangsters and paramilitary agents to attack labor organizations and leftist groups in the city. Over the following days, thousands were brutally killed in the streets of Shanghai and then throughout southern China. Chiang emerged as the undisputed leader of the GMD and its army, now cleared of Communists and other rivals to his power. Communists such as Zhou Enlai and Mao Zedong barely escaped alive and fled into the countryside. The ranks of the CPC were decimated; tens of thousands died. The bloodbath ended the united front between the Communists and Nationalists. In the following year, Chiang established a new Republic of China government in Nanjing, with himself at its head. The bloody events in far-off China attracted little attention in the United States. Chiang was a shadowy figure who was largely unknown to Americans, and the Communists were an even bigger mystery.

The American response to Chiang and the powerful group of associates and relatives around him who led China for the next several decades occupies a preeminent place in the overall story of U.S.-China relations. Few, if any, foreign leaders so beguiled, confused, frustrated, angered, and divided Americans as intensely as Chiang. During his long reign as the leader of the Republic of China from 1928 to his death in 1975, Chiang elicited sentiments ranging from genuine reverence to utter disgust. He was seen as a saint, as the savior of the Chinese people, and as a military genius but also as a buffoon, crook, and despot. He was alternately viewed as America's best hope for China and the principal reason for the failure of America's efforts to befriend and support the Chinese people. Even in death, Chiang continues to challenge Americans. In recent years, important documentary evidence on Chiang has been released, and American historians have begun to see him in substantively new ways: he is emerging as neither simple hero nor villain but as a decidedly more complicated figure than was previously imagined. The updated picture of Chiang's personality, drawn largely from his now-available diary and other personal papers, presents him as decidedly nationalistic, mercurial, and martyr-like, qualities that made him both elusive and driven.[2] Even Beijing, which long vilified Chiang as the supreme enemy of the Chinese people and an unrepentant anti-Communist, now welcomes reconsiderations of Chiang's place as an important leader in modern Chinese history. The mainland, in the hope of reuniting Taiwan, has even intimated that Chiang's worldly remains would be welcomed for final burial in his home village near Shanghai, an honor of signal importance.

Chiang was born in 1887 near the treaty port of Ningbo in Zhejiang Province. He gravitated toward the military for his career, studied in an imperial army academy in Japan, and then joined Sun Yatsen's revolutionary movement. In 1924, Sun appointed him to lead the Huangpu (Whampoa) military academy in Guangzhou to train officers for Sun's revolutionary army. Chiang's connections with the military remained an important base for him throughout his life. Unlike Sun, Chiang was vehemently anti-Communist and after the 1927 bloodbath remained obsessed with the Communist presence in China. He conducted one massive extermination campaign after another to eliminate the red bandits, as he called them. Besides his military base, his support came from the wealthiest families of the country, especially the legendary Song (Soong) family, one of the world's most formidable clans in the first half of the twentieth century.

The founder of this lineage was Han Jiaozhun (1863?–1918), the name given to a boy who grew up on the southern Chinese island of Hainan. In 1878, the restless youngster traveled with an uncle to Boston to look for work. He spent a short time working in a tea shop but then left to be a cabin boy on a U.S. Coast Guard cutter. The ship's captain, a devout Methodist, helped convert Han to Christianity, and in 1880 he was baptized at the Fifth Street Methodist Church in Wilmington, North Carolina. Han became Charles Jones Soong, the name by which he became known as one of the most important persons of modern China. Benefactors helped him enter Trinity College (now Duke University) in 1881 to gain preparatory education before he enrolled in Vanderbilt University in Tennessee, where he received a degree in theology in 1885. The next year, North Carolina Methodists sent Soong, after eight fortuitous years in America, to Shanghai to serve as a missionary. Soong helped found the China YMCA, but he had more success publishing and selling Bibles than he did in winning converts. He left evangelical work, though he remained sincerely devout his entire life and became one of the most successful businessmen in China. He threw his substantial wealth behind fellow Methodist and Nationalist Sun Yatsen.

As important as he was to Sun and the 1911 Revolution, Charles Soong became legendary in Chinese history because of his progeny: all six of his children would play prominent roles in the politics and economics of twentieth-century China. They were also all closely associated with America. Charles sent all six children to America for their education, including primary and secondary for some and college for all. Soong's eldest daughter, Ailing, graduated from Wesleyan College in Macon, Georgia, and married banker Kong Xiangxi (H. H. Kung), a Christian with degrees from Oberlin and Yale who led the Central Bank of China and was China's minister of finance in the 1930s. Qingling, also with a degree from Wesleyan, married Sun Yatsen and played a prominent role in the Chinese political left her whole life. Mayling attended Wellesley College and married Chiang Kaishek in 1927. Two years later, it was she who persuaded him to convert to Christianity. Song Ziwen (T. V. Soong), the eldest son, received degrees from Harvard and Columbia and served as China's finance minister and foreign minister in the 1930s and 1940s. The two youngest sons, Zian and Ziliang, who graduated from Harvard and Vanderbilt University, respectively, became prominent bankers in the country and in world finance. Notably, after the 1949 revolution, most of them, the most prominent exception being Qingling, moved to the United States rather than to Taiwan to spend the rest of their lives. Even Mayling, better known as Madame Chiang Kaishek, settled in New York after her husband's death in 1975 and lived quietly on Long Island for her last thirty years. The Soong clan had a wide array of powerful friends in American religious, educational, business, and political circles and played an incalculably influential role in the fate of Republican China and in its relationship with the United States. More than any other force in the Chinese elite, the Soongs, even with the many differences among themselves, were responsible for sustaining America's faithful attachment to Chiang Kaishek and the Nationalists for more than three crucial decades.

Real assassins, not the phantoms that had haunted Paul Reinsch's deteriorating mind, acted in the darkness of night on September 18, 1931, in China's northeast. Rogue junior officers in a Japanese army unit stationed in Manchuria exploded a small device that slightly damaged a section of the South Manchuria Railroad, which was owned by Japan. The Japanese military immediately blamed the Chinese for what is now known as the Mukden, or Manchurian, Incident. The conspirators hoped to embarrass Chinese authorities, provoke large-scale Japanese military action against China, and push their civilian and military superiors in Tokyo to take control of as much of Manchuria as possible. The scheme succeeded on all counts.

Tokyo blamed Chinese lawlessness in the region for the explosion, using it as a pretext to send thousands of troops into the area from their colony in Korea, allegedly to restore order and "protect" Japanese economic and strategic interests, which were indeed substantial. Manchuria, comparable in land mass to France and Germany combined, possessed vast natural resources, including arable land, coal, ore, timber, hydropower, harbors, and living space. Over the years, the Japanese established major investments in the area and conducted far-ranging commercial dealings. Two hundred thousand Japanese nationals lived in Manchuria, which was also the ancestral and cultural homeland of the Manchus, but 28 million resident Chinese constituted 98 percent of the population. Since the end of the nineteenth century, China, Russia, Japan, and other powers had fought two major wars and engaged in countless battles for control of the vital region adjacent to Korea. In the weeks following the staged incident, Japan quickly occupied major cities and then assumed control of virtually all of Manchuria, tearing it away from China. So began the "barefaced rape of Manchuria," in the words of John Leighton Stuart, a famous American missionary educator in China and president of Yanjing University (Yenching University.) Although the central Chinese government under Chiang Kaishek mounted no military resistance to the aggression, it appealed to the League of Nations and the international community for help. In March 1932, a Japanese-engineered Manchurian independence movement established the puppet state of Manchukuo with the last Manchu emperor of China, Puyi, as the nominal leader of the fiction. All of Manchuria was taken from China and thus began fourteen years of military conflict between Japan and China.[3]

The incident shocked Americans. A number were living in Manchuria at the time, and their reports from the scene universally rejected the Japanese version of events and graphically described Japanese brutality. Sherwood Eddy, the influential and articulate YMCA leader who had worked in India, China, Korea, and Japan for much of his life, was on an evangelistic tour of China and in Manchuria through the crisis. He vividly communicated his observations and outrage to the American public, press, and political leaders. His reports included descriptions of Japanese atrocities against innocent Chinese and declared that the whole affair was clearly premeditated. He previously had not been anti-Japanese, but "Japan Threatens the World" was the title of his article for the *Christian Century*. "The situation is critical and grave developments are imminent," he wrote from Asia. After he returned to the United States, he spoke to large audiences around the country about what he had seen. Thousands of people attended his lectures, in which he denounced Japan's aggression. He feared the actual breakup of China, with Japan taking over the north, communism dominating in the central provinces, and a bankrupt and tottering central government around Shanghai. He announced that a new world war could be in the making.[4]

Reports such as Eddy's exposed the Japanese rationale as a flimsy pretext for aggression, but the ultimate purpose of the audacious act seemed unclear. Initially the possibility of a wholesale invasion of Manchuria seemed beyond reason, even for the ambitious Japanese army, and yet the Japanese military moved so quickly and forcefully that its premeditation and determination was unquestionable. Washington condemned Japan's actions and warned Tokyo not to engage in further aggressive behavior. President Hoover; his secretary of state, Henry L. Stimson; and much of the rest of the international community believed that Japan's actions in Manchuria challenged the entire edifice of great-power stability that had been erected after World War I. The incident violated agreements made at the 1922 Washington Conference, the many peace efforts of the League of Nations, and the much-heralded Kellogg-Briand Pact of 1928 that supposedly outlawed war as an instrument of national policy. At the same time, the Hoover administration, which was mired in the two-year-old Great Depression, faced widespread domestic discontent, soon dramatically symbolized by the protest march and encampment in the nation's capital of tens of thousands of impoverished World War I veterans and family members who demanded payment of promised bonuses for wartime service. The other major power with substantial interests in the region, Great Britain, was preoccupied with a financial crisis so severe that London took the extreme step of going off the gold standard. It did so on virtually the same day as the staged explosion in Manchuria.[5]

The episode was the most serious international crisis the Hoover administration had faced, and as events unfolded over the following months, it slowly forged a response that tried to express U.S. outrage and the possibility of future military action on its part. At the same time, it avoided committing the country to a path that could lead to immediate military involvement in a distant part of the world that most Americans believed did not warrant the shedding of American blood. Antiwar sentiment ran strongly in every sector of society, from Wall Street bankers to peace activists, despite the American public's widespread sympathy for China and antipathy toward Japan. Finally, in early January 1932, three months after the initial provocation, Washington issued what became known as the Hoover-Stimson Doctrine, a statement of moral condemnation of Japanese aggression and declaration of nonrecognition of the territory seized through military means. The statement rejected all Japanese rationales for their actions, calling them totally unfounded; highlighted their violation of a string of international norms of conduct and official protocols signed by Japan and others; and affirmed America's continued support for the Open Door Policy for China, including equal access to commercial opportunity and support for China's territorial integrity. The Hoover-Stimson Doctrine, however, proposed no specific measures, including economic sanctions, to counter the aggression. The American public endorsed the condemnation of Japanese aggression and the president's statement. Within weeks of the declaration of the doctrine, however, the Japanese military even more brazenly attacked the densely populated city of Shanghai to intimidate the Chinese, who continued to protest Japanese actions in Manchuria. Ground and air forces targeted not just military and political sites but also the civilian population, killing thousands and leaving hundreds of thousands homeless and destitute. This first use of terroristic aerial bombardment, including firebombing against civilians, stunned the world. For months, Japan waged a virtual undeclared war against China. Japan was compiling "a sinister record," the *Christian Century* declared in an editorial in April. On May 15, rightist junior officers in the navy and army burst into the home of the country's prime minister, Inukai Tsuyoshi, and assassinated him because of his efforts to rein in the military. Civilian rule in Japan effectively ended with his death and did not return until after World War II.[6]

In light of what we now know about the path to World War II, the Hoover-Stimson Doctrine is often characterized as being woefully inadequate, if not a form of appeasement of aggression that opened the way to global war. It has been described as simply waving a gun everyone knew was empty. A stronger response, it has been argued, might have frustrated the growth of militarism in Japan and possibly averted an eventual showdown in the Pacific with the United States. However, such post hoc assessments obscure an appreciation of the Hoover-Stimson Doctrine as an element in the long continuum of American attachment to China and as a reluctance to intervene directly in Chinese affairs. The U.S. position had very little to do with any existing material stake in China but everything to do with America's attitude, developed over many years, of simultaneously coveting China and considering itself China's special protector and benefactor. The American position was not the result of any close political relationship with China's actual government or its leaders at this time. In personal terms, America's leaders were much closer and more familiar with the civilian Japanese leadership than with the Chinese. Chiang Kaishek was still an undefined figure at the time, even to many in Washington.[7]

Several years after the crisis, Henry Stimson's detailed account of the events highlighted this special American sentiment toward China. U.S. relations with China and Asia, he wrote, differed from those of any European power. Europe was "remote" from Asia, he offered, while America was "adjacent" to Asia. Europeans were "absentee landlords; we, a neighbor." Asian affairs affected America in unique ways, and he vividly explained, as others had before him, that "the Pacific Ocean is no longer a barrier, but a means of communication" for America. Events had forced him to acknowledge this psychological reality, he said. American sentiment toward Asia was not a function of trade volume or an interest in expanding commerce but was a matter of the actual peace and security of the North Pacific, "our part of the world." The American response to the crisis, Stimson noted, rose from an "instinctive" feeling about Asia among the American people, which in turn profoundly affected Washington. At one point in the crisis, Stimson met with the Japanese ambassador and gave his "unvarnished account" of his critical "attitude and feelings" about Tokyo's action. The ambassador, according to Stimson's personal diary, confessed that he was "fairly overwhelmed" by the reaction of the American press against his country and was "very despondent."[8]

In contrast to the American position, the British response, which was initially critical of the behavior of the Japanese in Manchuria, broke with Washington's unequivocal moral condemnation of Japan's actions. London refused to back the Hoover-Stimson declaration and high officials openly downplayed the entire Manchuria matter. Washington even heard reports from field officers that the British leadership had "complete indifference" to the events in China. Stimson later described London's official reaction to his note as an open "rebuff" of the American concern about China. France also did not support Washington. Britain and France dawdled, hoping the matter would go away, and deferred to the response of the League of Nations. Its Lytton Commission studied the situation for a year before announcing something that everyone already knew, which was that the state of Manchukuo was a fabrication of Japan and that the Chinese protest was largely defensible. The report, however, avoided labeling Japan an aggressor and made no recommendations about how to counter its actions. Nevertheless, the report outraged Tokyo, which was increasingly ruled by the military. It left the league in the spring of 1933 and revoked its acceptance of international treaties that constrained its power. The differences between London and Washington over the handling of the Manchurian Incident irritated American officials long after the crisis had passed. Henry Stimson made a point of highlighting the conflict with the British in his memoir of the crisis, suggesting that the British government's position actually resulted from a selfish business community that wanted to avoid jeopardizing its position in Asia. Stimson's view reversed Lenin's theory of imperialism, which maintained that conflicting great-power financial interests produced war: in this case, Stimson argued that London placed British economic self-interest above moral, political, and legal principles and thus acquiesced to aggression in order to avert conflict.[9]

From the start of the crisis, American popular sentiment clearly favored the Chinese over the Japanese. International lawlessness had to be stopped, it was agreed, and an unusually diverse array of voices called on Washington to take a firmer stance against Japan than it did initially. On the left, socialists such as Norman Thomas condemned Japan, fearing its action would encourage wider reactionary activity, and Margaret Lamont, wife of the activist Corliss Lamont, called for an American boycott of Japanese goods and helped found the American Boycott Association. Scores of leading Americans endorsed the effort. Longtime friends of China such as John Dewey and liberals such as Jane Addams and Dorothy Detzer, executive secretary of the Women's International League for Peace and Freedom, feared Washington would sacrifice China to Japan. As it became clear that Japan would not desist, they even called on Washington to sever relations with Tokyo. The missionary community largely sided with China and turned against Japan, though a few missionaries associated with that country urged moderation in the American response. Columbia University president and Nobel Peace Prize recipient Nicholas Murray Butler criticized the Hoover administration for not doing more to oppose Japanese aggression, as did Harvard president and political scientist A. Lawrence Lowell. On February 17, 1932, a month after Stimson articulated the doctrine and after the attack on Shanghai, Lowell called on the president and Congress to end all commercial relations with Japan. Within days, thousands of civic leaders, including 150 college presidents and professors, issued similar statements. Business leaders also voiced their condemnation of Japan's aggression. One prominent organization was the Committee on Economic Sanctions, organized by the respected and vocal Twentieth Century Fund. The committee included the wealthy Boston merchant Peter A. Filene; Wall Street attorney and future secretary of state John Foster Dulles; San Francisco banker William H. Crocker, top General Motors executive James D. Mooney; president of the U.S. Chamber of Commerce Silas Strawn, and other financiers and industrial leaders from around the country. Unexpectedly, even leading political figures associated with isolationism, such as Republican senator William E. Borah of Idaho, powerful chair of the Senate Foreign Relations Committee, condemned Japan's actions and called on the Hoover administration to take a firmer stand against Japan, though he opposed economic sanctions. Borah had for many years expressed sympathy with Chinese efforts to throw off foreign domination. On the other hand, the ultranationalist press, such as the Hearst papers, opposed any measure other than military buildup.[10]

The threat Japan posed to the established international order rather than the specific plight of China was what appeared to concern most Americans who spoke out against the Manchuria crisis. Some even expressed frustration about China's political discord and the inability of its leaders to effectively govern the country. The danger to international peace and China's fate, however, were clearly linked. Because of its size, significance, and historical connection to the United States and other major powers, China was not just any country that suffered aggression. China was an essential element in the global balance of power. In the thinking of many Americans in the 1930s, the control of China would determine the future of the international community. China could be the tinderbox of a world conflagration.

Tokyo underestimated the strength of the American reaction to its actions in Manchuria, believing that the American response would be commensurate to the extent of its material stake in China, which was modest. Though Tokyo expected American displeasure with its actions, it thought that Americans would come to accept Japan's assertion of its control over Manchuria as no different from America's hegemony over the Caribbean and Latin America. Commentators said that Japan was simply enforcing its version of a Monroe Doctrine for Asia. After all, the United States had colonized the Philippines, Guam, Puerto Rico, and Hawaii and had repeatedly intervened militarily in the Caribbean and Central America throughout the 1920s. Tokyo believed its actions were consistent with existing norms of Western great-power behavior and was shocked by Washington's adamant opposition. Why the United States decided to oppose Japan with such vehemence and moral rectitude in a corner of the world so far away perplexed it and disrupted its calculations. Tokyo failed to appreciate the strength of America's historic attachment to China.[11]

When Walter Lippmann, the grand observer of American politics, wrote about the origins of World War II, he wondered about this same question, the "mystery of our China policy," as he put it. How did America and Japan get into terrible conflict over "an Oriental people from whom they are separated by the immense distances of the Pacific Ocean"? He offered trenchant observations that still speak to this question today. Lippmann dismissed the idea that business interests and simple profits had much to do with U.S.-Japan tensions in the 1930s. He believed that the two sides could easily have constructed a working relationship on a commercial level. (In fact, trade between the two powers substantially increased during the decade before Pearl Harbor.) Rather, Lippmann saw the source of the conflict as originating from something more important and basic to Americans that led them to see Japan's expansion as anathema to core American values and interests. Lippmann identified the powerful and yet intangible cultural impulse that animated much American behavior in Asia and the world: the open door as an expression of an essential national identity. "It is evident," he wrote, "that the Open Door meant something more to Americans than a commercial policy. . . . The missionary zeal with which we have propagated it touches chords of memory and of faith, and is somehow the expression of the American political religion." Americans cherished liberty and opposed tyranny, he claimed, and therefore opposed imperialism whenever it appeared. According to Lippmann, the open door was "at bottom" "a short name for the American way of life projected abroad."[12]

Lippmann spoke perceptively but imprecisely. For example, he did not see that America's open door moralism was selective. It had waged wars of conquest and acted as an imperialist on many occasions. The United States adopted a closed door policy on Asian immigration and in its colonies. It was only with China that America developed a peculiar sentimentality and emotionalism. To Americans, China was not just any country that suffered predation. It was a country in which Americans had invested special significance and meaning for its own definition and future. China, many Americans had early concluded, was too important to fall under the domination and control of anyone else, perhaps even the Chinese themselves.

The Chinese government under Chiang Kaishek responded weakly to the amputation of Manchuria from China. As angered as he was personally, Chiang believed the Chinese Communists were an even greater threat to the country and to his government than the Japanese. The cancer within had to be eliminated before treating the ailment from without. His so-called anti-Communist extermination campaigns continued to take priority, which disaffected an increasingly larger number of his countrymen, including those in his own party and military, who wanted national unity against foreign invasion. Chiang, believing his forces were too weak to resist Japanese aggression, decided to stall in order to build his military forces and strengthen his control over a country that was only nominally unified and was still fragmented by regionalism and political differences.[13]

The Depression and the rise of fascism in Europe commanded the attention of Washington under Franklin D. Roosevelt. The new president inherited the Hoover-Stimson Doctrine from his predecessor and continued its critical moral stance toward Japan but took no action against Tokyo. And like Hoover, Roosevelt had a unique personal connection to China. Though he had never personally visited or lived in China, as his predecessor had, Roosevelt grew up hearing stories about the colorful Delanos, his mother's side of the family. His maternal grandparents, Warren and Catherine, were among the legendary first "China Hands" and had lived in China for years. It was where they made the family fortune. One of the legendary China traders was Amasa Delano. FDR's mother, Sara, and his aunts had also lived in Hong Kong and China in the 1860s when they were young, and they regaled the family with vivid stories of their exotic experiences. They left delightful journals about their lives in distant China. This family history provided the president with a sentimental link to Asia, and he regularly referred to this part of his pedigree to enhance his claim to expertise on China. On a number of occasions, he used this family history to suggest that he had inherited more than mere lineage from his relatives; he had also somehow psychically received their lived experiences and insights about China. Outgoing secretary of state Henry Stimson recalled that in a 1933 meeting about the presidential transition, the president-elect told him that he had a "personal hereditary interest in the Far East." In explaining his support for the high-minded Hoover-Stimson Doctrine, FDR informed Raymond Morley, one of his closest advisors, that he "always had the deepest sympathy for the Chinese." He used his China card in admonishing his treasury secretary, Henry Morgenthau Jr., in a 1934 memorandum about the banking situation in China. "Please remember," the president wrote, "that I have a background of a little over a century in Chinese affairs." In a frank discussion about the complicated situation in China in 1943, FDR invoked his genealogy to remind the tough, experienced General Joseph Stilwell, who had returned from the China field, that the president really knew what the best course of action was for the United States in China. "You know," said the president, "I have a China history."[14]

Despite Roosevelt's personal feelings about China, official U.S. support for China and antipathy toward Japanese expansionism changed little in the mid-1930s. Though Roosevelt wanted to find ways to aid the Chinese government and provide moral encouragement, he also wanted to avoid any measure that might provoke conflict with Tokyo. Though some advocated toleration of Japanese behavior, interest in and sympathy for the Chinese soared in the 1930s among the American people. American writing about China had a long and rich tradition, and since the turn of the century American readers had received a steady stream of titles. *The Awakening of China* by the prolific Methodist bishop Rev. James Bashford; *The Road to Cathay* by Merriam Sherwood; *China: The Collapse of a Civilization* by Nathan Peffer; *China Revolutionized* by John Stuart Thomson; *Sister Martyrs of Ku Cheng* by D. M. Berry; and the deliciously mistitled *New Thrills in Old China* by the very straight-laced missionary Charlotte E. Hawes, are just a few of the hundreds of titles, sometimes sensational and sometimes inspirational, that appealed to everyday American audiences. No other country so stimulated the imagination of the American people for as long.[15]

Even the popular entertainer and social commentator Will Rogers was taken with China. Throughout the 1920s and 1930s, the influential Rogers wrote about China regularly in his weekly column, which was syndicated by the *New York Times* and carried in more than 600 newspapers around the country. He had tens of millions of regular readers. Styling himself as a straight-shooting, untutored cowboy from Oklahoma, Rogers spoke for the common man of middle America and lampooned politicians; the rich, famous, and powerful; and pretension of any kind. He was especially short with self-righteousness, religious and otherwise. Few people, nations, or events were immune to his irreverent commentary, but when it came to China, Rogers was curiously respectful, even admiring. He praised its ancient culture, its nonaggressive ways, and the practicality, diligence, and commitment to family of its people. In a 1927 column ridiculing the idea of America bringing "progress" to China, Rogers emphasized China's inherent wisdom and solidity: "China knows," he wrote, "that their government will be existing, that they will be living the same 1,000 years from now as they are today." No one in the West knew where the Chinese were going, even in the next few years, and yet "we call them 'heathens.'" Rogers sardonically concluded, "Why, they forgot more about living than we will ever know."[16]

At the same time, he saw that America and China had something fundamentally in common. "We are kinder like China," he once wrote; "we are so big and powerful that we get along in spite of all the bad management we have." He believed that the people of China were very much like everyday Americans: the Chinese worked hard, wanted to be left alone, were modest and down to earth, and just wanted to see the world get along. His observation was regularly repeated by others through the years. The great power pillage of China dismayed him, and he expressed open and heartfelt sympathy for the plight of the Chinese people. In 1927, in the midst of much public discussion about another foreign intervention in China, Rogers wrote in his newspaper column: "I never felt as sorry for anyone in my life as I do for them [the Chinese people]. Here they are, they have never bothered anyone in their whole lives. They have lived within their own borders, never invaded anyone else's domains, worked hard, got little pay for it, had no pleasures in life, learned us about two thirds of the useful things we do, and now they want to have a Civil War. . . . But poor old China, [the foreign powers] just ain't going to allow them to have a nice little private war of their own. No, we must get in it." For Rogers, the inoffensive, hard-working, but oppressed people of China embodied the underdog, long the worthy recipient of support and sympathy in American history. China's very backwardness was endearing.[17]

Even science provoked curiosity and speculation about China and its people. In the 1920s, sketchy reports from paleontologists in China began to tell of astounding fossil discoveries in digs near Beijing. Researchers had found 500,000-year-old fragments of what appeared to be one of the earliest ancestors of homo sapiens. *Sinathropus pekinensis*, or Peking Man, as it was named, fascinated specialist and lay audiences around the world, prompting speculation that China's ancient civilization might have been much more ancient than assumed. Beijing became not just the political capital of a country—it became a site, possibly *the* site, of the origin of modern humans. For the first time, substantial physical evidence appeared to confirm Darwin's theory of evolution as applied to humans. Peking Man emerged for some as the long-sought "missing link" in evolutionary science. Further discoveries of unprecedentedly rich caches of hominid remains in the 1930s, including full skullcaps, led paleontologists to speculate that northern China was the possible "evolutionary Garden of Eden." European and American scholars flocked to the digs and wrote breathtaking articles for the world's press about their findings. The Rockefeller Foundation funded the ongoing excavations, and for the next twenty years, until the fossils mysteriously disappeared during World War II, China continued to fire imaginations about human origins. Even though late-twentieth-century science has established Africa as the origin of modern humans, the saga of Peking Man and the mystery of the missing bones continue to provoke political and scientific controversy today and are linked to Chinese national pride and identity.[18]

Peking Man, Will Rogers, and the missionaries, travelers, and returned businessmen who wrote about China in the first decades of the twentieth century generated a rich storehouse of popular lore about and curiosity in the country and prepared the way for a remarkable growth of interest in China in the 1930s. Suddenly Americans began to think about China in ways that brought the Chinese people even closer than before. Among the many books and articles published on China at that time, three stand out. Their immense popularity serves as evidence of the deep reservoir of American interest in China. During a time when European cultures and events commanded the attention of university scholars, China appealed to many hearts and minds on the Main Streets of America.

The most famous of these 1930s works is Pearl Buck's *The Good Earth,* a novel that had modest literary merit but an astonishing ability to touch its Great Depression readers. It topped the list of best sellers for two years after its release in 1931, selling close to 2 million copies. *The Good Earth* was made into a stage show and then a successful Hollywood movie in 1937, attracting 23 million viewers. It helped win the Pulitzer Prize for literature in 1932 and the Nobel Prize for literature in 1938 for Buck, the first American woman writer to receive the award. The Hollywood adaptation won several Academy Awards. *The Good Earth* "created" the Chinese people for a whole generation of Americans. It is often said that the novel was the single most influential book about China published in America, but even this is an understatement. Pearl Buck has been the most widely read Western writer about China since Marco Polo and the most widely translated author in American literature; the novel is available in almost 150 languages. The appeal of *The Good Earth* continues today; it is still read in secondary schools and colleges throughout the country, and it was a selection for Oprah Winfrey's book club in 2004.[19]

Pearl Sydenstricker (1892–1973) was born in 1892 in West Virginia to missionary parents during their home leave. Taken to China soon after her birth, Pearl spent much of the rest of the next forty years in various missionary communities along the Yangzi River. She attended Randolph-Macon Women's College in Virginia, where she majored in English. She married agronomist John Lossing Buck in 1917. The two lived in north China's countryside for six years before settling in Nanjing to teach; they separated in the 1930s. During her years of living among Chinese peasants and urban dwellers, Pearl Buck, who was fluent in Chinese, developed a genuine affection for the common people and rued the ignorance about them in America. She was often critical of missionaries in China for being detached from the masses (even when she was a missionary for the Presbyterian Church), and her writing mirrored the feelings of the more sympathetically inclined among the Western missionaries. The Chinese in *The Good Earth* are presented as superstitious and abysmally poor but also hardworking. They are crude but capable of basic human dignity, simple-minded and yet heroic, victimized periodically by the whims of nature and human foolishness and cruelty. They lived in a state of nature where the fundamental life experiences of hope, tragedy, suffering, and joy could be expressed unmediated by complicating politics, religion, or high learning. Buck's naturalistic prose moved her readers, leading them to empathize closely with her characters and their trials and tribulations. *The Good Earth* vividly recounts the vicissitudes of a simple rural family's life. The locations and chronologies are vague, but the characters are colorful and seemingly timeless. Buck presented her Chinese not so much as unique individuals but as "universal types" that were fully accessible to American audiences.

A few comments from the enthusiastic reception of the novel provide insight into why the novel so successfully won American sympathy for the Chinese downtrodden. "As far as the spiritual content of Wang Lung [the main protagonist] is concerned," wrote a reviewer for the *Christian Century*, "it would not have differed greatly had he toiled on the Nebraska prairie rather than in China." Mitchell Kennerly, a leading New York publisher, said after he read a few pages of the novel, "I forgot I was reading about Chinese men and women. . . . It was as though I was living with these men and women, different from us only in the clothes they wore and the land they live in." The Book of the Month Club, which selected the novel for its list, described "the people in this rather thrilling story" as "not 'queer' or 'exotic'" but as "natural as their soil. . . . They are so intensely human that after the first chapter we are more interested in their humanity than in the novelties of belief and habit." Critic Dorothy Canfield Fisher said the novel "makes us belong to the Chinese family as if they are cousins and neighbors." Literary scholar Carl Van Doren wrote that "*The Good Earth* for the first time made the Chinese seem as familiar neighbors."[20]

Unlike the caricatures of Chinese as simpletons and evildoers that had populated much English-language yellow peril pulp fiction and film up to then, Buck's characters appeared fully and endearingly human. Years of published memoirs of returned visitors and missionaries to China had prepared the American public for Buck's effective portrayal of naïve, elementally decent Chinese peasants. In dozens of books and hundreds of articles, the patronizing missionary stories had described the backwardness of the heathen masses in China but also their capacity for sincere spiritual and cultural conversion. Buck's approach in *The Good Earth,* and in the many other successful novels and stories about China that Buck subsequently published, resonated with Protestant America. Her writing combined realistic description, an optimistic tone, and a formality that together seemed "biblical" in style, as many reviewers, including the Nobel Prize awards committee, noted. Her soft patronizing made the Chinese less threatening; her affection for and understanding of them, with their strengths and foibles, encouraged empathy. *The Good Earth* was not just the "'Book of the Month' or book of the year, but the book of our Time," effused the usually unsentimental Will Rogers, who read the book while on his way to visit Manchuria in 1931. The image of the everyday Chinese has never been the same in America since *The Good Earth* and the other novels Buck published about China in the 1930s and 1940s. On the occasion of the eightieth anniversary of the publication of the *Good Earth,* Amazon.com commended it to its customers as a "brilliant novel" and a "universal tale of the destiny of man."[21]

Buck wrote at a time when the American public was especially receptive to a sympathetic, almost affectionate, portrayal of a victimized people. Just six months after she published *The Good Earth,* the Mukden Incident occurred, beginning two years of crisis in Manchuria. China was on the front page of the daily paper for months, and when Buck returned to the United States to live in 1934, she became a popular speaker about the situation in the country. Buck continued to write about the tribulations of the peasants and Chinese resistance to Japan in a series of well-received novels: *Sons* (1933), *The Mother* (1933), *A House Divided* (1935), *The Patriot* (1939), and *Dragon Seed* (1942). When Japan's all-out war against China began in 1937, Buck became an even more valued interpreter of China to America. Highly critical of Chiang Kaishek, the Nationalists, and the Communists, Buck had few political friends in China, but her support for organizations such as United China Relief and her attachment to the Chinese common people helped rally the sympathies of Americans. Buck's China was beyond politics. After World War II, she continued to be a prodigious writer and was a respected advocate of a variety of liberal causes, including gender and racial equality, international human rights, and Amerasian children, but she never recaptured the eminence of her early years. After the Communist victory in 1949, China changed dramatically, and her moment had passed. She never returned to her beloved adopted country after her departure in 1933 and when she tried forty years later, as she was approaching the end of her life, Beijing curtly rebuffed her efforts to visit in 1972. Beijing described her work as slanderous against the Chinese people and denied her an entry visa. She died the next year.

Buck's phenomenal success has overshadowed an array of remarkable authors who published dozens of volumes of fiction and nonfiction about China in the same time span. These included crusty war correspondent Jack Belden; Nathaniel Peffer, a China scholar who lived in the country for twenty-five years as the correspondent for the *New York Tribune*; and the enigmatic anti-Communist George Sokolsky. Women writers were even more colorful and effective cultural interpreters. Agnes Smedley, Anna Louise Strong, Helen Foster (who also was known as Nym Wales and as Helen Foster Snow), Emily Hahn, and Ida Pruitt, who was born in China, all grew up in modest circumstances in America's hinterland, but their cultural or political iconoclasm prompted them to remove themselves to distant Asia, where they led eventful lives for many years. They found the tumultuous setting inviting for their rebellious souls. They wrote about the challenges of China's rural life, its mounting revolutionary movement, unusual cultural and political personalities, women, and the onslaught of Japanese aggression, all topics that related to American curiosity about China and the drama of civil war, rebellion, and social transformation. In contrast to their culturally conservative missionary sisters in China, these remarkable women led lives of political, gender, and even sexual freedom that they could never have enjoyed in America, factors that contributed to their status as successful writers and as controversial subjects.[22]

In addition, native Chinese writers came to prominence in the prewar years for the first time in American history. Though some Chinese, such as Wong Chin Foo, Yan Phou Lee, Yung Wing, and Wu Tingfang, had published in English in periodicals and books about China in the late nineteenth and early twentieth centuries, none made the impact that Hu Shi (1891–1962) and Lin Yutang (1895–1976) did during the 1930s. Both had completed graduate study in the West, Hu Shih at Columbia with John Dewey and Lin at the University of Leipiz and Harvard, and both were multitalented literary critics, essayists, political actors, and philosophers. Both had far-reaching influence in academic circles in America and China. Lin Yutang, whom Pearl Buck encouraged to write for Americans, published a series of best-selling volumes of social commentary, history, fiction, politics, and philosophy for general audiences in America. His literary productions provided Americans with the opportunity to read about China from the perspective of a native who could write engagingly in English. *My Country and My People* (1935) became a best seller the year of its release. *The Importance of Living* (1937) was a Book of the Month Club selection and was the best seller in nonfiction for all of 1938. It is still in print today. Lin then published *The Wisdom of Confucius* (1938), *Moment in Peking* (1939), and *Between Tears and Laughter* (1943). He published thirty books in English during his productive career.[23]

Next to Pearl Buck, the journalist Edgar Snow (1905–1972) is the most influential writer about China who emerged in the 1930s. *Red Star over China,* Snow's classic book that idealized the Chinese Communists, deeply influenced public opinion in China and America immediately upon its publication in 1937 and long afterward. It was based on unprecedented extensive interviews with the CPC's top leaders—including Mao Zedong, Zhou Enlai, Zhu De, and Lin Piao—and his extended visit to Communist-controlled areas in 1936. Because of this, the book has been widely described as the journalistic scoop of the century. Until *Red Star* appeared, China's Communists were known as only a shadowy group that obsessed Chiang Kaishek. No one in the West, and few in China outside of the "liberated" areas, knew what the Communists believed and wanted. Snow helped shape an image of Chinese Communists as a powerful and positive force shaping

China that influenced millions: President Roosevelt himself read the book to learn about the CPC.

Landing in China in 1928, Snow, a young journalist from Missouri, became captivated with the country and wound up staying until 1941. Like Pearl Buck, he became identified with China for the rest of his life. Snow at first admired Chiang Kaishek but steadily distanced himself from the Chinese leader and instead associated himself with the anti-Guomindang students and intellectuals whom he met while teaching journalism at Yanjing University in Beijing. His liberal politics brought him to the attention of the underground Communist movement, and in 1936, he received an invitation to visit Yan'an, where the CPC ended its epic Long March. His ten weeks there changed his life forever and what he wrote helped reshape American views of revolutionary China and Chinese Communists.

Rumor, misinformation, and speculation had surrounded the Chinese Communist movement since its birth in the early 1920s. Were they really dedicated followers of Marx, Lenin, and Stalin who sought a proletarian revolution? Or were they some sort of agrarian rebels, radical rural populists who only wanted to improve the lives of China's destitute peasantry? Were they adjuncts of Moscow, ruthless bandits, or independent crusaders rooted in China's native soil? Was Mao Zedong, their leader, even alive or dead? Few knew the answers for certain because the nature of Chinese Communism challenged Western interpretations.

As early as 1920, Paul Reinsch, the former American minister to China and a China specialist, declared that China's rural conditions could never sustain Bolshevism. China did not fit the Marxist mold, he said, though anti-foreign appeal could take root there. Pearl Buck believed that Chinese communism was indigenous to the country and not a Russian transplant. Guomindang brutality and abysmal conditions in the countryside created conditions that were favorable to the growth of communism, and she predicted its further rise. Nathaniel Peffer did not think that the Communists were real "communists"; instead he saw them as an "anomaly" in China. China scholar Owen Lattimore claimed that what was called "communism" in China was simply a label, "more convenient than accurate," because the movement differed with both Marxist theory and Russian practice. Other reports appeared that favorably described improved living conditions, social equality, and women's emancipation in the Communist base areas. The trouble with the reports was that they were largely secondhand and unconfirmed. No non-Communist Western journalist had actually been in

Communist-controlled territory, which the Guomindang had blockaded. The CPC base area was a mystery.[24]

After Chiang's attempt to eradicate his erstwhile Communist allies in 1927, he launched one campaign after another to finish the job. The Communists retreated into remote rural areas to try to rebuild their forces. After the Manchurian crisis of 1931, they joined a growing chorus calling for national unity to oppose Japanese aggression. But Chiang was unresponsive to the rising call for national resistance and unrelenting in his anticommunism. In the fall of 1934, he forced the Communists to withdraw from their southern base areas. They began a "long march" to escape him, moving north toward the front against Japan. One year and 6,000 circuitous miles later they arrived near Yan'an, which became known as the Communists' "capital" for the next decade. During the ordeal, the Communists lost 90 percent of their forces but generated many stories of heroics and sacrifice that increased the popular belief that they were a force of destiny. Along the way, the CPC elevated Mao Zedong to the position of its top leader, a position he retained for the rest of his life.

In contrast to the fantastic and intriguing descriptions of the Communists during these years, writers who were supportive of the Guomindang wrote about Communist atrocities in the countryside and the successes of the government's efforts to eradicate the red menace. However, these reports were unsubstantiated. In addition, the ability of the Communists to resurface after repeatedly being written off simply added to their mystique. As late as 1935, the respected journalist Nathaniel Peffer, writing about the Communist movement, admitted that "we actually know nothing about it." Everything that had been written about the Communists, he observed, was "propaganda, special pleading, guesswork or hearsay."[25]

Edgar Snow's firsthand reports therefore stunned the reading public when he released them after he returned to Beijing from Yan'an. For the first time, a credible, independent Western journalist offered what appeared to be an unbiased history of the Communist movement and a firsthand description of life in the areas under its control. The Communists and their followers whom he met were far from the monsters the Guomindang press had projected. They appeared to be disciplined, respectful, and determined social rebels and patriots in Snow's account. They upheld education and social equality for women. Their economic program was one of radical rural reform—they wanted to redistribute land and reduce taxes to decrease the burdens of the peasantry, not eliminate private property. They did not support any sort of socialism at this stage of their revolution. Theirs was a national revolution against the land-based gentry and against foreign domination. Snow found the atmosphere in the Communist area relaxed and the peasants who supported the party the sort of hardworking, unassuming farmers that Pearl Buck had brought to life in her novel.

More stunning than Snow's description of everyday life under the Communists was his presentation of the biographies of the Communist leaders, which were based largely on the accounts they gave him. They emerged as a colorful, diverse group with a wide variety of social and even ethnic backgrounds. What seemed to bind them together was their unflinching dedication to their cause and their lack of pretentiousness. Perhaps the most sensational part of Snow's book was the story of Mao Zedong's life, which was presented in his own words. It was and remains his only "autobiography." Snow's vivid description of his personal impression of Mao helped begin the construction of an image of Mao as legendary populist leader. Snow's version of Mao's story was not hagiography, which could be easily discounted; instead, it was something more effective: Snow was clearly captivated by the charismatic Communist leader and conveyed his powerful persona to Americans.

Snow's description begins, "I met Mao soon after my arrival: a gaunt, rather Lincolnesque figure." He was "an accomplished scholar of Classical Chinese, an omnivorous reader, a deep student of philosophy and history, a good speaker, a man with an unusual memory and extraordinary powers of concentration, an able writer, careless in his personal habits and appearance but astonishingly meticulous about details of duty, a man of tireless energy, and a military and political strategist of considerable genius. It is an interesting fact that many Japanese regard him as the ablest Chinese strategist alive." He was not a "savior" of China; no single person could be, Snow wrote, possibly making a dig at Chiang Kaishek, who did have biblical pretensions. In Mao, Snow observed, one felt "a certain force of destiny."

> You feel that whatever extraordinary there is in this man grows out of the uncanny degree to which he synthesizes and expresses the urgent demands of millions of Chinese, and especially the peasantry—those impoverished, underfed, exploited, illiterate, but kind, generous, courageous and just now rather rebellious human beings who are the vast majority of the Chinese people. If these demands and the movement which is pressing them forward are the dynamics which can

regenerate China, then in this deeply historical sense Mao Tse-tung may possibly become a very great man.

With the help of an American, the legend of Mao had begun.[26]

Snow's influence went beyond the shores of America. It may have even been greater within China itself. Snow published his accounts of his Yan'an journey in Chinese even before *Red Star* was published in the United States. Many young Chinese students were so inspired by what they read of Mao and his sacrificing comrades that they began dangerous pilgrimages to the Communist base area. Because of his influence, Snow was accused of being a Communist himself or at least an apologist. Though unquestionably impressed by the Communists, Snow maintained that he had no secret agenda and only reported what he saw and felt honestly. In fact, the Communist Party in the United States attacked Snow and his book as being anti-Soviet and unflattering to Stalin. Snow emphasized the CPC's independence from Moscow and portrayed Mao as a great leader who was beholden to no one, including Stalin. Snow's praise for the unique national characteristics of China's Communist movement displeased the American Communists, who carefully toed Moscow's line. In the reading of some, the Chinese Communists possibly were not Communists at all, only "so-called communists," a description that continued to be used, even within the highest levels of government in Washington. As the book reviewer for the *New York Times* observed, "the significance of Red China," if one interpreted Edgar Snow's book correctly, "is not that it is red but that it is Chinese."[27]

If Snow had been alone in his awe of the Communists, he could have been easily dismissed, but the remarkable thing was that Snow's impressions were echoed by a number of other Americans, including those with impeccably respectable political credentials, who had personally met the Communists. One of the most interesting of these was Evans Carlson, an American marine whom Roosevelt depended on for information about the Chinese Communists. Carlson, like Snow, developed a deep personal affection for the Communist leaders. Next to his father, Carlson said, he never loved another man more than Zhu De, the leader of the Red Army. Carlson may have been extreme for an American, but he was not alone in his admiration of the Communists.[28]

A third book published in the 1930s spoke to American interest about China in a very different way than did the *Good Earth* or *Red Star over China*. It spoke to audiences not especially invested in souls or in politics. Carl Crow (1884–1945) was a prolific journalist and Missourian, like Edgar Snow, and a longtime resident of China, like Pearl Buck. Like the other authors, Crow, who arrived in Shanghai as a United Press correspondent in the midst of the 1911 Revolution, developed a genuine attachment to the Chinese people during his twenty-five years in China.

Crow pursued a variety of occupations in China: he founded the *Shanghai Evening Post,* one of the city's leading newspapers; established the first Western advertising agency in Shanghai in 1911; and even worked for George Creel's Committee on Public Information during World War I to help shape an appealing image of America for dissemination in China. Crow became expert in the art of marketing, whether it involved a national image or a consumer product. He also educated mass audiences about China. Important Americans turned to him for advice and consul about the country. One of his most successful books was *Master Kung: The Story of Confucius,* which probably did more to popularize understanding of the philosopher than any other book published in America. During World War II, he stayed in the China Theater, wrote about the progress of the war for American audiences, and provided intelligence to the Office of Strategic Services. He returned to the United States in 1945 but died soon afterward.[29]

In his lifetime, Crow wrote fifteen books, almost all of them about China and Asia. He wrote about travel in China, the foreigner's life in tawdry 1930s Shanghai, the eminence of Confucius, and China's valiant resistance against Japanese aggression. But his most famous book, *Four Hundred Million Customers,* which he published in 1937 just before Japan launched its war of conquest, established him as a popular expert on doing business in China. The book was a great success in America, and although it seemed to pass forever into irrelevance after the 1949 Revolution, the booming business relationship between China and America in the twenty-first century has given it and Crow new life. A new edition of *Four Hundred Million Customers* is now available. Crow was one of the first Americans to think seriously about how to buy, sell, and promote products in China, the great dream of countless businessmen in America, past and present. Unlike Buck and Snow, who seemed insuppressibly earnest, Crow was often whimsical in his observations on how the Chinese went about their daily lives, characterizing them as charming and shrewd people. This made his book something more than a book about economic behavior. *Four Hundred Million Customers* can be said to be market research on the habits and psychology of the Chinese, who have been called the most materialistic people on earth. Crow showed that the Chinese were simultaneously a world apart from and essentially like Main Street Americans.

In a light, entertaining way, Crow described how Chinese came to smoke American cigarettes, use American lipstick, sew with American needles, and eat American raisins. The Chinese, however, were particularly demanding and careful consumers, and Crow advised American merchants to understand Chinese buying ways. Americans should not assume, for example, that it was Yankee marketing ingenuity that got Chinese women "on the cosmetic road to beauty." No, he wrote, 5,000 years ago, "Chinese girls were plucking useless hairs from their eyebrows and putting rouge on their cheeks." Crow emphasized that Chinese buying habits had been established over millennia and that they were far from being naïve or indiscriminate shoppers. American marketers had to appreciate the texture of Chinese skin, Chinese courting habits and customs, and Chinese standards of beauty. Crow also wrote about the Chinese as entrepreneurs who were savvy and original in their own ways. He described the quick ability of Chinese to manufacture what we today call unlicensed knockoffs of any popular foreign-made item; the central role of "friendship," or connections, in doing business; selling below cost to capture a market and accumulate quick capital; indirection and obscurity in negotiating transactions and agreements; and the canny ability of Chinese businessmen to cut costs to an absolute minimum, all familiar practices to Americans doing business in China today.[30]

The popularity of a book about doing business in China in the late 1930s might seem to be a mystery for those who think of China then as a desperately poor and increasingly radicalized country, the view that was portrayed in the work of Pearl Buck and Edgar Snow. Indeed, China in the 1930s was a terribly poor nation. Small-scale subsistence farming supported almost 75 percent of population and accounted for 60 percent of the gross domestic product. Some 3 million Chinese died of starvation in a 1928–1930 famine and another 5 million or so perished in 1936. Foreign interests dominated the "modern" transportation sector (shipping and railways), industry and manufacturing, urban commerce, finance, and utilities. Foreigners by the tens of thousands lived in privilege in defined concessions administered by the foreign powers, largely outside Chinese laws and customs. The wealthy foreigners, of which there were many, enjoyed opulent existences in isolation from the unwashed Chinese masses; enjoyed their own race tracks, swimming pools, and golf courses; and built splendid mansions that rivaled any grand bourgeois edifice in their home countries. China, which had been a "high-income" country before the nineteenth century, had in 100 years been reduced to a "poor and underdeveloped nation beset with very large political and economic problems," in the understated words of Albert Feuerwerker, the eminent economic historian of China.[31]

But China was also a country with a growing urban life and an appetite for foreign-produced goods and foreign investment opportunities. It was a country with a population close to 500 million, 100 million beyond the enticing title of Crow's book. By 1938, European and Japanese investment in China amounted to more than $2.5 billion, a sum that at the time was larger than in any other underdeveloped country but Argentina and British South Asia. American investments were third in size behind those of Japan and Great Britain. American tycoons such as railroad baron E. H. Harriman and John D. Rockefeller had aggressively pursued investment opportunities in China since the turn of the century. The dream of enjoying an even larger portion of the China market continued to fuel American imaginations, sustained in part by the example of the legendary success of North Carolinian James B. Duke and his cigarettes.

According to company history, Duke immediately appreciated the business significance of an 1881 invention that could roll a virtually limitless number of cigarettes and at a speed no human could. Upon hearing of the capacity of this machine, he asked for an atlas of the world, identified China as the country with the largest population on earth, and declared, "That is where we are going to sell cigarettes." And he did. The Chinese had known about tobacco since the sixteenth century, but within a few years after the first American-manufactured cigarettes appeared in China in 1890, sales soared. In 1902, Duke and other importers sold 1.25 billion cigarettes in China; in 1912, the number increased to 9.75 billion; and in 1916, it was 12 billion. In 1928, the United States alone exported more than 11 billion cigarettes to China. In 1915 and for at least the next decade, Americans exported more cigarettes annually to China than to the rest of the world combined. Duke's astounding success moved him to declare in 1916 that "we have made big progress in China" but that further possibilities "there can hardly be overestimated." The lure of the "inexhaustible" China market had captured him. (Today, over 350 million smokers in China consume more tobacco products than any other country in the world.)[32]

With Duke's success no doubt in mind, Carl Crow tried to get other Americans to appreciate China's economic value as he did. Think "pig bristles," he asked his readers of *Four Hundred Million Customers*. Think about the declining quality of the bristles in your toothbrushes. More than likely they had come from China, the dominant supplier to the world. The best bristles came from faraway Sichuan, on the border of the "mysterious and inaccessible Tibet," but government suppression of banditry and Communists had upset the supply. So, Crow advised, when you brush your teeth, "reflect on the smallness of the world" and yourself as a "neighbor of the 400 millions of China."[33]

Within months of publishing his whimsical vignettes, Crow was moved to issue a much more serious work, *I Speak for the Chinese*. Earnest plea replaced witticisms. Crow's book title was not an appropriation of a Chinese voice but rather a desperate advocacy. In July 1937, a minor skirmish between Chinese troops and Japanese soldiers at the Marco Polo Bridge (Lugouqiao) southwest of Beijing escalated into full-scale war. Popular Chinese sentiment against Chiang Kaishek's government and against Japan had grown steadily since the Mukden crisis of 1931–1932. Chiang's focus on eliminating the Communists above forging national unity against the foreign aggressor had alienated his countrymen. In December 1936, tensions came to a head when several of Chiang's most senior generals arrested the Chinese leader in what has become known as the Xi'an Incident. The generals insisted that Chiang reorganize the national government to make it more representative, end the civil war, and commit to a policy of national salvation through a unified front against Japan. Chiang at first refused, and only the intervention of the Communists during the negotiations saved his life. The Communists pledged to subordinate themselves to his Nanjing government in order to unify against Japanese aggression. Chiang reluctantly agreed and was released on Christmas Day 1936. The new national unity government accounted for the stiff Chinese resistance at the Marco Polo Bridge seven months later.

In August 1937, Tokyo ordered its military to invade full force into China and attack Shanghai, the vital center of modern Chinese life and commerce. For three months, the Chinese courageously resisted the attack before the city fell. The devastation was tremendous and many Chinese were killed. Images of the Japanese destruction of the city circulated around the globe and won sympathy for the Chinese. Crow recounted the cruel history of Japanese depredation against the Chinese and warned that the Japanese grand objective was nothing less than remodeling "the world's civilization along superior Japanese lines." The conquest of China was just the beginning. Crow directed his final words to the American audience. He warned, "After China, what?" More and more Americans also wondered. This was the start of the devastating Sino-Japanese War that would continue for eight long years.[34]

In December, the Japanese army advanced into Nanjing, the national capital. Chiang Kaishek was removing his government 1,000 miles inland to Chongqing, and the former capital was almost without defense. In a horror that ranks among the worst atrocities in history, over seven weeks, Japanese soldiers murdered and terrorized the civilian population of the ancient city. Soldiers raped tens of thousands of women and slaughtered tens of thousands of noncombatants. Some estimates of the number killed reach as high as 300,000. Americans read graphic eyewitness accounts of the "rape of Nanking," as it was already called at the time in major U.S. media outlets. *Life* magazine, the influential news photo journal, published gruesome photographs of the results of Japanese military cruelty. At the time, *Life* called it possibly "the worst holocaust in modern history." *Look* magazine ran photos of Japanese soldiers bayoneting bound Chinese prisoners under the headline "Killing for Fun." The unprovoked Japanese sinking of the USS *Panay*, an American gunboat that was helping Chinese evacuate from Nanjing during the pillage of the city, further encouraged American sympathy for the Chinese and antipathy toward Japan.[35] W. H. Auden and Christopher Isherwood, the great Anglo-American writers, published a report after a tour of China at this time. Included in it was "In Time of War," a long verse that ends with

> And maps can really point to places
> Where life is evil now:
> Nanking; Dachau.[36]

Japan soon occupied the cities and vital economic resources of most of coastal China. Important Americans began to conclude that war with Japan was inevitable. For geopolitical, economic, and moral reasons, support for China's resistance against Japan was increasingly seen as necessary for America's security.[37]

In addition to the popular press and government sources of information on China, Main Street Americans had another and perhaps even more influential source of information about events in China: the missionary network. Missionaries were everywhere in China and sent reports about the actions of the Japanese soldiers. As literal, personal testimony, these reports had a profound effect. An especially poignant one, written in Nanjing on Christmas Eve 1937, combined deep affection for the Chinese, revulsion against Japanese brutality, American patriotism, and personal honor and devotion and was widely circulated among religious circles in the United States. The unidentified American author graphically described the horror of the Japanese army's attack. The beautiful city of Nanjing was now "laid waste, ravaged, completely looted, much of it burned. Complete anarchy has reigned for ten days." We have "to stand by while even the very poor are having their last possessions taken from them—their last coin, their last bit of bedding (and it is freezing weather) . . . while thousands of disarmed soldiers who have sought sanctuary with you, together with many hundreds of innocent civilians are taken out before your eyes to be shot or used for bayonet practice and you have to listen to the sound of the guns that are killing them; while a thousand women kneel before you crying hysterically, begging you to save them from the beasts who are preying on them. . . . This is a hell I had never before envisaged, but hell it is none the less."[38]

Rev. John Magee, an American Episcopalian missionary who had lived in China since 1912 and led the Nanking Committee of the International Red Cross in 1937, also witnessed the rape of Nanjing. Risking his own safety, Magee left the sanctuary of the so-called safety zone for foreigners and went out to document the massacre. With a 16mm movie camera, Magee took hours of footage of beheadings, rapes, and other carnage. His footage was smuggled out of China and made its way back to the United States, where news publications reproduced frames and select government and private audiences viewed horrifying clips.[39]

Returned missionaries in America rallied to support China and pressed Washington to do something to impede Japan's aggression. The Roosevelt administration still faced strong sentiment against actions that some feared would provoke Japan and lead to war. Arguing against measures against Japan, influential diplomat and recently returned ambassador to the Soviet Union William C. Bullitt declared, "We have large emotional interests in China, small economic interests, and no vital interests." The strident isolationist organization America First Committee argued, "We sympathize with China. But we must not plunge America into war . . . for sentimental reasons." But public sentiment steadily grew in support of sanctions on American trade with Japan. Accounts of Japanese atrocities in China so upset FDR that he did not want them read at Cabinet meetings. However, he directed Secretary of State Cordell Hull to find a way to leak them to the public, "so that the American people might get the real Chinese background for the sake of the future." In the fall of 1938, FDR authorized a $25 million loan to Chiang's government. The amount was small, but it was symbolic of American feeling toward China and the start of what would become a steady flow of American material and financial support for China's war effort. Washington moved toward taking economic sanctions against Japan, which, in fact, became the proximate reason for Tokyo's attack on Pearl Harbor.[40]

Many Americans had sympathy for other victims of aggression and fascism in the mid-1930s, especially Ethiopia and the Spanish Republic, but Japan's action in China provoked even greater reaction, both because of the shocking reports from the field and because of the place China had long occupied in many American hearts. According to *Fortune* magazine, a 1938 survey found that more Americans were disturbed by the events in China than by the Nazi advance into Austria. A wide range of Americans from different walks of life—class, ethnic, and political—pressed Washington to do something about Japanese aggression and challenged prevailing isolationist sentiments in the country and those who wanted to maintain stability in U.S.-Japan relations. The value of bilateral trade with Japan was upward of seven times that between China and the United States, and Japan was the third-largest purchaser of American products in the world. Yet popular sentiment overwhelmingly sided with China.[41]

FDR and his closest advisors also decisively favored the Chinese over Japan but wanted to avoid actions that might precipitate hostilities. As Hoover had done before, FDR verbally denounced Japanese militarism. He condemned Japan's actions in Manchuria, characterizing them as part of a "reign of terror and international lawlessness" and a threat to the "very foundations of civilization," and like Hoover, he took no specific action against Tokyo. In mid-1938, however, the administration began to take concrete steps aimed at weakening Japan's capacity to make war, even as it tried to keep the focus of its attention on Europe. In September 1938, Washington banned the sale of American scrap iron to Japan. In July 1939, it terminated the bilateral commercial treaty with Japan, which opened the way to further actions, including banning the sale of aviation fuel and lubricants. War in Europe erupted in September 1939. And then in July 1941, Washington froze all

Japanese assets in the United States, ending the flow of oil that Japan desperately needed. When Congress passed the Two-Ocean Navy Act in 1940, authorizing funds for a huge buildup of the U.S. naval fleet, Tokyo concluded that it had to act against the United States before it developed an overwhelming military advantage. At the same time, Tokyo watched as Washington increased its economic and military assistance to China, Tokyo's main objective, which stubbornly refused to succumb to foreign domination.[42]

One of the most prominent groups that wanted to rally American support for China was the American Committee for Non-Participation in Japanese Aggression. Formed in 1938 by two returned China missionaries, the organization hoped to weaken Japan's military power by ending key American exports. Hoover's secretary of state, Henry L. Stimson, served as its honorary chair. Other prominent officers included publisher William Allen White, retired Harvard president A. Lawrence Lowell, and Rear Admiral Harry E. Yarnell, the former commander of the U.S. fleet in Asia. Other influential supporters included business leaders such as Henry Harriman, former president of the U.S. Chamber of Commerce; John D. Rockefeller Jr.; Henry Luce, publisher of *Time* and *Life* magazines; Dr. Walter Judd, another returned China missionary; and social activist Helen Keller. Hundreds of local civic and volunteer organizations, running from liberal to conservative, including church groups, labor unions, business associations and women's organizations, affiliated with the committee. By the spring of 1939, according to a poll the committee conducted, 70 to 80 percent of 453 American newspapers backed government action to limit American trade with Japan.[43]

Japanese aggression ignited Chinese Americans to rally to the support of China. Because law and social prejudice had largely excluded them from America's political life and relegated them to the social margins since the nineteenth century, many Chinese Americans believed that their destinies were inextricably linked to the future of their land of ancestry. Chinese Americans thought they would have rights and receive respect only when China itself became a modern, strong country, and they had long followed events in Asia. They had played an important role in supporting Sun Yat-sen's revolutionary movement and in the establishment of a republic. In 1905, Chinese in Hawaii and the U.S. mainland sparked a boycott of American goods to protest American anti-Chinese immigration legislation. The Japanese invasion of China in 1937 provided a new opportunity and a challenge.

Chinese Americans from all political persuasions, left and right, could alert America to China's plight and appeal to America's conscience and self-interest. Protest slogans such as "Racial Freedom and Liberty Forever" and "To Save China, to Save Ourselves" reflected the Chinese American view that their racial fate was intertwined with that of China. Chinese Americans called on Americans to donate funds for Chinese war relief and to support measures to end American trade in military-related material that could help the menacing Japanese military.[44]

For the first time, sympathetic ears heard the Chinese American plea. Chinese Americans rallied and paraded in the streets of San Francisco, New York, and other American cities with supporters from all walks of life and backgrounds. Their efforts raised hundreds of thousands of dollars for China's war effort. They picketed ships at harbors along the Pacific Coast that were loading scrap iron and other war materials bound for Japan and asked longshoremen to respect their picket lines. Union members joined the protest despite the threats of ship owners. The largest of these protests was a five-day picket on the San Francisco waterfront against a Japanese-owned ship that was to carry scrap iron. Some 5,000 picketers carried placards reading "Stop Sending War Supplies to Japan!," "Imperial Japan needs American Scrap Iron, Oil, Cotton to Kill Chinese Civilians Boycott Japan! Stop Japanese Aggression!," and "Bandages for China—Bullets for Japan. Why?" America and China were becoming allies against a common enemy.[45]

Another form of support for China developed through the personal efforts of a very different sort of American. After retiring from the U.S. Army Air Corps in 1937, Texan Claire Chennault became Chiang Kaishek's air force advisor just before the outbreak of hostilities. Chennault helped organize and train a fledgling Chinese air fighting force and then was instrumental in obtaining planes and pilots from the United States for Chiang. His original American Volunteer Group, better known as the Flying Tigers because of their insignia, consisted of 300 American military pilots and crew. Their exploits against Japanese bombers and fighters became legendary. Though ostensibly a private force hired by the Chinese government, the American Volunteer Group had the secret sanction of the president and federal monetary support before it was incorporated into the American air command force during World War II. It was a not-so-secret "covert operation." The colorful group included a number of individuals who went on to have important careers. Among them was the journalist Joseph Alsop, air transport businessman Robert Prescott, Medal of Honor pilot and author Gregory

'Pappy" Boyington, and U.S. Senator Ted Stevens. Scores of memoirs, fond accounts, and histories and the 1942 film *Flying Tigers,* starring John Wayne, immortalized the group.

The private citizen most responsible for rallying the United States to China's cause was the powerful publisher of the Time/Life news empire, Henry Robinson Luce. He and his wife, Clare Boothe Luce, an accomplished writer and political figure in her own right, played an enormous role in influencing public opinion through their media and social connections. As prominent political conservatives, their effort to have the United States oppose Japanese aggression brought them into conflict with isolationists, many of whom were fellow Republicans. The Luces, however, represented a growing number of important conservatives who closely identified America's future interests with Asia and the Pacific.

The explanation for Henry Luce's view is in significant part biographical. Though he was from a long line of New Englanders and had been educated at Yale, Luce was also very much a product of China. His missionary father had gone to China in 1897 and served there for much of the rest of his life, even acting as the vice-president of Yanjing University. Henry was born in 1898 in Qingdao, on the Shandong Peninsula. He learned Chinese before English and lived for his first thirteen years in China before leaving for education in the United States. Because of the cut of his clothes and foreign manner, the students at Luce's prep school called him "Chink."[46]

He and a Yale friend founded *Time* magazine in 1923, which quickly became phenomenally successful as the country's first national news periodical. Through the years, *Time* kept China in the attention of its readers. It put Chiang Kaishek on its cover five times before the magazine honored him and Madame Chiang as "Man and Wife of the Year" in 1937. An artist's full-color rendering of the two, appearing wise and determined, looked out at the reader.[47] Luce had closely followed developments in China through his contacts with Ida Pruitt, Edgar Snow, and other returned friends from China. His periodicals carried extensive features on the rise of the Communists in China and the advancing aggression of Japan. As early as June 1940, even as the Nazis were overrunning Europe, Luce maintained that the growing conflict in the Pacific was "far more important even than speedy aid to the Allies." He soon became a prime mover in a remarkable private effort to advance ties with China. In early 1941, Luce worked with prominent public figures in the country to launch one of the most effective humanitarian support groups ever in America, United China Relief. With John D.

Rockefeller III, Paul Hoffman of the Studebaker auto company, Thomas W. Lamont of Morgan Bank, David Selznick of Hollywood, Wendell Willkie, Pearl Buck, and other leading public figures, Luce and United China Relief raised $50 million in aid for China. In his fund-raising letter for the organization, Luce wrote that American support "will help to confirm, perhaps for years to come, the widespread belief in China that America feels kindly toward China." Then in early 1941, the Luces accepted an invitation from the Chiangs to visit China. The trip invigorated Luce's connection with China and inspired a missionary's zeal to help realize China's national salvation under Christian leadership. It was a passion that remained with Luce for the rest of his life.[48]

In China, the Luces visited with the Chiangs, others in the Soong clan, and national elite and toured the area still under the control of the central government. Everywhere they went and everyone they met inspired them. Chiang, in Henry Luce's view, was the greatest leader in Asia since the grand eighteenth century ruler of China, the Emperor Kangxi. Chiang and Madame, Luce maintained, would be honored for "centuries and centuries." The struggling country was being remade in America's image. Luce declared, "I see America and the 20th century stamped all over them." What Luce saw during his tour of China confirmed the expansive vision he presented in his famous editorial, "The American Century," published in *Life* in February 1941 just before the Luces left for China. America, Luce had proclaimed, was to be the Good Samaritan for all the people of the world. Through its generosity, help, leadership, and example, America would fulfill its destiny and become the leading power of the world. The twentieth century would be just the first, great "American Century." China was a key test case.[49]

Shortly after their return, the Luces reported on their China journey to a select gathering of the American cultural and political elite at the Waldorf-Astoria Hotel in New York City. Clare Boothe highlighted the commonality of America and China's national purposes, arguing that the Chinese were "our spiritual allies and our fellow Christians." They desperately needed America's help against Japan. The heroic foreign mission effort and the Christian leadership of the country, according to Clare Boothe, was "one of the most gallant and beautiful stories of the modern world."[50]

At about the same moment, across the continent, the president of Stanford University, Ray Lyman Wilbur, a close friend of Herbert Hoover and secretary of the interior under him, published "Our Pacific Destiny" in the

Pacific Historical Review. Wilbur had delivered the remarks to Charter Day celebrations at the Los Angeles and Berkeley campuses of the University of California a few months earlier and like the Luces viewed Asia as the source of America's future greatness. Like Henry Luce, Wilbur had relatives who were China missionaries.

With Britain valiantly holding out against Nazi Germany, Hitler about to invade the Soviet Union, and Washington providing billions of dollars in aid to Britain, France, and the Soviet Union, Wilbur's address seems odd to a reader today who might have assumed that the European war would be the preoccupation of the day. But that was not the case. There is no mention of Hitler's conquests or the danger of fascism in Wilbur's comments. Instead, Balboa and his "discovery" of the Pacific garner more attention than anything else. There is no mention of the danger of aggression against the United States. Though Wilbur, who tried to be scrupulously nonpolitical, said something about the "hideous nightmare" in Europe, he devoted almost all of his erudition to the historic importance of the Pacific to America. As so many had before him, Wilbur fixed his eyes on the positive possibilities: "we have entered upon a Pacific era," he declared; "in comparison with the Pacific, the Mediterranean is but a small lake." Wilbur encouraged his audiences to work for international understanding and cooperation and overcome the complications of racial prejudice, religious differences, population growth, and economics. There was no mention of the Japanese occupation of China, but Wilbur reminded his audiences of the closeness and importance of China to America throughout history. Wilbur ended by reminding his audience that it is the Pacific Ocean that "cradles the climate of California on which our future depends." Difficult times lay ahead, he conceded, but he expressed confidence that the future held "a glorious destiny for the peoples of the Pacific."[51]

A month later, the Roosevelt administration froze Japanese assets in the United States and put an embargo on further American exports of oil and steel to Japan. For moral reasons as much as for geopolitical ones, America had to stand with China. "Japan has no friends in this country, but China has," observed Secretary of Interior Harold Ickes. Popular opinion had turned intensely antagonistic against Japan: polls showed that up to 75 percent of Americans who were surveyed endorsed opposition to Japan even at the risk of war. At the same time, nearly two-thirds did not support the idea of war against Germany, even at this late date. Believing that its back was against the wall and time was running out, Tokyo decided it had no alternative but to strike against American naval power in the Pacific. The military began to map its attack against Hawaii.[52]

In a last effort to avert catastrophe, FDR's secretary of state, Cordell Hull, delivered an ultimatum to Japan on November 26, 1941. His so-called Open Door Note affirmed the long-established position of the United States in support of Chinese territorial integrity and equality of commercial opportunity in China, but it also called "for the peace of the Pacific," including the withdrawal of all Japanese military forces from China and nonsupport for any government in China other than the existing Republic of China then in Chongqing. Not surprisingly, Tokyo refused. Its naval fleet departed from Japan on the same day Hull delivered his demand and surreptitiously sailed east toward Hawaii. America's entry into the global conflagration of World War II came about as a direct result of its firm and provocative (to Japan) commitment to China.[53]

On December 7, 1941, a few hours after Japan's attack on Pearl Harbor, Henry Luce's ailing father passed away, but not before confiding in his son that America "will now see what we mean to China and China means to us." Henry Luce told friends the next day that he was gratified that his missionary father had lived long enough to know that America was finally "on the same side as the Chinese." More than a poignant moment of a son and a dying father, the story is emblematic of the deeply intimate connections that bound many Americans and Chinese through revolution and war. Beyond politics or strict geopolitical calculations, sentiment, or what some labeled "sentimentality," decisively directed the path of history.[54]

5

Allies and Enemies

The time is short; the enemy is sly;
And all who once loved peace and sorely tried;
But she shall take her people this reply:
"Our cause is common, and your pride our pride
Your triumph ours: sacred as ours, your loam,"
When she does through the far horizon, home.

Anonymous American, for Madame Chiang Kaishek, 1943

Chiang Kaishek, as did many others in China, expressed relief when the mighty United States declared war on Japan on December 8, 1941, and became China's powerful ally against the common foe. No longer did China have to fight Japan alone, as it had since 1937. At the time of the attack on Pearl Harbor, Japan occupied most of China's long coastline, Manchuria, north China, and major cities along its eastern seaboard and threatened the inland centers of Chinese resistance, especially the wartime capital of Chongqing in distant Sichuan Province. Chiang had moved the capital from Nanjing in 1937 just before the Japanese seized the city. Japanese bombers regularly rained horrible devastation on Chongqing's civilian population, but because of difficult terrain and distance, the Japanese army had been unable to advance into the area. The military conflict had reached a stalemate. Though Tokyo had established a puppet Chinese government in occupied Nanjing, as it had in Manchuria, the militarists had been unable to crush Chinese resistance. Japan's empire was about to reach its greatest extent, stretching from Northeast Asia and Korea through China and parts of South Asia and completely over Southeast Asia, the Philippines, and Indonesia.

President Franklin D. Roosevelt was pleased to establish a fighting alliance with Chiang's China, as he and other American officials had worried that China's resistance would collapse, allowing Japan access to the rich resources of the Chinese mainland and the opportunity to deploy its forces elsewhere. "I really feel that it is a triumph," he told British leader Lord Mountbatten not long after the attack on Pearl Harbor, "to have gotten the 425 million Chinese people on the Allied side. They will be very useful 25 or 50 years hence, even though China cannot contribute much military or naval support at the moment." For the first time in its history, China found itself in the role of a major military ally on the side of the United States and Britain, which itself had repeatedly fought China in the past.[1]

Throughout the 1930s, China had enjoyed the moral support of many in America, but sympathy translated into substantial material aid from Washington only slowly, even after Japan had launched its war of conquest in 1937. Faced with congressional sentiment against actions that might draw the United States into conflict overseas again, Roosevelt, who may have wanted to do more for China than political conditions allowed, could only verbally condemn aggression and permit a small amount of American military assistance to reach China. Not until as late as the summer of 1941, six months before Pearl Harbor, did the covert, volunteer Flying Tigers, the American air group that would became legendary for its exploits, begin their operations in Southeast Asia to help the Chinese.

Once China became one of the major theaters of military operations in the global war, it assumed a new importance for the United States. It engaged a substantial portion of Japan's fighting forces that otherwise would have been directed against the British in South Asia or the Americans in the Pacific. FDR understood that if nothing else, China tied down Japan's army, and his task was to keep China in the war fighting the Japanese. Through the war years, billions of dollars in U.S. assistance went to the Chinese central government to help it in this fight. Beyond practical military matters, China's political significance in American thinking grew as the war progressed and Americans considered the world's new power realities.

Though the idea that the two countries shared a fond friendship widely circulated before the war, the global conflict elevated the relationship to heightened strategic levels. Every day Americans read glamorized accounts of the exploits of Clare Chennault's Flying Tigers, fighting in the air over the faraway rugged mountains of southeastern China. They learned about the exhausting work of bringing supplies to the heroic free Chinese over the remote and treacherous Burma Road. Beyond politics and policy, the war experience helped transform the relationship between the two countries and changed the way Americans would think about the Chinese. Chinese and Americans found themselves committed to each other in deeply existential ways: love, fidelity, and sacrifice all became features of the relationship. For many, the war and its aftermath confirmed the conviction that the fates of America and China were intimately intertwined.

Americans in the twentieth century used the word "destiny," but in less transhistorical ways than their nineteenth-century counterparts who thought in more millennial ways. The idea of a special mission for America never disappeared, however, and a special feeling about China continued to inspire Americans to think in terms of grand history at work in that distant land. The size and population of the country, its dire circumstances under invasion, and the scale of its human drama all imbued China with singular importance and, for many Americans, accentuated its profile in their thinking. *Chinese Destinies* is the title American rebel Agnes Smedley gave to her book of biographies of everyday people she met when she visited the country in the early 1930s. After meeting Mao Zedong in the Communist capital of Yan'an, Edgar Snow described him as a man with "a certain force of destiny" about him. The American publishers of a collection of Chiang Kaishek's writing entitled the volume *China's Destiny.* "Our destiny," Soong Mayling herself declared, "is with the democracies." During the war years, many Chinese and Americans embraced the idea that the political fates of China and America were fundamentally entwined. From the left, respected China specialist Owen Lattimore observed before Pearl Harbor that "the old structure of power in Europe has done forever. . . . The center of gravity has shifted to China. First and last, that is what concerns America. . . . And as China goes, so goes Asia." A few years later, from the right, General Douglas MacArthur offered the same vision: "Europe is a dying system. It is worn out and run down. . . . The lands touching the Pacific with their billions of inhabitants will determine the course of history for the next ten thousand years."[2]

During the war years, the governments of the two countries grew closer than ever before and closer than they have been since then. But beneath the genuine friendship between the peoples and governments, tensions roiled and would later completely undermine the relationship. The Nationalists frustrated and then angered American leaders, who saw Chiang and the Chinese elite as inept and corrupt. Then, the rise and triumph of communism in China in 1949 provoked an epic turn in American attitudes toward China. The Chinese revolution and the overthrow of the Nationalists stunned Americans, such as MacArthur, who had concluded that the outcome of the war against Japan in Asia would determine the world's future. Communism now threatened to consume the vast Eurasian land mass and thus imperil the destiny of the whole world. The declaration of the founding of the People's Republic of China in October 1949 thrust the country to the top of the U.S. political agenda, sharply divided Americans, and ignited one of the most acrimonious debates in modern American political history. China the friend and ally became China the enemy. The "China question" has never been the same since. And then, in late 1950, just a few years after Chinese and Americans had fought shoulder to shoulder against Japan, they began to kill each other in Korea. Their countries had become mortal enemies; each saw the defeat of the other as essential for nothing less than national survival. Cold War contention and conflict with China, not intimacy, became America's reality.

In 1941, the picture did not seem so complex. Chiang Kaishek was the undisputed leader of China. He had the official backing of all resistance forces, including the Communists, who endorsed the national united front against Japan that was established after the Xi'an Incident in 1936. Chiang and the political forces around him also enjoyed an alliance with the United States and the unreserved admiration of both wealthy and well-placed American friends and many ordinary Americans. Roosevelt elevated Chiang to one of the "big four" leaders of the Allied Powers, joining himself, Churchill, and Stalin, that would determine the political contours of the postwar world. In late 1943, Chiang met with the other leaders at the Cairo Conference, where they discussed the future of Asia after the defeat of Japan. Roosevelt once even suggested to Chiang that China would take the prime responsibility for the occupation of Japan after the war. For the American people, Chiang was the heroic leader of free China. He was widely hailed as a "military genius" and a scholar-statesman. Christian Eddy, the influential leader of the YMCA, anointed him China's "Christian General." For Eddy, there were no other world leaders than President Roosevelt and Chiang for whom Christians "should more earnestly pray."[3]

Washington, however, was not oblivious to the political tensions within China that lay just beneath the surface of unity. Animosity between the Nationalists and Communists did not disappear with the formation of the formal united front. The national government under Chiang was supposed to accept Communists and end its efforts to eliminate them. The Communists, in turn, were to recognize the national leadership of Chiang and place their fighting forces under his command. But the two continued to war against each other even as they fought the Japanese. In late 1940, armies of the two forces clashed in southern Anhui Province when Nationalist soldiers ambushed Communist troops, leaving thousands dead or wounded. The New Fourth Route Army Incident, as it has been called, ended effective military coordination between the two sides.

Washington worried that Japan would exploit the simmering disunity in China. Because intelligence conflicted and was unreliable, Washington faced continual difficulties determining exactly what was going on in China. American leaders turned to unofficial and unusual sources of information to try to understand the situation there. Secretary of the Treasury Hans Morgenthau enlisted the aid of an unlikely intelligence agent: Ernest Hemingway, one of America's literary giants. In early spring 1941, Hemingway and his new wife, Martha Gellhorn, spent four months in Asia reporting on the region at war. Their principal interest was China, but they also traveled to Hong Kong and Burma. Gellhorn, an important journalist, submitted dispatches to *Collier's* while Hemingway reported for *PM,* a new progressive tabloid in New York. The couple ranged far and wide in their travels, from Chengdu at the foot of the Tibetan plateau in western Sichuan to Rangoon. They met the political and military elite of the National government, including Chiang and Soong Mayling and her relatives who dominated the government hierarchy. They met Zhou Enlai, the top representative of the Communists who was living in Chongqing at the time. They ventured to the front lines and traveled at night to avoid Japanese forces. Unknown to their Chinese hosts, Morgenthau had asked Hemingway to gather information about the government's use of American aid and confidentially report to him. Morgenthau was responsible for overseeing the distribution of U.S. aid that was flowing to the Chinese government. From 1941 to 1945, the United States sent some $1.5 billion to Chiang's government, and Morgenthau wanted to know how and where the money was being used.[4]

Hemingway had never traveled to Asia before and knew little about its history or culture, but he had established himself as an astute journalist during several visits to Spain in the late 1930s. Just before his departure for Asia, he published *For Whom The Bell Tolls,* which drew from his observations of life and politics in the Spanish Civil War. Hemingway's China writing is modest in scale compared to his famous work on Spain—he published just seven news articles from his trip and a secret report to Morgenthau—but they provide a unique American cosmopolitan's view of the complex situation in China on the eve of America's own entry into the Pacific War.

Hemingway and Gellhorn put themselves into difficult and occasionally dangerous situations to get their stories. They had terrifying flights in rickety old planes that flew over Japanese lines at night; they convoyed over horrible, muddy roads in rusty jeeps and over water in barely serviceable boats with rotting hulls; and they slept in hovels not much better than what the average, and pitiable, Chinese foot soldier had to endure. They went by horse and trekked by foot. They survived Japanese bombing raids and close encounters with enemy ground forces. They also experienced the contrasts of war when they were wined and dined by the Nationalist elite in Chongqing, who lived in luxury. They were treated as international celebrities, and the Nationalist government gave them long personal audiences with Chiang and Soong Mayling. At the same time, they met other American writers and journalists along the way, including the correspondent for *Time* magazine, Theodore White, who with Annalee Jacoby would write the highly influential book *Thunder out of China*, which presented a damning portrait of the Nationalist regime. Hemingway also spent many hours with William J. Lederer, then a naval lieutenant on a Yangzi River gunboat, who in 1958 would co-author *The Ugly American*, the influential novel that critiqued America's approach to the Cold War in Asia.

Because Morgenthau had asked Hemingway not to publish anything that might aggravate tensions between the Nationalists and Communists, Hemingway was careful not to be critical of the Chinese rivals or write anything controversial about them. Instead, he focused on the danger of Japan to America, especially to critical sources of raw materials in Southeast Asia, and on the heroic resistance of the Chinese. His most inspired writing described an extraordinary feat of human engineering and construction that, for Hemingway, was emblematic of China itself. On April 10, Hemingway flew from Chongqing to Chengdu, a nearby ancient city and the location of important military facilities for the National government. For several days, he watched in awe as 100,000 Chinese workers toiled on the construction of a massive airfield intended to accommodate the heavy bombers Chiang hoped Washington would soon send to use against Japan's home islands.

In just a few weeks, the Chinese government had drafted these workers from areas still under its control. Responsibility for the project fell to Chen Loh-kwan, a 38-year-old Chinese engineer and a graduate of the University of Illinois. The huge airfield was to be more than a mile long and 150 yards wide. It would be one of the world's largest airfields when completed and was to be operational in just 100 days. It had to have a five-foot-deep mul-tilayered base and top, but except for one lone steam shovel, all the work was to be done by hand. The backs of thousands carried away soil and de-bris from the cleared area and carried in rock crushed by other humans. One-hundred-man teams pulled ten-ton rollers back and forth to pack and smooth the runway. Through the dust and din of construction, Hemingway could hear countless voices singing work songs, the undertone, he described "as of surf breaking on a great barrier reef." He continued, "I saw some-thing that made me know what it would have been like to have ridden some early morning up from the south out of the desert and see the great camp and work that went on when men were building the pyramids." Hemingway carefully described the scale and division of labor: during twelve-hour work-days, 60,000 men hauled 7.8 million cubic feet of gravel eight miles to the site and 35,000 others crushed rock with hand-held hammers. They relied on 5,000 wheelbarrows and 200,000 baskets to carry the dirt and rock they moved. They also constructed two aqueducts each ten miles long to bring water to the runway. Bare feet mixed tons of concrete; no machinery was used. For their pay, the workers received the equivalent of forty ounces of rice a day, most of it in kind.

After witnessing the stunning monumental construction spectacle, Hemingway concluded that nothing was impossible for the Chinese if they put their minds to a task. As Gellhorn, who wrote six articles about their China travels for *Collier's Weekly,* put it: "Time does not matter in China. Four years of war is a long time. But perhaps if your history goes back 4,000 years, it does not seem so long. The Chinese are born patient, and they learn endurance when they start to breathe. No, time does not matter in China."[5]

After he returned to America, Hemingway sent a long report to Morgen-thau that presented his views of the political situation in China. He focused on the relationship between the Communists and Nationalists. Hemingway favored neither side but emphasized their deep enmity. The bitterness be-tween the two sides "can not hardly be exaggerated," he wrote, to the ex-tent that Nationalist leaders seemed to see the Communists as a greater danger than even the Japanese. Communism, according to them, was a

"HEART DISEASE" whereas the Japanese invasion was only a "SKIN DIS-EASE." The united front was largely a fiction. To forestall war between the two, Hemingway recommended that the United States insist that it would in no way finance a civil war. Many of the wealthy and powerful Chinese Nationalists were even pressing Chiang to go after the Communists and make peace with Japan. Chiang did not come off well in Hemingway's report, which indicated that Chiang's accusations against the Communists were often contradictory and misleading. The Communists also spread propaganda and inflated their role in the war against Japan. The only individual who truly impressed Hemingway was Communist leader Zhou Enlai, whom he met in Chongqing. Zhou, according to Hemingway, was "a man of enormous charm and great intelligence." Hemingway's candor never appeared in print for public consumption. Instead, the reading public learned from Hemingway's and Gellhorn's dispatches only that China was mightily resisting Japan under the leadership of the indomitable Chiang, his captivating wife, and their Westernized close associates. Hemingway wrote that under Chiang's leadership and with American aid, China would stop Japan, which "can never conquer China." The American public remained largely unaware of China's internal political tensions and divided rule.[6]

In November 1942, Chiang Kaishek's wife, Soong Mayling, traveled to the United States as a private citizen to obtain medical treatment for a variety of chronic ailments. After spending several months at the hospital of the medical school at Columbia University, Soong embarked on a grand tour of the United States to promote U.S.-China relations. She was stunningly attractive, appealing, and successful. The profoundly warm reception for Soong from everyday Americans and their leaders was extraordinary and has rarely, if ever, been repeated by any foreign visitor.[7]

Soong Mayling captured the hearts and imaginations of Americans across the land, and her tour revealed all the elements of the especially affectionate relationship that had developed between China and the United States during the war years. Soong, who held no governmental position and wielded no formal power, spoke to enormous crowds across the country. Part glamorous celebrity, part elegant regent, part sacrificing Joan of Arc (or Woman Warrior), Soong possessed a magnetic charm and impressive speaking ability that won people to her cause. But personality alone only partially explains the connection she made with Americans. She seemed to embody her nation: she was the soulful and civilized China that suffered under a common treacherous enemy, that cherished the same noble cultural and political ideals as Americans did, that possessed an enduring human dignity that would lead to triumph over adversity and unite with America to form a "new and better world," as Soong repeatedly announced China would do. This charismatic and articulate English-speaking woman personified the China that America had created in its own image during many years of interaction.

In February 1943, Soong traveled to Washington, D.C., where she stayed in the White House as the guest of President Roosevelt and First Lady Eleanor Roosevelt. On the 18th, she addressed the full Senate and then the House, becoming the first Asian and first private citizen ever to address Congress (and only the second woman to do so, the first being Queen Wilhelmina of the Netherlands). Though she was sensitive about issues related to her race and sex, she displayed confidence and grace, and her eloquent performance swept the tough audiences off their feet. Veteran political journalist Frank McNaughton, who witnessed her on Capitol Hill, reported that he had never seen anything like the reception America's political leaders gave her. Senators felt they were in the presence of "one of the world's great personalities." She spoke to the House from notes but "without glasses, without a single bobble or ill-timed pause, in a rich concise voice that clipped of the words better than most Americans can pronounce them. House members were stunned at her command of English, the lack of any accent, the craftsmanship of her combination of words, her calm assurance and her stage presence. Congressmen were wholly captivated by her personality, amazed by her presence, dizzied by her oratorical ability." Clare Booth Luce once praised her for being able to speak "flawless, tumbling, forthright *American.*" But beyond her personal charisma, Soong delivered messages to her American audiences that resonated deeply with notions of themselves and their national image and the historic association with China. "Coming here today," she declared in the Senate, I feel that I am "coming home." The Chinese people can tell you, she declared, that "fundamentally we are fighting for the same cause, that we have identity of ideals."[8]

Indeed, as *Life* observed, she seemed to speak "for Americans as well as Chinese" when she proclaimed that "we" had to have vision in making a "better world" so that "peace should not be punitive in spirit and should not be provincial or nationalistic or even continental in concept, but universal in scope and humanitarian in action." Soong's last major speech in America was on April 4, 1943, before an overflow crowd of more than 30,000 people in the Hollywood Bowl. While squadrons of bombers flew overhead,

Soong spoke about China's terrible suffering during the long conflict with Japan and its contribution to the global fight against war and militarism. She pledged China's commitment to helping construct an America-inspired vision of a future world where "we shall not permit aggression to raise its satanic head and threaten man's greatest heritage: life, liberty, and the pursuit of happiness for all peoples." An estimated 250,000 Americans heard her message in person during her three-month speaking tour.[9]

The exigencies of war transformed the social relationships and identities of Americans. For Chinese Americans, the war provided an opportunity to confirm their membership in the American family, something that racial prejudice and immigration laws had long denied. In 1943, they joined others in successfully lobbying Congress to repeal central features of the Chinese exclusion acts, which had been on the books for sixty years. The cruel discrimination based on race that forbade Chinese from immigrating to the United States and becoming naturalized citizens violated the lofty principles of America's democratic fight against fascism and militarism, and Congress ended the long-standing insult in order to strengthen the wartime alliance. Although Chinese ancestry had long been a stigma in the United States, war shifted it toward a positive good. Chinese Americans could proudly claim both their Chineseness and their Americanness. After the outbreak of war, a fifteen-year-old Chinese American girl in Berkeley, California, proudly declared in an "I Am an American" essay contest, "I am an American-born Chinese" adding that Madame Chiang Kaishek was her "heroine." She wrote that her uncle was in the U.S. army and another worked in a nearby shipyard. Her sisters served in civilian defense. "I belong to a club where I learn better citizenship" and "help my church collect money for the United China war relief." Perfectly attuned to the new climate in the country, the teenager emphasized "that which helps China helps America."[10]

As Chinese Americans were becoming full Americans, white Americans were becoming Chinese, at least in the movies. The tradition of white actors donning "yellow face" makeup and displaying quirky body language to play Chinese characters in films had long been a part of the American film industry. D. W. Griffith was one of the first directors to present such a spectacle. In 1919, after he released *Birth of a Nation,* he directed *Broken Blossoms,* a film about doomed interracial love featuring Lillian Gish as a white woman and Richard Barthelmess as a Chinese, or the Yellow Man, as the character was called. Grotesque portrayals of Chinese by white actors in Charlie Chan and Fu Manchu films entertained American audiences for decades in the interwar years. Marlene Dietrich and the Chinese American actress Anna May Wong starred in Josef von Sternberg's *Shanghai Express* (1932), Frank Capra presented *The Bitter Tea of General Yen* (1933), and Victor Mature led the cast in the dreadful *Shanghai Gesture* (1941). Characters in "yellow face" populated these major and many other minor films. An exception to the demeaning characterizations in these efforts was the film version of *The Good Earth*, based on the Pearl Buck novel set in China. The 1937 film reflects the growing sympathy for the downtrodden Chinese; its characters were intended to be fully human for American audiences and elicit their sympathy. Unlike the earlier crude portrayals that made little pretense of striving for ethnic authenticity, *The Good Earth* tried to do so, as the book had done. Luise Rainer won the Academy Award for best female actress for portraying the steadfast and suffering O-lan.

After Pearl Harbor, Hollywood released a steady stream of films with themes invoking America's China connection. Among these are *Across the Pacific* (1942) with Humphrey Bogart, *China* (1943), *Night Plane from Chungking* (1943), and *God Is My Co-Pilot* (1945). But the film *Dragon Seed* (1944) was the most striking presentation of yellow-face actors who elicited empathy, including Walter Huston and Katherine Hepburn, who played Jade, the central character who champions anti-Japanese resistance among Chinese villagers. American audiences are encouraged to identify with the "Chinese" Hepburn, who is made up with heavy eye and skin cosmetics. She and the other actors all speak in an English that is presumably supposed to sound like Chinese in literal translation. Though unmemorable cinematically, the film strikingly dramatizes the possibility of creating a common national and racial identity. The suffering of war made it plausible for a white American to become an appealing Chinese.

Though Soong Mayling's triumphant tour of America symbolized the high point of Chinese and American public comity, the political and military relationship between the two countries was fraying. American disenchantment with Chiang and his government came not just from liberal journalists such as Edgar Snow, but from tough, unsentimental military men, the most prominent of whom was General "Vinegar" Joe Stilwell, FDR's first military representative to the Chiang government. Stilwell's nickname derived from his well-known blunt manner and acerbic tongue. In China and

Burma, Stilwell had come to conclude that Chiang was incompetent, foolish, and opportunist, preferring to preserve his fighting forces for a future battle against the Communists rather than use them against the immediate Japanese enemy. Chiang had gathered around himself cronies and grafters who siphoned resources meant for the fight against Japan into their own pockets. Stilwell was a first-class professional and a seasoned China hand. He spoke Chinese fluently and had lived and worked in China for many years. His conflict with Chiang became legendary and emblematic of the frustration of the United States with corruption and deception among China's leaders.

In early 1942, only weeks after the United States entered the war in the Pacific, Washington pressed Chiang to accept Stilwell as his chief of staff and give him executive authority over China's national military forces. Washington wanted Stilwell to reorganize the army into a more effective fighting force through improving officer training, force deployment, and coordination of the various military factions. Stilwell was eminently suited for the task: he was a tough West Point graduate who had accumulated extensive field experience in the Philippines, World War I, and Central America. He came from a long line of Yankees, some of whom had fought in the Revolution. He was also the most knowledgeable person about China in the American military.

Stilwell had first visited China in 1911, just after the Republican Revolution, while he was serving in the Philippines. Between the two world wars, Stilwell was stationed in China three times, accumulating ten years of direct experience in the country, including as the military attaché to the U.S. embassy in Beijing. He learned Chinese ways and built friendships with Chinese from various walks of life. From early 1942 to 1944, Stilwell served in the China-Burma Theater, where he made extraordinary efforts to support the warmaking ability of the Chinese national government. But Chiang and the rivalries and disputes within the national government constantly infuriated him. He openly referred to Chiang as "the Peanut," a derisive reference to the leader's shaved head and his mediocre abilities. Moreover, the comfortable life style of the rest of the Nationalist leaders in Chongqing and their detachment from the hard reality of the Chinese people embittered him. Stilwell's contempt for Chiang and the Nationalist government, which became openly known only in the postwar years, highlighted the conundrum Washington encountered in its China policy. The actual, troubled relationship could hardly be more at odds with the grand unity that Soong Mayling promoted during her tour and the public pronouncements FDR issued. Though the United States publicly promoted China as one of the great powers for freedom in the world, many in Roosevelt's administration privately believed that the Chinese government was autocratic, ineffectual, and resistant to American tutelage. Chongqing was far from being a paragon of democracy and nationalist resistance. Instead, the leaders of the national government, and Chiang Kaishek in particular, inspired loathing from individuals, such as Stilwell, who dealt with them face to face.[11]

Stilwell's antipathy toward Chiang was reinforced by his deep and genuine fondness for the common people of China. They were, he wrote in his private diary, "fundamentally great, democratic, misgoverned. No bars of caste or religion [divided them]. Honest, frugal, industrious, cheerful, independent, tolerant, friendly, courteous." He accused the Nationalists of "corruption, neglect, chaos, economy, taxes, words and deeds. Hoarding Black market, trading with enemy." In contrast, the goal of "Communist program" was to "reduce taxes, rents, interest. Raise production, and standard of living. Participate in government. Practice what they preach." And coming from Stilwell, a man who prided himself in his straightforwardness, these words were a high compliment. Stilwell's private solution to the China tangle went so far as to consider the "elimination of Chiang K'ai-shek."[12]

Stilwell, with Roosevelt's backing, demanded full command of the Chinese military, but Chiang refused to submit. In the end, Roosevelt, who had little leverage over Chiang, recalled Stilwell from China and replaced him with Albert C. Wedemeyer, a colorless, unseasoned general but one who was more supportive of Chiang. Wedemeyer served as Chiang's chief of staff without drama or notable success for the rest of the war. Postwar revelations about Stilwell's experiences, however, would forever taint Chiang's reputation among many Americans.

The disenchantment with the Chiang regime corresponded to a growing appreciation in the United States of the Communists and their leaders. Their commitment and will to fight and to rid their country of the enemy was clear to all who came in contact with them. Journalists and government reports told of their self-sacrifice and success against the Japanese. The resistance and determination of the Communists became legendary and contrasted sharply with the behavior and decisions of the seemingly feckless Chiang. While much of the fascination with the Communists grew out of frustration over Chiang's seeming lack of will and competence to defeat the Japanese, the Americans who interacted with the Communist forces frequently came away with powerfully positive impressions of them. This was due, in part, to a reaction against the Nationalists. Accounts of endemic corruption; autocratic, even "fascist" behavior; arrogance; and detachment from the masses of Chinese people among Chiang and his followers became increasingly common in the American press. As the fortunes and reputation of the Nationalists fell, those of the Communists rose. But in many of the accounts of Americans who met Communists and spent time in China, there was something more than a search for a better fighting ally for the United States. These Americans believed that their values and outlook were actually closer to those of the Communists and their people's army than to the Nationalist leaders.

Before the late 1930s, few Americans knew anything about the Chinese Communists. American officials paid them little attention, believing they were of minor consequence. American knowledge of internal Chinese politics was at best superficial. Chinese Communists were assumed to be little different than Soviet-inclined Communists in America or in Europe. The growth in American understanding of the Chinese Communists came slowly.[13]

The first Americans who met any real Chinese Communists, as opposed to hearing about them through the Chinese media and the political grapevine, were themselves leftists, such as Earl Browder, a future leader of the American Communist Party; activist and writer Anna Louise Strong; and Agnes Smedley, a labor organizer and supporter of revolutionary causes. Strong and Smedley repeatedly returned to China over the years, socialized with top leaders of the CPC, and became especially well known for their effusive praise of the Communist movement in China. Not surprisingly, their reports about the Communists were highly sympathetic and portrayed them as dedicated to the welfare of the downtrodden Chinese masses and the liberation of their nation from imperialism and feudalism. Mao and his followers were seen as heroic fighters against the privileges and oppression of a corrupt elite and foreign invaders.

Missourian Edgar Snow, liberal though not as left leaning as the other writers, remains the most influential writer about the Chinese Communists, perhaps in any language. His report on the journey to the Red Capital of Yan'an in 1937 captivated imaginations around the world, including Chinese students, who avidly read his work in translation. In Snow's telling, the Communists were tough, charismatic, dedicated patriots who were determinedly opposed to the hated Japanese. But they were also social rebels who seemed to eschew Marxist dogma in favor of agrarian reform, the people's livelihood, and democratization of the country. So undoctrinaire did the Chinese Communists appear in Snow's telling that the American Communist Party criticized Snow as encouraging anti-Stalinism.

Snow was not the only American who came away from China with respect for, even awe of, the Communists in the late 1930s. One of the most unusual and curious of these was an American marine officer by the name of Evans Fordyce Carlson, the first American military observer who lived with the Communists. He later became famous for his legendary exploits as a commander of marines who fought with great success against Japanese forces at Guadalcanal, Saipan, and elsewhere in the Pacific. He claimed that the effectiveness of Carlson's Raiders, as they were called, came from lessons he gained from his time with the Chinese Communists, especially about the importance of close ties between officers and their men and the use of untraditional field tactics against the enemy. Hollywood immortalized his field exploits in the classic war film *Gung Ho!* After the war, he was promoted to the rank of brigadier general because of his heroic actions.

Carlson was the most unlikely of Americans to develop what can only be called an infatuation with the Communists. He was the son of a minister and a Bible-quoting, flinty New Englander whose family went back to the Puritans. His forebears fought in the American Revolution. He never finished high school but instead joined the army. In the 1920s, after he fought against leftist rebels led by Augusto Sandino in Nicaragua, he was ordered to China as an intelligence officer. He studied the language and became closely familiar with the people and terrain of the country. In 1935, he was appointed to help command FDR's military guard at the presidential retreat in Warm Springs, Georgia, and it was during that duty that he became friends with the president and his staff and family. FDR took a particular liking to Carlson, and when Carlson was sent again to China for intelligence work, FDR asked him to send confidential reports back to him, though they were to be addressed to his secretary and not to the president directly. Side comments FDR made in meetings indicate that he read Carlson's reports. They offer an unusually candid and personal picture of one American's encounter with China at war and especially of the Communist fighters.

As a Marine Corps captain, Carlson arrived in China in late 1937 to gather information for naval intelligence. The U.S. military wanted to know about the strength of the Chinese Communists and the reasons for their reported success against the Japanese. For the next six months, Carlson traveled throughout China's hinterland, often in the company of members of the

Red Army. On foot, on horseback, and in combat, Carlson closely observed the life and operations of the Communists, both the rank and file and the leadership. What he saw and experienced made a profound impression on him. Years later, he said in an interview that what he saw convinced him that the Communist approach to the war against Japan "was the one best calculated to defeat Japan in the long run." Moreover, he said, he found that the Red Army leaders "were different from any I had formerly met in China. They were selfless men who used their power to improve the welfare of those they led. They were incorruptible."[14]

Carlson's surviving reports corroborate his memory. One of these, composed on Christmas Eve 1937, overflowed with excitement. The Communist élan, Carlson wrote, their fighting methods, their motivation, the relations between officers and men were all a breath of fresh air to him. He and many of the other American military personnel detested the empty formalism and incessant intrigue that seemed to characterize the Nationalist elite. The Communists displayed none of that but rather were tough, down-to-earth fighters determined to liberate their country from the invaders. They had deep ties with the peasants in the countryside, who provided them with sustenance and intelligence about the enemy. They appeared to be more "American" in their unassuming manner and values than the country's putative Christian leaders, with their obscurantist and hierarchical Confucian ways.

The legendary leader of the Red Army, Zhu De (Chu Teh), especially impressed Carlson. Zhu De "is a kindly man, simple, direct and honest," he wrote, "a practical man. He is humble and self-effacing. And yet he is forthright in military matters. He has the tenacity of a Grant and the kindliness of a Lee." Carlson later added that Zhu De also had the "humility of Lincoln!" After meeting Mao Zedong at Yan'an, Carlson wrote that Mao was "a dreamer," "a genius" who was not committed to the immediate class struggle but would help China through a period of democracy and development with a mixed economy. He would encourage private enterprise and even foreign investment and would enter into a coalition government with the Nationalists. "The Chinese Communist group (so-called)," wrote Carlson to the president, "is not communistic in the sense that we are accustomed to use the term." Rather, Carlson called them "liberal democrats" or "social democrats" who just wanted "equality of opportunity and honest government." Communism in the "Russian sense" was "wholly at variance with Chinese psychology and Chinese tradition."[15]

Several years later, the leader of the American military observer unit that traveled to Yan'an to meet the Communists came away with impressions very similar to Carlson's. Colonel David D. Barrett was another military "old China hand." He spent nearly all of his twenty-seven years in the U.S. Army in China, including as the military attaché to the U.S. embassy in Beijing. He spoke fluent Chinese and had an abiding affection for the Chinese people. The Chinese, he wrote in his memoir, "are on the whole the smartest, the most attractive, and in some ways the most civilized and on the average the handsomest people in the world." In the summer of 1944, General Stilwell sent Barrett to lead a team of twenty select U.S. military and diplomatic personnel to Yan'an, where they were to establish a formal liaison with the Communists. Among them were two Japanese Americans sent as interpreters to help interrogate the Japanese prisoners the Communists held. Although its official title was the United States Army Observer Group to Yan'an, it became more popularly known as the Dixie Mission. The name may have referred to the fact that they were venturing into rebel territory or because of the number of southerners in the U.S. group.[16]

For almost the next three years, the United States maintained this unique link with the Communists. The reports of the American diplomatic and military personnel in the Dixie Mission provide captivating descriptions of their experiences. However, the importance of the mission goes far beyond the record of colorful personal experience in China. The mission was one of the most important sustained contacts the United States had with the Chinese Communists, including their leaders, and with that contact, Washington received continuous intelligence about the Communists. Important members of the mission, including Barrett himself and diplomatic personnel such as John S. Service and John Paton Davies, who later were attacked during the McCarthy witch-hunt of the 1950s, submitted detailed reports on the Communists that expressed high regard for their egalitarianism, their tactical success against the Japanese, and their high fighting spirit. The Communists were earthy, dedicated, practical fighters. They behaved with none of the indirection and ceremony that infuriated no-nonsense Americans. Chongqing had ubiquitous secret police, constant rumors of political intrigue, and a depressing atmosphere of gloom and graft. The national leaders lived apart from the people in posh elegance. In contrast, Yan'an's atmosphere was positive and open. The Communists seemed to have excellent relations with the common people. The Chinese Communists were certainly the "good guys" at the time, though Barrett later admitted that he may have been naïve. The Americans ate, drank, and danced with the Communists; played baseball with them; and went behind enemy lines with them. The reports of journalists who also made their way to Yan'an during these months often went even further than the military and diplomatic dispatches. Barrett described the journalists as going "ga-ga" over what they thought they saw in Yan'an. "A Chinese Wonderland City" was the headline of the article New York Times war correspondent Brooks Atkinson wrote after visiting Yan'an in the fall of 1944. The Communist system there, he said, was an "agrarian or peasant democracy" that was largely self-sufficient; it was not a burden on the local peasantry. Even Mao grew his own vegetables.[17]

Many of these Americans concluded that the Chinese Communists were unlike other Communists who promoted class warfare, advocated for a proletarian state, and spoke in Leninist, formulaic jargon. Some of these observers were inclined to be sympathetic to the Communists because of their own left-leaning views, but others who were politically conservative, such as Patrick J. Hurley, who had been Herbert Hoover's secretary of war, a brigadier general, and then U.S. ambassador to China in 1944–45, also advanced the idea that Mao and his comrades were a legitimate political force in China and should be incorporated into the national government. Perhaps more than any other leading American official during World War II, Hurley helped popularize the idea that the Chinese Communists were not "genuine" Communists.

After conversations with top officials in Moscow in 1944, including Foreign Minister Vyacheslav Molotov, Hurley concluded that the Russians did not trust the Chinese Communists because they did not believe the Chinese were faithful to communist doctrine. Stalin himself described Mao and his comrades as just "margarine Communists," meaning they were not the real thing. In China, Hurley shuttled back and forth between Chiang in Chongqing and Mao in Yan'an to broker a deal that would end the internecine fighting and bring about a coalition government for national resistance against Japan. He got as far as having Mao agree to bring the Communists into the national government while recognizing Chiang as China's top leader. The Communists endorsed the idea of a coalition government based on the "principles of Sun Yat-sen" that would be "a government of the people, for the people, and by the people." The national government would uphold all basic democratic rights and liberties for the people as expressed in the U.S. Constitution and Declaration of Independence. During his mission, Hurley repeatedly reported to FDR that "the Communists are not in fact

Communists" and that the Soviets did not "recognize the Chinese Communist Party as Communists at all." Hurley repeatedly used the phrase "so-called Communists."[18]

In retrospect, there are a variety of possible explanations for these positive assessments of the Communists. They might have been due to the contrast the Communists presented to Nationalist corruption, Chinese Communist duplicity, American ignorance and naïveté, or even deliberate misinformation on the part of leftist-inclined American officials who hoped to sabotage American support for Chiang Kaishek. The latter sensational accusation formed the core of the "Who lost China?" crusade in America that erupted as the Communists marched toward victory at the end of the 1940s. The view that American officials in China submitted false reports and deliberately worked to undermine Chiang's government is the least persuasive explanation. The evidence for this accusation, which destroyed the careers of leading China specialists, was never sustained. The witch hunt was a product of the advent of Cold War anti-communism. There is more to support the other explanations: the Communists did much to orchestrate the visits of foreigners to areas under their control and Americans, even veteran political observers, did not fully grasp the peculiarities (or, as the Chinese Communists would say, the originality) of the Chinese Communist approach. The attention to the peasantry and land reform, the idea of a democratic transitional stage in the Revolution, the appeal to national unity in the anti-Japanese effort that won a wide range of popular support, the barely concealed antipathy to the Soviets—all appeared to represent a break with doctrinaire Stalinism. Americans who thought the Chinese Communists were some sort of hybrid political animal were in fact accurate. The Chinese Communists never fit stereotypical molds and from Mao to Deng, they regularly eluded easy characterization or prediction.

Yan'an and Chongqing were very different places, and the fact that Americans of all political persuasions favorably compared the social atmosphere and morale in the Communist areas with those in the Nationalist cannot be easily dismissed as fabrication or foolishness. By the 1940s, the Communists had indeed won the sympathies of many Chinese from a wide variety of backgrounds with their devotion to the anti-Japanese cause, their appeal to the masses of the Chinese people, and their self-sacrificing zeal. The Americans saw the respect the soldiers and the citizenry had for the Communists. They had grown from a small beleaguered band at the start of the war against Japan into a potent political force that controlled "liberated areas" of almost 90 million people, an army of 1 million soldiers, and a militia of 2 million more. The Communists also seemed to become personally fond of the Americans they met during the Yan'an days and appreciated American directness and plain living. Mao and his comrades even enjoyed watching Laurel and Hardy movies with the Americans, who had brought the films to Yan'an for entertainment. American journalists, visitors, and members of the Dixie Mission made such a positive impression on Mao and other Communist leaders that they apparently sincerely believed that they would be able to continue to cooperate with the United States after the defeat of Japan.[19]

In contrast to the growing positive picture of the Communists was the increasingly negative portrayal of the national government in Chongqing. Stilwell's antipathy to Chiang was not widely known, but other Americans began to conclude that Chiang and his government were inept and corrupt. As early as mid-1943, *Time* magazine's top reporter in China, Theodore White, began to send back highly critical reports about the situation in the regions the Nationalists controlled. U.S. ambassadors to China Nelson Johnson and then Clarence Gauss, who had both lived for decades in China, were themselves increasingly critical of Chiang, as were most of the other American diplomatic staff throughout China.

Despite their deep misgivings about Chiang, Roosevelt and then Truman nevertheless tried to find a way to strengthen the position of Chiang's government and forestall civil war in China in the midst of the fight against Japan. The United States continued to pour generous amounts of military aid to the Nationalists and then helped them occupy territory formerly held by the defeated Japanese. American support for Chiang was understandable. He and other Nationalist leaders were familiar to Americans. They had attended American universities and military academies. Many were Christian and had forged warm personal friendships with American social, religious, cultural, and political leaders. They were not Communists. And, as Chiang made sure, there were no viable alternatives to his regime and himself.

One top emissary after another went to China to seek a way to end the internecine fighting, which undermined the effort to forge a stable and reliable Asian ally for the United States. The stature of these representatives— Vice-President Henry Wallace in 1944, General Patrick Hurley late in 1944, and George C. Marshall, the esteemed military leader of World War II, from late 1945 to early 1947— indicate the seriousness with which Washington took the situation in China. When Japan finally surrendered in August 1945, many Americans hoped that China, in close alliance with the United States, would assume the leadership role in Asia. Along with the United States, Britain, France, and the Soviet Union, China became one of the permanent members of the new United Nations founded in 1945.

Marshall, who had served in China for three years in the late 1920s, when he headed the U.S. Army's Fifteenth Infantry Regiment, which was stationed in Tianjin, attempted to use the good offices of the United States to broker a coalition government in China during his mission to postwar China. For brief moments, the Nationalists and Communists stopped fighting and Marshall succeeded in obtaining support from both sides for his efforts. The two parties initially saw Marshall as an impartial negotiator and welcomed his involvement in their rivalry, but repeated failures to reach lasting agreements led to frustration and accusations against Marshall from all. Chiang accused Marshall of favoring the Communists, and the Communists accused Marshall of duplicity and covertly aiding the Nationalists. The reality was that the enmity, suspicion, and ambition of both sides that had accumulated over twenty-five years were insurmountable. In mid-1946, total civil war broke out and violence engulfed the country. In early 1947, Marshall called it quits and returned to the United States, where he forged the most celebrated part of his career as secretary of state and architect of the reconstruction plan for Western Europe that now carries his name. That success has overshadowed his failure to effect reconciliation between Communist and Nationalist forces in China.[20]

In the massive Chinese civil war, Chiang and the Nationalists had significant numerical advantages in terms of troops, weapons, and logistical superiority and achieved initial successes on the battlefield against the Communist armies. The Nationalist army numbered more than 3 million men and the Communists' 1 million. Within two years, however, the fortunes and numbers of the two sides reversed. By the end of 1948, the Nationalists faced clear defeat. "Historians a hundred years hence will agree that the death knell of Western democratic civilization was sounded in China in the autumn of 1948," pronounced the well-known American church leader Henry P. Van Dusen, president of Union Theological Seminary, as the Communists advanced to victory. The defeat of the Nationalists forced Chiang and his remnant forces to retreat from the mainland to Taiwan, an island redoubt, while the Communists triumphantly celebrated their victory. Mao Zedong's declaration of the founding of the People's Republic of

China on October 1, 1949, formally marked the end of Nationalist rule. The United States, which had supported Chiang for so long, viewed this turn of events as a defeat of disastrous proportions to its foreign policy.[21]

The "China question" ignited a storm of controversy in the United States that deeply divided Americans. The specific issues were weighty: there were questions about what had been the actual quality, capability, and strength of Chiang's government; about the nature and ambitions of the victorious Chinese Communists; about the relationship of the Soviet Union to the new government in China; and about the extent to which the United States could still try to determine the future of China. There were no easy answers. There was only the enormity of China, the complexity of its problems and politics, and the difficulty Americans had with understanding a country so very different from their own. In addition, a unique emotionality complicated the American response to postwar developments in China. Personal sentimentality, fears, and long-standing attachments, all inheritances from the past, played important roles in explaining the American response to the Chinese revolution.[22]

An individual whose personal and professional lives sharply mirrored the quixotic relationship between America and China was John Leighton Stuart, one of the longest-serving missionaries in China, the founding president of Yanjing University (whose campus would later be known as Peking University), and the last American ambassador to serve on the mainland before the 1949 Revolution. Stuart was born in China, lived most of his life there, and developed a heartfelt attachment to the Chinese people. During his many years in the country, he developed associations with virtually the entire Chinese political and intellectual elite. In 1945, *Time* honored him as "perhaps the most respected American in China," but he also later suffered the ignominy of being the only American Mao Zedong ever singled out to ridicule personally and publicly in the title of one of his most famous essays, "Farewell, Leighton Stuart!" To this day, in China, millions of Chinese know nothing about Stuart other than what they read from Mao: Stuart was simply part of the imperialist detritus washed away by the Revolution. Mao's characterization was done for political purposes in 1949, but now, with the advance of U.S.-China relations, Stuart's reputation is slowly being restored to the respected status of decades ago.[23]

Stuart was born in 1876 in Hangzhou, one of China's most scenic and historic cities. Because of its central location and economic importance, Hangzhou became a site of sustained efforts of foreign missionaries. Stuart's ancestors were ministers and missionaries as far back as the early American republic. John Linton Stuart, Leighton's own missionary father, began his lifelong stay in Hangzhou in 1868, and his mother founded the Hangzhou School for Girls. The two served most of their lives in China, had their family there, and died in Hangzhou, where they are still buried.

Stuart was the eldest of four sons, all born in China. Though his parents, who were originally from the American south, sent him back to the United States for education, he was said to have never felt completely American and to be more Chinese in temperament. In Alabama, where the Stuart boys attended school, their look and manner were supposedly so "Chinese," that even decades later Leighton recalled people making tactless remarks like, 'Oh, they do look like Chinese, don't they?'" Their cousins were even ashamed to be seen with them. After studying at Hampden-Sidney College and Union Theological Seminary in Richmond, Virginia, Leighton Stuart returned to China in 1904 with a bride. He worked there for most of the rest of his life, in total fifty years.[24]

Stuart first taught at missionary schools in the Hangzhou area and then at the Nanjing Theological Seminary. Liberal in theology, Stuart openly expressed his respect for Chinese tradition and culture, angering conservative missionaries who emphasized the superiority of the West and the backwardness of the Chinese and all their heathen beliefs. Stuart shared his colleagues' dedication to mission, uplift, and the providential responsibility of Americans to bring Jesus to China, but he also harbored a deep fondness for the Chinese people and their striving for progress and modernity. He supported the 1911 Revolution—he is said to have been the only non-Chinese present at the founding ceremony of the Republic of China. He condemned Japanese encroachment on China and endorsed the ideas of national self-determination propagated by his friend and confidant, Woodrow Wilson.

In 1919, Stuart was offered the presidency of Yanjing University, a new school founded through the merger of several American Christian colleges in China. Over the next thirty years, he built Yanjing into one of the finest institutions of higher learning in the country by raising its academic standards, expanding the student body and faculty, building a substantial endowment, and linking it to important American universities, including Harvard, Princeton, Wellesley, and the University of Missouri. He was an indefatigable fund-raiser and with the help of Rev. Henry W. Luce, fellow missionary to China and father of the famed publishing magnate, Stuart built a beautiful campus in the northwest section of Beijing. After 1949, Peking University, an illustrious Chinese university that had been located near the Imperial Palace in the inner city, moved to the Yanjing campus and incorporated Stuart's institution. During his long tenure at Yanjing, Stuart drew close to a wide range of Chinese political and intellectual leaders, from Chiang Kaishek to Zhou Enlai, from the traditional Confucianist Chen Lifu to cultural liberal Hu Shi. Former students of his college went on to assume high positions in both the Nationalist and Communist Parties.[25]

The challenges Stuart faced in China through the years reflected the United States' general dilemma with China. He possessed a sincere affection for the Chinese people, but Chinese politics continually challenged him. He preferred Chinese reformers and liberals but played to the realities of power politics and dealt with brutal warlords and autocrats. In the early 1930s, he openly condemned the rise of communism in China, seeing it as a threat to the American effort to make China a Christian country, and favored the rise of the Christian Chiang Kaishek and the Nationalists. He initially praised their efforts to unify China and developed close relations with the powerful Soong family. But by the late 1930s, Stuart, like other Americans, found increasing fault with the Nationalists. He criticized the rampant nepotism and corruption he saw in their ranks and expressed a grudging respect for the Communists, whom he also believed were not genuine "Bolsheviks." They were a movement based on "agrarian discontent," he said, and he thought they might even help the development of democracy in China. Never, however, did he consider the atheistic Communists to be a viable replacement for the Christian Nationalists, as unpalatable as they were.

Stuart forcefully advocated for American support for China's resistance against Japan after it invaded in 1937, and he refused to retreat from the Yanjing campus in Beijing for the safety of unoccupied China or the United States. He remained at his post and proudly flew the American flag at the university. On the morning of the attack on Pearl Harbor, the Japanese seized Stuart, who evidently ranked high on their list of Americans to control, and held him prisoner for almost four years. Several times he thought he would be lined up and shot, but his treatment was relatively benign. One of his fellow prisoners was Henry S. Houghton, the medical doctor who led the famous Rockefeller-founded Peking Union Medical College, who apparently was assigned to keep Stuart in good physical condition so that he might be used as a bargaining chip in future negotiations with the Chinese government. The end of his incarceration came with the defeat of Japan and the end of the "thirty years' nightmare" of Japanese subjugation of China. Stuart returned to his life in Beijing.[26]

During his mission to China, in early July 1946, George C. Marshall personally asked Stuart to become the U.S. ambassador. Stuart had just turned 70 and wanted to retire, but Marshall insisted and Stuart agreed. When Marshall announced Stuart's appointment, he praised him as "the most highly respected foreigner" in the country and one who had the trust and admiration of both Nationalists and Communists. When he arrived in Nanjing, the seat of the national government, to assume his post, Stuart received warm wishes and gifts from the leaders of both parties. However, by the end of the month, the two sides had resumed their civil war. Stuart personally witnessed the collapse and then the complete defeat of the Nationalist government.

Like Stuart, Washington clearly favored the Nationalists over the Communists, and the United States continued to provide hundreds of millions of dollars of military aid to Chiang to support his struggle against the Communists. From the end of World War II, Washington provided $2.5 billion of aid to the Nationalists, most of it military. As late as April 1948, Truman signed a bill that provided $400 million in aid for the Nationalists, but it was not enough to save the Nationalists. They steadily lost ground to Mao's Red Army, and then in 1948 Chiang's armies suffered horrendous defeats. Hundreds of thousands of troops defected to the Communists. By the end of the year, the Communists were poised to cross from the north over the mighty Yangzi River, which roughly divided China in half. Despite political pressure from Chiang's supporters in the United States to provide even greater amounts of aid to the Nationalists, the Truman administration began quietly to reassess its China policy. Truman had never been fond of Chiang and his government. Alarmed by the mounting tensions with the Soviet Union in Europe, the president began to believe that the Nationalists were a lost cause, no matter how much material assistance the United States provided, and a diversion from the confrontation with the Soviet Union in Europe. The Truman administration had no good policy options in China, and it wanted to avoid being drawn into an endless civil war it clearly could not control. When Soong Mayling came to the United States for a yearlong visit in 1948, she was coolly received by Truman and she failed to gain the military aid her government wanted.

In the spring of 1949, Ambassador Stuart still hoped to find a way to prevent a complete rupture with the Communists, despite his support for the

Nationalists. As early as March 1949, Stuart requested Secretary of State Dean Acheson's permission that he try to meet Communist leaders to seek "a better mutual understanding." Stuart wanted Washington's authorization that arranging such meetings be left to his own "discretion." As the Nationalist government prepared to abandon Nanjing to the Communists, Stuart wondered whether he should flee with the National Government, as other foreign emissaries were doing, or remain in place. In his private diary, Stuart expressed his wish to stay in Nanjing and not go with the Nationalists to Guangzhou in the south. The order from his superiors in Washington that he stay, at least for the time being, sustained his hope that some sort of communication with the Communists could develop. Then, on the evening of April 24, the Communists entered Nanjing. Early the next morning, several Red Army soldiers entered his bedroom and awakened him from his sleep. Communist authorities later explained that the soldiers were unsupervised country rustics who had been out exploring the city's sights and knew nothing about diplomatic protocol. Though Stuart saw an increase in anti-American propaganda, few restrictions were placed on his activities and he went about his business much as before. Communist leaders back in Beijing, where the new capital would be located, noted with interest that U.S. Ambassador Stuart remained in Nanjing.[27]

In early May, Huang Hua, a close associate of Zhou Enlai and head of the Communist office of relations with foreign governments in Nanjing, approached Philip Fugh, Stuart's Chinese personal secretary, to initiate a series of conversations. Huang Hua had been a student of Stuart at Yanjing University, where he had been student body president. He had also been a liaison with the Dixie Mission in Yan'an. Stuart, as an "ordinary citizen" and not a government official, met with Huang, and the two discussed the sensitive issue of the possible U.S. recognition of the new Communist government when it was established. Over the next several weeks, Stuart continued to wonder about the possibility of finding a way to maintain contact with the Communists. On June 26, Huang Hua unexpectedly extended a personal invitation from Mao and Zhou Enlai to Stuart to visit Beijing as a "private individual," ostensibly to visit his Yanjing University and celebrate his birthday with friends. Mao was said to describe Stuart "as an old friend of many [in the] CCP" and his party as having nothing to hide from the Americans. Two days later, the invitation was again extended: Stuart recorded in his diary that his impression was that Mao and Zhou would "heartily welcome me."[28]

The rancor of the Communist media's public attacks on the United States for its imperialism and its backing of the Nationalists mounted, but privately the top party leaders apparently were curious to see if there might be a way to develop direct contact with Washington, if for no other reason than to see if a wedge could be driven between Chiang and Washington. In the United States, though, supporters of the Nationalists were attacking Truman for not doing enough for Chiang. Communism had to be fought globally, and in the eyes of some conservatives, the mounting Cold War would be won or lost in Asia, not Europe. They were already highly critical of Truman's distancing from the Nationalists. When Truman and Secretary of State Dean Acheson finally answered Stuart, their response was sharply and unequivocally negative. They ordered Stuart not to go to Beijing under any circumstances. Truman could not be seen as authorizing such an affront to the Nationalist government, which the United States continued to recognize officially.

On August 2, 1949, Stuart and other leading members of the U.S. embassy flew out of the country. It would be thirty years before Washington posted another ambassador in the China mainland. By that time, in 1979, Stuart's former student, Huang Hua, was China's foreign minister.[29]

As Stuart was leaving China, Washington released the "China White Paper," an official study of U.S. relations with China. As a disclosure of policy and intelligence reporting, it was unprecedented in American diplomatic history. The more than 1,000-page narrative and supporting documents, many of them previously highly classified, recounted the long and, in the view of the state department authors, positive and constructive history of American policy toward China. However, the main purpose of the study was political rather than academic. The formal letter of transmittal of the report from Secretary of State Dean Acheson to President Truman maintained that the United States had been a true and generous friend to the Chinese people, including in its support for the Nationalist government, which had received billions of dollars in U.S. aid. The United States had done all it could to help the Nationalists remain in power, but events in China were now beyond the control of Washington. The Nationalist government would have to fend for itself, the paper maintained, and, though the turn of events was calamitous, China appeared to be lost to communism. America would have to wait for a future return of China's traditional "democratic individualism" to resume the historical friendship between the two countries. The Truman administration had hoped that the position paper would quiet the vociferous China lobby. However, it only enraged them further; they attacked the White Paper as an apology for surrender and appeasement. For the following decades, conservatives and others connected to the China lobby relentlessly attacked liberals and Democrats for being responsible for the "loss of China" and for being soft on communism generally. Their campaign made China policy into a partisan domestic issue of the most sensitive kind.

At the same time, Mao responded to the release of the White Paper with a vituperative attack under his name against the Truman administration. Turning Acheson's words and logic against the United States, Mao penned five fiery, sarcastic editorials to explain why the Chinese revolution had been inevitable and was a great advance for the Chinese people over domestic reaction and foreign imperialism. Mao said he welcomed the publication of the White Paper because it unintentionally revealed that the United States, in documenting the extent of its support for the now-discredited Chiang, was no sincere friend of the Chinese people. The White Paper was an admission of full guilt. The sharpest of Mao's essays was devoted to attacking John Leighton Stuart by name. Mao's derisive editorial entitled "Farewell, Leighton Stuart!" ("*Biele Situ Leideng*") hailed the emissary's withdrawal from China and disabused any in China who still thought of him and the United States as true friends. Mao labeled Stuart a "loyal agent of U.S. cultural imperialism in China" and saw his return to the United States as "a symbol of the complete defeat of the U.S. policy of aggression."[30]

After returning to the United States in late 1949, Stuart gave talks to select groups of old China hands about witnessing the Revolution and the developing situation in China. In line with the growing anti-Communist militancy in the country, Stuart unrelentingly condemned the Communists and said nothing about his personal contact and exploratory conversations with Huang Hua just months before. According to Stuart, the Communists were turning China into "a police state." "They are fanatical in their leadership," he told an elite group in New York. All was not lost, however, as he hoped Chinese tradition might still moderate Marxist-Leninist ideology and American students might be allowed in China. American recognition of the new regime, he noted, would be difficult but not completely out of the question. As it turned out, developments far beyond Washington's control would preclude such possibilities for decades.[31]

Stuart died in the United States in 1962, and his last wish that his remains be buried in China, where his wife and parents rested, remained unfilled because of the total rupture in U.S.-China relations. Stuart's wish was in accord with Chinese tradition, which held that one's eternal resting place should be with one's ancestors in Chinese soil. For almost fifty years, Stuart's ashes waited in limbo in America, and it was not until 2008 that authorities in China finally allowed Stuart to return to his home city of Hangzhou. His remains were reinterred as the "Star Spangled Banner" and "Amazing Grace" played in a solemn ceremony attended by city officials and surviving Yanjing University alumni.

City officials have also reopened Stuart's former spacious residence as a public museum. Located in the old downtown of the city, the Stuart Museum has been nicely restored to show how Stuart once lived his life as a devoted educational missionary. Plentiful storyboards, photographs, and memorabilia tell the long story of his sincere devotion to the Chinese and his intimate connections to their modern political and cultural history. A beautiful porcelain vase that Zhou Enlai gave Stuart in 1946 sits in a prominent glass case; Stuart took the treasure with him when he left the country. It and many of his other personal items and Chinese art were also returned from America for display. Most interestingly, the bilingual storyboards now respectfully describe a man whose friendship with the Chinese people transcended government politics. Gone is Mao's vituperation. The vicissitudes of Stuart's life and the location of his final resting place are dramatically emblematic of the intimate connection many Americans developed with China. In effect, Stuart became one with the country.

The constant element in Stuart's views, like that of other leading Americans, was an abiding belief in the deep importance of China to America and that China could be remade in America's image. James C. Thomson Jr., a China specialist who was born in China to missionary parents, once accurately described Stuart as forming part of a "constituency" of "traders, bankers, churchmen, military men, journalists and academics" who "shared a paramount interest in the promise of China and a belief in an activist American role in keeping open that promise." As late as the start of the Korean War in June 1950, 2,000 American missionaries continued to live and work in China. They soon had to follow Stuart and leave the country. Stuart wrote in his 1952 memoir that the future of the Pacific depended on the existence of a strong, united, and independent China. China's "national freedom" and "her fine national culture," he wrote, were "vitally related to the peace of the Pacific and the progressive welfare of all mankind." He had devoted his life to those ends, as had thousands of other Americans.[32]

On October 1, 1949, from atop Tian'anmen Gate in Beijing, Mao Zedong proclaimed the founding of the People's Republic of China. Some in America rejoiced, believing that the Communist victory signaled the victory of the Chinese people over imperialism and domestic reactionaries, as Mao put it. Several days after Mao's declaration, hundreds celebrated in San Francisco's Chinatown. For many other Americans, the victory of the Communists in the Chinese civil war was an unmitigated disaster. The apparent fall of the most populous country in the world into the camp of America's mortal enemy in the Cold War was a defeat of epic proportions: not only was it the end of more than 100 years of an especially close and special bond between America and China, but the triumph of the Chinese Communist Party imperiled the very security of the United States.

In contrast to the Truman administration's focus on the Cold War in Europe, many, especially powerful conservatives, lobbied for heightened attention to the Asia front. They saw calamity in the deteriorating fortunes of the Nationalists and called for invigorated efforts to stop communism in Asia. William C. Bullitt Jr., the first U.S. ambassador to the Soviet Union, who had become a militant anti-Communist, was one of the first to publicly sound the alarm when he published an article in *Life* magazine at the end of 1947. "The cause is a common cause," he wrote, emphasizing the importance of the alliance with the struggling Nationalists. "If China falls into the hands of Stalin, all Asia, including Japan, sooner or later will fall into his hands. The manpower and resources of Asia will be mobilized against us. The independence of the U.S. will not live a generation longer than the independence of China." Minnesota member of Congress Walter Judd, a former medical missionary to China and one of the stalwart backers of Nationalist China in Washington, declared in Congress in August 1949 that the Communist victory was a "mortal peril to all Asia" and that the Communist conquest of Asia would constitute "a mortal peril to Europe and to the United States."[33]

Bullitt and others who became known as the "Asia-Firsters" in the Cold War continued their loud chorus after Mao proclaimed victory. In the early 1950s, Bullitt even called for an American invasion of China. Senator Robert A. Taft of Ohio, a contender for the presidency and a conservative leader of the Republican Party, sounded the same theme: "The Far East," he declared, "is ultimately even more important to our future peace than is Europe."[34]

With the scales seemingly tipped in favor of Moscow, powerful and influential Americans condemned the policies of Roosevelt and Truman that they felt had led to the debacle. In their view, American actions that were a product of ignorance or possibly even of treason—there were Communists in the State Department, they claimed—had led to the "loss of China." A "China lobby," a loose coalition that included newspaper publishers Henry Luce (*Time* and *Life*), William Randolph Hearst (Hearst empire), Roy Howard (Scripps-Howard), William Loeb (*New Hampshire Morning Union*), and Robert R. McCormick (*Chicago Tribune*); military and political figures such as former president Herbert Hoover, Douglas MacArthur, Claire Chennault, Patrick Hurley, Albert Wedemeyer, and Harold Stassen; and industrialists such as William Reynolds and others condemned the Truman administration and called for an aggressive campaign to support free China under the Nationalists. In Congress, this cause was championed by a "China First" bloc that was led by Senators William Knowland of California, H. Alexander Smith of New Jersey, and Pat McCarran of Nevada and Representatives Walter Judd of Minnesota and John Vorys of Ohio. The fate of America, in their view, was inextricably linked to the reversal of the Communist victory in China.

The inspiration of the stalwart supporters of the Nationalists in the country was part political partisanship and part genuine conviction. It was under the watch of Democrats that the rise of global, monolithic communism appeared to rise to challenge the international order established by the United States in the aftermath of World War II. Democrats seemed vulnerable to the charge that they had underestimated, or even misunderstood, the menacing aspects of communism, an evil that some on the right had long believed was even worse than fascism. Others deeply differed from the Atlantic orientation of many among the eastern seaboard elite that dominated national politics. Asia, not "old Europe," was where the fight against communism would be won or lost. In geopolitical terms, the future of America lay in the contest for Asia, including the possible reversal of the Communist victory in China. None in the China lobby were resigned to the defeat of the Nationalists.

Clare Boothe Luce was an articulate and glamorous female member of this powerful group. She was one of the most influential and accomplished women in America. She had been a Park Avenue socialite, a successful playwright, and a New York editor, and in 1935 she had married Henry Luce. Together the two played a prominent role in shaping the image of China in the American mind. China, she once declared, was "the greatest country in the world in terms of what counts most—individual human souls." In 1942, Luce was elected to the House of Representatives from Connecticut. She served two terms. In 1948, she delivered the keynote address to the Republican National Convention, and in 1953 President Eisenhower appointed her U.S. ambassador to Italy.[35]

In June 1949, as the Chinese Nationalists faced defeat, she delivered a long address at a New York banquet for Rev. Paul Yu-Pin, Catholic archbishop of Nanjing, who was visiting the United States. Her stern remarks criticizing the Roosevelt/Truman policy toward China are an indication of the passion conservatives felt about the situation in China and the prospect of a Communist China. Although Luce did not accuse leading American officials of national betrayal, as some other conservatives did, she characterized U.S. policy as incomprehensibly wrong, and in essence, helpful to Soviet ambitions to control the world. A "free China, friendly to the U.S.A., opposed to Communism" was, in her view, "essential" to American interests in Asia. U.S. policy, however, had failed utterly to seek that end. Instead, U.S. policy had "led step by step towards the collapse of a free China and the erection of a vast Soviet Empire in the Pacific." She accused some in Washington of harboring "intellectual puppy-love raptures for Communism" that led to the grievous wartime agreements made at Teheran and Yalta that she believed favored the Communists. Luce, who had recently converted to Catholicism, identified "Original Sin" as responsible for the failure of American intellectuals and others to appreciate the full evils of communism. She remained adamantly hostile toward Beijing for the rest of her life, though ironically it was she who first introduced Henry Kissinger to Richard Nixon in 1967. The two would lead the way to the resumption of relations between China and the United States.[36]

Others believed the Communists had triumphed on the mainland due to a conspiracy. They wanted to know "Who lost China?," the battle cry based on the prideful assumption that China had somehow previously belonged to America. How could China, with its long history of friendship with the United States; the extensive religious, economic, and social ties between Americans and Chinese; and the billions of dollars of assistance given to the Chiang government by the United States have fallen to the Communists, these critics asked? Dean Acheson's China White Paper, which maintained that the incompetence and venality of the Chiang government explained the setback in American policy and loss of China to communism, failed to quiet the rage. Critics believed that only betrayal could explain the defeat and accused the Roosevelt and Truman administrations of being riddled with Communists who had undermined Chiang and U.S. policy in China. The crusade to ferret out the responsible elements led to government investigations, and although no subversion was ever proven, dedicated and professional junior officers and advisors in the State Department were dismissed. The honest reports they had submitted from the field in China telling of the debilitated state of Nationalist China were taken as evidence of disloyalty, if not criminality. Truth was sacrificed with the scapegoats. In early 1950, Senator Joseph McCarthy expanded the crusade and made sweeping accusations about rampant infiltration of Communists in the federal government and American life more generally. The fear of being seen as soft on communism in China and in Asia generally straitjacketed honest assessments of events in Asia for decades to come.

Then in June 1950, less than nine months after the founding of the People's Republic of China and as Chinese Communist and Nationalist forces were still fighting in outlying regions of the China mainland, North Korean Communists invaded the south, setting off the Korean War. International agreements during and after the World War had divided the country, which had been a Japanese colony for forty years, to facilitate the establishment of a provisional Korean government. The division along the 38th parallel was to be temporary, but the Communists in the north and the anti-Communists in the south quickly established formidable and mutually hostile regimes that contended for legitimacy and territorial control. The military forces of the two sides sparred continuously along the new border for two years before the 1950 attack and full war. The North Korean offensive almost succeeded in driving the South Korean and U.S. occupying forces off the peninsula, but after Douglas MacArthur's daring amphibious landing at Inchon in September, the United States reversed the advance of the North Koreans, who soon had to retreat back across the 38th parallel. Then, in a fateful decision, Washington decided to order its forces to join the South Koreans in crossing north of the 38th parallel to eliminate the North Korean regime. They quickly advanced through the country and then further northward toward the Yalu River, the boundary with China. Commanding U.S. general Douglas MacArthur, who had long thought about invading Manchuria and was convinced that the Chinese would never be so foolhardy as to enter the war and take on the United States, ordered his forces to continue to go toward the border. China's top leaders wanted no war with the United States, and they agonized over their response to Mac-Arthur's provocative advance. After much difficult deliberation, they reluctantly concluded that the survival of the infant People's Republic of China required them to drive the U.S. forces away from the border and back into South Korea. Hundreds of thousands of Chinese troops were sent into battle, and after suffering horrible losses, they pushed the Americans out of the north and back into the south. The brutal, ugly conflict then stalemated at the 38th parallel, the original demarcation of the two Koreas. The war sputtered on until June 1953, when a cease-fire was finally reached.[37]

In a famous speech to the pro-Nationalist China Institute in New York City in May 1951, just a few months after Chinese and American forces first engaged one another, Assistant Secretary of State Dean Rusk, who would become one of the architects of America's disastrous intervention in Vietnam in the 1960s, condemned Communist China for fighting in Korea for a foreign master, the Soviet Union. China had become a huge "Slavic Manchukuo," he said, invoking the Japanese puppet regime that had been established in Manchuria. The Communist government in Beijing did not represent the true interests of the Chinese people; "it is not Chinese," Rusk declared. His was a gratuitous insult to the proudly nationalistic Communists, a reaffirmation to the beleaguered Nationalists now protected by the United States on Taiwan, and copy for the domestic China lobby in America. It was a distortion of Chinese communism, which was in no way subservient to Moscow, and it would haunt the United States and hobble policy for decades. Rusk had created a phantom China that existed only in his nightmare. If anything, it was Chiang's exile government on the small island of Taiwan that resembled a "proxy" regime, but for U.S. rather than Soviet interests. Whether American leaders approved or not, the People's Republic of China was the firmly established government of 500 million people and was its own master.[38]

By the time of the armistice in mid-1953 that suspended the war in Korea, 40,000 Americans and more than 200,000 (and perhaps as many as 400,000, including Mao's own son) Chinese had died, largely fighting each other. One to two million Koreans, mainly civilians, had been killed in the brutal war. China and America were now sworn enemies, with blood debts against each other. Eternal hostility appeared to be their fate.

For Beijing, the war's end in a standoff with the imperialist United States was celebrated as a victory and confirmation of the strength and virtue of the new People's Republic. The rapacious United States had been successfully resisted, just as had Japan and the domestic reactionaries. For Washington and the American people, the distant and protracted conflict had been exhausting and unpopular. It also reinforced assumptions that communism was a global, monolithic philosophy with evil intentions. The ghastly losses the Asian Communists had suffered was taken as evidence of the length they would go to achieve their ambitions and their callous disregard for human life. As President Eisenhower wrote Winston Churchill after the end of the war, the United States could not afford to go "slinking along in the shadows, hoping that the beast will finally be satiated and cease his predatory tactics before he finally devours us." Survival depended on defeating communism. U.S. policy hardened against Beijing. Washington engaged in a barely secret war against the Chinese Communists by actively supporting hostile forces along China's borders and within the country itself; American military, economic, and ideological support for Chiang's rival regime escalated; and the U.S. banned any level of intercourse with the mainland, commercial, cultural, or social. The Communist regime was deemed illegitimate. The passports of American citizens contained the explicit directive that the document was invalid in those portions of China controlled by the Communists. China was forbidden to Americans.

6

Transformations

China has a limitless capacity to fascinate.

Richard Nixon, 1989

For thirty years following its founding, the People's Republic of China (PRC) and the United States constructed one of the strangest (and most strained) relationships in modern history. Regular governmental relations did not exist from 1949 to 1979. Aside from a few rare exceptions, there were no tourists or travelers, no journalists, and no business or trade between the two countries. No books, newspapers, or movies were sent legally from one country to the other. There were no direct mail, telegraph, or telephone communications. The leaders and peoples of the two countries were informed about the other largely through third parties and specialists who studied from afar but had no firsthand contact. It was a great interregnum, years of animus and distance that interrupted what had been a long and close engagement. The two had angrily divorced in 1949 but were unable to go their own separate ways, their mutual hostility perversely binding them together. It was a relationship without precedent in international relations, one of mutual ignorance that encouraged extremism and flights of imagination, both nightmares and dreams.[1]

The United States and the Soviet Union established full diplomatic relations just sixteen years after the Bolshevik Revolution and had never broken off business or social contact, as had happened with China. Even as the United States prosecuted a "cold war" against the Soviet Union, it pursued a hot-war policy in Asia against communism, with China as the center of the perceived danger. Millions of Asians in Korea, Vietnam, and other nations in Southeast Asia died as a result of the brutal civil wars that became internationalized because of America's hostility toward Beijing. The reason the United States was fighting in Vietnam, according to Richard Nixon just a few years before he became president, was to stop Beijing's alleged drive to conquer Asia. The Vietnam War, the most agonizing for the United States in its history, was fought largely as a proxy conflict with China.[2]

While the United States dismissed the real China of 500 million people on the mainland—John Foster Dulles, President Dwight Eisenhower's secretary of state, famously declared that the People's Republic of China was merely a "passing phase"—Washington promoted the fantasy that the Nationalist government on Taiwan was the true China. Chiang Kaishek, swept off the mainland by Mao's forces, had brought 3 million troops and other followers to the island, where they settled among 12 million local residents in order to sustain the Republic of China. But Chiang's "China" was a fiction. It existed only because of American military, economic, and political backing, without which it would have disappeared quickly. It, not the Beijing regime, was a passing phase of the government of the Chinese people.

The Cold War shaped global politics for a good part of the twentieth century. It has been perceptively described as a contention between two hostile state enterprises determined to organize the world in their respective global visions of what constituted the good, the modern, and the progressive. They sought to subordinate and simplify all international and domestic affairs to serve their mutual superpower contestation. But despite the efforts of the two protagonists, the global Cold War was jagged, fractured, uneven, and often beyond their control.[3]

Mao's China, contrary to the beliefs many Americans first held about the Communist revolution and so-called monolithic communism, was never subordinate to Moscow but fiercely maintained its principles about what it thought best for its revolution and for the Chinese people. In a basic way, Beijing shaped the conduct of the Cold War as much as and perhaps even more than Cold War politics affected life in China. While Washington and Moscow each considered the other their most powerful and challenging adversary, China impudently disrupted the binary geopolitical order they tried to impose. China even helped define the stages of the Cold War. Far from being a simple adjunct to Soviet power, as many in America initially believed, China pursued an independent foreign policy based on its own definition of interests, both ideological and national. From the late 1940s to the early 1960s (what can be called Cold War I), Beijing allied itself with Moscow and with what Washington considered to be revolutionary Asia and the most violent theater of the Cold War. In Europe there was a tense standoff, a stalemate, while in Asia there was open military conflict. Asia was the meeting ground where the forces of communism and anti-communism clashed, seemingly deciding the world's future in "hot wars." There was nothing "cold" about the wars in Asia. But then in the 1970s, after Richard Nixon's adventure in China, a new, second phase of the Cold War (Cold War II) emerged in which China allied with the United States against its former ally, the Soviet Union. China's switch in sides contributed to the immense pressures that eventually helped produce the collapse of the Soviet Union.[4]

In the first stage of the Cold War, Washington's avowed purpose was to do everything it could to isolate and weaken revolutionary China in Asia. In turn, Beijing focused its anti-imperialist energies principally on the United States. The antagonism between the two was exceptional and mutual. There is no question that Washington's continued recognition and extensive material support of the Nationalist government on Taiwan; its military interventions and encouragement of hostile regimes around the entire periphery of China; and its fueling of covert actions within China itself, such as in Tibet and along the China coast, are evidence of Washington's particularly provocative and aggressive hostility against the Beijing regime. Washington's anti-China animus far exceeded that of its close allies such as Britain and France. Britain never broke off diplomatic ties with China after 1949 and France established full diplomatic recognition of the PRC as early as 1964. Britain and France never invested much political or military capital in Chiang's regime. If the United States had ended its recognition and support for the Nationalists on Taiwan, U.S.-China relations would have been far less hostile and might have achieved an earlier rapprochement.[5]

The United States even openly and repeatedly threatened to use nuclear weapons against China, during the Korean War, during the French effort to retain control of Vietnam in 1954, and during confrontations between the Communists and Nationalists in 1954–1955 and 1958, when the two sides battled over Nationalist-held offshore island groups along the China coast. In 1955, President Eisenhower seriously considered blockading much of the China coast to support the Nationalists' retention of offshore island groups. And as he once famously declared at a press conference during the crisis, he saw no reason why America's nuclear weapons "shouldn't be used just exactly as you would use a bullet or anything else" against the Chinese

Communists. Through the 1950s and 1960s, the danger of China actually escalated in the eyes of American leaders, justifying the serious contemplation of the battlefield use of the nuclear option, while the Soviets, who at least talked about "peaceful coexistence," appeared to become less threatening and more reasonable.[6]

By the early 1960s, it was evident to many observers of global politics that the putative Sino-Soviet monolith was irrevocably fracturing due to profound national and ideological differences between Moscow and Beijing. In 1960, Moscow abruptly withdrew more than 1,000 Soviet technical experts from China, tore up hundreds of contracts and cooperative agreements, and destroyed factory blueprints in a rage over Beijing's criticisms of the Soviet Union for its abandonment of communism and its interference in China's internal affairs. In 1962, when border tensions between India and China erupted into armed conflict, Moscow openly sided with New Delhi against Beijing, its supposed Communist ally, even as Moscow was embroiled in the Cuban Missile Crisis with Washington. In 1963, Beijing issued a comprehensive polemic against Moscow, accusing it of abandoning revolution and the struggle against U.S. imperialism. China styled itself as the new center of world revolution and suggested that Moscow had more in common with Washington than with Beijing and other revolutionary forces around the world. President John Kennedy thought the Soviets had to be so concerned about the Chinese that he directed Averell Harriman, one of his closest aides, to approach Soviet leader Nikita Khrushchev in person with a proposal to consider taking "action" against China's nuclear weapons facilities. Khrushchev, though he had no love for the Chinese, did not accept Kennedy's provocative proposal, and the Chinese successfully exploded their first nuclear device the next year.[7]

Washington was especially worried about Chinese Communism in these years. It saw its leaders as still heady in their triumph and determined to support anti-Western movements throughout Asia and Africa in the wake of decolonization. Nonwhite revolutionary China appeared to appeal to the restless millions throughout the former colonial world as they became increasingly important in international politics. But an additional element fueled American animosity. The long-held and fond notion that America and China's destinies were inextricably entwined had a contrary side: many in America harbored a deep fear of China. A Chinese incubus had to be isolated. A "yellow peril" arising from irreconcilable Chinese racial and cultural differences that went beyond ideological differences threatened America's fate. Nineteenth-century racial fears were given new life in the Cold War.

Many Americans, including Presidents Eisenhower and Kennedy and their closest advisors, shared the belief, for example, that because of their vast numbers and brutal culture, the Chinese attached a lower value to human life than did Westerners, a conviction that Westerners had commonly voiced in the previous century. Dillon Anderson, Eisenhower's national security advisor, publicly asserted that the United States was fully prepared to use nuclear weapons against "700 million Chinamen" on the mainland in the 1950s. "Good God," he once said in explaining the policy, "they can breed them faster in the zone of the interior than you can kill them in the combat zone." Eisenhower himself was convinced that the Chinese valued life less than Westerners did. He once told his Cabinet that the Chinese had "peculiar attitudes" about the value of human life and would consider the starvation of 50 million Chinese a national "gain." John Foster Dulles, Eisenhower's secretary of state, claimed that China's leaders were "absolutely indifferent to the prospect of losing millions of people" in a conflict. In contrast, life in the West, he said, "is weighed carefully—to understate our attitude." In these views, the Chinese were less than fully human.[8]

In the 1960s, such views increased as Americans grew even more alarmed about China's rise. President John Kennedy commonly talked about the China danger. When he hosted the French minister of culture, Andrew Malraux (a leftist author who in 1933 had written *Man's Fate*, one of the great classic novels about modern China), in the White House in 1963, Kennedy described a China, which was then constructing a nuclear capability, as the "great menace in the future to humanity, the free world, and freedom on earth." Kennedy told Malraux that in his opinion, the Chinese "would be perfectly prepared to sacrifice hundreds of millions of their own lives" in their aggressive policies. Kennedy repeatedly expressed his fear to others. The French did not share Washington's antagonism toward China, and the de Gaulle government established full diplomatic relations with Beijing the following year.[9]

Public opinion polls in early 1964 found that a great majority of Americans saw China as the greatest threat to world peace, even more dangerous than the Soviet Union, which seemed to be mellowing under post-Stalin leaders. Two out of three persons polled believed that China was America's number one menace, and many cited a racial/cultural reason for their fear. They believed that a cataclysmic clash "between the East and West" was in the making, in which "the yellow people will turn on the white race." Survey respondents offered evidence to support their view: "human life has no value" for the Chinese; their leaders were "yellow fanatic rulers"; they were a "hungry, over-populated country" that had to expand to survive. Some voiced support for an alliance with the Soviets against the Chinese, for at least the Russians were a "western nation" and had a Christian heritage. Even as the United States was locked in an arms race with the Soviets, Americans were enjoying regular visits from the Bolshoi Ballet. There was no such cultural exchange with China.[10]

American public opinion and Washington's policy toward China were in accord in these years. In 1964, when President Lyndon Johnson and Congress committed U.S. combat forces to the conflict in South Vietnam, the ostensible reason given was support for the regime in Saigon in its efforts to fight domestic subversion and aggression from the north. But behind all the trouble was Communist China, according to Johnson. At Johns Hopkins University in April 1965, the president presented the broad context for America's deepening involvement in Southeast Asia, a region of the world that was virtually unknown to most Americans at the time. "Over this war," he pronounced, is "the deepening shadow of Communist China." Beijing was urging Hanoi's aggression and was "helping the forces of violence in almost every continent." Vietnam was just "part of a wider pattern of aggressive purposes." Washington saw Vietnam as the critical battleground upon which the United States had to turn back aggressive Chinese communism. Vietnam, it was claimed, was "China's war."[11]

Despite considerable evidence that the Vietnam conflict was a civil war and the Vietnamese Communists were independent of foreign control, American officials continued to use the specter of China to justify its mounting involvement. Stopping China, with its militant hordes, was the reason to fight. Johnson's secretary of state, Dean Rusk, raised the yellow peril rationale as late as 1967. When he was asked at a press conference why he thought the security of the United States was at stake in Vietnam, an unequivocal Rusk said that soon there would be "a billion Chinese on the Mainland, armed with nuclear weapons," adding that the "free nations of Asia" "don't want China to overrun them on the basis of a doctrine of world revolution." The United States was obligated to help defend these struggling allies. "After all, he reminded the reporters, "World War II hit us from the Pacific, and Asia is where two-thirds of the world's people live." The United States was "both a Pacific and an Atlantic power." Within a few days, newspapers around the country ran an editorial cartoon drawn by the popular Herblock that showed Rusk releasing a menacing dragon out of a sack labeled "Vietnam Rationale." "China is the enemy" is emblazoned on the monster. "Dean," says an onlooking President Johnson, "I think you've let the dragon out of the bag."[12]

In 1968, China ranked lower in American eyes than even North Vietnam, which American B-52s were then carpet bombing. Then, in 1969, Soviet and Chinese forces clashed in bloody border fighting that threatened to expand into general conflict. At the same time, Moscow signaled its interest in engaging Washington in negotiations to limit the number and types of strategic nuclear weapons each side could have. For many Americans watching the widening dispute, China embodied the worst, and most dangerous, of the two perils, the Red and the Yellow.

African Americans often held views about China that contrasted quite sharply with those of whites. In the nineteenth and early twentieth centuries, African Americans saw little that China could offer them. Chinese immigrants in America, as members of a despised racial caste, were commonly seen as occupying a position in the racial hierarchy even lower than did blacks after emancipation. African Americans sometimes sympathized with Chinese, who could not become naturalized American citizens, but they also could see them as threatening to their own tenuous economic position. Chinese and African American workers occasionally found themselves competing for the same jobs. After the Civil War, white planters brought Chinese laborers into the south to replace free blacks who wanted their own land in the Mississippi delta. In the 1920s and 1930s, leading African American thinkers and writers argued that China's suffering under European exploitation paralleled the conditions of life under Jim Crow in America and supported anti-imperialist movements in China. But they also often expressed greater interest in Japan, as the self-proclaimed "champion of the darker races" of the world. Many African Americans even accepted Tokyo's rationale for its mounting aggression against China, which was that Japan had assumed the burden of ridding the Chinese masses of the yoke of white colonialism.[13]

After Japan's brazen seizure of Manchuria in 1931, some African Americans began to turn away from Japan, which they now saw as a part of the imperialist club, and identify with Chinese resistance and their nascent revolution. Langston Hughes, who visited China in 1933, loudly condemned

Japan's militarism. He met Song Qingling, Sun Yatsen's widow; Lu Xun, China's leading cultural figure; and others on the Chinese left. He deplored the treatment of China by the West and Japan. In 1937 he composed his famous poem "Roar China," which ends shouting

> Crush the enemies of land and bread and freedom!
> Stand up and roar, China!
> You know what you want!
> The only way to get it is
> To take it!
> Roar, China![14]

More and more African Americans began to see China's fight against Japanese militarism as part of the freedom movements of the 1930s that included Ethiopia's resistance to Italian colonialism. The famous singer and actor Paul Robeson was most prominent among those who sided with the Chinese against Japan and saw their plight as akin to the beleaguered Republican forces in Spain under attack by fascism. The "Chinese people," he declared, were "heroically defending the liberties of *all* progressive humanity." Robeson took up the study of the Chinese language and recorded an album of Chinese patriotic and folk songs with the Chinese singer Liu Liangmo that included "*Qilai*" ("The March of the Volunteers"), which became China's national anthem. In 1949, Robeson loudly hailed the founding of the PRC.[15]

By the 1950s and 1960s, black curiosity about revolutionary China rose in inverse proportions to the decline of China in the estimation of mainstream America. The more Washington demonized the Chinese, the more glorious (or at least intriguing) China seemed to many blacks. African American journalist William Worthy may have been the first American reporter to travel to China after 1949. Working for the *Baltimore Afro-American*, he defied Washington's travel ban and spent more than a month in China in 1956–1957. After his return, the State Department, in a highly publicized case, seized his travel documents because of his defiance of U.S. law. W. E. B. Du Bois, one of the world's great intellectuals, who had turned to communism in the 1950s out of bitterness against the West, had long followed events in Asia, believing that the future of the region would inevitably influence African Americans and their struggle in America. In his famous 1914 essay "The World Problem of the Color Line," Du Bois noted that the colored races were coming increasingly into contact. "We are nearer China today," he wrote, "than we were to San Francisco yesterday." In the 1930s, Du Bois believed that Japan, as an advanced nonwhite nation, was a positive model for African Americans and its seizure of Manchuria was an effort to "uplift" Asia. In 1936, when he visited Shanghai as a correspondent for the African American newspaper *The Pittsburgh Courier*, he found the city supposedly under Chinese administration depressing. Blatant European mistreatment of the Chinese on Shanghai's streets reminded him of the brutalization that blacks faced in Mississippi. The Chinese, however, displayed no resistance or anger, just acquiescence, and he found Japan and the proud Japanese much more to his liking. But in the 1950s he rued his earlier comments about China and Japan and concluded that People's China had become the beacon of light illuminating the way forward for the oppressed people of color of the world. China was now the source of inspiration for his hopes for racial liberation.[16]

In 1959, Du Bois, and his wife Shirley Graham Du Bois, traveled to China at the personal invitation of Mao Zedong, to celebrate Du Bois's ninety-first birthday. They were extraordinarily moved by their experiences in China, which included personal meetings with the chairman and other top Communist leaders, the privilege of delivering a lecture on his birthday to 1,000 students and faculty at Peking University that was broadcast nationally in China and to the world, and weeks of gracious and generous Chinese hospitality. The visit left an indelible impression on the great scholar and activist. Du Bois, who had become a resident and citizen of Ghana several years before, was convinced that People's China was now Africa's natural friend and ally in the world and encouraged China-Africa ties. He was so moved by his visit that he composed the longest poem of his life to salute and honor China. "I Sing to China" gushed with exuberant optimism about revolutionary China and its vital meaning for the oppressed downtrodden everywhere. It ends with a resounding declaration and urgent plea

Shout, China!
Roar, Rock, roll River;
Sing, Sun and Moon and Sea!
Move Mountain, Lake and Land,
Exalt Mankind, Inspire!
For out of the East again, comes Salvation!
Leading all prophets of the Dead—

Osiris, Buddha, Christ and Mahmoud
Interning their ashes, cherishing their Good;
China save the World! Arise, China![17]

Du Bois was not alone in praising revolutionary China. A pantheon of black radicals in America came to believe that their liberation was inextricably connected to China's destiny. On the final page of *The Autobiography of Malcolm X,* the black leader commits himself to learning African languages but also to learning Chinese, which seemed to him the future's "most powerful political language."[18] Robert F. Williams, a leader of a local NAACP chapter in North Carolina who advocated armed self-defense against white violence, was another early proponent of what became known as Black Power. After death threats and an indictment on charges of inciting insurrection, Williams went into exile for eight years in the 1960s, first to Cuba and then to China. From abroad, he published a stream of commentaries that called for black revolution in America. In 1962, he published the provocative *Negroes with Guns,* which helped inspire Huey Newton to form the Black Panther Party. During his several years in China, Williams told Mao about the plight of African Americans and prompted the Chinese leader to proclaim his support for the black struggle in America. Mao, citing Williams as his inspiration, penned his "Statement Calling on the People of the World to Unite to Oppose Racial Discrimination by U.S. Imperialism and Support the American Negroes in Their Struggle against Racial Discrimination." It was one of two commentaries Mao issued in explicit support for the black struggle in America; the second was published after the assassination of Martin Luther King Jr.[19]

Years later, Williams returned to the United States from China and assumed a position at the University of Michigan's Center for Chinese Studies. In February 1971, he published "On the Platform with Mao Tse-tung," an opinion piece in the *New York Times.* He wrote that China "left the greatest imprint upon my life" and described the country as being "a variety of worlds with a variety of people bound by profound human qualities." The most important were those of "morality and selflessness," qualities he said "the Western world must cultivate if it is to survive." He concluded his heartfelt essay by saying that China was not a "fearful dragon" but was a "plodding dragon making her way toward the top of humanity." When Williams died in 1996, he was buried in a grey Chinese suit that Mao Zedong had given him thirty years earlier. The icon of the civil rights movement, Rosa Parks, delivered his eulogy.[20]

Huey P. Newton read Mao's writings voraciously when he was a student in Oakland's Merritt College in the mid-1960s and the chairman's rhetoric shaped the early ideological profile of the Black Panther Party he helped found in 1966. Among the most prominent of black revolutionary organizations, the Black Panther Party advocated armed defense against the police and the end of white capitalist rule. Members raised funds for the new organization by hawking copies of *Quotations of Chairman Mao* on Berkeley street corners. Mao's words inspired much of Newton's sloganeering: "seize the hour" became Newton's "seize the time." Newton favored Mao's aphorisms, for example "political power grows out of the barrel of a gun" and "revolution is not a dinner party." When he visited China in September 1971, Newton, like other radicals before him, was captivated by what he encountered. Like Du Bois and Williams, Newton thought he saw the future in Mao's revolutionary China. In his autobiography, *Revolutionary Suicide*, which was written soon after he had returned from his journey, he wrote that he had found a profound personal "sensation of freedom" in China, "as if a great weight had been lifted from my soul and I was able to be myself, without defense or pretense or the need for explanation." "I felt absolutely free for the first time in my life," Newton wrote, "completely free among my fellow men."[21]

A shared revolutionary romanticism helps explains this adoration of Mao's China. China in these decades was in the grip of Mao's vision of utopia, which featured an ethos of exaggerated self-reliance and communist purism. The individual could remake the world through will alone, disregarding social and political realities, in the name of the infinitely powerful "people" or "masses." This vision appealed to dreamers and poets and demagogues alike, and Mao was all of these himself. But there was more to the association than a shared radical aesthetic. Many radicals, not just African Americans, found Mao's messianic message irresistible and chose to disbelieve the real consequences of his extremism. The horrendous human costs of the Great Leap Forward and then the Cultural Revolution were dismissed as the regrettable price of human progress or simply the fabrications of reactionaries to discredit the brave new emerging world. Black revolutionaries and others around the world in these heady years of the ascendancy of "Maoism" saw a China they wanted to see and what they believed would be their own destinies as long as they struggled in the proper way. This infatuation recalled the celebration of Stalin's Soviet Union in the 1930s by those searching for a liberated future. But there was more. China was a country of nonwhites who suffered physical and emotional abuse by the Great Powers that easily compared to racist brutality in segregated America. The oppressors of the Chinese people seemed closely familiar: when Langston Hughes celebrated the founding of new China in 1949, he explained the Revolution to his African American readers back home with the statement that "Chiang Kai-shek was a Chinese Uncle Tom." China, though, was not a blank slate upon which any radical fantasy could be projected. Mao's millennialism was not empty fabrication so much as terrible folly, a flowering plant atop a moldering grave. As had many American travelers, missionaries, and social reformers before them, revolutionaries of the 1950s and 1960s saw only the blossoms and discovered a China that resonated with their own aspirations and illusions. For them, China and the Chinese people embodied a tangible form of their imagined, desired future.[22]

Dreams and nightmares about revolutionary China came easily to Americans who had no direct connection with the country. From the political right and from the left, from Washington officials to revolutionaries on the streets of West Oakland, from farmers in the Great Plains to intellectuals in New York, many thought about China in exaggerated terms. Some Americans believed China was the greatest danger to peace and civilization, while the Black Panthers hailed Mao as their great revolutionary inspiration. The vacuum in America's knowledge because of the paucity of diplomatic, cultural, or social contact made possible academic careers that aimed to present informed, dispassionate opinion and scholarship on China. More than any other individual, John King Fairbank helped shape the modern understanding of China in America. For some fifty years, Fairbank, a historian, political advisor, commentator, and academic empire builder at Harvard University, commanded the field of China studies. His attitude, as he articulated it in *Chinabound,* his aptly entitled 1982 memoir, was that China more than simply mattered to America; it was fundamental to the country's very existence. Just as the irresistible urge to spread the Word had moved his missionary uncle in the nineteenth century, he wrote, so was there an inspired purposefulness in his own academic career. "America's salvation," he was convinced, would be "through China studies." He was a "missionary in reverse," spreading knowledge about China to an exceedingly unenlightened America, a most dangerous condition for the country and the world.[23]

Fairbank was born in South Dakota, a place one might not think would produce a scholar of distant China, but the Plains and Midwest states were the homes of an unusual number of Americans whose lives became linked with China. Perhaps they found some basic things in common with the Chinese: the rhythm of rural life, the solidity of continental insularity, plain speaking, and lack of pretense perhaps help explain the mutual attraction. (Xi Jinping, China's current leader, continues this pattern: he made a special connection with the Iowa hosts he befriended on his first trip to America, when he was a young and up-and-coming official). China was also a place that appealed to Fairbank's pioneer soul. China, as he recalled in his memoirs, was "an unknown horizon, waiting to be explored and cultivated."[24]

After studying Chinese at Harvard and Oxford, Fairbank arrived in China in early 1932 and traveled to Beijing, whose immense enclosing walls, which no longer exist, were "overwhelmingly awesome" to the budding scholar. Wilma Cannon, a Radcliffe graduate and daughter of the head of the Harvard Medical School, joined him in Beijing, where an American missionary married them. Wilma also became a China specialist and later served in the U.S. diplomatic corps in China. The young couple quickly inserted themselves into the small and close-knit community of foreign scholars, missionary educators, and Western-oriented Chinese intellectuals and officials, a coterie that became the core of Fairbank's extended network for the rest of his life. They traveled widely and stayed for four years, followed by two other extended visits to China in the 1940s. During these long sojourns, the couple immersed themselves in China's vast land, culture, and people. They became critical of the privileged status foreigners enjoyed in the country (though as young newlyweds, they had four servants in their comfortable Beijing home) and the inability of the ruling Nationalist Party to improve the welfare of the masses of people. Fairbank identified with the rising discontent in the country and predicted early on that China would one day see an epic social revolution that would change the course of history.[25]

In 1935, Fairbank assumed a position as a historian back at Harvard, where he built one of the most successful careers in American academia. He was a capable scholar and program builder who, unlike many other China specialists at the time, focused on the modern period, the mid-nineteenth century to the present. The study of European history dominated scholarship at Harvard in the prewar years, and few there (or anywhere else in American higher education) devoted serious attention to Asia. Fairbank and his colleague, Japan historian Edwin O. Reischauer, challenged the prevailing

Eurocentrism by offering engaging courses, including their legendary "rice paddies" class that tutored legions of students over the decades about the histories of the countries of East Asia; building the eminent collection of the Yenching Library; producing generations of stellar graduate students who went on to populate American universities and colleges; and hosting leading scholars from Asia to come to America. They promoted the publication of pioneering scholarship and drew on the funds of wealthy benefactors and foundations to build the young field of China and Asia studies. Their efforts helped transform not just a specific geographic field of inquiry but also the way American specialists thought about non-European areas of the world. Fairbank was central in constructing what became known as "area studies," a unique American approach that brought together specialists from the social sciences and humanities to study a specific region of the world deemed important for the United States. Fairbank's approach to China became a model for the study of non-Western societies in American universities.

Fairbank developed strong opinions about Japan's encroachment in China in the late 1930s and called for American support for Chinese resistance. He advocated specific measures such as military assistance. China, he declared before Pearl Harbor, was defending "the cause of civilization as we know it." Later, as the Communists approached victory, Fairbank tried to educate Washington and the American public about what was happening in that vital area of the world. He had long concluded that Chiang Kaishek and the Nationalists were a lost cause and that a Chinese mass revolution was inevitable. In November 1948, he wrote that the Communists had already won the support of the "vast majority of the poor peasants" and that they would triumph. He believed that the American preoccupation with the Soviet Union blinded the country to Chinese realities. In his view, Americans had to accept the fact that the Chinese Communist movement "is not only genuinely Communist but also genuinely Chinese."[26]

In 1949, he accepted the Revolution as a verdict on Chiang and basically agreed with the conclusion of the U.S. State Department's White Paper that China's situation, as regrettable as it was, was beyond the ability of America to control. He rejected the argument advanced by political conservatives that America had "lost" China. The conservative outcry tapped into beliefs about American exceptionalism and America's global mission and went far beyond policy debate. China's loss to communism, in the conservative view, was more than a geopolitical defeat: it was simply unacceptable and inconceivable, suggesting a violation of basic American identity. This incendiary accusation, which blamed Democrats and liberals, became a staple in American partisan politics from the late 1940s through the 1950s.

In contrast, Fairbank believed that the Chinese revolution was a product of endemic Chinese realities and the latest expression of the Chinese drive to reach modernity and national greatness. Though communism was "bad in America," according to Fairbank, it was "good in China" because it tried to represent the people's aspirations. He had no sympathy for the Communists, but his assessment grew out of his appreciation of the very different histories, cultures, and social orders of the two countries. Fairbank wanted to see America develop a thoughtful approach that did not simply push China further away and alienate the country he loved. America needed to help Asia develop and "modernize," not pursue military confrontation. He propagated this message consistently for the next forty years. He, along with a number of other scholars, favored recognition of the new regime in Beijing as the de facto government of the Chinese people and as a necessary requirement if America was to stay connected with the Chinese people.[27]

Fairbank's effort to be nonideological and his genuine sympathy for the Chinese people led him to press for what he called an understanding of China under revolution. For decades after 1949, Fairbank patiently urged attention to China, opposed policies that he felt kept Americans and Chinese ignorant about each other, and advocated appreciation of the deep historical and social currents that lay just beneath the tumult and rhetoric of Chinese communism. He wanted Americans to recognize the very different histories and cultures of the two countries as a way of understanding political behavior: China's long experience was with autocracy, centralization of authority, and a collectivist experience that emphasized the social group, while the American experience was with democracy, decentralized authority, and individualism. China often experienced desperate poverty and social upheaval and tragedy, while America's history recorded much prosperity and considerable social cohesion, notwithstanding important exceptions. Both imperial and modern China had experienced humiliation at the hands of foreign peoples, including Americans. The United States had never been conquered and occupied. Americans had to appreciate the resulting nationalism of the Chinese and the success of the Communists in capturing the patriotic sentiments of the people. Moreover, much about the Chinese Communist revolution fit the pattern of dynastic change in China's long imperial past. Marxism and Maoism was the new Confucian orthodoxy, power was centralized and absolute, and Mao was the new occupant of the throne. Fairbank carefully advised that the "patterns of past institutions may be fruitfully kept in mind when looking at current configurations," as understanding the present would be impossible otherwise. Communist China, he instructed in the memorable title of one of his articles for *Foreign Affairs,* was now the "People's Middle Kingdom," a modern, revolutionary state with ancient cultural and political legacies.[28]

At times, Fairbank sounded as if he was trumpeting the familiar trope of an unchanging, static China (Henry Kissinger's recently published book *On China* perpetuates this view), but his purpose was more to highlight the deep historical and social structures that continued to shape China's present rather than to suggest that nothing important had changed. His attention to real historical continuities and parallels aimed to respond to those who used a simplistic Cold War framework to interpret complex developments in China. From another direction, however, younger scholars and some of his own students on the left later accused Fairbank of underappreciating the significance of the genuinely new and positive in revolutionary China, which they saw as opening a portal to a utopian future for humankind.[29]

Today, in light of the tremendous growth in sophistication of American scholarship and a popular understanding of China that appreciates the complexity, discontinuities, and contingencies of Chinese history, Fairbank's views can appear naïve and prone to serve expedient political purposes. But in the 1950s, Washington's political leaders largely resisted moderate and well-considered ideas. The country was engulfed by the McCarthyite Red Scare, which went after many China hands and propagated a Chinese Communist bogeyman. Eminent scholars such as Owen Lattimore and O. Edmund Clubb and dedicated foreign service officers such as John Service, John Vincent Carter, and John Paton Davies did not escape the witchhunt, and their reputations were smeared and their careers ruined. For the rest of his life, Fairbank believed that the removal of these and other experienced specialists helped pave the way for the unnecessary and tragic crusade in postwar Asia that was capped by America's disastrous descent into the Vietnam debacle. Washington had made policy without the input of the knowledge and practical experience of these individuals, who had known communism and Asian nationalism in the field. Washington's misguided policies, he wrote, were made by leaders who were themselves "truly representative" of America's "profound public ignorance" of Asian realities. America's setbacks in Asia were self-inflicted. At the height of the global

Cold War, Fairbank counseled that Americans and Chinese still had "to learn to live on the same planet."[30]

For their part, however, China's leaders exhibited little interest in learning to live with the United States and improving understanding. From the late 1950s into the late 1960s, China's politics turned increasingly fanatical under Mao's obsession with using mass revolutionary campaigns to try to industrialize and build a new socialist society. His Great Leap Forward, which envisioned leapfrogging forward in steel production by encouraging the construction of backyard furnaces and the collectivization of agriculture beginning in 1959, proved ruinous and led to massive starvation in the early 1960s. Insisting on keeping "politics in command" and "continuing the revolution under the dictatorship of the proletariat," Mao launched the Great Proletarian Cultural Revolution in 1966, which virtually dismantled state and party structures in the name of opposing bureaucracy, or what was called "revisionism." Chaos and destruction became so bad that the army had to step in to maintain a semblance of order. Mao encouraged the people to turn on themselves and their leaders (except himself) to prove their worthiness to revolution, but the result was horrific tragedy, cruel vendettas, personal ruin, and mass demoralization. Mao destroyed his own revolution in the name of revolution.[31]

Mao was no authoritarian like Stalin, who favored institutionalized terror to build a vision of socialism. Mao was in some ways the exact opposite, which is why he never was comfortable with his bureaucratic Soviet allies. He broke with them a brief decade after the founding of the PRC. Through the 1960s, Beijing and Moscow became increasingly hostile to one another, and their armies clashed along their long border. There was no Communist monolith. In contrast to the stodgy Soviets, Mao had strong tendencies toward what could be called an idealized anarchism. He was deeply suspicious of administration and order of any sort. He hoped to realize a society based on mass self-sacrifice and revolutionary morality in accord with his messianic vision of a classless world. The result was not virtue, equality, and self-motivation, however, but dystopia, but more akin to a *Lord of the Flies* nightmare in which atavistic factionalism and inhumanity consumed all than to Orwell's *1984*, which was modeled on Stalin's Soviet Union. The victims in China were also the perpetrators.

Because the United States was mired in Vietnam, Democrats and President Lyndon Johnson could not take initiatives to end the stalemate in U.S.-China relations. The breakthrough came from a completely unexpected political actor, Richard Nixon, who called for new thinking about China in a famous essay published in *Foreign Affairs* in 1967. In "Asia after Viet Nam," an opening shot for his run for the presidency, Nixon offered a vision of American policy after extracting itself from the Vietnam disaster. His candor was striking: Vietnam had taken its toll on the United States, and the United States could no longer play the role of the world's policeman. It had to accept the limits of its power. As for China, Nixon signaled that he was ready to see a change in the relationship. The United States, Nixon declared, had to come to grips with the "reality of China."[32]

About the time when Nixon's article appeared, John Fairbank bumped into Henry Kissinger on the air shuttle between New York and Boston. Both were Harvard professors, and the two discussed how U.S.-China relations might be reconstructed. Fairbank later recalled the discussion and remembers that he explained aspects of traditional imperial Chinese statecraft to the ambitious political scientist, especially the imperial tributary system in which leaders from afar journeyed to Beijing as guests of the emperor to pay their respects and in return receive his commendation. Fairbank told Kissinger that as the presumptive holder of the Chinese throne, Mao could not leave the country, but the American president could go just about anywhere in the world. Kissinger never forgot Fairbank's tutorial and later gave the China scholar the impression that the conversation the two had on the plane had "changed history." Kissinger would become President Nixon's national security advisor and co-architect of the new China policy and it would be Nixon, of course, who traveled to Beijing to meet the chairman.

China occupied an important dimension in the personal and professional lives of many American presidents in the twentieth century. Theodore Roosevelt received the Nobel Peace Prize for successfully negotiating the end of the Russo-Japanese War that was fought over the control of Northeast Asia. Woodrow Wilson took a keen interest in the 1911 Republican Revolution and took the lead in extending recognition to the new Chinese Republic. Herbert Hoover had lived in China before his presidency and faced the Manchurian Crisis of 1931 while he was in office. Franklin Roosevelt reveled in his family's China connection and promoted Chiang Kaishek to a position of world leadership. Harry Truman faced the momentous problems of responding to China's civil war, the challenge of the 1949 Communist revolution, and the Korean War. Dwight Eisenhower endured perpetual crisis in the China area, as the Communists and Nationalists constantly clashed along the China coast and threatened to reopen their massive civil war. As he confessed at his last press conference before leaving office in 1960, Eisenhower said that what he most regretted during his time in the White House was that he had not made progress on the "China question." John Kennedy feared that the imminent Chinese acquisition of nuclear weapons would alter the world balance of power and doom the United States. China lurked in his nightmares about the future of all of Southeast Asia. And Lyndon Johnson committed America to its most disastrous war, in large part in the name of stopping Chinese Communist expansionism in Southeast Asia. But the president who is and will likely remain most identified with the challenge of China is Richard Nixon. Immodestly, but not incorrectly, he called his visit to China in February 1972 the "week that changed the world." Nixon did fundamentally change the relationship between the two countries in what arguably is the most dramatic diplomatic episode in American presidential history, and his visit did transform world politics.

Nothing in Nixon's early public life indicated that he would be the president who would end decades of U.S.-China hostility and open the way to the normalization of relations. In fact, in his early career Nixon distinguished himself as one of the most belligerent anti-Chinese Communist politicians in America. When he ran for the Senate from California in the fall of 1950, he unfairly attacked his opponent, Helen Gahagan Douglas, as being soft on communism. He smeared Douglas and other Democrats, including Dean Acheson and President Truman, for appeasing Communists in Asia and allowing "Free China" to fall. This was all done for partisan politics. As Eisenhower's vice-president, Nixon was chosen to appeal to the Republican right wing. He frequently presented himself as one of the most loyal supporters of the Chinese Nationalists and as a proponent of an aggressive U.S. military posture toward Beijing. Nixon called for threatening "massive retaliation" against China, which meant the use of nuclear weapons, if it involved itself in Southeast Asia. His tough stance against Beijing went even further, at least rhetorically, than Eisenhower's hard-line secretary of state, John Foster Dulles. When Nixon visited Taiwan in 1953, the media prominently featured him meeting Chiang Kaishek and saluting his leadership of "Free China." The Republic of China, Nixon declared "will be a bastion of cultural strength, of spiritual strength, and a sample for all free people to see, and for people who want to be free as well." Dulles thought Nixon had gone too far in his exaggerated rhetoric and tried to rein in the vice-president. In 1956, when he visited Taiwan again, Nixon again presented himself as one of the most determined backers of Chiang and his regime. Nixon told Chiang of his "admiration for your unyielding stand against communism" and declared, "Let there be no misapprehension about our own steadfastness in continuing to support the Republic of China."[33]

When he ran for the presidency against John Kennedy in 1960, Nixon again resorted to the right-wing tactic of accusing Kennedy of being soft on communism. Nixon levied the charge during the famous television debates between the two candidates when they discussed the confrontation over the offshore island groups in the Taiwan Strait that had brought the United States and China dangerously close to armed conflict repeatedly in the 1950s. Nixon tried to paint Kennedy as inexperienced, while Kennedy characterized the stance that Eisenhower and Nixon had adopted as ill advised. Their actual positions were not as opposed as the rhetoric suggested. Though he failed in his presidential bid, Nixon continued to rail against the Chinese Communists. As the Sino-Soviet split erupted into plain view in the early 1960s, he publicly opposed any American effort to take advantage of discord among the Communists and any suggestion that the United States might soften its stand against Beijing to exploit the division. During the escalation of the American intervention in Vietnam, Nixon endorsed the growing effort in order to stop what he referred to as "Peking's drive for conquest."[34]

In private, however, Nixon was less ideological than his quotable remonstrations suggested. His comments as vice-president made within the confines of the White House and in private gatherings reveal a different Richard Nixon. There are hints that Nixon was captured by a "China mystique" even as he railed against Beijing. During a Christmastime party at his Washington home in 1959, Nixon, while munching on an egg roll, shocked one of his guests with an offhand comment. "Someday," he mused through bites of the finger food, "I'm going to China." When pressed, he made clear he was not speaking of Taiwan and seeing Chiang Kaishek again. Chiang, Nixon declared in the privacy of his own home, was "a stupid man. . . . He is a small man, only capable of running a small island." Nixon said it was the real China he wanted to see. Nixon raised the idea of a mainland China visit on other private occasions in 1960 and speculated about the inevitability of serious Sino-Soviet discord and about the opportunities such a split might present to the United States. The enormous political capital he would gain if he was able to get into China also clearly dazzled him.[35]

As he prepared for another run for the presidency in the mid-1960s, Nixon completed a political makeover. He offered himself as a statesman of international stature to offset his reputation as a political ideologue. His public comments indicated that he could think in terms of hard geopolitical realities, especially about the decline in the relative power of the United States in world affairs after Vietnam and the need to take dramatic steps to reposition Washington in the Cold War. Hailing from California on the Pacific, he emphasized America's stake in Asia especially because many of his financial and political backers, such as U.S. Senator William Knowland of California, had long-standing personal and business interests in Asia. Nixon, who unsuccessfully ran for governor of California in 1962, represented the move away from the Europe centered vision of the country of his Washington predecessors to one that took greater account of the Pacific. In his memoirs, Nixon recalled having fond glimpses of the blue ocean during his formative childhood years in southern California, where he returned to live after serving as vice-president.

Perched on the Pacific in the 1960s, Nixon closely watched the growing call for change in Sino-American relations in academic and policy circles. In 1966, the Senate Foreign Relations Committee under J. William Fulbright conducted a high-profile review of U.S. policy toward Vietnam and China. "It is of great importance that we try to learn something more about the strange and fascinating Chinese nation," Fulbright announced in his remarks that opened the hearing, "about its past and its present, about the aims of its leaders and the aspirations of its people." A parade of virtually every China specialist in America, including John Fairbank, came before the committee to emphasize the dangerous ignorance and distance that separated the two countries. The pundits and scholars were nearly unanimous in their call for a new policy that could find a way to establish cultural and social contacts with the largest country on earth. They feared miscalculation might lead to escalation of hostilities to the level of open war with Beijing. Nixon himself began to muse about the possibility of enlisting China against the Soviet Union, an audacious idea that would be heretical among conservatives and liberals alike. After winning the presidential election in 1968, he immediately directed his assistants to begin a thorough but quiet reassessment of U.S. policy toward China to see what new initiatives could be taken to end the long standoff. Nixon had begun what would be his epic journey to the East.[36]

As Nixon and other American leaders groped for a way out of the impasse in U.S.-China relations, Beijing's leaders, most importantly Chairman Mao himself, began their own strategic reassessment, prompted by the rapidly escalating hostility with Moscow and Beijing's international isolation due to the ravages of the Cultural Revolution. The possibility of major military conflict with Moscow had grown appreciably, and China's leaders sensed acute vulnerability. Mao and other top leaders began to think in new ways about the United States, previously their number-one enemy. Moscow, not Washington, now loomed as the greater perceived threat. Independently and haltingly, both China and the United States each began to try to signal to the other that the time had come for a change. Interpreting the signals, however, proved to be exceedingly difficult in the absence of regular, high-level direct contact and because of the extraordinarily sensitive political implications of a new relationship. The first tentative moves appear almost comically oblique in hindsight. But discretion, even deliberate obfuscation, was necessary because of the high political stakes. Leaks or missteps could result in embarrassment or even political sabotage from powerful opponents who were resistant to a radical new direction in U.S.-China relations.

Even Mao had to move carefully. In January 1969, China's main paper, the *People's Daily,* published a full translation of Nixon's presidential inaugural address on its front page, but without comment. Today, one can see that the speech contained a subtle but positive gesture toward China that may have been the reason for its prominent display, but at the time, its unexplained appearance was puzzling to Chinese readers and professional China-watchers in the United States alike. Later in the year, Nixon tried to send a message through Pakistan and other third parties who had good relations with Beijing that he was interested in opening a channel of communication with China. Both Mao and Nixon attempted to communicate through other intermediaries and lower-level representatives, but it was unclear whether anyone was listening, let alone understanding intent, on the other side. Then, in October 1970, Mao made the dramatic move of having his old friend from Yan'an days, the journalist Edgar Snow, stand at his side on the reviewing platform atop Tian'anmen Gate during the high-profile National Day celebrations. It was a week before the *People's Daily* published a photo of the remarkable scene of the two, the chairman with the American. Again, however, the meaning was unclear. Was this a hint of movement in what had been decades of glacial immobility and hostility? As ever, American officials were deeply suspicious of Beijing. And in Beijing, powerful figures opposed a shift in attitude toward Washington. Several months later, Mao took the unprecedented step of telling Snow that Nixon was welcome to visit China "as a tourist or as President." Mao's message, however, was not conveyed through American bureaucratic channels to Nixon for months. Snow had to make the invitation public in an article he published in Henry Luce's *Life* at the end of April 1971.[37]

As dramatic as Mao's message was, it had actually been preempted by an episode now legendary in popular memory: Ping-Pong diplomacy. In early April, when the American table tennis team visited Japan to participate in the World Championship tournament, leading members of the American and Chinese teams unexpectedly encountered one another away from the tables. There were some awkward moments but also an exchange of trivial friendship mementos. Not long afterward, the leading member of the Chinese team, star player Zhuang Zedong, extended a surprise invitation to the American team to visit China. Back in Beijing, Mao had learned of the initial contact between the two sides and approved Zhuang's idea of an invitation, recognizing it as a wonderful political opportunity. The American players eagerly accepted. Zhuang said it was the photo of Mao with Edgar Snow in October 1970 that prompted his initial friendliness toward the Americans. A few days later, the Americans were in the People's Republic, the first "nonpolitical" group from the United States in decades. Though it seemed that ordinary people had brought the two sides together, Ping-Pong diplomacy was a product of quiet, high level efforts to initiate change. Still, its seeming serendipity and the charm of the casual athletes and coaches captured imaginations in both countries. *Time* magazine featured the long haired, multiracial American team atop the Great Wall on its cover on April 26, 1971. The tremendous excitement the visit unleashed revealed that the time had finally come for a new relationship between the two countries.

More than a political connection, the emerging U.S.-China relationship was also a phenomenal cultural moment. As *Time* announced in Chinese Communist red and yellow on its cover, "China: A Whole New Game—First Color Photos: Yanks in Peking." The content of the headline resembled those seventy years earlier that had announced the victorious entry of American soldiers into Beijing to suppress the Boxer uprising, but the times were now entirely different. The long standoff between Chinese Communists and American imperialists was about to shift from tense confrontation to wary but respectful engagement. The Yanks were now welcomed as friends and as a counterweight against a common foe. China's ties with the Soviets had always been uneasy, and the resumption of ties with the United States, which developed remarkably quickly, was helped along by the arousal of dormant channels formed through the long historical experience of the two nations.[38]

In early July, Henry Kissinger conducted the first of what would become many visits to Beijing, this one completely clandestine. Using stories about illness or visits to girlfriends to cover his disappearance from public, Kissinger slipped out of Pakistan and flew to Beijing on a mission that subordinates had arranged. Beijing was still unsettled by the ongoing Cultural Revolution and from the airport, "a large limousine, with curtains drawn" whisked him quietly to the leadership compound of the Communist Party. There he met Zhou Enlai and other top Chinese leaders and conducted substantive discussions, including about the arrangements for Nixon's trip, which the never-humble president would later compare with Marco Polo's legendary journey to the "magic kingdom."[39]

Kissinger could barely contain himself upon his return to Washington and composed a remarkable secret report on his experiences for the president. The usually imperturbable national security advisor exuberantly tried to describe the indescribable. "My two-day visit to Peking resulted in the most searching, sweeping and significant discussions I have ever had in government," Kissinger began. His talks with Chinese leaders prepared the way for Nixon's visit and "may have marked a major new departure in international relations." Nothing less than the transformation of "the very framework of global relationships" was possibly in the works. Mere words seemed inadequate to convey the complete feelings of the former professor: "It is extremely difficult to capture in a memorandum the essence of this experience. Simply giving you a straightforward account of the highlights of our talks, potentially momentous as they were, would do violence to an event so shaped by the atmosphere and the ebb and flow of our encounter, or to the Chinese behavior, so dependent on nuances and style." For Kissinger, the experience went beyond politics and he had to resort to the gustatory to convey a sense of his extraordinary experience to the president. His extensive discussions with Zhou, he wrote, "had all the flavor, texture, variety and delicacy of a Chinese banquet." "Prepared from the long sweep of tradition and culture, meticulously cooked by hands of experience, and served in splendidly simple surroundings, our feast consisted of many courses, some sweet and some sour . . . it was a total experience." Kissinger summarized his tantalizing, "for your eyes only" classified report to Nixon with uncharacteristic emotion: "I am frank to say that this visit was a very moving experience. The historic aspects of the occasion: the warmth and dignity of the Chinese; the splendor of the Forbidden City, Chinese history and culture; the heroic stature of Chou En-lai; and the intensity and sweep of our talks combined to make an indelible impression on me and my colleagues." Kissinger was optimistic that care and finesse could win the day, and if so, he ended, "we will have made a revolution."[40]

On February 21, 1972, President Richard Nixon, who had made his career as one of America's arch anti-Communists, stepped off Air Force One at the Beijing Capital Airport (then not much more than a dusty airstrip, unlike today's mammoth transportation hub) and walked spiritedly down the steps to meet Premier Zhou Enlai, the veteran Communist mandarin. Nixon extended his hand in a deliberate gesture of friendship meant to displace the image of Secretary of State John Foster Dulles turning his back to snub Zhou's effort to shake hands at the 1954 Geneva Conference. It did not matter that the insulting incident may never have actually occurred; it had become part of international lore. It was plausible enough, as it perfectly symbolized America's visceral hostility toward Red China. The international media recorded Nixon's firm handshake to mark the start of a new era in global politics.[41]

Nixon's grasp of Zhou's hand on the tarmac may be the most enduring image from his week in China, but it is another handshake that was the most implicative. Within hours after Nixon's plane touched down in Beijing, Zhou Enlai summoned the president to meet Chairman Mao. Despite all the advance planning, Nixon and his team did not know whether they would actually get to meet the elderly and ill Chinese leader. The Chinese organizers also apparently did not know if or when Mao would be able to see Nixon. Mao, however, was eager to meet the American president and could not wait. He required an immediate audience with the visitor from afar. Led into Mao's library parlor lined with reading material, Nixon came face to face with the living legend. Mao took the moment to grasp Nixon's hand, held it long and firmly for "as long as a minute," and looked straight into the president's face, according to Nixon. Mao had donned a new suit, slipped on new leather shoes, and had a fresh haircut. For Mao, it was a supreme moment in his life as peasant revolutionary and then as the revered leader of the world's largest country. Mao had met Americans before in Yan'an: journalists and writers, military men stationed to work with the Communists, after

1949 a handful of leftist supporters and American expatriates in China, and even Vice-President Henry Wallace, but Nixon was different. He embodied American capitalism and was the leader of the most powerful nation on earth. For Mao, it had long been the United States, not the Soviet Union or any other country, that most fascinated him. America had been his "most respected enemy." Now Nixon was in Mao's own quarters. It was a singular moment in the long history of U.S.-China relations.[42]

Nixon did not meet Mao again on this trip, but over the next several days, American and Chinese leaders discussed a wide range of matters, though they did not arrive at any substantive specific agreements. Getting to know one another was enough for the time being. The press learned almost nothing of the discussions among the leaders but were offered gorgeous photo opportunities of the president and first lady visiting the Great Wall, the Ming tombs, the Forbidden City, and model factories and attending one of Jiang Qing's revolutionary ballets, the *Red Detachment of Women,* which ends with a unit of female Communist fighters avenging themselves by dispatching an evil landlord with a barrage of bullets. When asked what his reaction was to this drama about bloody class revenge, words failed the nonplussed Nixon and he could only smile weakly. But the overall image of the Nixon trip that endured in the American imagination was one of their national leader enjoying a fascinating wonderland full of positive possibilities. Nixon brought American public opinion about China to a new place.

Geopolitics had been the immediate policy concern that brought the two governments together. For their own separate reasons, both China and the United States saw the Soviet Union as their principal threat and regarded their incipient anti-Soviet partnership as promising. It was the political glue that brought the two sides together and bound them for the next decade. Other sensitive matters, such as China's claim to the island of Taiwan, where the Republic of China, with the backing of the United States, continued to maintain that it represented the Chinese people, and the American morass in Vietnam, were left largely unresolved and took second seats to the task of reestablishing amicable relations against a common foe. Even trade and economics played a negligible role in the discussions of the state leaders, though American businessmen quickly flocked to China, sensing a renewed business opportunity. In just one year after Nixon's trip, the United States became China's third-largest trading partner, largely because of Chinese purchases of American agricultural products. The amount was still small, however. The boom in U.S.-China business lay in the future. No one at the time could have predicted the astonishing growth of China's economy beginning in the 1980s and its importance for the American economy.[43]

The opening of China and America to one another woke dormant wells of fascination, sometimes from unexpected places. Brooke Astor, who had married the great-great-grandson of John Jacob Astor of the early China trade and was one of the wealthiest women in America, was one of the first private citizens to promote cultural exchanges between the two countries. The New York socialite and philanthropist funded the construction of the Astor Court in the Metropolitan Art Museum. This first permanent cultural exchange project between the two countries began in the late 1970s and recreated a Ming dynasty scholar's home that featured authentic construction techniques, furniture, and art work. Scores of Chinese craftsmen were flown to New York for their unique skills and tools. Astor consulted eminent scholars to ensure that her re-creation was historically faithful. Expense was no obstacle. Astor, an accomplished author, also wrote frequently about her love of China and her experiences there, including the years of her adolescence when she lived in prerevolutionary Beijing. Her father had been the commander of the marine detachment stationed in the city. She wrote of her own visit to China in 1979 that it was "one of the great experiences of my life." The elderly Astor mused that it had seemed "inevitable that I would return to China to rediscover not only the mystery and the beauty of the land, but also to rediscover myself."[44]

Other American travelers to China returned to report what they saw in glowing terms. It was as if the years of animus between the two countries had vanished overnight. The quick change amazed Fairbank, who thought the rapturous descriptions of Mao's China delivered by the steady flow of Americans bordered on the inane. Delegation after delegation of groups from civic, professional, and political groups offered breathless accounts about the mysterious country. The energetic descriptions of Chinese graciousness, adorable schoolchildren, self-reliance, and earnest civic unity amused Fairbank. He knew the power and attraction that Chinese hospitality and performance could have over American innocents. What the visitors were seeing in China was a state presentation of revolutionary idealism, a mass staging of a script akin to Jiang Qing's model operas that depicted heroic self-sacrifice and the triumph of the virtuous class underdog. After leading a delegation of Chase Manhattan Bank top executives to China in 1973, David Rockefeller announced in the *New York Times* that he had witnessed remarkably "high morale and community of purpose" in China and, moreover, "general economic and social progress" was "impressive." The symbolic representative of American capitalism concluded, incredibly, that "the social experiment in China under Chairman Mao's leadership is one of the most important and successful in human history." China scholar James C. Thomson Jr., the son of China missionary parents, saw the new China craze sparked by Nixon's visit as the latest manifestation of a "virtual China obsession" that Americans had expressed periodically from the earliest days of their nation.[45]

The new American infatuation with China amazed veteran writer Stanley Karnow, who was in the press corps for Nixon's trip and would later receive awards for his history of the Vietnam War. Karnow had been stationed in China during the Pacific War as a member of the U.S. military and was one of America's most experienced journalists on Asia. He was also near the top of Nixon's enemies list because of his critical reporting on the Vietnam War. Karnow was no Sinophile and was shocked that not only travelers of liberal inclination, such as Shirley MacLaine, or banker Rockefeller, but also seasoned journalists such as James Reston, Harrison Salisbury, and even the conservative Joseph Alsop returned with glowing reports about China's progress. Americans had magnified communism's failings in the past, Karnow observed, but now they leaped "to the other extreme of portraying the country in nothing but euphoric prose." Writing just a year after the Nixon trip, Karnow turned his pen on his fellow reporters and found that they, like the general American public, had swung from "extreme hostility to extreme affection" in the blink of an eye. The explanation, he offered, was the "peculiarly American passion about China." This wide-eyed fascination with Mao's China was the most recent version of a deep-seated sentimentality and paternalism.[46]

China's Spartan anti-consumer culture also appealed to many Americans who at the time were weary of materialism and self-indulgence. But there was something more than naïveté or sentimentality. China could mirror back a new image of America unlike that of any other country on earth. Actor Shirley MacLaine's published account of her visit to China in 1973 is especially revealing in its description of the extraordinary effect China could have on visiting Americans at this time.

MacLaine, who had been invited by the Chinese government to lead an American women's delegation, gathered a politically and racially diverse group of women from around the country to participate in a grand tour of the country. It was an opportunity of a lifetime: just a handful of Americans had had any personal experience in the new China, a country that piqued personal and political imaginations. China also had a special attraction for MacLaine. It was an ancient land of culture and mystery for her, but it was also a place that the Washington establishment had demonized for decades. Americans had been forbidden to visit the country, and forbidden fruit always has an attraction. MacLaine was a liberal feminist activist and had devoted herself to the recently failed presidential campaign of George McGovern. Though it appeared to her that progressive change was stumbling in America, perhaps it was forging ahead elsewhere. What had Mao and the Chinese been able to do in creating a new human being? China seemed to offer the chance to see both the venerable old and the possibilities of the new. "I had dreamed of China since childhood," MacLaine wrote in her 1975 memoir about her trip, *You Can Get There from Here*. She was eager to go.

MacLaine's group visited cities and rural areas, schools, factories, and farms. They met Chinese men and women who described the ways the Revolution had transformed their lives for the better and their commitment to building a new, clean society out of the degraded and poor China of the past. The moving testimonies and the everyday lives she was presented led MacLaine to conclude that "the Chinese way might be the way of the future." It was a country of wonder and dramatically positive change, in her view. She believed she saw real equality developing between men and women there. Freed from American preoccupations with sex and gender-defined roles for men and women, in China she reveled in "the ease of equality," which she said the group saw "all around us every day." She found the collectivity, the commitment to working for the common good, and the submerging of competitiveness profoundly liberating. She felt reborn through the experience of a "shared humanity." It is no wonder that MacLaine's glowing descriptions of China, similar to those others presented after their visits, disturbed Karnow, the hard-nosed journalist.[47]

Karnow saw MacLaine and other Americans who praised Mao's communism as the latest in a long tradition of American romanticizing of China, be it imperial, republican, or communist. Karnow called their glowing reports sentimental; they suspended critical facilities and glorified the Revolution. But MacLaine's account was much more than a paean to socialism. It is as much or perhaps even more a commentary on what China meant to the women in her delegation as Americans. Revolutionary China challenged basic assumptions the women had about their own personal and social identities, their political values, and life's higher meaning.

Something indescribable transformed MacLaine while she was in China, she reported. She stopped smoking two days after she arrived there and then abandoned other stubborn nervous habits. She felt comfortable, immersed among the masses, with their hard work, plain living, and selflessness. She felt liberated from the self-centeredness of individualism and American crass materialism. "I was extraordinarily happy," she declared. China was completely different from anything she had experienced before, including the Soviet Union. The Chinese were genuinely happy, it seemed to her. This was not the socialism she had encountered before. China's ongoing revolution, she believed, showed that humans could change and improve. Chinese socialism was enabling "the better side of human nature to dominate," and if ancient China could change, "then absolutely anything is possible." In the moment of that revelation, MacLaine declared, "my life changed." Curiously, it was collectivist China that led her to the realization that she was meant to be an artist and devote herself to that most individualistic of endeavors. China helped her identify her personal path to self-actualization.[48]

China was a special alterity for MacLaine and other Americans. It was not just another foreign and unfamiliar place, but a location where they were inspired to look within and reconsider the "American way" of life. Other locations in the world may have stimulated similar radical departures from the conventional, but those usually evinced more spiritual and socially detached responses. Perceived differences in gender roles also played an important role in MacLaine's admiration of People's China. Her belief that Chinese women and men had attained a high level of equality profoundly impressed her. But American male visitors to China in the 1970s also concluded that China seemed to offer a completely different social and political path that, though radically different, was also intimately and irrevocably connected to America. Communist China was the antipode to capitalist American egoism and consumerism and inspired flights of imagination about the possibilities for more meaningful personal and national futures.

Not long after she had returned to America, MacLaine found herself in a Las Vegas resort parking lot at daybreak. She had performed on stage in that most decadent of American cities and was tired and still a bit exhilarated from her work. All of sudden, she reflected again on her recent China trip. She suddenly realized that because of it, she had become a happier and more fulfilled person. She had come to see that human change was possible, not just for herself but for others and for the country and the world as well. A warm wind blew over her, she wrote, "the same wind that blew in China, blowing across oceans, valleys, and mountain ranges, all the way across the world to Nevada." This was a wind of "possibility, a wind of hope." It was a wind of the future, she thought. It belonged to no one and to everyone.[49]

In early 1975, George Herbert Walker Bush, the future president, headed the U.S. Liaison Office in Beijing, which served as a quasi-embassy after Nixon's trip and before full diplomatic relations were established in 1979. He read MacLaine's book. The patrician Bush, who had been the U.S. ambassador to the United Nations and head of the Republican National Committee, felt quite differently about China than MacLaine. China did not move him as it had the actress, but he was curious to know what she had thought about the country. Her "naivete" and her admiration of Mao put him off, he wrote in his private journal. He was especially disturbed by the attention other Americans were giving her book. He recorded that it was being widely reviewed back home and was "the main subject" of discussion among foreigners in China, even among his well-heeled American friends. MacLaine, he complained privately, was getting a great deal of publicity and had "disproportionate influence in the United States." Her message, to his displeasure, had found a receptive audience. Her narrative clearly resonated with many other Americans.[50]

The China of Mao that MacLaine had encountered and praised, however, was short lived. In 1976, the chairman died and with him, his vision of radical human transformation and continual revolution. Other Chinese leaders with very different visions of attaining Chinese greatness and destiny quickly came to the fore, most importantly Deng Xiaoping, once a trusted comrade of Mao and a veteran Communist leader. Deng did not share Mao's vision of limitless human transformation based on self-sacrifice and moral exhortation. By the time Mao died, China was exhausted from the leader's endless political campaigns and convulsive upheavals and was ready to follow the route of economic development based on material incentives, profit making, and privatization that Deng espoused. His would be a revolution against Mao's revolution. The model schools and rural communes became things of the past, as did the myth of a revolutionary China that would help America become something greater and better. Deng and his China would see the possibilities of American business and investment as the way to attain prosperity and dreams of greatness. It was not coincidental that his new vision for China became established policy at the same time that the United States and China formally and finally established full diplomatic relations with each other. Nineteen seventy-nine marked the beginning of a new China and of a new stage in U.S.-China relations.

A small number of Chinese semi-official delegations visited the United States in the 1970s after the Nixon breakthrough. Their published accounts reveal palpable curiosity about the country that had long been demonized in their own. The noise, hustle and bustle, and material abundance of American cities overwhelmed them. They noted the bewildering diversity of American everyday life and both the seamy and exhilarating sides of America's cultural cornucopia. None of their published accounts reveal an infatuation like that of many American accounts of China in the 1970s or anything approaching an interest in emulating the American way of life. By the 1980s, however, as greater numbers of Chinese visited America or had more access to unfiltered information as a result of Deng Xiaoping's open policy, more ordinary Chinese began to develop a richer picture of American life, one that was better informed and more thoughtful than accounts that emphasized American "capitalist decadence." Criticisms were still common about American racism, violence, and class differences but powerful challenges to the negative, one-sided accounts of the past began to appear. Chinese observers expressed frank admiration of the American work ethic, the energy of American everyday life, and the spirit and practice of American democracy. One bold poster on the Democracy Wall, the location of a short-lived flowering of open expression in Beijing in 1979, declared, "The United States Is a Paradise of Democracy." "The United States is more democratic than we are," wrote the author. America had much more than mere "things" to offer China—it had a vitality and value transcending the material that China needed if it was to rise to its future greatness. By the early 1980s, especially for growing numbers of young Chinese, an idealized America had become a nation that was essential for their personal and national futures, if not necessarily an attractive alternative to their own.[51]

In 1984, another Hollywood personality visited China, but as president of the United States. It was already a very different place than what MacLaine had seen a decade before. For Ronald Reagan, China was not a possible alternative reality, but it was a country with which his America was intimately, uniquely bound in geopolitical ways. He spoke of a new convergence of interests, both security and economic, and conjured a mental visualization of this grand strategic binary. China and America were "two great and huge

nations on opposite sides of the globe," he declared. "We are both countries of great vitality and strength," the president declared to students at
Shanghai's Fudan University. "You are the most populous country on Earth;
we are the most technologically developed. Each of us holds a special weight
in our respective sides of the world." And in an eloquent expression, Reagan
declared that between China and America "there exists a kind of equipoise."
The relationship "speaks of a fine and special balance." It was an exquisite
way of describing what he saw as the vital interconnectedness of the two
countries that went beyond the usual diplomatic claptrap. It was not an original vision by any means—it was in fact a restating of visions that harkened
back to the very beginnings of the "city on the hill," his oft-repeated admiring
reference to America. And Reagan, despite the pronounced anti-communism
and hostility toward Beijing he had expressed before he entered office, let it
be known that as president, he fully appreciated the growing importance
of China to America. During his China visit, Reagan broadcast back to the
United States an address in which he emphasized this view and the great
areas of common interest the two shared in economics and security. He emphasized that many predicted that the "21st century will be the century of
the Pacific." His journey to China, he was certain, would help advance the
historic relationship between the two nations and would help forge a
"stronger U.S.-China relationship."[52]

Beyond economics and geopolitics, political leaders such as Nixon and
even Reagan helped form a powerful psychological connection between everyday Chinese and Americans. In addition to the focus on policy and power,
Americans developed an attitude toward China that went beyond identification of formal interests, as important as they were. There was something
even grander and more epic in the American connection with China. The
moral sociologist and China-watcher Richard Madsen called this American
penchant a "new sentimental mythologizing." He observed that for the
United States, China became a canvas upon which Americans painted a re-
vitalized American Dream of a nation that was capable of doing something
positive, exhibiting national goodwill, and realizing creative opportunities.
The China opening had helped lift a dejected America out of the Vietnam
miasma and discard the feeling that it was a nation that could only make
war and destroy. Instead, the China opening seemed to point to new, exciting possibilities ahead and a sense that China and America had a special
affinity for one another. Each country appeared destined to help the other
obtain a brighter future. The Cold Warrior and cynical politician Nixon had

contributed to this optimistic projection. His description of his frequent interactions with China, which continued well beyond his presidency, went beyond the geopolitical and encouraged romanticism about the country. He noted that China had a special effect on other Americans. "China," he pointed out in the aftermath of the bloody Tian'anmen tragedy in 1989, "had a limitless capacity to fascinate." He was speaking about others whose hopes for a liberalized China had been dashed by the military suppression in Beijing, but he could also have been speaking for an array of other Americans, from W. E. B. Du Bois to Shirley MacLaine to himself.[53]

7

Old/New Visions

The virtuous American
And the Chinese make manifest
Their destinies in time.
All patriots were brothers once:
Let us drink to the time when they
Shall be brothers again. *Gam bei!*

Premier Zhou Enlai toasting President Richard Nixon in the opera *Nixon in China*

John Adams's *Nixon in China* is celebrated as among the greatest American operas. Aside from its considerable artistic merit and its imaginative staging of Nixon's historic visit to China, the completion of the opera itself came at a critical political moment in U.S.-China relations. In the mid-1980s, when Adams was completing his work, U.S.-China relations were unsettled. As critical as the relationship appeared to be for existing international relations, the direction of their future contact was uncertain. This ambiguity is reflected in Adams's artistic conceptualization and interpretation. The opera leaves the audience wondering what Nixon's journey might ultimately mean and highlights the persistent question of what the intertwined destinies of the two countries will be.

The concluding moment of Adams's epic is given to the Zhou Enlai character, the most thoughtful and paradoxical personage in an assemblage that includes Nixon, Pat Nixon, Henry Kissinger, and Mao Zedong. Adams elevates the interactions between these well-known personalities to the level of a transhistoric moment based on the dramatic reconnection of two peoples and two states that Nixon's visit to Beijing in 1972 initiated. It is the cerebral Zhou to whom Adams and the librettist Alice Goodman give the last word, not the president who is the ostensible central character of the opera. In the closing moments of the opera, Zhou struggles with grand, nagging existential questions: What can be controlled or determined? Are we captured by our outsized ambitions, our hubris? Are we giants in command of our destiny or only minor actors in an inexorable current of history beyond human control? Zhou also grapples with an uncertainty that has occupied the center of America's relationship with China since its earliest days: What do America and China ultimately mean to one another?[1]

In the concluding scene of the opera, a sleepless Zhou reflects alone in the stillness of the night on the frenetic activities of the past few days of Nixon's visit and wonders what was actually done and what might be done further. "How much of what we did was good?" he asks himself, a question not limited to the Nixon's visit but to something much greater, to human history itself. His soliloquy seemingly ends with an existential lament. "Everything seems to move beyond our remedy," Zhou sighs, "At this hour nothing can be done." But then he collects himself, draws from within, and quietly calls out, "To work! Outside this room the chill of grace lies heavy on the morning grass." The opera ends.[2]

A decade after the Nixon visit in the mid-1980s, anti-Soviet concerns continued to anchor the U.S.-China bilateral relationship. Some called it an alliance against Moscow. During his own 1984 visit to China, President Ronald Reagan emphasized the common interest the two states shared in opposing Moscow. Commercial matters, independent of security concerns, had only begun to occupy an important position in the relationship, but it was unclear just how significant the economic relationship could be. An unholy alliance against a shared enemy that was clearly in serious internal and international trouble and an awkward economic relationship between the world's leading capitalist country and socialist China left many wondering where Beijing and Washington were headed. Would the relationship fall apart with the collapse of the Soviet Union? Could the United States and China build new foundations upon which to forge a stable, even amicable, relationship? The deep rot from the years of mutual recriminations after 1949 could still easily fell any timber.

Today, in the twenty-first century, few question the critical importance of the relationship for the two countries and the centrality of economics within it. The China-America connection, it is now widely accepted, is likely to determine each country's future. The idea is now so apparent that the intimate link is often assumed to have been inevitable. But it was not always so. If anything, uncertainty about China's economic importance to America was the accepted wisdom well into the twenty-first century. China's economic rise and its perceived critical importance to America were certainly not inexorable, let alone inevitable. A review of the relatively short history of the U.S.-China business relationship reveals that the assumption of an assured boom is a recent idea that was driven by dreams as much as ledger calculations. Business ventures require careful calibration, but they also involve a leap in faith about the future and an assumption of risk. And there was, and continues to be, considerable risk in the ongoing story of America's business ties with China.

In July 1971, the *New York Times* bluntly reported that Nixon's announcement about his China trip "virtually had no effect on the stock market," the given reason being that few American businessmen saw any significant economic opportunity in the enormous shift in foreign policy. Per capita income in China was then about a paltry $100 annually, hardly an amount that inspired visions of a boundless market for American goods. China's economy was highly centralized and rigidly planned. There was no private ownership of productive property. Individual entrepreneurial activity was actively banned and suppressed with deadly purpose. Eighty percent of the population was rural and poor. If anything, the political shift toward the China mainland appeared to threaten established U.S. business with a relatively prosperous Taiwan, where American companies had significant and profitable ties. The Shanghai Communiqué, a joint statement of the United States and China that was issued at the end of Nixon's 1972 trip, devoted just two brief sentences to economic matters.[3]

In 1972, U.S.-China bilateral trade in goods totaled less than $96 million dollars. A headline in the *Wall Street Journal* cackled "Illusory Market: Trade with China, Long a Dream of Americans, Remains Only a Mirage; Peking Policy Limits Imports; China's Potential Exports Unlikely to Spur Demand; Want to Buy Any Pig Bristle?" Three years later, even as tourism to China began to increase, American business was still not especially sanguine about economic prospects in China. Trade had not developed in any significant way and analysts were predicting an actual shortfall in business activity for the year. China, with a trade deficit and an inconsequential consumer market, held little promise for American marketers. The *New York*

Times declared that "No Great Leap Forward" in Sino-American business relations was in store.[4]

In the late 1970s, as Deng Xiaoping systematically dismantled Mao's "politics in command" approach to the economy and replaced it with a bottom line of material incentives and tangible results, American business began to take note of the possibilities for profit. As in the days of old, Americans began to speak carefully of the "China market" and identify themselves with their nineteenth-century Yankee trader predecessors who dreamt of an inexhaustible outlet for American goods in China's vast, stirring population. *The Economist* put China's attraction simply in an article title that said it all: "China: Over 900m Customers." Deng's new approach, which was revolutionary in its own way as it reversed Mao's autarchy and collectivism, would attain prosperity through several key measures: returning farmland to rural families, who could use it largely as they saw fit; inviting foreign investors to take advantage of plentiful Chinese labor; purchasing technology and manufacturing equipment from abroad; privatizing state-owned enterprises; and establishing special economic zones that were exempt from many labor, business, investment, and tax codes and levies as a way of attracting foreign companies. Suddenly China appeared to be moving toward a market-driven economy. Though it was not clear how far Deng would go, let alone how permanent the changes would be, capital from eager overseas Chinese in Hong Kong, Taiwan, and Southeast Asia soon began to flow into China. Asian manufacturers saw the chance to exploit China's vast labor force to produce goods for foreign consumers. American companies hoped to sell to China or to extract raw materials; hotel, oil, agriculture and medical, and aircraft companies were among the earliest to venture to China. "China is emerging as American industry's most promising new frontier," declared the *New York Times* when diplomatic relations were normalized in 1979, invoking the eternal allure of the "frontier," America's traditional location for adventure and profit. A symbol of this new relationship was the return to China's markets of that most all-American of products, Coca-Cola, which had established a niche for itself in prerevolutionary China. Other American consumer products, from cosmetics to cigarettes, followed. When Deng visited the United States in January 1979, he held highly publicized meetings with the CEOs of Ford, Boeing, Coca-Cola, and Exxon.[5]

Yet as late as Ronald Reagan's presidency in the mid-1980s, important sectors of American business remained skeptical, even hostile, to the idea that the United States could or even should seek closer economic ties with

China for any reason or that such ties might be of benefit to American business. In 1984, on the eve of Reagan's trip to China, the *Wall Street Journal* published a scathing article criticizing Washington's eager pursuit of commerce with China. Advantage had all gone one way, the business paper claimed, with the United States sending weapons, advanced technology, and manufacturing know-how to China but receiving little in return other than "panda bears." Militarily weak China was of little strategic help against the Russians, the paper said, and the United States had much more important ties to cultivate with Taiwan, South Korea, and Japan, America's traditional allies in Cold War Asia. The *Wall Street Journal* conceded that a case might be made on humanitarian grounds for American economic investment in China but not on the basis of self-interested commercial opportunity, because China's condition was simply one of "pitiful economic development."[6]

Then, in June 1989, the horrifying suppression of young dissenters in Beijing's Tian'anmen Square confirmed the worst suspicions of Americans who thought Chinese communism could never change. Brutal autocracy would smash any challenge, political or economic, and in the minds of many Americans, the two dimensions were intimately connected. Economic liberalization required or would eventually produce political liberalization, which in turn was necessary for a genuine market-driven economy. Deng's image in America instantly changed from the champion of reform to the butcher of innocent students. The American pursuit of Chinese business stalled.

In the fall of 1990, more than a year after the Tian'anmen crackdown, the *Wall Street Journal* continued to be bearish about China. The business climate in China remained dismal, in its view, and the prospects for a more "capitalist" China appeared as distant as ever. American business worried about the hard-line political climate in the country, bureaucratic inefficiency, problematic quality control, high costs, and meager profitability. "The balloon is out of the China bubble," the paper quoted a China business specialist as saying. The gloomy picture sent American businesses elsewhere in Asia or to Eastern Europe for opportunities. American business had understood that investing and doing business in China required a long-term vision, but now, the paper reported, even the long term seemed almost impossibly distant. "There used to be a missionary aspect to it," meaning doing the brave work of business in China, an American businessman familiar with China declared, "with the board of directors having a vision of an enormous consumer market—you know, two billion armpits in need of deodorant." But Tian'anmen had dashed that pretty picture. The *New York*

Times prominently quoted a European diplomat's statement that "no one cares about China anymore." Many Americans agreed, and with the collapse of the Soviet Union in December 1991, China seemed to diminish in importance even further. A common enemy no longer provided the basis for a U.S.-China alliance.[7]

The attitude of others in American business, however, was radically different. Dreams encouraged them to take on significant risk. American manufacturers, not marketers, began to see China's potential as a generator of goods for Americans and began to pour huge investments into China. In 1990, the footwear giant Nike, an early pioneer of manufacturing in China, ran five factories in south China that made 650,000 pairs of shoes a month. (In 2014, Nike has more than 240,000 workers at almost 200 factories in China.) Exports largely from Nike and other American companies back to the United States began to soar, up to more than $12 billion a year and rising quickly. Despite the American public's concern about China's human rights record, the status of Tibet, environmental degradation, worker rights, and other highly sensitive issues, the Chinese economy grew astronomically in the 1990s, stimulated to a great degree by trade with the United States and foreign investment into China. No other country in history had ever grown so rapidly over such a sustained length of time. In 2000, China's total foreign trade reached $475 billion. From 1985 to 2010, the value of U.S.-China bilateral trade in goods soared from $7 billion to $365 billion, making China America's most important trading partner. China's huge domestic market continued to attract many American businessmen, but so too did an immense work force and low production costs, prompting a torrent of outsourcing to China. U.S.-based manufacturers competed with products made in China costing 50 percent less than their goods. "The China price" became the "three scariest words in U.S. industry," declared *Bloomberg Businessweek,* but it was also the lure that brought American manufacturers to China and helped make it the workshop of the world. China attracted staggering amounts of foreign investment, more than any other developing country in the world. In 1993, approved foreign investment in China, which had amounted to about $20 billion annually in the late 1970s, climbed to more than $110 billion, almost twice that of the year before. For most of the 1990s, China was second only to the United States in the world in receiving direct foreign investment. As to the future of China as a market, the horizon for American companies appears boundless. Apple's CEO Tim Cook announced in 2012 that China will one day become the largest market for Apple Inc., one of the world's most valuable companies. With China, he said, "the sky's the limit." Apple manufactures almost all of its hundreds of millions of iPhones and iPads in China and now sells a rapidly increasing amount of those products inside China. Four large Apple stores already operate in Beijing alone. Greater China sales of these products is already approaching 50 percent of the value of those sold in all of the Americas.[8]

What made all this possible? Explanations abound: China's immense, disciplined but hungering work force was ready for capitalist exploitation. China's smart central planners learned from the experiences of the neighboring Economic Tigers in Asia, such as Japan, South Korea, Taiwan, and Singapore, and their successful export-oriented growth strategies. China could grow using foreign markets as they did. The years of enforced austerity and stifled entrepreneurial ambition had never eliminated the dream (or Mao's nightmare) of producing for the market and profit making. Pent-up traditional Chinese business savvy that was dormant under Mao simply sprang back to life once the political strictures were lifted.

All these internal factors are undeniably relevant in explanations for the rise of China as an economic powerhouse, but there is an additional critical external explanation to consider. The support of many people in American business and in government was an essential element in China's meteoric rise in the late twentieth and early twenty-first centuries. Through Republican and Democratic administrations alike, despite raging partisanship in Congress over China policy, popular outrage and criticism against China on issues ranging from human rights to environmental degradation, and several sensational confrontations, the United States forged an approach to China that on the whole favored and supported its rapid economic growth. The rise of China as a global economic power was not Washington's doing, but America played a pivotal, even decisive, role in making it possible. And more than profit calculations underlay this attitude: There was a strong element of faith that went beyond the ledger books. It required taking risks, making choices, and envisioning immense future possibilities.

Before he was elected president, Ronald Reagan vociferously condemned communism in China and provocatively (from China's viewpoint) endorsed efforts to strengthen ties with Taiwan, America's stalwart ally. He sounded like Richard Nixon in the 1950s. A few years later, in the mid-1980s, however, President Reagan praised developments in China and even referred to it publicly as a "so-called Communist country." He may have been unaware that right-wing Republicans in the 1940s and 1950s had labeled

Americans who called Mao and his comrades "so-called communists" as traitors and dupes. Reagan as president had come to accept the proposition that China was on a trajectory to become increasingly like America. He and other leading officials of his administration saw huge promise in the changes in China and felt that China could offer America incomparable opportunities, economic as well as political. The Reagan years, in the view of veteran journalist and China-watcher James Mann, were "golden years" and a "halcyon era" in U.S.-China relations, during which Reagan and other leading officials in his administration were enamored by the prospects of the China connection. They had, Mann observes, using a description that runs throughout the long history of the relationship, a "romantic view" of China.[9]

George Herbert Walker Bush, after Richard Nixon, was the president with the most foreign policy experience of any modern president. As the former head of the U.S. Liaison Office in Beijing in the 1970s before the normalization of relations, he believed he had a special personal understanding of the country because of the years he had lived there. In the Oval Office, Bush took a commanding role in directing China policy, including in the tense aftermath of the suppression of protestors in Beijing's Tian'anmen Square in 1989. Bush resisted strong pressures from the public and from members of both parties in Congress to go far beyond verbal condemnations and enact harsh sanctions against China's government to punish its brutality and assist antigovernment activists. Bush opted to keep the United States quietly engaged with China, especially in the economic realm. He took his strongest stand in keeping China eligible for most-favored-nation trading status, which would allow the business relationship to continue to grow, and stubbornly resisted annual efforts to link the renewal of that status to improvements in China's human rights record. To widespread and bipartisan dismay, Bush twice vetoed bills from Congress that aimed to tie China's most-favored-nation status to its human rights record. Democrats accused him of "kowtowing" to China. Here was a Republican president who was "soft" on communism, it was said.

By the time he left office, Bush had not only succeeded in maintaining a policy of engagement with China but had even increased cooperation, especially in the area of commercial relations. Though the Soviet Union was gone, and with it the central rationale for U.S.-China cooperation since Nixon's visit in 1972, Washington increasingly saw China as having direct importance to American commercial well-being. The Bush and Clinton administrations successfully shifted the anchor of America's relationship with China from national security to economics. It would become the locus of the new "convergence of interests" between America and China, according to Wang Jisi, one of the leading specialists on U.S.-China relations in China.[10]

But in the first two years of Clinton's presidency, the China policy of the United States was still in transition and not at all predictable. Instead, it was marked by acrimony and conflict with Beijing. Candidate Clinton had actually campaigned against Bush's engagement policy and attacked the incumbent for abandoning the moral core of America's responsibility to global human rights. President Clinton endorsed the view that renewal of most-favored-nation status should be conditional on changes in the Chinese government's behavior. Beijing refused to change, let alone cooperate with Washington, and countered with harsh accusations about the meddling of a superpower in the country's internal affairs. At the same time, Beijing found powerful and sympathetic allies in American big business to pressure the White House to drop its crusade. China's domestic economy boomed in the Clinton years, posting startling 13–14 percent annual gains in gross national product. The International Monetary Fund declared that China had become the third-largest economy in the world. In mid-1993, the Clinton administration adopted the Bush approach of making economic considerations primary, and bilateral commercial ties boomed. Several serious military and political clashes between the two states barely ruffled business activities. At the end of his administration, President Clinton led Congress to grant China permanent most-favored-nation status in American trade policies and supported Beijing's effort to join the World Trade Organization (WTO), a move that was essential to China's continued commercial revolution. U.S.-China bilateral trade reached $116 billion by the time Clinton left office in 2000, up from just $1 billion in 1978. (In 2014, bilateral trade approaches $500 billion and mutual investment totals over $80 billion.) In contrast to his early presidency, at the end of his terms Clinton was widely seen as China's great friend in America, or as even the "Manchurian Candidate" as his detractor, *The National Review*, racially caricatured him on its March 1997 cover.[11]

In 2001, the WTO accepted China as a member, an event described by Michael H. Armacost, former U.S. ambassador to Japan, as a "landmark event" in China's economic development and for international trade more broadly. Bill Clinton hailed it as a "once in a generation" achievement. After it achieved WTO status, China significantly cut a wide variety of tariffs and barriers to imports and opened broad and important sectors of its domestic economy, including telecommunications, banking, insurance, and other financial services, to foreign investment and involvement. Beijing promised to abide by international rules protecting foreign intellectual property. In turn, China's growing number of investors and traders gained increased access to markets and commercial opportunities in the United States and around the world. It was a major step in China's integration into the global market economy and strengthened China immeasurably, despite some vocal predictions to the contrary.[12]

Similar to Clinton in his first year in the presidency, George W. Bush initially adopted a get-tough policy against China. Bush saw China not as a "strategic partner," the label Clinton used to characterize the relationship, but as a "strategic competitor" and even a potential danger to the United States. Under the influence of crusading neoconservatives among his close advisors, Bush declared provocatively that the United States would do "whatever it takes" to defend Taiwan against the mainland. It appeared that he was breaking even with his father's strategic engagement approach toward China. But the events of 9/11, the declared war on terror, other security concerns, and the seemingly inexorable economic growth of China turned Bush around and his attitude shifted dramatically. The warm relationship he cultivated with Beijing made him a *lao pengyou,* an old friend of China. He traveled there several times during his presidency in high-profile visits that emphasized an American commitment to nurturing a positive relationship with Beijing. Washington dropped China from the list of worst human rights violators, and, in 2008, Bush and his wife attended the opening ceremony of the Beijing Olympics, the most prominent head of state to do so. In contrast to the direction of China policy in the early days of his administration, the construction of stable and constructive relations with China became the most positive foreign policy achievement of the George W. Bush administration. Bringing China into the web of established international finance, business, and commerce further entrenched China in accepted norms of behavior, it was claimed. The Bush administration was the turning point in confirming the essential importance of the China relationship to the United States.[13]

Barack Obama, like his predecessors and other presidential aspirants, dwelled on the negatives of China during the campaign for the presidency. Criticizing Beijing on its human rights record, its violations of intellectual property rights law, its unfair trade practices, and its currency manipulation had become standard fare for all national-level political campaigns. But once in office, Obama largely dropped the China-threat rhetoric and resumed the effort to forge an engaged relationship with the PRC, as the previous seven presidents had done. What played well in campaign politics did not play well in the Oval Office with its responsibilities of wielding actual power. President Obama repeatedly expressed his view that the two countries were becoming more and more dependent on one another, especially economically, and he actively sought to shape the relationship into one that could be dispassionately managed both administratively and diplomatically. Cold War "zero-sum game thinking" and rivalry would not dictate the future, in his view, as the two states would maturely work out the inevitable differences that were bound to develop between them. China and the United States would seek to be collaborators, not adversaries. Obama's positive approach encouraged Chinese leader Xi Jinping to express his own hope that China and the United States would construct a "new great power relationship" and avoid the type of contention that had scarred previous epochs, when an established power and a rising one had confronted each other and clashed.

When viewed in the relatively short term, Washington's China policy over the last quarter-century appears extraordinarily volatile, uncertain, emotionally fraught, contentious, and divided along highly ideological and partisan lines. No other foreign policy challenge has been as unsettled and controversial for the American public. When one takes two steps back and views the same period with a longer historical sensibility, however, a far different picture emerges. Over the last thirty years, a form of strategic vision that promotes U.S.-China relations has emerged as the strong position of most well-informed China-watchers and political and business elites, and that position has become one of the central components in the foreign policy of the United States. This vision of positive engagement with China did not emerge from any deliberate planning process but appears to have simply evolved over time through a succession of presidential administrations. China and the United States, the conventional wisdom now holds, are locked together in a long-term relationship that, if handled sensitively and carefully, will not only bring benefits to both sides but will also serve global stability and prosperity. Human rights concerns, continuing authoritarian rule, and accusations of the abuse of ethnic nationalities certainly continue to rankle the American public, but U.S. policy devotes little attention to such matters now. Rather, cooperation, engagement, even partnership are the words used to describe the U.S.-China connection, the *zhong-mei lianxi,* that has over time become steadily closer, more predictable, and more mutually advantageous.[14]

High-profile conflicts have certainly punctuated the history of the last thirty years. They have been mostly political/military and moral in nature: the U.S. bombing of the Chinese embassy in Belgrade in 1999 that killed three Chinese reporters; the clash of military aircraft over the southern China coast in 2001; continuing tensions from Chinese military threats against Taiwan and from disputes about sovereignty over islands in the South China seas; breaches of national cybersecurity; the highly sensitive issue of Tibet; violations of human rights; and mistreatment of democracy activists. The economic relationship, in contrast, has been comparatively stable, despite serious disputes over copyright infringement and currency valuation. The economic dreams of both sides clearly are propelling the relationship in a way that seeks to avert confrontation that would lead to financial catastrophe. Former U.S. ambassador to China and Republican presidential contender Jon Huntsman Jr. articulated this succinctly in 2013 when he wrote, drawing on the vocabulary of the nuclear arms race, "For better and for worse, America and China are bound together in a form of mutually assured economic destruction." Saying the same thing but in a more positive way, Secretary of State Hillary Clinton declared during a 2012 visit to Beijing that she and President Barack Obama had repeatedly said that "the United States believes that a thriving China is good for America, and a thriving America is good for China." In an expansive, metahistorical way, Clinton also presented a hopeful vision of the future. At a global town hall meeting just before leaving her post, she emphasized that China and the United States must find a way to forge interdependence and avoid a zero-sum geopolitical game. "Historically, a rising power and a predominant power have had clashes, whether they were economic or military. Neither of us wants to see that happen." "The United States and China," she famously offered, "will together defy history."[15]

Some serious American observers of the relationship challenge such thinking as based on myth, fiction, fantasy, or self-delusion. Americans, some of these critics say, cyclically romanticize China and invoke the ability of America to shape another people's fate, to bring progress and benevolence to others. No other nation historically seems to inspire similar fantasies, either about itself or about America's fate. Romance with China, it is said, will be followed by disenchantment and animus, reactions to an inevitable outrage or provocation. It is self-deception to think that China can ever be a true partner with America. Critics point to China's centralized Communist system, the systematic suppression of human rights and democratic processes, the habitual violation of norms governing international behavior, and China's historical drive to establish regional hegemony. They claim to have seen no appreciable change in basic attitude. The idea that economic reform will inevitably lead to a mellowing of Communist authoritarianism or that time will erode Chinese territorial ambitions prevents leaders, it is said, from recognizing the existential danger of the China threat. These same critics urge the United States to confront China now from a position of strength rather than in the future, when China will be able to challenge American supremacy.[16]

Parallel to the embrace of economic China by business and political leaders was the return of widespread alarm over its rise. The American popular imagination became preoccupied with the China threat. Both profit and paranoia animated relations. For many Americans, Deng Xiaoping's very success appeared to create a China that was more threatening than Mao's revolutionary, but isolated and poor, country. One would have thought that China's embrace of profit making, of entrepreneurialism and private ownership, of economic integration with the capitalist West would have been universally welcomed, but Deng's success in what many in the West saw as an effort to replace socialism with capitalism actually provoked a more frightening image of a Chinese colossus. Could Chinese merchants really be more successful in doing business than Yankee traders? Could hardworking Chinese factory workers under communism outproduce hardworking Americans under capitalism?

Perhaps not intentionally, much of the alarmist literature of the late twentieth century resembled the yellow peril literature of the late nineteenth century. In 1997, journalists Richard Bernstein and Ross H. Munro published one of the first nonfiction books to predict unmitigated disaster with China's post-Mao rise. *The Coming Conflict with China* was soon joined by a river of writing forecasting a dire, horrible future for America at China's hands. The titles told it all: *Red Dragon Rising: Communist China's Military Threat to the United* States (1999); *The China Threat: How the People's Republic Targets America* (2000); *Hegemon: China's Plan to Dominate Asia and the World* (2002); *China: The Gathering Threat* (2005); *America's Coming War with China* (2006); *Death By China* (2005); *Showdown: Why China Wants War with the United States* (2006); *The Coming China Wars: Where*

They Will Be Fought and How They Can Be Won (2007); and *In The Jaws of the Dragon: America's Fate in the Coming Era of Chinese Hegemony* (2008). Snarling dragons typically emblazon the dust jackets of these books, which are generally long on misinformation and short on facts and reason. Their success in the marketplace has less to do with the complex reality of China's economic and social transformation than with pandering to deep-seated fears rooted in historical ignorance and racial stereotypes. They are more revealing about Americans' imagination about their own country, anxieties about maintaining unchallenged power, and desire for complete, assured security than they are about real dangers to the nation. Exaggerated, ill-informed speechmaking echoed the same sentiment in Congress: A malevolent China threatened America and the world. In 1999, the U.S. House of Representatives released what is popularly known as the Cox Report, which alleged that the top leadership in China had for years directed a systematic effort to steal secret advanced nuclear weapons research from and harbored hostile intentions toward the United States. The Cox Committee urged the United States to take aggressive steps against China to prevent it from developing into a military power. Though the allegations were refuted by informed security specialists and no alleged thefts were ever confirmed, the government report strengthened popular fears about China. Magazine covers of respected American periodicals reflected this fear, often featuring a menacing Chinese eye (a "racial eye") in their illustrations. "How We Would Fight China," an article in the June 2005 issue of *The Atlantic* was characteristic. The cover illustration highlights the vengeful glare of a Chinese military sailor. The China in the view of this literature is irrevocably hostile to the West, America in particular; self-aggrandizing and territorially aggressive; voracious in its appetite for raw materials, markets, and global power; and amoral, uninterested in and incapable of adhering to civilized, established international norms. The threat arises both from China's Communist system and from its national character, and America is vulnerable.[17]

John Updike, one of America's most celebrated writers, is an unlikely contributor to this peril literature, but his *Toward the End of Time* (1997) is emblematic of the cultural fear the rise of China has triggered in America. China served as a backdrop to several of Updike's earlier works, most importantly his well-known *Rabbit, Run* (1960) which is about the confines of American middle-class life but begins with the protagonist hearing about Chinese soldiers fighting in Tibet and the escape of the Dalai Lama. Later, an important scene in the novel occurs in a suburban Chinese restaurant. In

The Coup (1978), Updike's novel on Africa written after he traveled there as a Fulbright lecturer, Chinese from the mainland appear as tourists, described by the novel's narrator as "a small closed flock of official visitors, in their blue-gray many-pocketed pajamas, their mass-produced wire-frame spectacles (no doubt of identical prescription) resting on the fat of their cheeks as they smilingly squinted up from their guidebooks." *Toward the End of Time* is a futuristic imagining of a dystopic America in 2020. The novel recounts the tortured life of a couple in an America after a four-month-long nuclear war between China and America has killed millions and devastated the country. The federal government has collapsed, Federal Express has assumed many of the responsibilities of civil administration, the country has Balkanized, and savagery stalks the land. "Metallobio" mutant life forms have appeared in the permanently contaminated atmosphere. The reader never learns the causes of the war or the details of its conduct; it serves only as the context for the principal character's lamentations about his existence and approaching demise. But the consequences of the "Sino-American Conflict," as Updike calls it, are ever present in the story of the war, at one point understood by its narrator as perhaps the just reward for America's sins against Native Americans. The war might very well have been, the narrator contemplates, "revenge administered by the Mongolian superpower of that Asian continent from which the North American aborigines had crossed the Bering land-bridge." Updike's georacial nightmare is a high-brow expression of the China threat from one of America's leading writers.[18]

More recently, acclaimed author Chang-Rae Lee, a professor of writing at Princeton University, published his vision of a dystopic and extensively Sinicized America. Set in a distant future, *On Such a Full Sea* describes a horribly divided, violent, and purposeless society that is simultaneously familiar and grotesquely strange. Characters wearing "hoodies" are terrorized by the "C-illness" and constantly use their electronic tablets, but their food (dumplings, onion cakes, "Shanxi-style smoked pork belly," and the like) and funeral customs are putatively Chinese. That is because many Americans descend from abroad. "Our people arrived from New China, truly ancient times," including the central character, Fan, a diminutive young woman who sets out from B-more (previously known as Baltimore) on a frightful journey to recover lost love. There are no Anglos, African Americans, and Latinos in America's cities, their remnants having merged into the multitude of descendants of the Chinese migrants, who were originally brought in by "fedcrated companies" for their labor. These Chinese eagerly came to America to escape their own polluted nation with its overextracted resources. Unlike Updike's futurology, however, Lee's work deliberately refuses to pander to latent yellow peril fears; instead, his novel reflects contemporary American unease about China. As the book's jacket describes, Lee's novel has "enormous contemporary relevance and insight into American anxieties about Chinese power and influence, and our own national prospects and legacies."[19]

China-mongering, however, is popular among authors who appeal to a broader mass audience. Tom Clancy, billed by his publisher as "the world's favorite international thriller author," envisioned future catastrophic wars between China in three of his products. In the book/video game *SSN* (1996), Clancy has China and the United States navies engaging in all-out combat in the South China Seas. In *The Bear and the Dragon* (2000), the United States comes to the aid of a besieged Russia whose Siberian territory has been invaded by oil-thirsty Chinese. American president Jack Ryan labels China's leaders "Klingons," the swarthy, villainous race of warlike aliens featured in the television series *Star Trek,* while Chinese foot soldiers are smeared with a common nineteenth-century epithet; they are simply dismissed as "Joe Chinaman." And in *Threat Vector* (2012), the very future of the world is at stake as the United States thwarts China's grab for global domination using cyberwarfare. All were best sellers.

These contrasting and competing visions of hope and fear, of profit and paranoia, of respect and revulsion have been not so much cyclical as simultaneous, parallel expressions of a unique American preoccupation with China. These attitudes have persisted throughout the long stretch of American history and emanate from an assumption that China, as friend or enemy, has special, transcendent importance to the continued flourishing of America. Rarely have Americans been dispassionate about China. It is the place of America's future or its horrifying nightmare. Europeans have commented on what they see as this peculiar obsessive American attitude toward China.[20]

An immense body of recent nonfiction writing has emerged that emphasizes the common, albeit uncomfortable, place that China and America occupy in the realm of national dreams and aspirations. In these writings by a variety of respected writers and China-watchers, the futures of the two are presented as deeply entwined and mutually constitutive. A good number of the titles of these works themselves suggest that the two powerhouses share linked fates, though not necessarily wholly positive ones. China scholars such as Richard Madsen (*China and the American Dream: A Moral Inquiry*; 1995), David M. Lampton (*Same Bed, Different Dreams: Managing U.S.-China Relations*; 2002), Warren I. Cohen (*The Asian American Century*; 2002), and Neville Mars and Adrian Hornsby (*The Chinese Dream*; 2010) consider the social, cultural, and ideological interconnections of the two countries as they enter an uncertain future together. Journalists Joe Studwell (*The China Dream: The Quest for the Last Great Untapped Market on Earth*; 2003), Helen H. Wang and Lord Wei (*The Chinese Dream*; 2010), and Anand Giridharadas (*Chinese Dreams*; 2011) seek to understand the hopes and fears of a Chinese people in the midst of social transformation and their implications for Americans. Writers Gerald Lemos (*The End of the Chinese Dream*; 2012) and James Fallow ("What Is the Chinese Dream?"; 2012) try to explain to Americans what the Chinese people want. Chinese dreams, many of these authors argue, are profoundly connected to American dreams. Likewise, American dreams figure prominently in those of the Chinese. Chinese and American dreams, whether shared or at odds with one another, are helping shape the hopes and aspirations of each country.[21]

American musings about American and Chinese dreams may have actually inspired China's top leader to identify and loudly declare a unique Chinese Dream that should serve as national inspiration. In late 2012, just two weeks after he was selected to head the Chinese Communist Party, Xi Jinping spoke at China's mammoth National Museum along the side of Beijing's Tian'anmen Square. The museum's mission is to present the almost two-million-year history of the territory known as China. After viewing an exhibition entitled *Road to Revival,* Xi proclaimed that "the great Chinese dream is the rejuvenation of the Chinese nation." The official media energetically promoted the concept across the country and encouraged the people to embrace the notion as a new rallying call. Xi's simple but vague formulation aimed to arouse a deep-seated and pervasive sentiment among the Chinese people. Almost universally, Chinese share the view that their nation has suffered a hundred years of humiliation and suffering at the hands of foreign rulers and imperialists, beginning in the first part of the nineteenth century. According to Xi, China has been deprived of its rightful status, and deserved position, as a great civilization and power. Its people have died countless horrible deaths at the hands of invaders and its national face was smeared in the mud of modernity. The great aspiration of the Chinese people, Xi said, is to return China not just to well-being but to its historical greatness in the family of nations. His dream is a dream of a future that will right a monumental and unforgivable historical wrong.[22]

The nerve Xi sought to touch was far from new; it was a pulsing sore point that had provoked Chinese patriotism from all walks of life since the mid-nineteenth century. It was as much a reason for the success of the Chinese Communist revolution as the demand for land, peace, and equality was. For most Chinese Nationalists, socialists, democrats, or Communists, their political agendas and programs had never been so much ends in themselves as the means to achieve the greater goals of national pride and reconstruction.[23]

What was different about Xi's formulation, however, was its curious resonance and connection with the concept of the American Dream. In fact, a column from New York Times writer Thomas L. Friedman entitled "China Needs Its Own Dream" may have been the actual inspiration for Xi's declaration. The op-ed piece was published just the month before Xi's speech and circulated widely in China. Friedman, best known for his book on globalization entitled *The World Is Flat* (2005), had long given close attention to China's rise and strongly encouraged Washington to adopt a collaborative approach with Beijing in world affairs in his many columns on developments in China. Regardless of whether there was any direct connection between Friedman and Xi's thinking, the time seemed to be right for China to have its own ambitious dream alongside that of America.[24]

Xi hoped his slogan would inspire Chinese to work hard, contribute to "rejuvenating" the nation, and support the Communist Party. China's dream, he later implied, was simply "communism," which would bring national revival. But the slogan, which aimed to provide guiding inspiration to the country, sparked a raging debate in China about how to define the Chinese dream, and everyone—People's Liberation Army soldiers, pop singers, academics, and social activists—seemed to have their own interpretation and vision. The Chinese Dream could even accommodate anti-party agitators who identified the future with the end of Communist rule. Comparisons were often explicitly made with the renowned American Dream. How did the two dreams differ? Was one more individualistic and materialistic, the other collectivist and nationalist? After he visited Beijing, Secretary of State John Kerry invoked the two dreams and called for America and China to work together, and with other countries, to realize a "Pacific dream." Many everyday Americans, anxious that their cherished goal of achieving a comfortable middle-class life could not be met, wondered if realizing the American Dream now depended on realization of the Chinese Dream. The two countries might need each other to reach their respective prosperity. In contrast, other Americans linked the putative erosion of the American Dream to the rise of China.[25]

But what is a "dream?" Is it not just a softer version of "destiny," another way of talking about something that we would like to see realized? In the nineteenth century, visionary Americans spoke of "destiny," but today we willful moderns often speak of dreams in ways that sound like fate, or certainly expectation. Many of us believe we are destined to meet our soul mate and that if we just work hard enough, we will certainly achieve our dream career someday.

The most evocative vision of imagined, converging national futures has come not from fiction writers or politicos but from an accomplished and diverse group of distinctly unsentimental economists and geopolitical specialists. Expressed in different ways, this vision anticipates and even encourages forging a common, interlocked fate that approaches a veritable apotheosis of 400 years of U.S.-China interactions. C. Fred Bergsten, one of the country's leading trade and economic specialists in and out of government, early emphasized the centrality of the U.S.-China economic and political relationship for global affairs. "The rise of China," he and his co-authors wrote in 2006, "is one of the most momentous developments of our time," one that "parallels the rise of the United States itself in the late nineteenth century." The two are, or soon will be, they wrote, the "two most important countries in the world" and their relationship will have profound implications for the "stability and well-being of the global community as a whole." Bergsten encouraged wise and prudent stewardship of this relationship from both sides, even going so far as to suggest formalizing its management in a "G-2," an informal "caucus of the two" whose effective functioning would be, in his words, "imperative if the world economy is to move forward." (The very name G-2, or Group of Two, highlights the importance of the two nations above all the major economies of the world, which today collectively meet as the G-20 or G-7). To construct the G-2, in Bergsten's view, the "United States should seek to develop a true partnership with China to provide joint leadership" over "the global economic system," even if this requires substantially altering the status quo way of conducting international relations in order to appeal to China. Such a partnership would properly be perceived by the Chinese as "accurately recognizing the new role of China as a legitimate architect and steward of the international economic order."[26]

In 2009, Zbigniew Brzezinski, Jimmy Carter's national security advisor, promoted the G-2 concept in Beijing at a high-profile celebration of the thirtieth anniversary of the normalization of relations between the two countries. And from another side of the political spectrum, Robert B. Zoellick, who was a leading trade and State Department official in the Bush administration, president of the World Bank, and advisor on international security to Mitt Romney, also actively uses the concept in his policy recommendations.[27]

Although the G-2 notion is by no means universally accepted by Washington insiders, it nevertheless highlights the critical importance of the China-U.S. relationship that almost all American political and economic leaders now acknowledge. The G-2 idea remains just a provocative vision that is far from being actually realized. But the most inspired expression of the G-2 notion came from the business historian Niall Ferguson, known elsewhere as an apologist for the British Empire, who coined the resonant neologism "Chimerica" to suggest the merging of the economic souls of the two powerhouses. He invokes the Chimera, the mythical beast containing multiple beings in one body, to express the reality of the "dual country" of "China plus America," a geopolitical mega-entity that accounted for a "tenth of the world's land surface, a quarter of its population, a third of its economic output and more than half of global economic growth" in the first eight years of the twenty-first century. But, hedging his bets, Ferguson also acknowledges the many commercial and political pitfalls that could turn the Chimerica into a real chimera, just an illusion after all. As a student of the past, Ferguson well knows that history is littered with the empty shells of prognostications that were once advanced with similar certainty.[28]

A famous promoter of close economic and political ties between China and America declared to a special gathering of New York businessmen and political elite that in just the previous few years, trade between the two countries had already soared to tremendous heights. The value of the trade was "but a tithe of the enormous trade that will take place with China," he declared with complete assurance, when China gets "into full fellowship with the rest of the world." How familiar this sounds! The comment was offered in June 1868 and the occasion was the visit to New York City of Anson Burlingame, the American diplomat who was in the service of the Chinese government, representing its interests to the United States. Burlingame was far from the first to embrace the golden promise of the China trade; others as far back as the earliest settlers of North America had similar dreams. American entrepreneurs today are just the latest in the string of Americans inspired by the lure of China. The centuries-long promise of China for America may finally be coming to fruition; journalist Thomas L. Friedman is completely convinced of it. "Our two economies and fates," he has declared, "are totally intertwined today."[29]

There was nothing inevitable about the rise of China and the formidable economic force it has become in a relatively short time. Nor were America and China destined to have the vital relationship they now have. Human choices made the difference. President Nixon did not have to pursue his daring effort at rapprochement. Chairman Mao did not have to turn to Washington to counter the Soviet threat. The "gang of four" in China could have remained in place to continue Mao's austere approach to communism. Deng Xiaoping might not have returned to China's leadership to oversee a market revolution. Bilateral negotiations might easily have broken down over sensitive issues such as Taiwan. Eight successive U.S. presidents did not have to conclude that encouraging China's economic rise was a good thing for the United States. One can easily reconstruct any of these moments and see that the outcomes were far from assured.[30]

Why did America's leaders choose to encourage China's economic growth and facilitate its rise as a global power? Opposition from all political quarters from those who were concerned about economic competitiveness, human rights, national security, or challenges to American hegemony, among other issues, could easily have scuttled the emerging connection. They still might. Some voices in America call the idea that China and America should, or even can, forge a long-term constructive relationship folly. Their vision of America's destiny is singular and hegemonic, one that distances the United States from China. Until now, however, America's leaders, by and large, have embraced the vision that America's fate lies in engaging China and increasing interdependence as good and necessary. Peril or profit: These ideas have long animated America's attitude toward China, and their improbable and unpredictable mix will continue to do so.

No other country has so inspired American imaginations over so long a time, from the beginning of the country to the present. England, Germany, Italy, and the other lands of ancestry for many Americans understandably inspired great personal interest and commitment. But although homelands resonate with sentiment about the past, they do not inspire references to destiny. Western Europe remains the undeniable fulcrum of American foreign policy, but in terms of the perceived future of the nation, no other country looms as importantly as China. America's relationships with Russia, Japan, India, Israel, Mexico, and others have been vital for many and have dominated policy concerns, but these have been episodic and tied to contemporary concerns. Japan provoked hatred during World War II and dread in the economic wars in the 1980s, but not many Americans believed that their nation's fate was tied to the island empire. To be sure, Americans at various times have considered other nations, such as Britain, essential to the future well-being of the country, and some Americans, including those who had had a personal relationship with China, such as Herbert Hoover, have dismissed China as inconsequential. China, it was said, was too poor, the people too backward, the huge country too difficult to govern. Yet what is remarkable from a historical perspective is the long persistence of the belief in a "China destiny" for America. From the earliest moments, Americans from many different walks of life—cultural figures, business leaders, politicians, social critics, journalists, radicals, and reactionaries—identified America's future with China. This persistent view of China as part of an imagined national destiny is a uniquely American one.

From the time of Columbus to today's Silicon Valley entrepreneurs, China has inspired American dreams and schemes. China and America are mirror opposites, counterpoised, at opposite ends of a balance beam, forever distanced yet forever connected. They are continental empires on the facing shores of a shared ocean that either links or separates, depending on one's point of view. China has always been America's farthest reach west, the ultimate frontier. America, for Chinese, has been revered as the "Gold Mountain," the popular name given to it in the nineteenth century. China today has become great again in part because Americans believed that China was destined to grow. One can see the power of self-fulfilling prophecy at work in all this. The vision of a G-2 may be the historical merger long predicted and advocated or it may just be the latest incarnation of an overblown ambition. But little suggests that China's rise will come to an end soon. In the twenty-first century, it is only American and Chinese machines that walk the surface of the moon; China landed its first craft on the moon at the end of 2013. In the not-distant future, brown Chinese eyes will view the blue earth from the lunar surface.

Hollywood is already imagining the link of America and China in space with *Gravity*, a 3D epic, winner of seven Academy awards in 2014, a film rich in metaphorical implications. *Gravity* focuses on the desperate efforts to survive in space of the American Dr. Ryan Stone, played by Sandra Bullock. She is stranded during a spacewalk when debris from the Russian destruction of one of its satellites crashes into her station and kills all her compatriots. Stone and her partner, played by George Clooney, drift untethered, seemingly destined for oblivion in deep space. Exhausted and near death, Ryan finally reaches an unstaffed Chinese space station, *Tiangong* (Heavenly Palace), but because she knows no Chinese, she is disoriented and does not understand the craft's labels and signage. Through grit and intelligence, however, she overcomes these obstacles and uses the reentry capsule, *Shenzhou* (Divine Craft), to return to earth. It is to China that the despairing American turns to rescue her from the possibility of drifting for eternity in the endless void of the universe.[31]

Americans, it has often been said, are a forward-thinking people. They are optimistic and confident, or certainly hopeful, that the future will be a better place. Political figures nurture such optimism in difficult economic or political times to lead the country forward and inspire people to work harder, fight tougher, and have the courage to weather a storm. It is the future that is important for Americans, and thus the idea of destiny, a confidence in fated greatness, runs through the arc of America's history and the dreams of its people. Few adhere today to the Puritan belief that God has already fully determined our fate, but many continue to believe without question that America is destined to be God's exceptional city upon the hill, as John Winthrop articulated in 1630.

Americans honor their country's glorious past because it established the foundation for an even better future. The American Revolution's leaders are the "founding fathers" who began the effort and whose promises are still to be fully realized. The past is respected, but rarely, except perhaps for those who romanticize the antebellum south or mythologize "rugged individualism," is the past seen as a better place, a place to which one would return.

Looking to the future and envisioning its contours is a much more pleasing activity for most Americans. It is a habit, a national trait, perhaps prompted by the constant energy of an exuberant market economy fully oriented toward the future and the national worship of the new. For most generations throughout American history, the future has been materially better and politically freer, or at least many have thought that to be the case. A brighter, promising, and more prosperous future is assumed to be an American birthright. It is called the American Dream.

Modern China, in contrast, has never been preoccupied with a future time. The Chinese have not been so optimistic, or so fortunate, a people. For so many, the future, until quite recently, has not been especially promising, while the mythic, untroubled past is something that is constantly recalled. The idealization of the past exerts a strong hold on the dreams and imaginations of many Chinese today, who understand the present as a declension from ancient wisdoms, harmony, and prosperity. Even Mao Zedong, when he described a glorious socialist future for the Chinese people, conjured the *taihe,* or Great Peace, the ancients spoke of, a time of harmony and abundance. His was a communism with traditional Chinese characteristics. The Chinese respect the "eight immortal sages" as those who are still relevant for them today. Xi Jinping's Chinese Dream itself is a rally call to recapture China's assumed historical eminence and well-being.

"Destiny" suggests inevitability or predetermined fate. But realizing a destiny requires human agency. The appropriate historical currents and the direction of those currents must be identified. We must act in accord with the will of history, but act we still must. Visionary Greeks, evangelical Protestants, Communist dialectical materialists, and others who want to make history have shared this mixed attitude toward human agency, as it provides the possibility of assigning epic meaning to our worldly endeavors, but only if we make the right choices with our lives. Karl Marx's proletarian revolution was inevitable, but only when wage slaves understood their exploited condition, threw off their chains, and made their history.

The word destiny conjures images of grand history, of a human pageant that can realize a glorious future; it suggests a long history of human endeavor and an appreciation of the need for purposeful will in order to realize greatness. It suggests inevitability—yes, with human intervention, but for the purpose of reaching an end that cannot be avoided. That perspective is nonhistorical, even anti-historical, for as the study of the past shows, it is contingency, accident, and surprise that mark the human record. Depressions, wars, and revolutions result from human will and accident. History, as we know, could have taken a variety of paths. Nothing was predetermined; nothing is completely predictable, let alone as certain as "destiny" or fate. We can only be confident of change.

History is not linear. In hindsight we give human activity and events shape and direction, but as we look to the future, none can be certain of anything except death and taxes. History is about human choice. Thus, nothing is fated about a China and America clash or embrace. Yet for now, it appears that the future of the two countries will be deeply intertwined. We share fateful ties. Everything else is prediction offered with varying levels of confidence and aspiration. Perhaps the most we can say is that we are left with a future with an "unpredictable fate" in America-China relations, the enigmatic notion used by the contemporary Chinese artist Li Chen for the title of one of his mysterious Buddhist/Taoist-inspired statuary.

Nothing in this book is intended to be a forecast, though one might think that the argument this study makes about the important place China has occupied in American thinking offers guidance for the future. One might conclude, for example, that the United States will inevitably abandon its support for Taiwan because of its obsession with China. But history might also support a different point of view: America's fears of China, sometimes dormant, sometimes visceral and open, might also sustain attachment to the island, even at the cost of angering the mainland. American views of China have always been quixotic. Americans reveled in the spectacle of the 2008 Beijing Olympics, which were meant to impress the world. But American commentators also openly expressed concern about the awesome opening ceremony that showcased mass human organization and extravagantly expensive spectacle. They wondered about the implications of such power beyond mere sport.

American visions of destiny with China can tell us more about America than about China. This book examines the ambitions and fears of leading, often visionary, Americans and what they thought would be essential for the growth, prosperity, protection, and stature of America in the world. They often saw America as inextricably tied to China or distanced from it for its own good. Their stories tell us much about their own self-conception and their sense of national identity and purpose. As we consider our frantic present, the past enables us to see how others have thought about China and thus fortifies us as we march forward into the future with an awareness of the continuities and challenges that this relationship embodies.

As we glide from historical reflection to prognostication about the future, we might still conclude that someday there will be a certain grand convergence in the trajectories of America and China. Capitalism and socialism, as two irreconcilable and distinct economic and social systems, may just be definable historical moments that are now slipping past. Capitalism and socialism are not eternal epochs. They came into being in particular historical circumstances and they may dissolve under different ones, and we might not yet have the vocabularies to talk about the emerging political/economic realities. The United States and China at one time seemed to occupy opposite ends of modernity's spectrum, but they could now be moving toward a center point, a synthetic union of aspects of market liberalism and social statism. A "United States of China" is what one American scholar recommends that China's leaders consider for the country's future. Perhaps there is "destiny" after all.[32]

Telegraph Hill is one of San Francisco's most prominent physical features, clearly visible to every ship entering the bay. In the 1850s, signal flags flew there announcing the arrival of vessels to the booming city. Many of those ships came from China and carried Chinese to America's shores. American goods flowed back out of the harbor to Asia. The back and forth continued unabated with only brief interruptions due to war. Today, Coit Tower sits atop Telegraph Hill, one of the city's iconic landmarks, built in the early twentieth century to beautify the city. At its base is a massive bronze statue of Christopher Columbus. It was a gift of the local Italian community to the city to celebrate one they claimed as its own. The great explorer, tall, erect, with grand visage, gazes over the city at his feet to distant shores, the ones he had hoped to reach in the fifteenth century. No matter he never made it to the Pacific, let alone to anyplace close to San Francisco. He is a symbol. In his left hand he holds a document declaring that he is on a mission from his Spanish sovereign. On his sword is inscribed his words "*buscar el levante por el poniente*," search for the East by way of the West. The search continues.

Afterword

This is a book of history written by a historian who is more comfortable viewing the past than the present and speculating about what the future might bring. About the only lesson that the study of history provides is that it is impossible to foresee the future in any confident and specific way. The historical record is full of surprise and contingency, not the inevitable or predictable. Change is the constant. At best, historians, who usually take a long view of the past, might see patterns or make educated comparisons, to make sense of the complexity of the human experience. This is what I have tried to do in this book. I leave it to other specialists, more confident in their faith in modeling or theory, to offer firmer predictions about the future of U.S.-China relations.

Several years ago, early in the current boom in the relationship between the United States and China, Joyce Seltzer of Harvard University Press asked if I might offer historical perspective on what was shaping up to be one of the central concerns of our era. Daily events confirmed that the continuing rise of China was transforming the world and that America's response to that development would have far-reaching implications for its own people and the peoples of all countries. As one who has spent much of his professional life studying the interactions of America and China, I realized that this was an opportunity I should take. But more than a chance to bring together intellectual strands from a career, writing this book, to my surprise, sparked an exploration of personal history. What I came to understand is that my life shaped the telling of the story and in many ways reflected and intersected with the larger historical experience. My own life belonged alongside the other personal stories that constitute so much of this book.

I cannot claim that my family's life in America begins with Jamestown, though my children can now trace part of their roots on their mother's side all the way back to one of the Mayflower voyages. I have no knowledge about whether any of my ancestors had anything to do with nineteenth-century Euro-American traders, missionaries, or merchants in China. There may be connections to be discovered, because my ancestral history on my paternal and maternal sides is found, respectively, in the Hangzhou and Guangzhou regions of China, both places of important American presence in the nineteenth century. I can document my lineage in America back to the early 1850s, when a great-grandfather on my maternal side landed with thousands of other Chinese migrants and settled in California. He came from the *siyi* area, home of much of the vast China diaspora of the nineteenth century. He may have had connections to the construction of the transcontinental railroad. His grandchildren, my mother and her siblings, were born in Washington, a small Sierra mining town not far from Lake Tahoe, and grew up in the San Francisco Bay town of Vallejo, the capital of California twice for brief periods. They were educated by Christian teachers who were among the few in the early twentieth century who were willing to have close contact with the heathen Chinese. With their Chinese faces and their American names, they embodied the human link of their land of ancestry with their land of birth. Several were named auspiciously: my elder uncles were Theodore and Taft (for the presidents) and Hiram (for a governor). My elder aunts were Alice (for Theodore Roosevelt's daughter) and Minnie (for the Indian princess Minnehaha). My mother was Helen (for Taft's daughter).

My father was an accomplished artist from the Hangzhou/Nanjing/Shanghai area whose most famous composition was a huge painting completed as a gift for Franklin D. Roosevelt on the occasion of his third election as president. Painted in China's wartime capital, Chongqing, it was created by Shuqi, my father, who hoped it would advance ties between the United States and China. Presented to U.S. ambassador Nelson Johnson, the painting made its way to the White House. It became in its day the most famous Chinese painting in America. Shuqi subsequently made his way to the United States, traveling with a diplomatic passport and the title of "Ambassador of Art and Goodwill." After Pearl Harbor, he had to remain in the United States for the war years, which is when he met my mother. Among those who favored his artwork was Pearl Buck. Henry and Clare Boothe Luce purchased his work for their art collection.

My father and mother lived in China for a short while after the end of the war and socialized with Nationalists and Communists alike. Shortly before they returned to the United States, Shuqi gave one of his paintings to U.S. ambassador John Leighton Stuart and inscribed his great respect for the diplomat in a colophon. In 2012, when I visited the Stuart Museum in Hangzhou, I was astonished to discover it prominently displayed among Stuart's treasured China keepsakes. I had not known about its existence beforehand.

I grew up in the hills of Oakland, across the bay from Burlingame, the town located on Anson Burlingame's retirement estate. Our home was a gathering place for Chinese intellectuals, artists, and political figures displaced from the mainland by the Communist revolution. Among my father's friends in America were Hu Shi, Chen Lifu, Zhao Yuanren, Soong May-ling, Song Ziwen, and many artist friends. I grew up reading books in my parents' library, including Theodore White's *Thunder out of China*, Madame Chiang Kaishek's *China Shall Rise Again,* and Carl Crow's *Master Kung: The Story of Confucius.* In middle school in the early 1960s, I participated in our school's model United Nations and was assigned, against my wishes, the position of opposing Red China's admission to the international body. I can't recall who won the debate. Around this same time, my mother took me to San Francisco to see the British journalist Felix Greene and his film praising the accomplishments of People's China. Masonic Auditorium was overflowing with people hungry to know something about the country so far removed by distance and politics from America. On another occasion, my mother introduced me to Pearl Buck when she visited San Francisco.

I read the first volume of George F. Kennan's memoirs as I traveled across the country by train to go to college. One of my dreams was to help America better understand China, as Kennan had done with Russia. At Princeton, I studied under eminent China scholars, became deeply disaffected from America because of the Vietnam War, and rejected any idea of joining the Washington establishment. I became radicalized and consumed the writings of Mao. In deciding where to go to graduate school, I turned down a chance to go to Harvard, where I would have studied with John F. Fairbank, and instead went to Stanford. I lasted less than two years because of my political activism and left academia for a decade.

In 1971, before Nixon's trip but after Kissinger's travel to Beijing, I made my first trip to China, along with a group of other Chinese Americans sympathetic to New China. I saw a China still in the midst of the Cultural Revolution. I never met Mao or Zhou but did meet other Chinese leaders. I also encountered the former Foreign Service officer John Service; Huey Newton from Oakland; and a couple of young Americans who had settled in Dazhai, a model farming collective touted as the future of Chinese socialism. It would be disbanded and discredited after Deng Xiaoping rose to power in the late 1970s. I met old Cantonese who had lived in America but returned to China after 1949. They had been labor organizers and leftists.

After returning to the United States with hundreds of slides and stories of idealized schools, factories, and communes, I became an instant "expert" on revolutionary China and was frequently invited to speak about my visit. There was still a dearth of Americans who had even set foot in post-1949 China. In February 1972, I spoke to a San Francisco audience just as Richard Nixon's plane set down on the tarmac in Beijing's Capital Airport. I watched with rapt attention as he shook Zhou Enlai's hand. The world has not been the same since.

I have traveled to China regularly since my first visit. The transformations I've seen have been nothing less than stunning. I have also lived and studied at Peking University on two extended stays, once in 1985 and most recently in 2012, when I taught for Stanford University's overseas studies program. My family and I stayed in a lovely restored traditional building on the shore of the campus's famous Weiming Lake. The building is known as the Packard Pavilion, named for David Packard, the founder of the computer giant that bears his name, who covered the costs of the renovation and to celebrate Peking University's centennial in 1991. Across the way in one direction from the residence is a memorial to the journalist Edgar Snow, whose work profoundly influenced U.S.-China relations. In another direction is a tribute to the Rev. Henry W. Luce, who spent his life as a missionary in China. It was constructed by his China-born son, Henry Luce, founder of what is now known as the Time-Life publishing empire. Overshadowing all is the famous Peking University water tower, which is enclosed in a multistory pagoda. It was constructed in the 1920s with funds from an American mining magnate. An easily overlooked plaque at the base of the tower tells of that American largesse. I came and went to the university through the famous Dongmen entrance, which is where W. E. B. Du Bois walked when he visited Peking University in 1959.

In 2012, I also spent several days in my paternal *lao jia*, my ancestral home village. Lizhang, a small and somewhat remote place, is located more than four hours by car from Shanghai. The name of the village honors my sur-name. A few hundred continue to farm, largely in quite traditional ways, but they enjoy a new prosperity, with televisions, imported cars, personal electronic devices, and WiFi in ample evidence. A few small one-room work-shops produce contracted items for distant American companies. One of these companies, Tommy Hilfiger, had Lizhang villagers stitch together fabric for its patriotic American Flag bedding line several years ago. A photo shows them hard at work, displaying, literally and symbolically, our inter-twined "destinies," in national and, for increasingly numbers of Americans, like myself, deeply personal ways.

On my maternal side, my ancestry in America traces back to the 1850s, when my great-grandfather traveled from the Pearl River delta in southern China and settled in the foothills of the Sierra Nevada. He and my other relatives were workers, craftsmen, shopkeepers, and miners in America. The village from which he came, like most of the others in that area of Guang-zhou, is more prosperous these days but little different in appearance. My distant relatives who still reside there had me drink from the village well when I visited in the 1990s. For them, the sip symbolized my continued fa-milial connection. One of the elders shared with me a genealogy that went back to the Song dynasty, 1,200 years ago. The family now extends throughout the world, to the United States, Canada, Australia, and Europe.

Notes

Introduction

Epigraph: Adam Smith, *An Inquiry into the Nature and Causes of the Wealth of Nations* (1776), book 1, chapter 8.

1. Apologies to those who live north and south of the United States. They are also Americans and live in America. In this book, I use the term "America" as most of those who live in the United States do, as roughly synonymous with the location and the name of the United States. I use America to emphasize the people and society of this country as distinct from the state, the United States.

2. William D. Phillips Jr. and Carla Rahn Phillips, *The Worlds of Christopher Columbus* (New York. Cambridge University Press, 1992), 134; Berthold Laufer, "Columbus and Cathay, and the Meaning of America to the Orientalist," *Journal of the American Oriental Society* 51, no. 2 (1931): 87–103; William Speer, *The Oldest and the Newest Empire: China and the United States* (Hartford, CT: S. S. Scranton, 1870), 24; Sydney Greenbie, *Gold of Ophir: The China Trade in the Making of America*, rev. ed. (New York: Wilson-Erickson, 1937).

3. Jonathan D. Spence, *The Chan's Great Continent: China in Western Minds* (New York: Norton, 1998), 18.

4. David Abulafia, *The Discovery of Mankind: Atlantic Encounters in the Age of Columbus* (New Haven, CT: Yale University Press, 2008), 10–30; Karen Ordahl Kupperman, *The Jamestown Project* (Cambridge, MA: Belknap Press of Harvard University Press, 2007), 3–4, 133–134, 151–152, 190–191; Charles Holcombe, *A History of East Asia: From the Origins of Civilization to the Twenty-First Century* (New York: Cambridge University Press, 2011), 1.

5. Andrew L. March, *The Idea of China: Myth and Theory in Geographic Thought* (New York: Praeger, 1974), 39.

6. On the allure of China, see Karen J. Leong, *The China Mystique: Pearl S. Buck, Anna May Wong, Mayling Soong, and the Transformation of American Orientalism* (Berkeley: University of California Press, 2005).

7. John K. Fairbank, "Introduction," in *America's China Trade in Historical Perspective: The Chinese and American Performance,* ed. Ernest R. May and John K. Fairbank (Cambridge, MA: Harvard University Press, 1986), 2. See also William L. Neumann, "Determinism, Destiny, and Myth in the American Image of China," in *Issues and Conflicts: Studies in Twentieth Century American Diplomacy,* ed. George L. Anderson (Lawrence: University of Kansas Press, 1959), 1–22.

8. Anders Stephanson, *Manifest Destiny: American Expansion and the Empire of Right* (New York: Hill and Wang, 1995), xi–xii. For the place of the Pacific in expansionism, see Norman A. Graebner, *Empire on the Pacific: A Study in American Continental Expansion* (New York, Ronald Press, 1955). For manifest destiny as ideology, see Albert Weinberg, *Manifest Destiny: A Study of Nationalist Expansionism in American History* (Baltimore, MD: Johns Hopkins University Press, 1935); and Michael H. Hunt, *Ideology and U.S. Foreign Policy* (New Haven, CT: Yale University Press, 1987).

9. Fairbank, "Introduction," 6, 7. A classic treatment of American images of China is Harold R. Isaacs, *Scratches on Our Minds: American Images of China and India* (New York: John Day, 1958). Recent versions include Carola McGiffert, ed., *China in the American Political Imagination* (Washington, DC: Center for Strategic and International Studies, 2003); and Oliver Turner, *American Images of China: Identity, Power, Policy* (London: Routledge, 2014).

10. "United States Policy toward Asia," *Department of State Bulletin* 22 (March 27, 1950): 467–472.

11. Advertisement, *The Atlantic,* April 2009, 49.

12. Keith Bradsher, "Hauling New Treasure along the Silk Road," *New York Times,* July 20, 2013.

1. Ties of Opportunity

Epigraph: Benjamin Franklin, *The Writings of Benjamin Franklin,* vol. 9 (New York: Macmillan, 1906), 387.

1. Giovanni Arrighi, *Adam Smith in Beijing: Lineages of the Twenty-First Century* (London: Verso, 2007), 38.

2. James R. Gibson, *Otter Skins, Boston Ships, and China Goods: The Maritime Fur Trade of the Northwest Coast, 1785–1841* (Seattle: University of Washington Press, 1992), 84–86.

3. Immanuel C. Y. Hsu, *China's Entrance into the Family of Nations: The Diplomatic Phase, 1858–1880* (Cambridge, MA: Harvard University Press, 1960), 3–17.

4. James Kirker, *Adventures to China: Americans in the Southern Oceans, 1792–1812* (New York: Oxford University Press, 1970), 3–4. See also Eric Jay Dolin, *When America*

First Met China: An Exotic History of Tea, Drugs, and Money in the Age of Sail (New York: Liveright, 2012).

5. Jonathan Goldstein, *Philadelphia and the China Trade, 1682–1846: Commercial, Cultural, and Attitudinal Effects* (University Park: Pennsylvania State University Press, 1978), 1–3, 34–40; Rodris Roth, *Tea Drinking in 18th Century America: Its Etiquette and Equipage* (Washington, DC: Smithsonian Institution, 1961), 61–91; Carl L. Crossman, *The China Trade: Export Painting, Furniture, Silver and Other Objects* (Princeton, NJ: Pyne Press, 1972), 4; John Kuo Wei Tchen, *New York before Chinatown: Orientalism and the Shaping of American Culture, 1776–1882* (Baltimore, MD: Johns Hopkins University Press, 1999).

6. Goldstein, *Philadelphia and the China Trade*, 8–23.

7. Ibid., 16–18; Benjamin W. Labaree, *The Boston Tea Party, 1773: Catalyst for Revolution* ([Boston]: Massachusetts Bicentennial Commission, 1973), 5–23; T. H. Breen, *The Marketplace of Revolution: How Consumer Politics Shaped American Independence* (New York: Oxford University Press, 2004), 294–331; James R. Fichter, *So Great a Proffit: How the East Indies Trade Transformed Anglo-American Capitalism* (Cambridge, MA: Harvard University Press, 2010), 17–25.

8. Philip Chadwick Foster Smith, *The Empress of China* (Philadelphia, PA: Philadelphia Maritime Museum, 1984), 3–30; "Salem," *Salem Gazette*, August 21, 1783, 3; Ledyard quote from Dolan, *When America First Met China*, 12. Ledyard and the celebrated American naval captain John Paul Jones had themselves planned an ambitious venture to participate in the China trade. See also James Zug, *American Traveler: The Life and Adventures of John Ledyard, the Man Who Dreamed of Walking the World* (New York: Basic Books, 2005).

9. Smith, *The Empress of China*, 3–8; Foster Rhea Dulles, *China and America: The Story of Their Relations since 1784* (Princeton, NJ: Princeton University Press, 1946), 1–2.

10. Philip Freneau, "On the First American Ship," in *The Poems of Philip Freneau: Poet of the American Revolution*, vol. 2, ed. Fred Lewis Pattee (Princeton, NJ: Princeton University Library, 1902), 261–262. Freneau dedicated this poem, dated 1784, to the *Empress of China*.

11. A. Owen Aldridge, *The Dragon and Eagle: The Presence of China in the American Enlightenment* (Detroit, MI: Wayne State University Press, 1993), 244.

12. Smith, *The Empress of China*, 31–36.

13. Quoted in Aldridge, *The Dragon and Eagle*, 122.

14. Samuel Shaw, *The Journals of Major Samuel Shaw: The First American Consul at Canton* (Boston: Wm. Crosby and H. P. Nichols, 1847), 167–168, 183.

15. Dulles, *China and America*, 5–7; Goldstein, *Philadelphia and the China Trade*, 30–31; David Igler, *The Great Ocean: Pacific Worlds from Captain Cook to the Gold Rush* (New York: Oxford University Press, 2013), 32; Fichter, *So Great a Proffit*, 1.

16. Jules Davids, "Introduction," in *American Diplomatic and Public Papers: The United States and China,* Series 1, *The Kearny and Cushing Missions,* vol. 1 (Wilmington, DE: Scholarly Resources, 1973), xi–xlviii; Fichter, *So Great a Proffit,* 5, 27, 264–271.

17. Dulles, *China and America,* 8–10; Yen-P'ing Hao, "Chinese Teas to America—a Synopsis," in *America's China Trade in Historical Perspective: The Chinese and American Performance,* ed. Ernest R. May and John K. Fairbank (Cambridge, MA: Harvard University Press, 1986), 21–22.

18. Hao, "Chinese Teas to America," 13–18, 28–30; Sucheta Mazumdar, *Sugar and Society in China: Peasants, Technology, and the World Market* (Cambridge, MA: Harvard University Asia Center, 1998), 115–116.

19. Gibson, *Otter Skins, Boston Ships, and China Goods,* 102–103.

20. Robert Gardella, *Harvesting Mountains: Fujian and the China Tea Trade, 1757–1937* (Berkeley: University of California Press, 1994); Roy Moxham, *Tea: Addiction, Exploitation and Empire* (London: Constable, 2003).

21. Quotes from R. David Arkush and Leo O. Lee, eds., *Land without Ghosts: Chinese Impressions of America from the Mid-Nineteenth Century to the Present* (Berkeley: University of California Press, 1989), 15–16.

22. Quote from Aldridge, *The Dragon and Eagle,* 87.

23. Quote from Aldridge, *The Dragon and Eagle,* 85–93; Jim Egan, *Oriental Shadows: The Presence of the East in Early American Literature* (Columbus: Ohio State University Press, 2011), 75–76; Manuscript Document Signed by Charles Biddle as Vice President of the Supreme Executive Council of Pennsylvania, Presided over by Benjamin Franklin, Offering Aid to Chinese sailors in U.S., May 30, 1786, http://www.pbagalleries.com/view-auctions/catalog/id/321/lot/687/?url=%2Fview-auctions%2Fcatalog%2Fid%2F321%3Fcat%3D3%2C38, accessed October 8, 2014; David Weir, *American Orient: Imagining the East from the Colonial Era through the Twentieth Century* (Amherst: University of Massachusetts Press, 2011), 19–22.

24. Aldridge, *The Dragon and Eagle,* 8, 25–30, 93–97, 265; Goldstein, *Philadelphia and the China Trade,* 23; Thomas Paine, "A Letter to Mr. Erskine," ca. 1797, in *The Complete Writings of Thomas Paine,* vol. 2, ed. Philip S. Foner (New York: Citadel Press, 1945), 737; Thomas Jefferson to G. K. Van Hogendrop, October 13, 1785, in *Papers of Thomas Jefferson,* vol. 8, *February 1785 to October 1785,* ed. Julian P. Boyd (Princeton, NJ: Princeton University Press, 1953), 633.

25. Aldridge, *The Dragon and Eagle,* 146–148.

26. Ibid., 196; Craig R. Hanyan, "China and the Erie Canal," *Business History Review* 35, no. 4 (1961): 558–566. Regarding American cities named Canton, I thank Xiaoxia Zhang for her unpublished paper, "Incantations of 'Canton': How a Chinese City Exported Itself to America," 2014.

27. Aldridge, *The Dragon and Eagle,* 21–22, 268; Washington to Tench Tilghman, August 29, 1795, http://founders.archives.gov/?q=Washington%2C%20George&s=211 1311211&r=24&sr=Tilghman, accessed 8 October 2014.

28. Amasa Delano, *A Narrative of Voyages and Travels, in the Northern and Southern Hemispheres: Comprising Three Voyages Round the World; Together with a Voyage of Survey and Discovery, in the Pacific Ocean and Oriental Islands* (Boston: E. G. House, 1817), 530–542.

29. Robert Bennet Forbes, *Remarks on China and the China Trade* (Boston: Samuel N. Dickinson, 1844), 14; Aldridge, *The Dragon and Eagle*, 118–119.

30. Shaw, *The Journals of Major Samuel Shaw*, 167–168, 183; Stuart Creighton Miller, *The Unwelcome Immigrant: The American Image of the Chinese, 1785–1882* (Berkeley: University of California Press, 1969), 16–64; Donald M. Murray, "Emerson's 'Language as Fossil Poetry': An Analogy from Chinese," *The New England Quarterly* 29, no. 2 (1956): 204–215.

31. Gibson, *Otter Skins, Boston Ships, and China Goods*, 103–104; Kenneth Pomeranz and Steven Topik, *The World That Trade Created: Society, Culture, and the World Economy, 1400 to the Present* (Armonk, NY: M. E. Sharpe, 1999), 99–105.

32. Thomas N. Layton, *The Voyage of the Frolic: New England Merchants and the Opium Trade* (Stanford, CA: Stanford University Press, 1997), 27–40; Goldstein, *Philadelphia and the China Trade*, 53–54; Jacques M. Downs, *The Golden Ghetto: The American Commercial Community at Canton and the Shaping of American China Policy, 1784–1844* (Bethlehem, PA: Lehigh University Press, 1997), 117–131.

33. "The Opium Trade—England and China," *Hunt's Merchants' Magazine and Commercial Review* 2 (May 1840): 394–413.

34. Bradford Perkins, *The Creation of a Republican Empire, 1776–1865: The Cambridge History of American Foreign Relations*, vol. 1 (New York: Cambridge University Press, 1993), 4, 8–9; Te-kong Tong, *United States Diplomacy in China, 1844–60* (Seattle: University of Washington Press, 1964), 3, 20, 22–27.

35. Samuel Flagg Bemis, *John Quincy Adams and the Union* (New York: Alfred A. Knopf, 1956), 484–486; Tyler Dennett, *Americans in Eastern Asia: A Critical Study of the Policy of the United States with Reference to China, Japan and Korea in the 19th Century* (New York: Macmillan, 1922), 105–108; William Earl Weeks, *John Quincy Adams & American Global Empire* (Lexington: University Press of Kentucky, 1992), 19–21, 33–34.

36. Adams to Richard Rush, December 30, 1842, quoted in Bemis, *John Quincy Adams and the Union*, 485n10. See also Greg Russell, *John Quincy Adams and the Public Virtues of Diplomacy* (Columbia: University of Missouri Press, 1995), 239, 242, 261; and Tan Chung, *China and the Brave New World: A Study of the Origins of the Opium War (1840–42)* (Durham, NC: Carolina Academic Press, 1978), 1–5.

37. Josiah Quincy, *Memoir of the Life of John Quincy Adams* (Boston: Crosby, Nichols, Lee and Company, 1860), 336–342; "J. Q. Adams on the Opium War," in *Proceedings of the Massachusetts Historical Society* 43 (February 1910): 295–325. Napoleon Bonaparte, believing that a foreign emissary meeting the emperor or any other sovereign was obliged to follow the etiquette required of the host country, had no problem with the *koutou*

and thought the British refusal to comply disrespectful and ill advised. He saw no difference between the Chinese practice and kissing the pope's toe or the king of England's hand. See Barry O'Meara, *Napoleon in Exile: or, A Voice from St. Helena,* vol. 1 (New York: William Gowans, 1853), 470–472.

38. Weeks, *John Quincy Adams & American Global Empire,* 19–21, 33–34.

39. Julian Sturgis, *From the Books and Papers of Russell Sturgis* (Oxford: Oxford University Press, 1893), 219–236. For a long analysis of Adams and a condemnation of his argument, see W. A., "Great Britain and China," *The Christian Examiner* 32 (July 1842): 281–319. The article turned Adams's use of China's violation of natural law as a justification for the war against Adams by arguing that the same logic would lead one to support a war to end slavery, clearly an abomination against the rights of man, in the United States. Downs, *The Golden Ghetto,* 140.

40. Richard E. Welch Jr., "Caleb Cushing's Chinese Mission and the Treaty of Wanghia: A Review," *Oregon Historical Quarterly* 58, no. 4 (1957): 328–357; John Belohlavek, "Race, Progress, and Destiny: Caleb Cushing and the Quest for American Empire," in *Manifest Destiny and Empire: American Antebellum Expansionism,* ed. Robert W. Johannsen, Sam W. Hayes, and Christopher Morris (College Station: Texas A&M University Press, 1997), 21–47.

41. Michael H. Hunt, *The Making of a Special Relationship: The United States and China to 1914* (New York: Columbia University Press, 1983), 18; "The Dinner at Faneuil Hall, on the 17th Instant," *Niles National Register,* July 1, 1843, 283.

42. Dulles, *China and America,* 25.

43. Claude M. Fuess, *The Life of Caleb Cushing,* vol. 1 (New York: Harcourt, Brace, 1923), 397–454.

44. "Monthly Commercial Chronicle," *Hunt's Merchants' Magazine,* January 1845, 74–80; "The Progress of American Commerce," *DeBow's Review* 2, no. 6 (1846), 396.

45. "Miscellaneous," *Niles National Register,* November 1, 1845, 136–137.

46. Karen Ordahl Kupperman, *The Jamestown Project* (Cambridge, MA: Belknap Press of Harvard University Press, 2007), 152–159; "The West and American Ideals," Commencement Address, University of Washington, June 17, 1914, in Frederick Jackson Turner, *The Frontier in American History* (New York: Henry Holt, 1920), 290–310. See also Dan E. Clark, "Manifest Destiny and the Pacific," *Pacific Historical Review* 1, no. 1 (1932): 1–17. This essay, the author's presidential address to the Pacific Coast Branch of the American Historical Association, inaugurated the journal.

47. Thomas Jefferson, "Instructions to Lewis," June 20, 1803, *Writings of Thomas Jefferson,* vol. 8, ed. Paul Leicester Ford (New York: G. P. Putnam's Sons, 1892), 194–199. On Jefferson's global vision, see Alan Taylor, "Jefferson's Pacific: The Science of Distant Empire, 1768–1811," in *Across the Continent: Jefferson, Lewis and Clark, and the Making of America,* ed. Peter Onuf, Douglas Seefeldt, and Jeffrey Harman (Charlottesville: University of Virginia Press, 2005), 16–44.

48. Dulles, *China and America*, 32; Charles H. Ambler, *The Life and Diary of John Floyd: Governor of Virginia, An Apostle of Secession, and the Father of the Oregon Country* (Richmond, VA: Richmond Press, 1918), 65–75.

49. Robert R. Russel, *Improvement of Communication with the Pacific Coast as an Issue in American Politics, 1783–1865* (Cedar Rapids, IA: Torch-Press, 1948), 11; Foster Stockwell, *Westerners in China: A History of Exploration and Trade, Ancient Times through the Present* (Jefferson, NC: McFarland, 2003), 86–94; quote in Dulles, *China and America*, 33–34.

50. See John L. O'Sullivan, "The Great Nation of Futurity," *United States Democratic Review* 6, no. 23 (1839): 426–430.

51. James K. Polk, "Third Annual Message," December 7, 1847, http://www.presidency.ucsb.edu/ws/?pid=29488; Michael P. Riccards, *The Presidency and the Middle Kingdom: China, the United States, and Executive Leadership* (Lanham, MD: Lexington Books, 2000), 18.

52. Asa Whitney, *A Project for a Railroad to the Pacific* (New York: George W. Wood, 1849).

53. "China and the Indies—Our 'Manifest Destiny' in the East," *DeBow's Review* 15 (December 1853): 541–571. The same idea is expressed in A. W. Ely, "The Empire of Japan," *DeBow's Review* 13 (December 1852).

54. Miller, *The Unwelcome Immigrant*, 19; Peter Schran, "The Minor Significance of Commercial Relations between the United States and China, 1850–1931," in *America's China Trade in Historical Perspective: The Chinese and American Performance*, ed. Ernest R. May and John K. Fairbank (Cambridge, MA: Harvard University Press, 1986), 237–258; Hao, "Chinese Teas to America," 12–31; Foster Rhea Dulles, *Old China Trade* (Boston: Houghton Mifflin, 1930), 115–116; Robert G. Cleland, "Asiatic Trade and the American Occupation of the Pacific Coast," in *Annual Report of the American Historical Association for the Year 1914*, vol. 1 (Washington, DC: American Historical Association, 1916), 283–289.

55. "Relations with China," *New York Times*, April 30, 1852, 2.

56. Matthew Perry with Francis L. Hawks, *Narrative of the Expedition of an American Squadron to the China Seas and Japan* (New York: D. Appleton, 1856), 95.

2. Physical and Spiritual Connections

Epigraph: Bret Harte, "What the Engines Said—Opening of the Pacific Railroad," *The Complete Poetical Works of Bret Harte*, vol. 8 (New York: P. F. Collier & Son, 1898), 304–305.

1. Karl Marx and Friedrich Engels, *Communist Manifesto*, in *The Marx-Engels Reader*, 2nd ed., ed. Robert C. Tucker (New York: W. W. Norton, 1978), 477.

2. George Richards, "Blood Is Thicker than Water," *The Century*, March 1918, 786–789; Paul H. Clyde and Burton F. Beers, *The Far East: A History of Western Impacts and*

Eastern Responses, 1830–1975, 6th ed. (Englewood Cliffs, NJ: Prentice Hall, 1975), 95–103; Paul H. Clyde, *United States Policy toward China: Diplomatic and Public Documents, 1839–1939* (Durham, NC: Duke University Press, 1940), 38–58.

3. See Kenneth Scott Latourette, *A History of Christian Missions in China* (New York: Macmillan, 1929).

4. Henry L. Stimson, *The Far Eastern Crisis: Recollections and Observations* (New York: Harper & Brothers, 1936), 13–14, 153–154; Tyler Dennett, *Americans in Eastern Asia* (New York: Barnes & Noble, 1941), 558.

5. Kenneth Scott Latourette, *The United States Moves across the Pacific: The A.B.C.'s of the American Problem in the Western Pacific and the Far East* (New York: Harper & Brothers, 1946), 55; Stimson, *The Far Eastern Crisis,* 153; John K. Fairbank, "The Many Faces of Protestant Missions in China and the United States," in *The Missionary Enterprise in China and America,* ed. John K. Fairbank (Cambridge, MA: Harvard University Press, 1974), 13; Edward V. Gulick, *Peter Parker and the Opening of China* (Cambridge, MA: Harvard University Press, 1973), 206.

6. Stuart Creighton Miller, *The Unwelcome Immigrant: The American Image of the Chinese, 1785–1882* (Berkeley: University of California Press, 1969), 57–60; Dennett, *Americans in Eastern Asia,* 555.

7. Jessie Gregory Lutz, "The Grand Illusion: Karl Gutzlaff and Popularization of China Missions in the United States during the 1830s," in *United States Attitudes and Policies toward China: The Impact of American Missionaries,* ed. Patricia Neils (Armonk, NY: M. E. Sharpe, 1990), 46–77.

8. Entry for April 1, 1832, Journal of Peter Parker, Box 4, Journal 5, Peter Parker Papers, Yale University Medical Library.

9. Letter published in the American Board of Commissioners for Foreign Missions report of 1833, quoted in Lutz, "The Grand Illusion," 53, emphasis in original.

10. Arthur Schlesinger Jr., "The Missionary Enterprise and Theories of Imperialism," in *The Missionary Enterprise in China and America,* ed. John K. Fairbank (Cambridge, MA: Harvard University Press, 1974), 336–373.

11. David Abeel, *Journal of a Residence in China and the Neighboring Countries* (New York: J. Abeel Williamson, 1836), 141–143.

12. Quotes from Gulick, *Peter Parker and the Opening of China,* 32–33. See also Eliza J. Gillett Bridgman, *The Life and Labors of Elijah Coleman Bridgman* (New York: Randolph, 1864); and Miller, *The Unwelcome Immigrant,* 62–68.

13. W. A., "Great Britain and China," *The Christian Examiner* 32 (July 1842): 281–319; "The Opium War and Its Justice," *The Christian Examiner* 30 (May 1841): 223–237; Peter Ward Fay, *The Opium War, 1840–1842: Barbarians in the Celestial Empire in the Early Part of the Nineteenth Century and the War by Which They Forced Her Gates Ajar* (Chapel Hill: University of North Carolina Press, 1975), 239–242; Michael C. Lazich, *E. C. Bridgman (1801–1861), America's First Missionary to China* (Lewiston, NY: Edwin Mellen Press, 2000), 214; Miller, *The Unwelcome Immigrant,* 102–103.

14. Louis B. Gimelli, "'Borne upon the Wings of Faith': The Chinese Odyssey of Henrietta Hall Shuck, 1835–1844," *Journal of the Early Republic* 14, no. 2 (1994): 221–245; Lazich, *E. C. Bridgman*, 13–59.

15. Stuart Creighton Miller, "Ends and Means: Missionary Justification of Force in Nineteenth Century China," in *The Missionary Enterprise in China and America*, ed. John K. Fairbank (Cambridge, MA: Harvard University Press, 1974), 249–282.

16. Clifton J. Phillips, "The Student Volunteer Movement and Its Role in China Missions, 1886–1920," in *The Missionary Enterprise in China and America*, ed. John K. Fairbank (Cambridge, MA: Harvard University Press, 1974), 91–109; Barlow and Eddy quotes from Schlesinger Jr., "Missionary Enterprise and Theories of Imperialism," 356.

17. Charles Ernest Scott, *China from Within: Impressions and Experiences* (New York: Fleming H. Revell, 1917), 10, 23, 90.

18. Jane Hunter, *The Gospel of Gentility: American Women Missionaries in Turn-of-the-Century China* (New Haven, CT: Yale University Press, 1984), 226.

19. Lutz, "The Grand Illusion," 46–47; S. Doc. No. 35-22, at 1208–1210 (1857).

20. William Speer, *The Oldest and the Newest Empire: China and the United States* (Hartford, CT: S. S. Scranton, 1870), 387; Foster Rhea Dulles, *China and America: The Story of Their Relations since 1784* (Princeton, NJ: Princeton University Press, 1946), 50.

21. Edward D. Graham, *American Ideas of a Special Relationship with China, 1784–1900* (New York: Garland Publications, 1988), 184–201; Speer, *The Oldest and the Newest Empire*, 387–388.

22. Speer, *The Oldest and the Newest Empire*, 387.

23. Miller, "Ends and Means," 281. Paul A. Varg says that there were fewer than 38,000 Protestant converts in 1899; see *Missionaries, Chinese, and Diplomats: The American Protestant Missionary Movement in China, 1890–1952* (Princeton, NJ: Princeton University Press, 1958), 13. See also Latourette, *A History of Christian Missions in China*, 780.

24. Michael H. Hunt, *The Making of a Special Relationship: The United States and China to 1914* (New York: Columbia University Press, 1983), 26–30; Lutz, "The Grand Illusion," 68; Arline T. Golkin, "American Missionaries and the Politics of Famine Relief to China," in *United States Attitudes and Policies toward China: The Impact of American Missionaries*, ed. Patricia Neils (Armonk, NY: M. E. Sharpe, 1990), 195–210; Latourette, *A History of Christian Missions in China*, 2–3.

25. Dennett, *Americans in Eastern Asia*, 563–576.

26. Speer, *The Oldest and the Newest Empire*, 671–672.

27. The *Missionary Herald* quoted in Graham, *American Ideas of a Special Relationship with China*, 223–227.

28. For a fascinating story, see Karen Sanchez-Eppler, "Copying and Conversion: An 1824 Friendship Album 'from a Chinese Youth,'" *American Quarterly* 59, no. 2 (2007): 301–339.

29. The material on Yung Wing is from Yung Wing, *My Life in China and America* (New York: Henry Holt, 1909); and Y. C. Wang, *Chinese Intellectuals and the West, 1872–1949* (Chapel Hill: University of North Carolina Press, 1966), 42–45.

30. Yung Wing, *My Life in China and America,* 159.

31. Liel Leibovitz and Matthew Miller, *Fortunate Sons: The 120 Chinese Boys Who Came to America, Went to School, and Revolutionized an Ancient Civilization* (New York: W. W. Norton, 2011), 231–233, 268–269.

32. See Alexander Saxton, *The Indispensable Enemy: Labor and the Anti-Chinese Movement in California* (Berkeley: University of California Press, 1971); Jean Pfaelzer, *Driven Out: The Forgotten War against Chinese Americans* (Berkeley: University of California Press, 2008); and William Alvin Bartlett, "Address," *The American Missionary* 37, no. 12 (1883): 367–370.

33. Karen Ordahl Kupperman, *The Jamestown Project* (Cambridge, MA: Belknap Press of Harvard University Press, 2007), 156, 312; Speer, *The Oldest and the Newest Empire,* 24. A curious side note: Speer, a nineteenth-century former missionary to China and Sinophile once claimed that in his misnaming, "Columbus meant *Chinese*" but called the people he encountered "Indians" because Europeans in the fifteenth century commonly called all of East Asia "the Indies." Only the "mere use of a general for a particular appellation," according to the minister, prevented "our Indians from being called by us 'Chinese'" (24).

34. John Kuo Wei Tchen, *New York before Chinatown: Orientalism and the Shaping of American Culture, 1776–1882* (Baltimore, MD: Johns Hopkins University Press, 1999), 76–79; James R. Fichter, *So Great a Proffit: How the East Indies Trade Transformed Anglo-American Capitalism* (Cambridge, MA: Harvard University Press, 2010), 51–52.

35. Quote from John H. Schroeder, "Rep. John Floyd, 1817–1829: Harbinger of Oregon Territory," *Oregon Historical Quarterly* 70, no. 4 (1969): 341.

36. Dulles, *China and America,* 33.

37. See Cong. Globe, 29th Cong., 1st Sess. (1846), 917–918.

38. William H. Seward, "Survey of the Arctic and Pacific Oceans," July 29, 1852, in *The Works of William H. Seward,* vol. 1, ed. George E. Baker (New York: Redfield, 1853), 236–253; Dennett, *Americans in East Asia,* 408–409, 420. Seward believed that the free immigration of Chinese into the United States was an essential element of both his Pacific vision and the promotion of trade between China and the United States. The idea of the inexorable westward movement of civilization is presented in Elias Lyman Magoon, *Westward Empire, or, The Great Drama of Human Progress* (New York: Harper & Brothers, 1856).

39. Speer, *The Oldest and the Newest Empire,* 3–6.

40. Ibid., 25–26, 36–41.

41. Ibid., 28–31.

42. Ibid., 437–492, 638, 656, 664; Bonaparte quotes on 664, 461.

43. Tchen, *New York before Chinatown*, 49–54; Frederick Wakeman Jr., "Voyages," *American Historical Review* 98, no. 1 (1993): 1–17; Peter Parker, "Public Notification," January 10, 1856, in *American Diplomatic and Public Papers: The United States and China*, Series 1, *The Treaty System and the Taiping Rebellion, 1842–1860*, vol. 17, comp. Jules Davids (Wilmington, DE: Scholarly Resources, 1973), 6–17.

44. W. A. P. Martin, *A Cycle of Cathay: or, China, South and North. With Personal Reminiscences* (New York: F. H. Revell, 1900), 383.

45. Robert L. Irick, *Ch'ing Policy toward the Coolie Trade, 1847–1878* (Taipei: Chinese Materials Center, 1982), 32–43.

46. Davids, *American Diplomatic and Public Papers*, xiii–xxxv.

47. See Denise Helly's introduction to *The Cuba Commission Report: A Hidden History of the Chinese in Cuba* (Baltimore, MD: Johns Hopkins University Press, 1993); and Moon-Ho Jung, *Coolies and Cane* (Baltimore, MD: Johns Hopkins University Press, 2006).

48. For this and following paragraphs, see Judy Yung, Gordon H. Chang, and Him Mark Lai, eds., *Chinese American Voices: From the Gold Rush to the Present* (Berkeley: University of California Press, 2006), 1–54; Yong Chen, *Chinese San Francisco, 1850–1943: A Trans-Pacific Community* (Stanford, CA: Stanford University Press, 2000); and Shih-shan Henry Tsai, *China and the Overseas Chinese in the United States, 1868–1911* (Fayetteville: University of Arkansas Press, 1983), 1–21.

49. "The Chinaman as a Railroad Builder," *Scientific American* 21, no. 5 (July 31, 1869): 75.

50. Chester A. Arthur, Veto Message, April 4, 1882, http://books.google.com/books?id =BaQyAQAAMAAJ&pg=PA4704&lpg=PA4704&dq=%22largely+instrumental+in +constructing+the+railways+which+connect+the+Atlantic+with+the+Pacific%22&s ource=bl&ots=bvg8HLAM6c&sig=4IFiNjPrNUYahIKatkKsRdgrB74&hl=en&sa=X &ei=5ns1VIOyA6nmsATumoC4CQ&ved=0CCQQ6AEwAg#v=onepage&q&f=false, and in Joint Committee on Printing of the House and Senate, *A Compilation of the Messages and Papers of the Presidents*, vol. 11 ([Washington, DC]: n.p., 1897), 4704. See also Gordon H. Chang, "China and the Pursuit of America's Destiny: Nineteenth-Century Imagining and Why Immigration Restriction Took So Long," *Journal of Asian American Studies* 15, no. 2 (2012): 145–169.

51. Scott Zesch, *The Chinatown War: Chinese Los Angeles and the Massacre of 1871* (New York: Oxford University Press, 2012); Craig Storti, *Incident at Bitter Creek: The Story of the Rock Springs Chinese Massacre* (Ames: Iowa State University Press, 1991).

52. Robert G. Lee, *Orientals: Asian Americans in Popular Culture* (Philadelphia, PA: Temple University Press, 1999).

53. See, for example, Miller, *The Unwelcome Immigrant*.

54. The tract is by Henry Josiah West. Senator John P. Jones (R-Nev) quoted in Andrew Gyory, *Closing the Gate: Race, Politics, and the Chinese Exclusion Act* (Chapel

Hill: University of North Carolina Press, 1998), 141–142. The congressional debate on restricting Chinese immigration is full of similar descriptions of a cultural war. See, for example, Senator James G. Blaine on February 14, 1879 (*Congressional Record,* 45-3, pp. 1299–1303), and Senator John F. Miller on February 28, 1882 (*Congressional Record,* 47-1, pp. 1482–1485).

55. See Stanford M. Lyman, "The 'Yellow Peril' Mystique: Origins and Vicissitudes of a Racist Discourse," *International Journal of Politics, Culture and Society* 13, no. 4 (2000), 683–747; and Richard Austin Thompson, "The Yellow Peril, 1890–1924" (PhD diss., University of Wisconsin, 1957).

56. Pierton W. Dooner, *Last Days of the Republic* (San Francisco: Alta California Publishing House, 1880). Other work in this genre include Henry Josiah West, *The Chinese Invasion Revealing the Habits, Manners and Customs of the Chinese, Political, Social and Religious, on the Pacific Coast* (San Francisco: Excelsior Office, Bacon & Co., 1873); Robert Wolter, *A Short and Truthful History of the Taking of California and Oregon by the Chinese in the Year A.D. 1899* (San Francisco: A. L. Bancroft, 1882); Oto Mundo, *The Recovered Continent: A Tale of the Chinese Invasion* (Columbus, OH: Harper-Osgood, 1898); and Marsden Manson, *The Yellow Peril in Action* (San Francisco: Britton & Rey, 1907). The 1880 short story "The Battle of Wabash: A Letter from the Invisible Police," by Lorelle [pseud.] (*The Californian,* October 1880), envisioned a monumental battle between millions of Americans against Chinese in the fields of Indiana in 2081. The Chinese army is manned by immigrants and their descendants and an expeditionary force from China. The Chinese crush the Americans, the republic falls, and the people are enslaved. See Limin Chu, "Images of China and the Chinese in the Overland Monthly, 1868–1875" (PhD diss., Duke University, 1965), 307–323.

57. Jack London, "The Unparalleled Invasion," in *The Strength of the Strong* (New York: Macmillan, 1914), 71–100. See also London's "The Yellow Peril," in *Revolution and Other Essays* (New York: Macmillan, 1910), 267–289.

58. John Berdan Gardner, "The Image of the Chinese in the United States, 1885–1915," (PhD diss., University of Pennsylvania, 1961), 45–47, 64–91; George H. Blakeslee, ed., *Recent Developments in China: Clark University Addresses* (New York: G. E. Stechert, 1913), 13, 16; Arthur H. Smith, *Chinese Characteristics* (1894; repr., Norwalk, CT: EastBridge, 2002), 11. See also Charles W. Hayford, "Chinese and American Characteristics: Arthur H. Smith and His China Book," in *Christianity in China: Early Protestant Missionary Writings,* ed. Suzanne Wilson Barnett and John King Fairbank (Cambridge, MA: Harvard University Press, 1985), 153–174.

59. John F. Miller, "Certain Phases of the Chinese Question," *The Californian,* March 1880, 428–435. See also A. A. Sargent, *Chinese Immigration* (Washington, DC: np, 1878); and Smith, *Chinese Characteristics,* 33. For a prominent example of the supposedly superior fearing the inferior, see Samuel Gompers, "Meat versus Rice: American Manhood against Asiatic Coolieism, Which Shall Survive?" (Washington, DC: American Federation of Labor, 1901).

60. Wu Tingfang, *America: Through the Spectacles of an Oriental Diplomat* (New York: Frederick A. Stokes, 1914), v.

61. Zhang Deyi, *Diary of a Chinese Diplomat,* trans. Simon Johnston (Beijing: Chinese Literature Press, 1992), 72, 77, 80–86, 92–93, 145–146.

62. R. David Arkush and Leo O. Lee, eds., *Land without Ghosts: Chinese Impressions of America from the Mid-Nineteenth Century to the Present* (Berkeley: University of California Press, 1989), 25–95. See also Merle Curti and John Stalker, "'The Flowery Flag Devils': The American Image in China, 1840–1900," *Proceedings of the American Philosophical Society* 96, no. 6 (December 20, 1952), 663–690.

63. Huang Zunxian, "Expulsion of the Immigrants," in *Land without Ghosts: Chinese Impressions of America from the Mid-Nineteenth Century to the Present,* ed. R. David Arkush and Leo O. Lee (Berkeley: University of California Press, 1989), 61–65.

64. Arkush and Lee, *Land without Ghosts,* 81–95.

65. Quote from Jonathan D. Spence, *The Search for Modern China* (New York: Norton, 1990), 233–234.

66. "How Great Is This 'Yellow Peril'?" *New York Times,* August 2, 1900, 6; Herbert Hoover, *The Memoirs of Herbert Hoover,* vol. 1, *Years of Adventure, 1874–1920* (New York: Macmillan, 1951), 35–72.

3. Grand Politics and High Culture

Epigraph: City Council of Boston, *Reception and Entertainment of the Chinese Embassy by the City of Boston* (Boston: Alfred Mudge & Son, 1868), 19. The remarks were made at a banquet honoring Anson Burlingame.

1. Two studies that focus on the early history of this "special relationship" are Edward D. Graham, "American Ideas of a Special Relationship with China, 1784–1900" (PhD diss., Harvard University, 1968); and Michael H. Hunt, *The Making of a Special Relationship: The United States and China to 1914* (New York: Columbia University Press, 1983).

2. Chester A. Bain, "Commodore Matthew Perry, Humphrey Marshall, and the Taiping Rebellion," *Far Eastern Quarterly* 10, no. 3 (1951): 258–270; Michael P. Riccards, *The Presidency and the Middle Kingdom: China, the United States, and Executive Leadership* (Lanham, MD: Lexington Books, 2000), 19–22.

3. S. Doc., No. 36-30, at 7–10 (1860); Foster M. Farley, "William B. Reed: President Buchanan's Minister to China, 1857–1858," *Pennsylvania History* 37, no. 3 (1970): 269–280.

4. Shih-shan Henry Tsai, *China and the Overseas Chinese in the United States, 1868–1911* (Fayetteville: University of Arkansas Press, 1983), 1–8, 24–28; John Schrecker, "'For the Equality of Men—For the Equality of Nations': Anson Burlingame and China's First Embassy to the United States, 1868," *Journal of American-East Asian Relations* 17, no. 1 (2010): 9–34.

5. *Banquet to His Excellency Anson Burlingame and His Associates of the Chinese Embassy by the Citizens of New York on Tuesday, June 23, 1868* (New York: Sun Book and Job Printing House, 1868), 9, 47.

6. Boston City Council, *Reception and Entertainment of the Chinese Embassy by the City of Boston* (Boston: Alfred Mudge & Son, 1868), 19.

7. Ibid., 41–43.

8. Schrecker, "'For the Equality of Men,'" 21, 33; Tsai, *China and Overseas Chinese in the United States,* 28–29; miscellaneous clippings, Anson Burlingame Papers, Special Collections, M0119/1/5, Stanford University Libraries, Stanford, California. Though Seward and Burlingame worked closely together, Seward believed that Burlingame was overly optimistic about the ability of China to change and receive influences from the West. See Olive Risley Seward, ed., *William H. Seward's Travels around the World* (New York: D. Appleton, 1873), 280.

9. Kristin L. Hoganson, *Consumers' Imperium: The Global Production of American Domesticity, 1865–1920* (Chapel Hill: University of North Carolina Press, 2007), 22.

10. John Russell Young, *Around the World with General Grant* (New York: American News Company, 1879), 311–316, 441–443.

11. Ibid., 286–453.

12. Paul A. Varg, *The Making of a Myth: The United States and China, 1897–1912* (East Lansing: Michigan State University Press, 1968), 14–16, 36–49; Brooks Adams, *America's Economic Supremacy* (New York: Macmillan, 1900); Hubert Howe Bancroft, *The New Pacific* (New York: Bancroft Company, 1899); Josiah Strong, *Expansion under New World-Conditions* (New York: Baker and Taylor, 1900); Jerry Israel, *Progressivism and the Open Door: America and China, 1905–1921* (Pittsburgh, PA: University of Pittsburgh Press, 1971), 6–11; Marilyn Blatt Young, *The Rhetoric of Empire: American China Policy, 1895–1901* (Cambridge, MA: Harvard University Press, 1968), 2–5, 228.

13. William Elliot Griffis, "America in the Far East: The Signal Gun at Manila," *The Outlook,* November 26, 1898, 761–766.

14. Albert J. Beveridge, "March of the Flag," September 16, 1898, in Beveridge, *The Meaning of the Times and Other Speeches* (Indianapolis: Bobbs-Merrill, 1908), 52. On the consideration of China in the decision to take the Philippines, see Julius W. Pratt, *Expansionists of 1898: The Acquisition of Hawaii and the Spanish Islands* (Chicago: Quadrangle Books, 1936); and A. Whitney Griswold, *Far Eastern Policy of the United States* (New York: Harcourt, Brace, 1938).

15. Alfred T. Mahan, *The Problem of Asia and Its Effect upon International Politics* (Boston: Little, Brown, 1900), 19, 170.

16. Albert J. Beveridge, "Our Philippine Policy," January 9, 1900, in Beveridge, *The Meaning of the Times,* 59; Theodore Roosevelt to Benjamin Ide Wheeler, June 17, 1905, quoted in Howard K. Beale, *Theodore Roosevelt and the Rise of America to World Power* (Baltimore, MD: Johns Hopkins University Press, 1956), 174, 175–193; Roosevelt, "The

Pacific Era," *The Pacific Era* 1, no. 1 (1907): 1–4. See also Theodore Roosevelt, "The Awakening of China," *The Outlook,* November 28, 1908, 665–667.

17. Mahan, *The Problem of Asia and Its Effect upon International Politics,* 146–202.

18. Ibid.

19. Walter Lippmann, *U.S. War Aims* (Boston: Little, Brown, 1944), 12–16; 33–34; George F. Kennan, "America and the Orient," in Kennan, *American Diplomacy, 1900–1950,* exp. ed. (Chicago: University of Chicago Press, 1984), 38–54. The specific history of the origin and formulation of the Open Door Notes is beyond the scope of this study. Suffice it to say that it is voluminous and diverse. Influential works include Hunt, *The Making of a Special Relationship;* Kennan, "Mr. Hippisley and the Open Door," in Kennan, *American Diplomacy, 1900–1950,* 21–37; William Appleman Williams, *The Tragedy of American Diplomacy,* new edition (New York: Norton, 1988); Young, *The Rhetoric of Empire;* and V. K. Wellington Koo, *The Open Door Policy and World Peace* (London: Oxford University Press, 1939).

20. Quote from Thomas F. Millard, "The Japanese Menace," *The Century Magazine* 91 (March 1916): 673–682. See also Mingchien Joshua Bau, *The Open Door Doctrine in Relation to China* (New York: Macmillan, 1923), 21. Bau cites James W. Bashford, *China: An Interpretation* (New York: Abingdon, 1916), 17–18, but Bashford provides no citation. Parker Thomas Moon, *Imperialism and World Politics* (New York: Macmillan, 1930), includes the quote but gives no citation (p. 321). In his classic biography of Hay, Tyler Dennett does not include the quote; see Tyler Dennett, *John Hay: From Poetry to Politics* (New York: Dodd, Mead, 1933). The original source for the Hay quote has eluded me. Kenton J. Clymer, *John Hay: The Gentleman as Diplomat* (Ann Arbor: University of Michigan Press, 1975), 143–156.

21. Young, *The Rhetoric of Empire,* 109–136; Graham, "American Ideas of a Special Relationship with China," 310–327.

22. Quote from Foster Rhea Dulles, *China and America: The Story of Their Relations since 1784* (Princeton, NJ: Princeton University Press, 1946), 68.

23. Graham, "American Ideas of a Special Relationship with China," 327–340; Mahan, *The Problem of Asia and Its Effect upon International Politics,* 172–173. See also John Berdan Gardner, "The Image of the Chinese in the United States, 1885–1915" (PhD diss., University of Pennsylvania, 1961), 92–123.

24. Demetrius C. Boulger, "America's Share in a Partition of China," *North American Review* 171, no. 525 (1900): 171–181; *North American Review* 172, no. 531 (1901). Other Americans expressed a guarded sympathy for the Boxers' anti-foreign sentiments, seeing them as genuine grievances. See, for example, Graham, "American Ideas of a Special Relationship with China," 364–366.

25. Hunt, *The Making of a Special Relationship,* 196–200; Michael H. Hunt, "The American Remission of the Boxer Indemnity: A Reappraisal," *Journal of Asian Studies* 31, no. 3 (1972): 539–559.

26. John Barrett, *North American Review* 175, no. 552 (1902), 655–663.

27. Wu Tingfang, *America, through the Spectacles of an Oriental Diplomat* (New York: Frederick A. Stokes, 1914), 186.

28. Kennan, "Mr. Hippisley and the Open Door," 37; Varg, *The Making of a Myth,* 105–171; Schurman to Secretary of State, December 3, 1921, in United States Department of State, *Papers Relating to the Foreign Relations of the United States, 1921,* vol. 1 (Washington, DC: Government Printing Office, 1921), 315–321. John King Fairbank believed that the Open Door Policy was not a break from the past but continued a long tradition in America's westward expansion. See Fairbank, *The United States and China,* rev. ed. (Cambridge, MA: Harvard University Press, 1954), chapter 14.

29. John Stuart Thomson, "The Genesis of the Republican Revolution in China from a South China Standpoint," in *Recent Developments in China,* ed. George H. Blakeslee (New York: G. E. Stechert, 1913), 77, 89. Thomson published two major books on China: *The Chinese* (Indianapolis: Bobbs-Merrill, 1909) and *China Revolutionized* (Indianapolis: Bobbs-Merrill, 1913).

30. My discussion of Sun is based largely on Marie-Claire Bergere, *Sun Yat-sen,* trans. from the French by Janet Lloyd (Stanford, CA: Stanford University Press, 1998).

31. American opinion of the Chinese revolution can be seen in periodical articles such as "The Chinese Rebellion," *The Literary Digest* 43, no. 18 (1911): 721–722; "Ending Manchu Rule in China," 43, no. 20 (1911): 837–838; "What Will Become of China?," 44, no. 1 (1912): 11–12; C. Brownell Gage, "My Experiences in the Chinese Revolution," *The Independent* 72, no. 3294 (1912): 129–135; and "Recognition of the Chinese Republic," *The Independent* 72, no. 3295 (1912): 209–211. See also Blakeslee, "Introduction," in *Recent Developments in China,* ed. George H. Blakeslee (New York: G. E. Stechert, 1913), x. See the discussion of the Chinese in Woodrow Wilson, *History of the American People* (New York: Harper and Bros., 1902).

32. "The Acting Secretary of State to Certain American Diplomatic Officers," March 19, 1913, in United States Department of State, *Papers Relating to the Foreign Relations of the United States, 1913* (Washington, DC: Government Printing Office, 1913), 170–171.

33. James Reed, *The Missionary Mind and American East Asian Policy, 1911–1915* (Cambridge, MA: Harvard University Press, 1983), 36–39.

34. Paul S. Reinsch, *World Politics at the End of the Nineteenth Century as Influenced by the Oriental Situation* (New York: Macmillan, 1900), 111; Tien-yi Li, *Woodrow Wilson's China Policy, 1913–1917* (New York: Octagon Books, 1969), 16–19.

35. See Guoqi Xu, *China and the Great War: China's Pursuit of a New National Identity and Internationalization* (Cambridge, UK: Cambridge University Press, 2005).

36. Li, *Woodrow Wilson's China Policy,* 139–158; Warren I. Cohen, "America and the May Fourth Movement: The Response to Chinese Nationalism, 1917–1921," *Pacific Historical Review* 35, no. 1 (1966): 83–100; Israel, *Progressivism and the Open Door,* 169–175; Noel H. Pugach, *Paul S. Reinsch: Open Door Diplomat in Action* (Millwood,

NY: KTO Press, 1979), 266–276; Lansing quotes from Erez Manela, *The Wilsonian Moment: Self-Determination and the International Origins of Anticolonial Nationalism* (New York: Oxford University Press, 2007), 184.

37. Quotes from Pugach, *Paul S. Reinsch,* 276–277; Paul S. Reinsch, *An American Diplomat in China* (Garden City, NY: Doubleday, 1922), vii–xii.

38. Pugach, *Paul S. Reinsch,* 280–284; Reinsch, *An American Diplomat in China.*

39. Ellen Paul Denker, *After the Chinese Taste: China's Influence in America, 1730–1930* (Salem, MA: Peabody Museum of Salem, 1985); Jonathan Goldstein, *Philadelphia and the China Trade, 1682–1846: Commercial, Cultural, and Attitudinal Effects* (University Park: Pennsylvania State University Press, 1977), 36–40; Ping Chia Kuo, "Canton and Salem: The Impact of Chinese Culture upon New England Life during the Post-Revolutionary Era," *New England Quarterly* 3, no. 3 (1930): 420–442.

40. Joan M. Jensen, "Women on the Pacific Rim: Some Thoughts on Border Crossings," *Pacific Historical Review* 67, no. 1 (1998): 3–38; *The First Ladies* exhibit, Smithsonian Museum of American History, Washington, D.C.

41. Hoganson, *Consumers' Imperium,* chapters 2 and 3; Yong Chen, *Chop Suey: The Story of Chinese Food in America* (New York: Columbia University Press, 2014), 21–91; and see Annelise Heinz, "Mahjong, American Modernity, and Cultural Transnationalism," Department of History, Stanford University, doctoral dissertation in progress.

42. Nathan Dunn, *"Ten Thousand Chinese Things": A Descriptive Catalogue of the Chinese Collection in Philadelphia, with Miscellaneous Remarks upon the Manners, Customs, Trade, and Government of the Celestial Empire* (Philadelphia: Printed for the Proprietor, 1839); Denker, *After the Chinese Taste,* 21–24; Goldstein, *Philadelphia and the China Trade,* 73–79.

43. Brantz Mayer, "A Nation in a Nut Shell," nd, np., newspaper clipping accompanying Nathan Dunn, *"Ten Thousand Chinese Things.' A Descriptive Catalogue of the Chinese Collection, in Philadelphia. With Miscellaneous Remarks upon the Manners, Customs, Trade, and Government of the Celestial Empire* (Philadelphia: np, 1839), held in Green Library, Stanford University.

44. John R. Peters Jr., *Miscellaneous Remarks upon the Government, History, Religions, Literature, Agriculture, Arts, Trades, Manners, and Customs of the Chinese* (Boston: Eastburn's Press, 1845); Ronald J. Zboray and Mary Saracino Zboray, "Between 'Crockery-dom' and Barnum: Boston's Chinese Museum, 1845–47," *American Quarterly* 56, no. 2 (2004): 271–307; Hiroko Uno, "Emily Dickinson's Encounter with the East: Chinese Museum in Boston," *Emily Dickinson Journal* 17, no. 1 (2008): 43–67.

45. See Alexandra Munroe, ed., *The Third Mind: American Artists Contemplate Asia, 1860–1989* (New York: Guggenheim Museum, 2009); Cynthia Mills, Lee Glazer, and Amelia A. Goeritz, eds., *East-West Interchanges in American Art: A Long and Tumultuous Relationship* (Washington, DC: Smithsonian Institution Press, 2012); and Gordon H. Chang, Mark Dean Johnson, and Paul Karlstrom, eds., *Asian American Art: A History, 1850–1970* (Stanford, CA: Stanford University Press, 2009).

46. Ernest F. Fenollosa, *Epochs of Chinese and Japanese Art: An Outline History of East Asiatic Design* (New York: Frederick A. Stokes, 1912), xxix, 2; Ernest F. Fenollosa, "The Coming Fusion of East and West," *Harper's,* December 1898, 115–122; Lawrence W. Chisolm, *Fenollosa: The Far East and American Culture* (New Haven, CT: Yale University Press, 1963), 89–101; David Weir, *American Orient: Imagining the East from the Colonial Era through the Twentieth Century* (Amherst: University of Massachusetts, 2011), 115–120. See also Van Wyck Brooks, *Fenollosa and His Circle, with Other Essays in Biography* (New York: E. P. Dutton, 1962); Ezra Pound, *Cathay* (London: E. Mathews, 1915); and L. S. Dembo, *The Confucian Odes of Ezra Pound: A Critical Appraisal* (London: Faber and Faber, 1963).

47. *Chinamania* exhibit, April 2011, Freer Gallery of Art, Washington, D.C.; Anna Mathilda Whistler to James Gamble, February 10, 1864, Whistler Archive, Archives, University of Glasgow; Linda Merrill, *The Peacock Room: A Cultural Biography* (Washington, DC: Freer Gallery of Art, 1998); Lee Glazer, "Stories of the Beautiful: Narratives of East-West Interchange at the Freer Gallery of Art," in *East-West Interchanges in American Art: "A Long and Tumultuous Relationship,"* ed. Cynthia Mills, Lee Glazer, and Amelia Goerlitz (Washington, DC: Smithsonian Institution Scholarly Press, 2012), 216–230.

48. Denker, *After the Chinese Taste,* 42–43; Warren I. Cohen, *East Asian Art and American Culture: A Study in International Relations* (New York: Columbia University Press, 1992), 37–73; Shelley Sang-Hee Lee, *Claiming the Oriental Gateway: Prewar Seattle and Japanese America* (Philadelphia: Temple University Press, 2011), 76–104.

49. One of Weber's most famous works is entitled "The Chinese Restaurant." Tobey quote from Kathleen Pyne and D. Scott Atkinson, "Landscapes of the Mind: New Conceptions of Nature," in *The Third Mind: American Artists Contemplate Asia, 1860–1989,* ed. Alexandra Munroe (New York: Guggenheim Museum, 2009), 94. On American Orientalism and the arts and women, see Mari Yoshihara, *Embracing the East: White Women and American Orientalism* (New York: Oxford University Press, 2003).

50. Arthur Christy, *The Orient in American Transcendentalism: A Study of Emerson, Thoreau, and Alcott* (New York: Columbia University Press, 1932). See also Lyman V. Cady, "Thoreau's Quotations from the Confucian Books in Walden," *American Literature* 33, no. 1 (1961): 20–32; Frederic Ives Carpenter, *Emerson and Asia* (Cambridge, MA: Harvard University Press, 1930); and Robert Detweiler, "Emerson and Zen," *American Quarterly* 14, no. 3 (1962): 422–438.

51. Israel, *Progressivism and the Open Door,* 6–8; Ernest Samuels, *Henry Adams: The Middle Years* (Cambridge, MA: Belknap Press of Harvard University Press, 1958), 292–294, 298–312, 320–322, 414; Paul A. Varg, *Open Door Diplomat: The Life of W. W. Rockhill* (Urbana: University of Illinois Press, 1952), 1; Vivien Greene, "Aestheticism and Japan: The Cult of the Orient," in *The Third Mind: American Artists Contemplate Asia, 1860–1989,* ed. Alexandra Munroe (New York: Guggenheim Museum, 2009), 63.

See also Henry Adams, *The Education of Henry Adams* (New York: Modern Library, 1931), 391–392. Adams greatly respected Hay and praised his efforts to uphold the Open Door Policy, against the pressures of "old Europe"; see Arthur E. Christy, *The Asian Legacy and American Life* (New York: John Day, 1942), 1–50.

52. Charles W. Eliot, "The Means of Unifying China," in *Recent Developments in China*, ed. George H. Blakeslee (New York: G. E. Stechert, 1913), 18; Henry James, *Charles W. Eliot: President of Harvard University, 1869–1909*, vol. 2 (New York: Houghton Mifflin, 1930), 217–218.

53. Thomas E. LaFargue, *China's First Hundred: Educational Mission Students in the United States, 1872–1881* (Pullman: Washington State University Press, 1987); Liel Leibovitz and Matthew Miller, *Fortunate Sons: The 120 Chinese Boys Who Came to America, Went to School, and Revolutionized an Ancient Civilization* (New York: W. W. Norton, 2011); Weili Ye, *Seeking Modernity in China's Name: Chinese Students in the United States, 1900–1927* (Stanford, CA: Stanford University Press, 2001).

54. The following discussion of Dewey in China draws from Jessica Ching-Sze Wang, *John Dewey in China: To Teach and to Learn* (Albany: State University of New York Press, 2007).

55. Israel, *Progressivism and the Open Door*, 182–190, 197–202.

56. John Dewey and Alice Chipman Dewey, *Letters from China and Japan*, ed. Evelyn Dewey (New York: E. P. Dutton, 1920).

57. Quotes from ibid., 165, 235–237.

58. Ibid., 154–157, 185, 207, 237.

59. Quotes in Jon Thares Davidann, *Cultural Diplomacy in U.S.-Japanese Relations, 1919–1941* (New York: Palgrave Macmillan, 2007), 1–3, 6–9, 46; Dewey and Dewey, *Letters from China and Japan*, 156–157, 173, 179, 255. On China and Japan, see Wang, *John Dewey in China*, 4, 71–72; and John Dewey, *China, Japan and the U.S.A.: Present Day Conditions in the Far East and their Bearing on the Washington Conference* (New York: Republic Publishing, 1921), 1–3, 6–9. After they returned from Asia, the Deweys wrote several books about their experience and published forty articles for the periodicals *New Republic* and *Asia*.

60. Jane M. Dewey, ed., "Biography of John Dewey," in *The Philosophy of John Dewey*, ed. Paul Arthur Schilpp (Evanston, IL: Northwestern University Press, 1939), 42; Zhixin Su, "A Critical Evaluation of John Dewey's Influence on Chinese Education," *American Journal of Education* 103, no. 3 (1995): 302–325.

61. Michael Sullivan, *The Meeting of Eastern and Western Art* (Berkeley: University of California Press, 1989), 261–263.

62. See Jacquelynn Baas, *Smile of the Buddha: Eastern Philosophy and Western Art, from Monet to Today* (Berkeley: University of California Press, 2005); Jacquelynn Baas, "Before Zen: The Nothing of American Dada," in Mills et al., *East-West Interchanges in American Art*, 52–65; Jeffrey Wechsler, ed., *Asian Traditions/Modern Expressions: Asian American Artists and Abstraction, 1945–1970* (New York: Harry N. Abrams, 1997);

and Bert Winther-Tamaki, *Art in the Encounter of Nations: Japanese and American Artists in the Early Postwar Years* (Honolulu: University of Hawai'i Press, 2001).

63. J. J. Clarke, *Oriental Enlightenment: The Encounter between Asian and Western Thought* (London: Routledge, 1997); Weir, *American Orient*, 239–244.

64. Maxine Hong Kingston to Garrett Hongo, August 4, 1992, in *Amerasia Journal* 20, no. 3 (1994): 25–26.

4. Revolutions and War

Epigraph: Will Rogers, "China Invented Everything," in *Will Rogers' Weekly Articles*, vol. 5, *The Hoover Years, 1931–1933,* ed. Steven K. Gragert (Stillwater: Oklahoma State University Press, 1982), 7–9.

1. Jonathan D. Spence, *To Change China: Western Advisers in China* (New York: Penguin Books, 1980), 174.

2. Jay Taylor, *The Generalissimo: Chiang Kai-shek and the Struggle for Modern China* (Cambridge, MA: Belknap Press of Harvard University Press, 2009).

3. Akira Iriye, *Across the Pacific: An Inner History of American-East Asian Relations,* rev. ed. (Chicago: Imprint Publications, 1992), 172–173; John Leighton Stuart, *Fifty Years in China* (New York: Random House, 1954), 111.

4. Jon Thares Davidann, *Cultural Diplomacy in U.S.-Japan Relations, 1919–1941* (New York: Palgrave Macmillan, 2007), 143–144; Sherwood Eddy, "Japan Threatens the World," *Christian Century,* March 16, 1932, 346–347; Sherwood Eddy, *The World's Danger Zone* (New York: Farrar & Rinehart, 1932), 3–12.

5. Hoover mentions his experience of living in Asia as providing help in his handling of the crisis. See Herbert Hoover, *The Memoirs of Herbert Hoover: The Cabinet and the Presidency, 1920–1933,* vol. 2 (New York: Macmillan, 1952), 362–378.

6. Editorial, *Christian Century,* April 20, 1932, 499.

7. In his 300-page account of the Manchurian crisis, Henry Stimson relegates Chiang Kaishek literally to a footnote; see Henry L. Stimson, *The Far Eastern Crisis: Recollection and Observations* (New York: Harper & Bros., 1936), 134n.

8. Ibid., 234–236; Stimson diary entry for January 30, 1932, Henry Lewis Stimson Papers, Manuscripts and Archives, Yale University. In 1950, President Harry Truman told Stimson that the tougher stance toward Japan that Stimson had advocated but Hoover had overruled would have prevented the outbreak of the Pacific War. Truman provided no evidence to support his contention. See Truman to Stimson, July 7, 1950, in *Mr. President: The First Publication from the Personal Diaries, Private Letters, Papers and Revealing Interviews of Harry S. Truman,* ed. William Hillman (New York: Farrar, Straus and Young, 1952), 55.

9. Stimson, *The Far Eastern Crisis,* 97–109; Christopher Thorne, *The Limits of Foreign Policy: The West, the League and the Far Eastern Crisis of 1931–1933* (London:

Hamish Hamilton, 1972), 288–303. See also A. Whitney Griswold, *The Far Eastern Policy of the United States* (New York: Harcourt, Brace, 1938), 410–435.

10. Justus D. Doenecke, *When the Wicked Rise: American Opinion-Makers and the Manchurian Crisis of 1931–1933* (Lewisburg, PA: Bucknell University Press, 1984), 24–50, 67–93; A. Lawrence Lowell, "Manchuria, the League, and the United States," *Foreign Affairs* 10, no. 3 (1932): 351–368.

11. Iriye, *Across the Pacific,* 172–188. See also Michael E. Chapman, "Fidgeting over Foreign Policy: Henry L. Stimson and the Shenyang Incident, 1931," *Diplomatic History* 37, no. 4 (2013): 727–748.

12. Walter Lippmann, *U.S. War Aims* (Boston: Little, Brown, 1944), 30–40; Lowell, "Manchuria, the League, and the United States," 368.

13. Taylor, *The Generalissimo,* 92–114.

14. R. J. C. Butow, "A Notable Passage to China: Myth and Memory in FDR's Family History," *Prologue* 31, no. 3 (1999): 159–177; Frank Freidel, *Franklin D. Roosevelt: A Rendezvous with Destiny* (Boston: Little, Brown, 1990), 442.

15. Michael P. Riccards, *Presidency and Middle Kingdom: China, the United States, and Executive Leadership* (Lanham, MD: Lexington Books, 2000), 91–93.

16. Will Rogers, "Will Rogers Holds China Should Send Out Missionaries," in *Will Rogers' Weekly Articles,* vol. 3, *The Coolidge Years, 1927–1929,* ed. Steven P. Gragert (Stillwater: Oklahoma University Press, 1981), 12–14.

17. Rogers, "Cheer Up! There's No Tax for Being Happy," in *Will Rogers' Weekly Articles,* vol. 5, *The Hoover Years, 1931–1933,* ed. Steven K. Gragert (Stillwater: Oklahoma University Press, 1982), 116–118; and Rogers, "Two Bulls in a China Shop," in *Will Rogers' Weekly Articles,* vol. 2, *The Coolidge Years, 1925–1927,* ed. Steven P. Gragert (Stillwater: Oklahoma University Press, 1980), 275–277.

18. Noel T. Boaz and Russell L. Ciochon, *Dragon Bone Hill: An Ice-Age Saga of Homo erectus* (New York: Oxford University Press, 2004), 1–5, 20–21; Sigrid Schmalzer, *The People's Peking Man: Popular Science and Human Identity in Twentieth-Century China* (Chicago: University of Chicago Press, 2008), 33–34, 44–45, 47.

19. Harold R. Isaacs, *Scratches on Our Minds: American Images of China and India* (New York: John Day, 1958), 155–158; Peter Conn, *Pearl S. Buck: A Cultural Biography* (New York: Cambridge University Press, 1996), xii–xiv.

20. Michael H. Hunt, "Pearl Buck—Popular Expert on China, 1931–1949," *Modern China* 3, no. 1 (1977): 33–64; quotes from Kang Liao, *Pearl S. Buck: A Cultural Bridge across the Pacific* (Westport, CT: Greenwood Press, 1997), 20, 67; and Karen J. Leong, *The China Mystique: Pearl S. Buck, Anna May Wong, Mayling Soong, and the Transformation of American Orientalism* (Berkeley: University of California Press, 2005), 27.

21. Liao, *Pearl S. Buck,* 23–26. In awarding its prize to Buck, the Swedish Academy passed over American writers including Theodore Dreiser, F. Scott Fitzgerald, William Faulkner, Upton Sinclair, and Ernest Hemingway, provoking criticism and resentment

among some. It was said that the academy was pandering to popular tastes, which in effect was another way of saying that Buck had been extraordinarily effective in bringing the Chinese to life for Americans. Will Rogers, "China and the Bucks," in *Will Rogers' Weekly Articles,* vol. 5, *The Hoover Years, 1931–1933,* ed. Steven K. Gragert (Stillwater: University of Oklahoma Press, 1982), 187–189. Pearl S. Buck's *Dragon Seed* (New York: John Day, 1942) was perhaps her second most commercially successful book. It too was made into a film of the same name and starred Katherine Hepburn as a brave Chinese woman who stands up against rapacious Japanese invaders. The role won Hepburn an Academy Award nomination.

22. Mari Yoshihara, *Embracing the East: White Women and American Orientalism* (New York: Oxford University Press, 2003).

23. Judy Yung, Gordon H. Chang, and Him Mark Lai, eds., *Chinese American Voices: From the Gold Rush to the Present* (Berkeley: University of California Press, 2006); Suoqiao Qian, *Liberal Cosmopolitan: Lin Yutang and Middling Chinese Modernity* (Boston: Brill, 2011).

24. Paul Reinsch, "Bolshevism in Asia," *Asia* 20 (April 1920): 310–312; Pearl S. Buck, "Communism in China," *The Nation,* July 25, 1928, 97–99; Owen Lattimore, *Manchuria: Cradle of Conflict* (New York: Macmillan, 1932), 97.

25. Joyce Kathleen Bibber, "The Chinese Communists as Viewed by the American Periodical Press, 1920–1937" (PhD diss., Stanford University, 1968), 1–51, 124–133, 174–176; Kenneth E. Shewmaker, *Americans and Chinese Communists, 1927–1945, A Persuading Encounter* (Ithaca, NY: Cornell University Press, 1971), 12–33.

26. Edgar Snow, *Red Star over China* (New York: Random House, 1938), 65–83.

27. Bernard S. Thomas, *Season of High Adventure: Edgar Snow in China* (Berkeley: University of California Press, 1996), 173.

28. Evans Carlson, *Evans F. Carlson on China at War, 1937–1941,* ed. Hugh Deane (New York: China and Us Publications, 1993).

29. Jerry Israel, "Carl Crow, Edgar Snow, and Shifting American Journalistic Perceptions of China," in *America Views China: American Images of China Then and Now,* ed. Jonathan Goldstein, Jerry Israel, and Hilary Conroy (Bethlehem, PA: Lehigh University Press, 1991), 148–168.

30. Carl Crow, *Four Hundred Million Customers* (London: Hamish Hamilton, 1937), 33.

31. Albert Feuerwerker, "Doing Business in China over Three Centuries," in "Chinese Business History: Interpretive Trends and Priorities for the Future," ed. Robert Gardella, Jane K. Leonard, and Andrea McElderry, special issue, *Chinese Studies in History* 31, nos. 3–4 (1998): 16–34; Albert Feuerwerker, *The Foreign Establishment in China in the Early Twentieth Century* (Ann Arbor: Center for Chinese Studies, University of Michigan, 1976).

32. Sherman Cochran, *Big Business in China: Sino-Foreign Rivalry in the Cigarette Industry, 1890–1930* (Cambridge, MA: Harvard University Press, 1980), 10–11, 224;

Carol Benedict, *Golden-Silk Smoke: A History of Tobacco in China, 1550–2010* (Berkeley: University of California Press, 2011), 1, 131–136.

33. Crow, *Four Hundred Million Customers*, 316–317. The toothbrush is said to have been invented in China in the fifteenth century and then brought to Europe by travelers.

34. Carl Crow, *I Speak for the Chinese* (New York: Harper Brothers, 1937), 80–82.

35. "The Japanese Conqueror Brings 'A Week of Hell' to China Nationalist Capital in Nanking," and "A Universal Cameraman Documents American History: 'The Panay Incident,'" *Life*, January 10, 1938, 50–51, 11–17; Ernest R. May, "U.S. Press Coverage of Japan, 1931–1941," in *Pearl Harbor as History: Japanese-American Relations, 1931–1941*, ed. Dorothy Borg and Shumpei Okamoto (New York: Columbia University Press, 1973), 511–549.

36. W. H. Auden and Christopher Isherwood, *Journey to a War* (New York: Random House, 1939), 274.

37. Iriye, *Across the Pacific*, 196–198.

38. Unattributed letter "mimeographed for distribution by the New York head-quarters of one of the largest national philanthropic organizations," as quoted in John W. Masland, "Missionary Influence upon American Far Eastern Policy," *Pacific Historical Review* 10, no. 3 (1941): 279–296.

39. See the 2007 documentary *Nanking*, directed by Bill Guttentag and Dan Sturman.

40. Freidel, *Franklin D. Roosevelt*, 292–294; Justus D. Doenecke and John E. Wilz, *From Isolation to War: 1931–1941*, 2nd ed. (Arlington Heights, IL: Harlan Davidson, 1991), 120–127; William L. Neumann, *America Encounters Japan: From Perry to Mac-Arthur* (Baltimore, MD: Johns Hopkins University Press, 1963), 253–255.

41. T. Christopher Jespersen, *American Images of China, 1931–1949* (Stanford, CA: Stanford University Press, 1996), 46; Doenecke and Wilz, *From Isolation to War*, 74.

42. Warren I. Cohen, *America's Response to China: A History of Sino-American Relations*, 5th ed. (New York: Columbia University Press, 2010), 130–138; Michael H. Hunt and Steven I. Levine, *Arc of Empire: America's Wars in Asia from the Philippines to Vietnam* (Chapel Hill: University of North Carolina Press, 2012), 71–76; S. C. M. Paine, *The Wars for Asia, 1911–1949* (New York: Cambridge University Press, 2012), 175–176, 181–183.

43. See Masland, "Missionary Influence upon American Far Eastern Policy"; and Donald J. Friedman, *The Road from Isolation: The Campaign of the American Committee for Non-Participation in Japanese Aggression, 1938–1941* (Cambridge, MA: East Asian Research Center, Harvard University, 1968).

44. See Renqiu Yu, *"To Save China, To Save Ourselves": The Chinese Hand Laundry Alliance of New York* (Philadelphia, PA: Temple University Press, 1992).

45. Kevin Scott Wong, *Americans First: Chinese Americans and the Second World War* (Cambridge, MA: Harvard University Press, 2005), 34–44; Lim P. Lee, "China-town Goes Picketing," in *Chinese American Voices: From the Gold Rush to the Present*,

ed. Judy Yung, Gordon H. Chang, and Him Mark Lai (Berkeley: University of California Press, 2006), 200–203.

46. Robert E. Herzstein, *Henry R. Luce, Time, and the American Crusade in Asia* (New York: Cambridge University Press, 2005), 21–25.

47. *Time,* January 3, 1938.

48. Herzstein, *Henry R. Luce,* 34; Alan Brinkley, *The Publisher: Henry Luce and His American Century* (New York: Alfred A. Knopf, 2010), 274–275.

49. Brinkley, *The Publisher,* 276–277; Herzstein, *Henry R. Luce,* 25, 36; Jerry Israel, *Progressivism and the Open Door: America and China, 1905–1921* (Pittsburgh, PA: University of Pittsburgh Press, 1971), 195.

50. Jespersen, *American Images of China,* 53–54.

51. Ray Lyman Wilbur, "Our Pacific Destiny," *Pacific Historical Review* 10, no. 2 (1941): 153–163.

52. Iriye, *Across the Pacific,* 216–226; Hunt and Levine, *Arc of Empire,* 75–76.

53. "United States Note to Japan November 26, 1941," *Department of State Bulletin* 5, no. 129 (December 13, 1941); Paine, *The Wars for Asia,* 185–186.

54. Brinkley, *The Publisher,* 280–281; Herzstein, *Henry R. Luce,* 39.

5. Allies and Enemies

Epigraph: Anonymous, "Three Sonnets Written for Madame Chiang," *Sonnet III,* composed after attending one of Madame's rallies in the United States, quoted in Jane Park, "'The China Film': Madame Chiang Kai-shek in Hollywood," *Screening the Past* 30 (2011), http://www.screeningthepast.com/2011/04/the-china-film/.

1. Michael P. Riccards, *The Presidency and the Middle Kingdom: China, the United States and Executive Leadership* (Lanham, MD: Lexington Books, 2000), 96.

2. Agnes Smedley, *Chinese Destinies: Sketches of Present-Day China* (New York: Vanguard Press, 1933); Edgar Snow, *Red Star over China* (New York: Random House, 1938), 67; Chiang Kai-shek, *China's Destiny,* trans. Wang Chung-Hui (New York: Macmillan, 1947); May-ling Soong Chiang, *This Is Our China* (New York: Harper & Brothers, 1940), 51. Lattimore and MacArthur quotes from William L. Neumann, "Determinism, Destiny, and Myth in the American Image of China," in *Issues and Conflicts: Studies in Twentieth Century American Diplomacy,* ed. George L. Anderson (Lawrence: University of Kansas Press, 1959), 18.

3. Frank Freidel, *Franklin D. Roosevelt: A Rendezvous with Destiny* (Boston: Little, Brown, 1990), 478; Sherwood Eddy, *I Have Seen God Work in China: Personal Impressions from Three Decades with the Chinese* (New York: Association Press, 1944), 55–56.

4. Peter Moreira, *Hemingway on the China Front: His WWII Spy Mission with Martha Gellhorn* (Washington, DC: Potomac Books, 2006).

5. "Ernest Hemingway Says Russo-Jap Pact Hasn't Kept Soviet From Sending Aid to China," *PM,* June 10, 1941, 4–5; "Ernest Hemingway Says We Can't Let Japan Grab

Our Rubber Supplies in Dutch East Indies," *PM*, June 11, 1941, 6; "Ernest Hemingway Says Japan Must Conquer China or Satisfy USSR Before Moving South," *PM*, June 13, 1941, 6; Moreira, *Hemingway on the China Front*, 119–125; "Ernest Hemingway Tells How 100,000 Chinese Labored Night and Day to Build Huge Landing Field for Bombers," *PM*, June 18, 1941, 16–17; Martha Gellhorn, "These, Our Mountains," *Collier's Weekly*, June 1941, 16–17, 38, 40–41, 44.

6. Hemingway to Morgenthau, July 30, 1941, in *Subcommittee to Investigate the Administration of the Internal Security Act and Other Internal Security Laws of the Committee on the Judiciary*, United States Senate, 89th Congress, 1st sess., February 5, 1965, 457–462; Ernest Hemingway, "After Four Years of War in China Japs Have Conquered Only Flat Lands," *PM*, June 16, 1941, 6–9.

7. Laura Tyson Li, *Madame Chiang Kai-shek: China's Eternal First Lady* (New York: Atlantic Monthly Press, 2006), 193–237.

8. Frank McNaughton, "Mme. Chiang in the U.S. Capitol," *Life*, March 8, 1943, 11–12, 14, 16; Li, *Madame Chiang Kai-shek*, 200.

9. "Editorial: Speech to Congress. Madame Chiang Kai-shek calls upon the U.S. to Join China in War and Peace," *Life*, March 1, 1943; Madame Chiang Kai-shek, Address at Hollywood Bowl, April 4, 1943, *Los Angeles Times*, April 5, 1943, 9; T. Christopher Jespersen, *American Images of China, 1931–1949* (Stanford, CA: Stanford University Press, 1996), 105–107; Li, *Madame Chiang Kai-shek*, 223–225.

10. K. Scott Wong, *Americans First: Chinese Americans and the Second World War* (Cambridge, MA: Harvard University Press, 2005), 109–124, 70–71.

11. The Stilwell story was first presented in *The Stilwell Papers*, ed. Theodore White (New York: W. Sloane Associates, 1948), and then by Barbara Tuchman in her classic book, *Stilwell and the American Experience in China, 1911–45* (New York: Macmillan, 1970).

12. Stilwell, *The Stilwell Papers*, 315–317.

13. Dorothy Borg, *The United States and the Far Eastern Crisis of 1933–1938: From the Manchurian Incident through the Initial Stage of the Undeclared Sino-Japanese War* (Cambridge, MA: Harvard University Press, 1964), 196–234.

14. Evans Fordyce Carlson, *Evans F. Carlson on China at War, 1937–1941*, ed. Hugh Deane (New York: China and Us Publication, 1993), 9–11.

15. Evans Fordyce Carlson, *The Chinese Army: Its Organization and Military Efficiency* (New York: Institute of Pacific Relations, 1940), 16–28, 37–49; Evans Fordyce Carlson, *Twin Stars of China: A Behind-the-Scenes Story of China's Valiant Struggle for Existence by a U.S. Marine Who Lived & Moved with the People* (New York: Dodd, Mead, 1940), 65–67; Carlson quoted in Kenneth E. Shewmaker, *Americans and Chinese Communists, 1927–1945: A Persuading Encounter* (Ithaca, NY: Cornell University Press, 1971), 82–106.

16. David D. Barrett, *Dixie Mission: The United States Army Observer Group in Yenan, 1944* (Berkeley: Center for Chinese Studies, University of California, 1970), 35.

17. John Colling, *The Spirit of Yenan: A Wartime Chapter of Sino-American Friendship* (Hong Kong: API Press, 1991); John Paton Davies, *Dragon by the Tail: American, British, Japanese, and Russian Encounters with China and One Another* (New York: W. W. Norton, 1972); Wilbur J. Peterkin, *Inside China 1943–1945: An Eyewitness Account of America's Mission in Yenan* (Baltimore, MD: Gateway Press, 1992); Koji Ariyoshi, *From Kona to Yenan: The Political Memoirs of Koji Ariyoshi,* ed. Edward D. Beechert and Alice M. Beechert (Honolulu: University of Hawai'i Press, 2000); John S. Service, *Lost Chance in China: The World War II Despatches of John S. Service,* ed. Joseph W. Esherick (New York: Random House, 1974); Brooks Atkinson, "Yenan, a Chinese Wonderland City," *New York Times,* October 6, 1944; Shewmaker, *Americans and Chinese Communists,* 202, 211; Barrett, *Dixie Mission,* 35–50; Li, *Madame Chiang Kai-shek,* 254–259.

18. Barrett, *Dixie Mission,* 62–63; Jonathan Fenby, *Chiang Kai Shek: China's Generalissimo and the Nation He Lost* (New York: Carroll & Graf, 2004), 438–439; Tang Tsou, "The American Political Tradition and the American Image of Chinese Communism," *Political Science Quarterly* 77, no. 4 (1962): 570–600.

19. Shewmaker, *Americans and Chinese Communists,* 82, 112–113, 159; He Di, "The Most Respected Enemy: Mao Zedong's Perception of the United States," *China Quarterly* 137 (March 1994): 144–158; commentary by Sidney Rittenberg after the screening of *The Revolutionary,* Stanford University, November 29, 2012.

20. For an interesting perspective on the Marshall mission from a Chinese historian, see Zi Zhongyun, *No Exit? The Origin and Evolution of U.S. Policy toward China, 1945–1950* (Norwalk, CT: East Bridge, 2003).

21. Quote is from Jespersen, *American Images of China,* 150.

22. For a conservative's view of these developments, see Lee Edwards, *Missionary for Freedom: The Life and Times of Walter Judd* (New York: Paragon House, 1990).

23. Yu-ming Shaw, *An American Missionary in China: John Leighton Stuart and Chinese-American Relations* (Cambridge, MA: Harvard Council on East Asian Studies, 1992), 149.

24. Biographical background on Stuart comes from Shaw, *An American Missionary in China*; and John Leighton Stuart, *Fifty Years in China: The Memoirs of John Leighton Stuart, Missionary and Ambassador* (New York: Random House, 1954), 17.

25. Shaw, *An American Missionary in China,* 47–58.

26. Stuart, *Fifty Years in China,* 126, 138, 141, 153.

27. Stuart to the Secretary of State, March 10, 1949, in *The Forgotten Ambassador: The Reports of John Leighton Stuart, 1946–1949,* ed. Kenneth W. Rea and John C. Brewer (Boulder, CO: Westview Press, 1981), 309–312, see also 322–335; John Leighton Stuart, diary entries for April 4–13 and 25, 1949, John Leighton Stuart Papers, Box 1, Hoover Institution Archives, Stanford University; Stuart, *Fifty Years in China,* 239–246.

28. Stuart, diary entries for May 13 and 27; June 3, 8, 26, and 28; and July 14, 18, 20, and 26, 1949; Simei Qing, *From Allies to Enemies: Visions of Modernity, Identity, and*

U.S.-China Diplomacy, 1945–1960 (Cambridge, MA: Harvard University Press, 2007), 145–149; He Di, "The Evolution of the Chinese Communist Party's Policy toward the United States, 1944–1949," in *Sino-American Relations 1945–1955: A Joint Reassessment of a Critical Decade,* ed. Harry Harding and Yuan Ming (Wilmington, DE: SR Books, 1989), 43–44.

29. Stuart, *Fifty Years in China,* 247–248; Nancy Bernkopf Tucker, *Patterns in the Dust: Chinese-American Relations and the Recognition Controversy, 1949–1950* (New York: Columbia University Press, 1983), 47–48, 27–29, 232–233; Qing, *From Allies to Enemies,* 144–149.

30. Mao Zedong, "Farewell, Leighton Stuart!," *Selected Works of Mao Tse-tung,* vol. 4 (Beijing: Foreign Languages Press, 1967), 433–440.

31. "Report of Conference with Ambassador J. Leighton Stuart," November 12, 1949, John Leighton Stuart Papers, Box 1.

32. James C. Thomson Jr. quoted in Shaw, *An American Missionary in China,* 137–138; James C. Thomson Jr., "Role of State Department," in *Pearl Harbor as History: Japanese-American Relations, 1931–41,* ed. Dorothy Borg and Shumpei Okamoto (New York: Columbia University Press, 1973); Stuart, *Fifty Years in China,* 280–282, 289.

33. William C. Bullitt, "A Report to the American People on China," *Life,* October, 13, 1947, 35ff; quote from *Congressional Record,* August 18, 1949, 11787–11788, in Edwards, *Missionary for Freedom,* 166.

34. Robert E. Herzstein, *Henry R. Luce, Time, and the American Crusade in Asia* (New York: Cambridge University Press, 2005), 94.

35. Ross Y. Koen, *The China Lobby in American Politics* (New York: Macmillan, 1960), 100; Jespersen, *American Images of China,* 180–182.

36. Clare Boothe Luce, *The Mystery of American Policy in China: An Address at Testimonial Dinner Honoring the Most Reverend Paul Yu-Pin, D.D., Archbishop of Nanking, New York, June 14, 1949* (New York: Plain Talk, 1949); Conrad Black, *Richard M. Nixon: A Life in Full* (New York: Plain Talk, 2007), 547.

37. Qing, *From Allies to Enemies,* 151–168; Michael Schaller, *Douglas MacArthur: The Far Eastern General* (New York: Oxford University Press, 1989), 159–160, 201–212.

38. Dean Rusk, "Chinese-American Friendship," [May 18, 1951], *Vital Speeches of the Day* 17, no. 17 (1951): 514.

6. Transformations

Epigraph: "Nixon Lauds Bush for China Policy," *New York Times,* June 25, 1989. The quote comes from a statement Nixon issued in the aftermath of the Tian'anmen crackdown.

1. Gordon H. Chang, "Are There Other Ways to Think about the 'Great Interregnum'?," *Journal of American-East Asian Relations* 7 (Spring–Summer 1998): 117–122.

2. Louise Hutchinson, "Nixon Cites Peking's Drive for Conquest," *Chicago Tribune,* February 11, 1966, 5.

3. See Odd Arne Westad, *The Global Cold War: Third World Interventions and the Making of Our Times* (New York: Cambridge University Press, 2005); and Thomas J. Christensen, *Worse Than a Monolith: Alliance Politics and Problems of Coercive Diplomacy in Asia* (Princeton, NJ: Princeton University Press, 2011).

4. For a prescient view, see John L. Melby, "The Cold War," *International Journal* 23, no. 3 (1968): 421–434.

5. James Peck, *Washington's China: The National Security World, the Cold War, and the Origins of Globalism* (Amherst: University of Massachusetts Press, 2006), 100, 104–107.

6. Gordon H. Chang, *Friends and Enemies: The United States, China, and the Soviet Union, 1948–1972* (Stanford, CA: Stanford University Press, 1990), 116–142.

7. Zhihua Shen and Danhui Li, *After Leaning to One Side: China and Its Allies in the Cold War* (Washington, DC: Woodrow Wilson Center Press, 2011), 117–166; Chang, *Friends and Enemies,* 228–252; Simei Qing, *From Allies to Enemies: Visions of Modernity, Identity, and U.S.-China Diplomacy, 1945–1960* (Cambridge, MA: Harvard University Press), 263–268.

8. Chang, *Friends and Enemies,* 170–174.

9. Ibid., 236.

10. Samuel Lubell, "Americans Change Views on Red China's Threat," *Boston Globe,* February 2, 1964, A4; Charles R. Kitts, *The United States Odyssey in China, 1784–1990* (Lanham, MD: University Press of America, 1991), 219.

11. *Public Papers of the Presidents of the United States: Lyndon B. Johnson, 1965,* vol. 1, entry 172 (Washington, DC: Government Printing Office, 1966), 394–399; Evelyn Goh, *Constructing the U.S. Rapprochement with China, 1961–1974* (New York: Cambridge University Press, 2005), 38–45.

12. "Secretary Rusk's News Conference of October 12, 1967," Department of State Press Release no. 227, October 12, 1967; Chang, *Friends and Enemies,* 261. See also "Must We Fight China in Vietnam?" *Harvard Crimson,* June 15, 1967.

13. Mark Gallicchio, *The African American Encounter with Japan and China: Black Internationalism in Asia, 1895–1945* (Chapel Hill: University of North Carolina Press, 2000), 2, 50–72; Destin K. Jenkins, "Two Sleeping Giants: African American Perceptions of China, 1900–1939" (Senior thesis, Department of History, Columbia University, 2010), 69–76.

14. Langston Hughes, "Roar China," in Hughes, *Good Morning Revolution: Uncollected Social Protest Writings,* ed. Faith Berry (New York: Lawrence Hill, 1973), 118–120.

15. Greg Robinson, "Internationalism and Justice: Paul Robeson, Asia, and Asian Americans," in *AfroAsian Encounters: Culture, History, Politics,* ed. Heike Raphael-Hernandez and Shannon Steen (New York: New York University Press, 2006), 260–276.

16. Bill V. Mullen, *Afro-Orientalism* (Minneapolis: University of Minnesota Press, 2004), 1–3; Jenkins, "Two Sleeping Giants," 97–99; W. E. B. Du Bois, "China and Japan," *New York Amsterdam News,* October 21, 1931.

17. W. E. B. Du Bois, "I Sing to China," [May 1, 1959], *China Reconstructs* 8 (June 8, 1959): 24–26; W. E. B. Du Bois, *The Autobiography of W. E. B. Du Bois: A Soliloquy on Viewing My Life from the Last Decade of Its First Century* (New York: International Publishers, 1968), 405–408; W. E. B. Du Bois "Our Visit to China," *China Pictorial,* March 20, 1959; Mullen, *Afro-Orientalism,* 33–41.

18. Malcolm X, *The Autobiography of Malcolm X* (New York: Grove Press, 1965), 386.

19. *Peking Review,* August 12, 1966, 12–13; "A New Storm against Imperialism: In Support of the Afro-American Struggle against Violent Repression," *Peking Review,* April 19, 1968, 5–6.

20. Robert F. Williams, "On the Platform with Mao Tse-tung," *New York Times,* February 20, 1971, 27; Timothy B. Tyson, *Radio Free Dixie: Robert F. Williams & the Roots of Black Power* (Chapel Hill: University of North Carolina Press, 1999), 307. For Williams's life in China, see Robert Carl Cohen, *Black Crusader: A Biography of Robert Franklin Williams* (Secaucus, NJ: Lyle Stuart, 1972).

21. Huey P. Newton, *Revolutionary Suicide* (New York: Harcourt Brace Jovanovich, 1974), 110, 322. See also Robin D. G. Kelley and Betsy Esch, "Black Like Mao: Red China and Black Revolution," in *Afro Asia: Revolutionary Political and Cultural Connections between African Americans and Asian Americans,* ed. Fred Wei-han Ho and Bill V. Mullen (Durham, NC: Duke University Press, 2008), 97–164; and Judy Tzu-Chun Wu, *Radicals on the Road: Internationalism, Orientalism, and Feminism during the Vietnam Era* (Ithaca, NY: Cornell University Press, 2013).

22. Langston Hughes, "The Revolutionary Armies in China—1949," *Chicago Defender,* October 8, 1949, reproduced in Hughes, *Good Morning Revolution: Uncollected Social Protest Writings,* ed. Faith Berry (New York: Lawrence Hill, 1973), 117–118.

23. John King Fairbank, *Chinabound: A Fifty-Year Memoir* (New York: Harper & Row, 1982), 4; John King Fairbank, *China: The People's Middle Kingdom and the U.S.A.* (Cambridge, MA: Belknap Press of Harvard University Press, 1967), v.

24. Fairbank, *Chinabound,* xiv–5.

25. Ibid., 38, 61–65; Paul M. Evans, *John Fairbank and the American Understanding of Modern China* (New York: Basil Blackwell, 1988), 14–47.

26. Evans, *John Fairbank and the American Understanding of Modern China,* 66–70; Fairbank, *Chinabound,* 324, 286, 312–316, 320–328. See also David B. Honey, *Incense at the Altar: Pioneering Sinologists and the Development of Classical Chinese Philology* (New Haven, CT: American Oriental Society, 2001).

27. Fairbank, *Chinabound,* 317; John King Fairbank, "Communism in China and the New American Approach to Asia," in *Next Step in Asia,* ed. John K. Fairbank, Harlan Cleveland, Edwin O. Reischauer, and William L. Holland (Cambridge, MA: Harvard University Press, 1949), 1–24; Joyce Mao, "The Specter of Yalta: Asia Firsters and the

Development of Conservative Internationalism," *Journal of American-East Asian Relations* 19, no. 2 (2012): 132–156; Nancy Bernkopf Tucker, *Patterns in the Dust: Chinese-American Relations and the Recognition Controversy, 1949–1950* (New York: Columbia University Press, 1983).

28. See John King Fairbank, *China Perceived: Images and Policies in Chinese-American Relations* (New York: Alfred A. Knopf, 1974); Evans, *John Fairbank and the American Understanding of Modern China*, 106–131; John K. Fairbank, *New Views of China's Tradition and Modernization* (Washington, DC: American Historical Association, 1968), 54; and John K. Fairbank, "The People's Middle Kingdom," *Foreign Affairs* 44, no. 4 (1966): 574–586.

29. John King Fairbank, *The United States and China*, new rev. ed. (Cambridge, MA: Harvard University Press, 1958); Xiaoqing Diana Lin, "John K. Fairbank's Construction of China, 1930s–1950s: Culture, History, and Imperialism," *Journal of American-East Asian Relations* 19, nos. 3–4 (2012): 211–234.

30. Alice Lyman Miller, "Some Things We Used to Know about China's Past and Present (But Now, Not So Much)," *Journal of American-East Asian Relations* 16, nos. 1–2 (Spring–Summer 2009): 41–68; Fairbank, *Chinabound*, 319–320; 349–351; John K. Fairbank, *Chinese-American Interactions: A Historical Summary* (New Brunswick, NJ: Rutgers University Press, 1975), 4.

31. Jian Chen, *Mao's China and the Cold War* (Chapel Hill: University of North Carolina Press, 2001), 163–276.

32. Richard Nixon, "Asia after Viet Nam," *Foreign Affairs* 46, no. 1 (1967), 111–125.

33. "Nixon Hits Failure to Aid Free China," *Los Angeles Times*, October 17, 1950, 15; "Nixon and Douglas Views Contrasted," *Los Angeles Times*, October 26, 1950, 4; "Nixon Hits Foe's Policy on Red China," *Los Angeles Times*, November 4, 1950, 12; "Nixon Again Assails Democrats' Policies," *New York Times*, July 3, 1954, 6; "Nixon Gives Chiang Ike's Note Promising Continued U.S. Help," *Daily Boston Globe*, July 8, 1956, 10.

34. "Battle of the Islands," *Time*, October 24, 1960, 26; "Nixon Warns U.S. to Shun Reds' Battle," *Chicago Tribune*, April 5, 1964, 3; "Nixon Cites Peking's Drive for Conquest," *Chicago Tribune*, February 11, 1966, 5.

35. See Karen Leong, *China Mystique: Pearl S. Buck, Anna May Wong, Mayling Soong, and the Transformation of American Orientalism* (Berkeley: University of California Press, 2005); James C. Humes and Jarvis D. Ryals, *"Only Nixon": His Trip to China Revisited and Restudied* (Lanham, MD: University Press of America, 2009), 7, 11–12; and Marvin Kalb and Bernard Kalb, *Kissinger* (Boston: Little, Brown, 1974), 217–219.

36. *Congressional Record*, March 7, 1966, in *U.S. Policy Toward China: Testimony Taken from the Senate Foreign Relations Committee Hearings*, ed. Akira Iriye (Boston: Little, Brown, 1968); Chang, *Friends and Enemies*, 282–284; Nancy Bernkopf Tucker, "Taiwan Expendable? Nixon and Kissinger Go to China," *Journal of American History* 92, no. 1 (2005): 109–135.

37. My discussion of the background to Nixon's trip to China is based on the rich archive of documents and analysis provided by the National Security Archive, George Washington University. It is available at www2.gwu.edu/~nsarchiv. Edgar Snow, "A Conversation with Mao Tse-tung," *Life* 70 (April 30, 1971): 46–48.

38. Guolin Yi, "The 'Propaganda State' and Sino-American Rapprochement: Preparing the Chinese Public for Nixon's Visit," *Journal of America-East Asian Relations* 20, no. 1 (2013): 5–28.

39. Henry A. Kissinger, *White House Years* (Boston: Little, Brown, 1979), 743.

40. Henry A. Kissinger, "My Talks with Chou En-lai," report to President Nixon, July 14, 1971, National Security Archive Electronic Briefing Book no. 66, document 40, http://www2.gwu.edu/~nsarchiv/NSAEBB/NSAEBB66/ch-40.pdf. On the Nixon trip, see Margaret MacMillan, *Nixon and Mao: The Week that Changed the World* (New York: Random House, 2007); and Chris Tudda, *A Cold War Turning Point: Nixon and China, 1969–1972* (Baton Rouge: Louisiana State University Press, 2012).

41. See Chang, *Friends and Enemies,* 318–332. Wang Bingnan, Zhou's longtime personal assistant, told the author that Dulles's slight of Zhou never happened.

42. He Di, "The Most Respected Enemy: Mao Zedong's Perception of the United States," *China Quarterly* 137 (March 1994): 144–158.

43. "Briefing of the White House Staff," July 19, 1971, National Security Archive, http://www2.gwu.edu/~nsarchiv/NSAEBB/NSAEBB66/#docs; Tucker, "Taiwan Expendable?," 109–135.

44. Brooke Astor, *Patchwork Child* (New York: Harper & Row, 1962), 1, 370–375; *Footprints: An Autobiography* (Garden City, NY: Doubleday, 1980).

45. Evans, *John Fairbank and the American Understanding of Modern China,* 295–296; David Rockefeller, "From a China Traveler," *New York Times,* August 10, 1973, 31; James C. Thomson Jr., "A Cycle of Cathay," *American Heritage Magazine* 23, no. 5 (1972): 4.

46. Stanley Karnow, "China through Rose-Tinted Glasses," *Atlantic Monthly,* October 1973, 73–76.

47. Shirley MacLaine, *You Can Get There from Here* (New York: W. W. Norton, 1975), 112–114, 146, 161, 193, 239, 244–245. MacLaine took a film crew to accompany the delegation. Their efforts resulted in *The Other Half of the Sky,* the title drawing from Mao's epigraph "women hold up half the sky." The film received an Academy Award nomination for best documentary.

48. Ibid., 160–163, 230, 244–247.

49. Ibid., 245–249.

50. George H. W. Bush, *The China Diary of George H. W. Bush: The Making of a Global President,* ed. Jeffrey A. Engel (Princeton, NJ: Princeton University Press, 2008), 223–224, 243. The politics and political culture of China repelled Bush, but he developed a personal fondness for much of Chinese life and ways. He even learned some Chinese during his tenure in Beijing.

51. R. David Arkush and Leo O. Lee, eds., *Land without Ghosts: Chinese Impressions of America from the Mid-Nineteenth Century to the Present* (Berkeley: University of California Press, 1989), 259–303; Jing Li, *China's America: The Chinese View the United States, 1900–2000* (Albany: State University of New York Press, 2011), 125, 145–174.

52. "President Reagan's Remarks at Fudan University in Shanghai, China 1984," April 30, 1984, http://www.reagan.utexas.edu/archives/speeches/1984/43084e.htm; "President Reagan's Radio Address to the Nation on the Trip to China, 1984," April 28, 1984, http://www.reagan.utexas.edu/archives/speeches/1984/42884e.htm.

53. Richard Madsen, *China and the American Dream: A Moral Inquiry* (Berkeley: University of California Press, 1995), 61–90.

7. Old/New Visions

Epigraph: John Adams, *Nixon in China* (1987), libretto by Alice Goodman.

1. These questions also preoccupied Chen Shi-Zheng, who directed the staging of *The Bonesetter's Daughter,* an opera based on the work of Amy Tan. See Sheila Melvin, "Multilayered Story, Multinational Opera," *New York Times,* August 31, 2008, Arts and Leisure Section, 21.

2. Adams, *Nixon in China,* act 3, available in CD set recorded 1988, Electra/Nonesuch. The last line plays on Zhou Enlai's name, which translates as "coming grace." Timothy A. Johnson, *John Adams's Nixon in China: Musical Analysis, Historical and Political Perspectives* (Surrey, UK: Ashgate, 2011), 154–159.

3. Leonard S. Silk, "Nixon, China and Wall St.," *New York Times,* July 21, 1971, 45. See also Dong Wang, *The United States and China: A History from the Eighteenth Century to the Present* (Lanham, MD: Rowman & Littlefield, 2013), 247–272.

4. "Illusory Market," *Wall Street Journal,* February 29, 1972, 1; Joseph Lelyveld, "Sino-American Relations: No Great Leap Forward," *New York Times,* November 24, 1974, 208.

5. "U.S. Trade with China Increases as Peking Acts to Lift Economy," *New York Times,* November 23, 1978; "China: Over 900m Customers," *The Economist,* October 14, 1978, 114; "New Trade Agreements Are Building Bridges to China," *New York Times,* December 24, 1978, F11; "Teng's American Business Trip: Goal of Modernization by 2000," *New York Times,* January 31, 1979, D1.

6. "Panda Bear Diplomacy," *Wall Street Journal,* April 16, 1984, 32; "Why Investors Are Sour on China: Many Doubt Its Market Will Open, or That They'll Ever Turn a Profit," *New York Times,* June 8, 1986, F7.

7. "Reality Check: After Tiananmen Square, Businesses Take a Harder Look at Opportunities in China," *Wall Street Journal,* September 21, 1990, R7; "Headaches in China for Investors," *Wall Street Journal,* February 5, 1990, D8; "Suddenly, China Looks Smaller in the World," *New York Times,* March 27, 1990, A15.

8. "Punishing China on Trade Punishes Its Free-Marketers," *Wall Street Journal*, May 24, 1990, A11; Nicholas R. Lardy, *Integrating China into the Global Economy* (Washington, DC: Brookings Institution Press, 2002), 1–5; Robert D. Hormats, "Forty Years after the Nixon Visit: Progress, Challenges, and Opportunities in U.S.-China Economic Relations," remarks at the Asia Society, New York City, March 6, 2012, http://www.state.gov/e/rls/rmk/2012/182523.htm. Hormats was undersecretary of state for economic, energy, and agricultural affairs when he gave this speech. "The China Price," *Bloomberg Businessweek*, December 5, 2004; Nicholas R. Lardy, *China in the World Economy* (Washington, DC: Institute for International Economics, 1994), 1–3; "Can Apple Win over China?," *Fortune*, October 29, 2012; "Apple's Record 51 Million iPhone Sales Trail Estimates, Is the Smartphone Market Saturated?," *Bloomberg*, January 29, 2014.

9. James Mann, *About Face: A History of America's Curious Relationship with China, from Nixon to Clinton* (New York: Alfred Knopf, 1999), 134–147.

10. See Robert S. Ross, "The Bush Administration: The Origins of Engagement," in *Making China Policy: Lessons from the Bush and Clinton Administrations*, ed. Ramon H. Myers, Michel C. Oksenberg, and David L. Shambaugh (Lanham, MD: Rowman & Littlefield, 2001), 21–44; Wang Jisi and Wang Yong, "A Chinese Account: The Interaction of Policies," in *Making China Policy*, 269–295.

11. Nancy Bernkopf Tucker, "The Clinton Years: The Problem of Coherence," in *Making China Policy: Lessons from the Bush and Clinton Administrations*, ed. Ramon H. Myers, Michel C. Oksenberg, and David L. Shambaugh (Lanham, MD: Rowman & Littlefield, 2001), 45–76; Mann, *About Face*, 274–368; Lardy, *Integrating China into the Global Economy*, 158; Hormats, "Forty Years after the Nixon Visit"; Chen Weihua, "Sunny Skies Shine on Sino-US Relations," *China Daily* advertisement in the *New York Times*, January 19, 2014, 14–15.

12. Lardy, *Integrating China into the Global Economy*, vii–4.

13. Chi Wang, *George W. Bush and China: Policies, Problems, and Partnership* (Lanham, MD: Lexington Books, 2009).

14. Andrew J. Nathan and Andrew Scobell, "How China Sees America: The Sum of Beijing's Fears," *Foreign Affairs* 91, no. 5 (September/October 2012): 32–47; Aaron L. Friedberg, "Bucking Beijing: An Alternative U.S. China Policy," *Foreign Affairs* 91, no. 5 (2012): 32–47, 48–58.

15. Ian Bremmer and Jon M. Huntsman Jr., "How to Play Well with China," *New York Times*, June 2, 2013, Week in Review, 7; "Clinton at U.S.-China Dialogue in Beijing," May 3, 2012, IIP Digital, http://translations.state.gov/st/english/texttrans/2012/05/201205034981.html#axzz2ccbEV1gg; "Secretary Clinton Holds a Global Townterview," January 29, 2013, http://www.state.gov/secretary/20092013clinton/rm/2013/01/203452.htm, accessed October 9, 2014; Hillary Rodham Clinton, "Remarks at the U.S. Institute of Peace China Conference," March 7, 2012, http://www.state.gov/secretary/20092013clinton/rm/2012/03/185402.htm.

16. See Richard Madsen, *China and the American Dream: A Moral Inquiry* (Berkeley: University of California Press, 1995); James Mann, *The China Fantasy: How Our Leaders Explain Away Chinese Repression* (New York: Viking, 2007); Jean A. Garrison, *Making China Policy: From Nixon to G. W. Bush* (Boulder, CO: Lynne Rienner Publishers, 2005), 114–118; various essays in Carola McGiffert, ed., *China in the American Political Imagination* (Washington, DC: Center for Strategic and International Studies, 2003); John J. Mearsheimer, "Clash of the Titans," *Foreign Policy* 146 (January/February 2005): 46–49; and Friedberg, "Bucking Beijing."

17. Chengxin Pan, "The 'China Threat' in American Self-Imagination: The Discursive Construction of Other as Power Politics," *Alternatives* 29, no. 3 (2004): 305–331; Stanley Lubman, "The Dragon as Demon: Images of China on Capitol Hill," *Journal of Contemporary China* 13, no. 40 (2004): 541–565. The formal name of the report is "The United States House of Representatives Select Committee on U.S. National Security and Military/Commercial Concerns with the People's Republic of China." The most authoritative refutation of the allegations is in Alastair Iain Johnston, W. K. H. Panofsky, Marco Di Capua, and Lewis R. Franklin, "Cox Committee Report: An Assessment," Center for International Security and Cooperation, Stanford University, December 1999, http://iis-db.stanford.edu/pubs/10331/cox.pdf. See also "China: Friend or Foe?" *Newsweek,* April 1, 1996; "The Next Cold War?" *Time,* June 7, 1999; and "How We Would Fight China," *The Atlantic,* June 1, 2005.

18. For the mass market, popular action writer Clive Cussler issued *Flood Tide* (1997), in which a Chinese overlord seeks to destroy America by the mass smuggling of illegal Chinese migrants into the country. Eric L. Harry's *The Invasion* (2000) is a 600-page futurology about a Chinese invasion via the Gulf of Mexico. Modern yellow peril literature echoes many of the themes found 100 years ago in work such as J. Pierton Dooner, *Last Days of the Republic* (1880); Robert Woltor, *A Short and Truthful History of the Taking of California and Oregon by the Chinese in the Year A.D. 1899* (1882); M. P. Shiel, *The Yellow Danger* (1898); J. Martin Miller, *China: The Yellow Peril at War with the World* (1900); H. G. Wells, *War in the Air* (1908); and Jack London, *The Unparalleled Invasion* (1910).

19. Chang-Rae Lee, *On Such a Full Sea: A Novel* (New York: Riverhead Books, 2014).

20. "America's Fear of China," *The Economist,* May 19, 2007; Thomas J. Christensen, "Fostering Stability or Creating a Monster? The Rise of China and U.S. Policy toward East Asia," *International Security* 31, no. 1 (2006): 81–126.

21. James Fallows, "What Is the Chinese Dream?," *The Atlantic,* May 9, 2012.

22. "Chasing the Chinese Dream," *The Economist,* May 4, 2013, 24–26; Orville Schell and John Delury, *Wealth and Power: China's Long March to the Twenty-First Century* (New York: Random House, 2013).

23. See Schell and Delury, *Wealth and Power.*

24. In turn, Friedman was apparently inspired by the writing of Chinese American author Helen H. Wang, who wrote *The Chinese Dream* (Bestseller Press, 2010), about China's rising middle class. Friedman's article "China Needs Its Own Dream" appeared in the *New York Times* on October 2, 2012, just a month before Xi's speech.

25. Chris Marquis and Zoe Yang, "Chinese Dream? American Dream?," *Danwei,* June 28, 2013; Qin Xiaoying, "The Chinese Dream vs. The American Dream," *China-US Focus,* April 27, 2013.

26. C. Fred Bergsten, Bates Gill, and Nicholas R. Lardy, eds., *China: The Balance Sheet. What the World Needs to Know Now about the Emerging Superpower* (New York: Public Affairs, 2006), 155–161; C. Fred Bergsten, "A Partnership of Equals: How Washington Should Respond to China's Economic Challenge," *Foreign Affairs* 87, no. 4 (2008): 57–69; C. Fred Bergsten, "Two's Company," *Foreign Affairs* 88, no. 5 (2009): 169–170; C. Fred Bergsten, Charles Freeman, Nicholas R. Lardy, and Derek J. Mitchell, *China's Rise: Challenges and Opportunities* (Washington, DC: Peterson Institute for International Economics, 2008), 22–23.

27. Richard C. Bush III, "The United States and China: A G-2 in the Making?," Brookings, October 11, 2011, http://www.brookings.edu/research/articles/2011/10/11-china-us-g2-bush; Robert B. Zoellick and Justin Yifu Lin, "Recovery Rides on The G-2," *Washington Post,* March 6, 2009, http://www.washingtonpost.com/wp-dyn/content/article/2009/03/05/AR2009030502887.html; "A Conversation with Robert Zoellick," Peterson Institute for International Economics, June 14, 2012, event transcript, http://www.iie.com/publications/papers/transcript-20120614zoellick.pdf.

28. Niall Ferguson, *The Ascent of Money: A Financial History of the World* (New York: Penguin, 2008), 332–340. A similar but less graceful formulation is offered in Handel Jones, *ChinAmerica: The Uneasy Partnership That Will Change the World* (New York: McGraw Hill, 2010). On China in the world, see David L. Shambaugh, *China Goes Global: The Partial Power* (New York: Oxford University Press, 2013).

29. "Remarks by Anson Burlingame," *Banquet to His Excellency Anson Burlingame: And His Associates of the Chinese Embassy: By the Citizens of New York, on Tuesday, June 23, 1868* (New York: Sun Book and Job Company, 1868), 11–19; Thomas L. Friedman, "Dear President of China," *New York Times,* December 15, 2014, Sunday Review, 1.

30. See Robert S. Ross, *Negotiating Cooperation: The United States and China, 1969–1989* (Stanford, CA: Stanford University Press, 1995); and Robert G. Sutter, *U.S.-China Relations: Perilous Past, Pragmatic Present* (Lanham, MD: Rowman & Littlefield, 2010).

31. The science fiction film *2012* (2009) contains a similar message. Cataclysmic geological and meteorological disasters threaten to extinguish life on Earth, and an American family and others are saved by going to China. There, they flee the utter destruction and find salvation by flying away on specially made arks that were secretly constructed in China's Himalayans. China enables them to fulfill their destiny, which was to help a remnant of humanity survive.

32. Scott Moore, "The United States of China," *New York Times,* March 11, 2014. The idea of a convergence of socialism and capitalism has also been expressed in China. See Shen Jiru, *Zhongguo bu dang bu xiansheng* [China Is Not Mr. No] (Beijing: Dangdai Zhongguo Chubanshe, 1998), cited in Jing Li, *China's America: The Chinese View the United States, 1900–2000* (Albany: State University of New York Press, 2011), 212.

Acknowledgments

This book draws substantially on the work of other scholars, and I thank them for their work. I cite many of their efforts in my endnotes. I thank Gu Ning, He Di, Denise Khor, Alice Lyman Miller, Simei Qing, and Lyman Van Slyke for reading large parts of the book manuscript or conversing about its ideas. They provided valuable insights and very useful and important suggestions for improvement and correction. I thank Shana Bernstein, Annelise Heinz, Eun Seo Jo, Kevin Kim, Beth Lew-Williams, Chris Suh, Xiang Zhai, and many other friends and colleagues in the United States and in China for providing critical research help and engaging conversations on America-China relations. Readers for Harvard University Press gave excellent comments and recommendations. Joyce Seltzer was the original inspiration for this book, and I thank her for her vision and determination. Her colleagues at HUP rendered wonderful assistance in production. Over the many years I have been at Stanford University, bright Stanford students have shared insights about America-China relations with me that are embedded throughout this work, and I thank them. Errors in the book are solely my responsibility. My colleagues at Stanford's Green Library and East Asia Library and the Hoover Institution Library and Archives provided invaluable assistance. Other librarians around the world responded to urgent inquiries about sources with efficiency, for which I am very grateful. I thank the Stanford Humanities Center for a productive year in residence, during which I was able to complete much of the writing of this book. A stay at the Stanford Center at Peking University also provided experiences and insights that enriched my thinking immensely.

Acknowledgments

I also thank my lovely, loving family, Vicki, Chloe, and Maya, for their support, care, patience, and affection. I thank them for the inestimable comfort and joy they offer every day. This book is dedicated to them.

Index

Abeel, David, 57–58
Adams, Henry, 122
Adams, John (composer), 237–238
Adams, John Quincy, and Anglo-Chinese
  war, 31–35, 50
African Americans: Chinese observations,
  85; attraction to revolutionary China,
  209–214
Alsop, Joseph, 163, 230
America and China: foreign policy (see
  Political relations, U.S.-China); different
  opinions of each other, 22–23; similarities,
  73, 125–126, 145; alarmist literature,
  249–250, 252–253; author's life as
  metaphor for interconnectedness, 263–267
America and China, relationship between:
  real vs. intangible influences, 5–6; special,
  8; and Opium Wars, 29–38, 51; and
  American paternalism, 105–106; America's
  position in Manchurian Incident, 138–140;
  during Japanese aggression, 161–167; with
  America's entry into World War II,
  169–171; unraveling, 170–171, 178–180;
  Reagan's expression of interconnectedness,
  234–235; interlocked future, 255–256. See
  also Hoover-Stimson Doctrine; Political
  relations, U.S.-China
American Committee for Non-Participation
  in Japanese Aggression, 162
American Dream, and Chinese Dream,
  252–255
American exceptionalism: and westward
  expansion, 42–43; fueled by evangelism in
  China, 64–65

American factories in China, 242–243
American imperialism: missionaries as
  cultural imperialists, 56, 59–61; Chinese
  observations, 86–87; late nineteenth
  century, 100–102. See also Open Door
  Policy
American intellectuals, interest in China,
  122–128
American representatives to China: Caleb
  Cushing, 35–39; Anson Burlingame, 51,
  92–96; Paul S. Reinsch, 114–116; military,
  178–180; John Leighton Stuart, 189–196
American Revolution, role of Chinese tea,
  15–16
Americans, impressions of visiting Chinese,
  84–87, 234
American transcendentalists, influenced by
  Eastern thought, 121
American Volunteer Group. See Flying Tigers
Amistad, 32
Anglo-Chinese war. See Opium Wars
Anglo-French War. See Opium Wars
Anti-consumerism, appeal to Americans,
  230
Apple, Inc., manufactured in China, 242–243
Arrow War. See Opium Wars
Art, East Asian, 117–121
Arthur, Chester A., 78
Asia: Europeans' search for passage, 1–2, 24,
  40–41; "hot wars," 203–205
Astor, Brooke, establishment of cultural
  exchange project, 229
Astor, John Jacob, 21–22, 229
Auden, W. H., 159

Barrett, David D., 107–108, 184
Beijing, destruction during Anglo-French
 War, 50
Benton, Thomas Hart, 70–71
Black Panther Party, influenced by Mao's
 writings, 213
Books and articles: "yellow peril," 81–82;
 The Good Earth, 146–149; American,
 about China, 149–151; Chinese, 150;
 Red Star over China, 150–154; *Four
 Hundred Million Customers*, 155–158;
 China-mongering, 249–252
Boston Tea Party, 16
Boxer Rebellion, 87–88, 106–107
Bridgman, E. C., 56, 57
Britain: control of China trade, 14–16; and
 Opium Wars, 29–32; missionaries'
 opposition, 57–58; reaction to Manchurian
 Incident, 139–140
Buchanan, James, 91
Buck, Pearl S., 146–151, 153, 155–156, 165,
 178, 264–265
Bullitt, William C., Jr., 160, 197
Burlingame, Anson, 51, 92–96, 256–257, 265
Burlingame Treaty, 92–96
Bush, George Herbert Walker: and Shirley
 MacLaine, 233; and U.S.-China policy,
 244–245
Bush, George W., and U.S.-China policy, 246

Canton system, 12–13
Capitalism: effect on Chinese labor, 242–243;
 and fear of Chinese economic gains,
 249–250
Carlson, Evans Fordyce, 154, 182–184
Cass, Lewis, 91–92
Catholic missionaries, 52–53
Central Pacific Railroad, and Chinese labor,
 77–78
Century of humiliation, 39. *See also* Treaty
 system, unfair to China
Chen, Lanbin, 51, 75
Chennault, Claire, 163, 169, 198
Chiang Kaishek, 111–112, 133–134;
 anti-Communist extermination cam-
 paigns, 143, 152; forced into unification,
 158; as undisputed leader, 171; Stilwell's
 disdain, 178–180. *See also* Chinese
 Nationalists; Guomindang (GMD); Taiwan
Chimerica, 7, 256
China: idealized versions, 46–47, 213–214,
 248–249; colonization, 50; Grant's visit,

96–99; losses in late nineteenth century,
 99; as emerging geopolitical concern
 for U.S., and Open Door Policy, 103–109;
 threatened with partition, 106; John
 Dewey's attraction to, 126–128. *See also*
 People's Republic of China (PRC); Taiwan
China, travel to: early, 18–19; clipper ships,
 22; tales, 26–27; defiance by William
 Worthy, 210; Henry Kissinger, 226;
 Richard Nixon, 227–228; reopened to
 Americans, 229–230
China and America. *See* America and
 China
China clippers. *See* Yankee clipper ships
"Chinamania," 120
China Repository, 54
China studies, John Fairbank's creation of
 field, 216
"China White Paper," 194, 195, 199, 216
Chinese Americans: galvanized by Japanese
 aggression, 162–163; naturalization,
 177. *See also* Immigration, Chinese in
 America
Chinese Characteristics, 83
Chinese civil wars, 132–133; Chiang's
 anti-Communist extermination cam-
 paigns, 143, 152; Xi'an Incident, 158; and
 façade of unity, 171–172, 175; America's
 efforts to avert, 187–188. *See also* Chinese
 Nationalists: vs. Communists
Chinese culture: mystique, 2–3, 122;
 multicultural history, 10–11; early
 Americans' interest, 23–25; Caleb
 Cushing's account, 38–39; as foreign to
 Americans, 38–39; learned through
 missionaries, 53; establishment of Astor's
 exchange project, 229
Chinese Dream, 252–255
Chinese economy: early, 2, 9–10; recent
 revolution, 7; Silk Road, 8; growth since
 1990, 242–243; during Clinton years,
 245–246; America's fears, 249–250;
 American encouragement, 257. *See also*
 Foreign trade
Chinese Education Commission, 66–67
Chinese Exclusion Act of 1882, 68–69, 81
Chinese government: Qing dynasty, 10–12;
 and Tongzhi Restoration, 92, 99; American
 advisors, 123
Chinese in America, travelers' impressions,
 84–87, 234. *See also* Chinese Americans;
 Immigration, Chinese in America

Chinese influence, artistic, 117–121
Chinese labor: coolie trade, 75–77; Central
Pacific Railroad, 77–78; airfield construc-
tion in Chengdu, 173–174; undergoing
capitalism, 242–243
Chinese military, changes during Tongzhi
Restoration, 92, 99
Chinese Museum, 117–118
Chinese Nationalists: vs. Communists,
171–172, 174–175 (*see also* 1949 Revolu-
tion); America's negative opinion, 187;
America's preference, 191–192; American
support following Revolution, 197–200
Chinese population: eighteenth century, 10;
growth under Manchus, 11; state of in
1930s, 156–157
Chinese religion, and Christian missionaries,
51–53
Chinese representatives in America: first, 51,
Yung Wing, 66–67
Christianity: conversion efforts (*see*
Missionaries); as justification for Opium
War, 33; and Taiping Rebellion, 61–63;
remaking China as Christian America,
64–65; and Boxer Rebellion, 87–88;
praying for China, 113
Cigarettes, imported to China, 157
Clancy, Tom, China-mongering in work,
252
Clinton, Bill, 245–246
Clinton, Hillary, 248
Cold War: "Asia First," 197–198; Chinese vs.
Russian agenda, 204–205; and U.S.
involvement in Vietnam, 208–209. *See also*
Asia: "hot wars"
Columbus, Christopher, accidental discovery
of America, 1–2, 262
Communism: as enemy, 171; American
conservatives against, 197–199; Chinese vs.
Soviet Union, 204–206, 219; seen as
positive for China, 217–218
Communist Party of China (CPC): emerging
from Versailles Treaty, 114–115; first
congress, 130; origins, 130–132; composed
of diverse thinkers, 131–132, 153; and
Chiang Kaishek's coup, 133; Edgar Snow's
reports, 150–154, 181–182
Communists, American: Edgar Snow
characterization, 154; accused, 199–200
Communists, Chinese: America's positive
opinion, 180–186; as "so-called Communists," 185–186; America's early opinion,

185–187; America's new infatuation, 230.
See also Communist Party of China (CPC)
Communists vs. Nationalists. *See* Chinese
civil wars; Chinese Nationalists: vs.
Communists
Confucianism, 10, 121–122
Conservatives: opposed to Roosevelt/Truman
policies, 197–200; blaming liberals for
"losing" China, 216–217
Coolie trade, 75–77
Cox Report, 250
Crow, Carl, 155–159, 265
Cultural Revolution. *See* Great Proletarian
Cultural Revolution
Cushing, Caleb, 35–39

Delano, Amasa, 26–27, 47, 143
Deng Xiaoping, 115, 131, 186, 233–234,
240–241, 249, 257, 266
Destiny: American concept, 3–4; U.S.-China,
3, 257–262; China's, 5–6; and westward
expansion, 43; Roosevelt's vision of Pacific,
102; concept during World War II, 170; vs.
dream, 255. *See also* Manifest Destiny
Dewey, John and Alice, 124–128, 129, 131,
140, 150
Dickinson, Emily, 118, 121
Dixie Mission, 184–185
Dooner, Pierton W., 81
Du Bois, W. E. B., 210–212, 236, 266
Duke, James B., 157, 158
Dulles, John Foster, 141, 204, 207, 221, 227
Dunn, Nathan, 117–118

East India Company: trade with China, 12,
14–15; and opium smuggling, 29–30
Economies. *See* Chinese economy; Foreign
trade
Eddy, Sherwood, 59, 136–137, 171
Education: roots in missionary work, 53–54;
Chinese in America, 66, 107, 124;
American university programs in China,
122–123
Eliot, Charles W., 83, 114, 123
Emerson, Ralph Waldo, 28, 121
Emigration, Chinese to various lands, 74–75
Empress of China, 16–19
Europe: period of ascendency, 9–10; trade
with China, 12–13. *See also* Britain; France,
conflicts with China; Soviet Union
Evangelism. *See* Missionaries
Expansionism. *See* Westward expansion

Factories in China, American companies, 242–243

Fairbank, John King, 3, 5, 214–220, 223, 229, 265

Fallows, James, 7, 253

Fenollosa, Ernest, 119–120, 129

Ferguson, Niall, 7, 256

Floyd, John, 41–42, 47, 69–70

Flying Tigers, 163–164, 169

Forbes, Robert Bennet, and trade with China, 27–28, 47

Foreign aid to China, 161, 172

Foreign trade: and search for passage to Asia, 2; China's attitude, 11–13; early Americans' desire for Chinese products, 14–15; tea, 16, 21–22; sea otter fur, 20–21; opium, 29–32; imposed on China, 51; other Asian countries, 240–241

Foreign trade, U.S.-China: British control, 14–16; Old China Trade, 18–21; state according to Robert Forbes, 27–28, 47; and opium smuggling, 30; during early republic, 46; *Four Hundred Million Customers*, 155–158; opened following Nixon's visit, 228–229; in 1970s and 1980s, 239–241; since 1990, 242; under Clinton, 245. *See also* American factories in China

Four Hundred Million Customers, 155–158

France, conflicts with China: Second Opium War, 50; Sino-French War, 99

Franklin, Benjamin, interest in China, 11, 23–24, 47, 121

Free trade, John Quincy Adams's views, 32–35

Freneau, Philip, 17–18

Friedman, Thomas L., 254, 257

Fulbright, J. William, 223

Fur trade, 20–21

Gellhorn, Martha, 172–175

Ginsberg, Alan, 129

Ginseng, imported to China, 18

The Good Earth (book), 146–149

The Good Earth (movie), 178

Grant, Julia, 117

Grant, Ulysses S., visit to Beijing, 96–99

Gravity, 259

Great Leap Forward, 219

Great Proletarian Cultural Revolution: launch, 219; appeal to Americans, 228–233

Griffis, William Elliot, and America's expansion to Philippines, 100–102

Group of Two (G-2) concept, 255–256

Guangzhou: early trade, 12, 18–20, 22; opium smuggling, 29–30; home of immigrants, 77; open hostility toward foreigners, 84

Guomindang (GMD), 111–112, 115; alliance with Communist Party of China (CPC), 132; misinformation regarding Communists, 152. *See also* Chiang Kaishek; Sun Yatsen

Gutzlaff, Karl, 60

Hale, Nathan Everett, 57

Hall, Henrietta Shuck, 58–59

Han Jiaozhun. *See* Soong family

Harriman, Averell, 206

Harriman, Edward Henry, 100, 157, 162

Harte, Bret, 49

Hay, John, 104–107, 122

Hayes, Rutherford B., 51

Hemingway, Ernest, 172–175

Holmes, Oliver Wendell, Sr., 95

Hong Xiuquan, 61–62

Hoover, Herbert, 88, 165, 185, 198, 200, 220, 258

Hoover, Lou Henry, 88

Hoover-Stimson Doctrine, 138–140, 143

Houqua. *See* Wu Bingjian

Huang Hua, 193–194

Huang Zunxian, 86

Hudson, Henry, 2

Hughes, Langston, 209–210

Hull, Cordell, 167

Human rights, Tian'anmen Square, 241–242

Huntsman, Jon, Jr., 248

Hurley, Patrick J., 185–186

Hu Shi, 125, 150, 191, 265

Immigration: Americans in China (*see* American representatives to China; Missionaries); effects on each country, 39–40, 68, 89

Immigration, Chinese in America, 65–70, 73–83, 85; mistreatment, 67–68, 74 (*see also* Coolie trade; Racism; "Yellow peril"); during colonization, 69; seen as divine plan, 74; legislation, 77; restrictions, 108. *See also* Chinese Americans

Imperial University. See *Tongwen Guan*

"Indians," as link to Asia, 69, 278n33

Isherwood, Christopher, 159

Index

Japan: American policy, acquiescence after World War I, 114–116; art, 119–121; compared to China, 127–128; and Manchurian Incident, 135–141, 144 (*see also* Hoover-Stimson Doctrine); attacks on Shanghai and Nanjing, 158–159; American sanctions, 161–162, 166; military, 168; African Americans' views, 209–211

Jefferson, Thomas: interest in China, 14, 21, 24–25; and western expansion, 41

Johnson, Andrew, 85

Judd, Walter, 162, 197–198

Karnow, Stanley, 230–231

Kennan, George F., 104, 108, 265

Kennedy, John F.: attitude toward China, 206–207, 221, 237, 265; vs. Richard Nixon, 222

Kingston, Maxine Hong, 129

Kissinger, Henry, 199, 218; meeting with John Fairbanks, 220; visits to Beijing, 226–227

Knowland, William F., 198, 223

Korean War, 6, 200–202

LaFarge, John, 119

The Last Days of the Republic, 81

Lattimore, Owen, 151, 170, 218

Ledyard, John, 17

Lee, Chang-Rae, 251–252

Leninism. *See* Soviet Union

Lewis and Clark Expedition, 41

Liang Qichao, 86–87

Lin Yutang, 150

Lin Zexu, 30

Lippmann, Walter, 104, 142

London, Jack, 81–82

Louisiana Purchase, 41

Lowell, A. Lawrence, 140, 162

Luce, Clare Boothe, 164–166, 176, 198–199

Luce, Henry Robinson, 162, 164–167, 198, 225, 264

Luce, Henry W., 164, 167, 190, 264, 266

Lynchings, 78

Lytton Commission report, 139–140

Macartney, Lord George, 14

MacLaine, Shirley, 230–233

Magee, John, 159

Mahan, Alfred Thayer, and "grand strategy," 101–103, 106

Manchurian Incident, 135–141; and Hoover-Stimson Doctrine, 138–139;

Britain's reaction, 139–140; as lead-up to World War II, 142

Manchus, 10. *See also* Qing dynasty

Manifest Destiny, 3–4, 42–43

Manufacturers, locating in China, 242

Mao Zedong: youthful philosophy, 125; early years, 131; Edgar Snow's account, 153–154; public attack on Leighton Stuart, 189, 195; proclamation of People's Republic of China, 197; influence on Black Panthers, 213; increasing fanaticism, 219–220; moves toward reconciliation with U.S., 224–225; meeting with Nixon, 227–228; death, 233

Marshall, George C., efforts to unify China, 187–188, 192

Marx, Karl, 50, 125

Marxism. *See* Soviet Union

Mayer, Brantz, 118

May Fourth Movement, 114, 126

McCarthyism, 6, 200, 218

McKinley, William, 4, 101, 104, 106

Melville, Herman, 27, 121

Mexican-American War, 4, 43

Miscegenation. *See* Race, advocates for miscegenation

Missionaries, 51–65; outlawed, 53; Peter Parker, 55, 57–58, 60–61; restrictions, 55; impact on Christians at home, 57; first female, 58–59; working with secular forces, 60–61; and Taiping Rebellion, 61–63; William Speer, 61–63, 71–74; successes after Second Opium War, 63; and national exceptionalism, 64–65; advocating for miscegenation, 72–73; and Boxer Rebellion, 87–88; reports on Japanese attacks, 160

Morgenthau, Hans, 172–174

Morris, Robert, 16–17

Morrison, Robert, 54

Most-favored-nation status, 244–245

Museums: Dunn's Chinese Museum, 117–118; collections of East Asian art, 120–121

Mutiny: *Amistad*, 32; *Robert Browne*, 76–77

Nanjing, Japanese attack, 159

Narrative of Voyages and Travels in the Northern and Southern Hemispheres, 26–27

Nationalist Party. *See* Chiang Kaishek; Chinese Nationalists; Guomindang (GMD); Taiwan

Natural law, John Quincy Adams's views, 32–34
Newton, Huey P., 213, 266
Nike, manufactured in China, 242
1949 Revolution, 188–189, 192
Nixon, Richard, 199, 203–205, 220–228, 230, 233, 237–239, 243, 244, 257, 265–266; proposal for new China policy, 220; stance against Communism, 221; desire to travel to China, 222; opening relations with China, 227–228, 234–236; effects of trip on economy, 239
Nixon in China, 237–238
Northern Expedition, 132–133
Nuclear weapons, America's threat against China, 205–206

Old China Trade, 18–21
The Oldest and the Newest Empire: China and the United States, 72–74
On Such a Full Sea, 251–252
Open Door Policy, 103–109, 112–113; notes of 1899, 105–106; unique to China, 142
Opium trade: conflicts, 29–34; imposed legality, 51
Opium Wars, 30–35; background, 29–30; America's position, 31; and John Quincy Adams, 31–35; as beginning of century of humiliation, 39; unequal treaty system, 49–51, 63; Christian view, 57–58; treaties after Second Opium War, 63 (*see also* Burlingame Treaty)
Oregon Territory, settling, 3, 36, 40–42, 69, 70

Paine, Thomas, interest in China, 24–25
Panama Canal, 102–103
Parker, Peter, 54–55, 57–58, 60–61, 75–76
Pearl Harbor, 161, 167–170, 178, 191, 216, 264
Peking Man, 145–150
People's Republic of China (PRC): proclaimed founding, 197; African Americans' revolutionary attraction, 209–214. *See also* China; Communists, Chinese
Perry, Matthew, 47–48, 91, 119
Peters, John R., 118
Philippines, as American acquisition, 101
Ping-Pong diplomacy, 225
Political relations: religious (*see* Missionaries); China's international system, 13–14; China's traditional system, 13–14; America's early nation building, 54; China's reformation, 92; sanctions against Japan, 161–162, 166

Political relations, U.S.-China: Treaty of Wangxia, 36–38; period of friendship and peace, 90–91; Burlingame Treaty, 92–96; Grant's visit to China, 96–99; changes during "gilded age," 99–100; Open Door Policy, 103–109; after World War I, 114–116; ruptured, 191–195, 203–204; Korean War, 200–202; anchored by anti-Soviet concerns, 219, 224, 228, 238; deterioration under Mao, 219–220; Nixon's move toward new policy, 223–228; reestablished diplomatic relations, 233–234; post–Cold War, 243–248; under Reagan, 243–244; under George H. W. Bush, 244–245; under Clinton, 245–246; under George W. Bush, 246; under Obama, 246–247; historic to present, 256–257. *See also* Cold War; Group of Two (G-2) concept
Polk, James K., 43

Qing dynasty, 10–12; 1911 revolution against (*see* Republican Revolution of 1911); and Tongzhi Restoration, 92, 99

Race, advocates for miscegenation, 70–73
Racism: George Washington's understanding of Oriental "race," 26; American attitudes toward Chinese, 78–84, 206–208; in American publications, 249–250
Railroads, laid by Chinese labor, 77–78
Rape of Nanjing, 159
Reagan, Ronald, 234–235, 240–241, 243–244
Red Star over China, 150–151
Reinsch, Paul S., 114–116, 135, 151
Remarks on China and the China Trade, 27–28
Republican Revolution of 1911, 109–112
Republic of China. *See* Guomindang (GMD); Taiwan
Revolution of 1911. *See* Republican Revolution of 1911
Ricci, Mateo, 52–53
Robert Browne, 76–77
Roberts, Issachar J., 61–62
Robeson, Paul, 210
Rogers, Will, 130,144–146, 148
Rong Hong. *See* Yung Wing
Roosevelt, Franklin Delano, 27, 151, 154, 160, 166, 169, 171, 176, 180, 187; personal connection to China, 143–144, 220, 264
Roosevelt, Theodore, and America's destiny in Pacific, 86, 94, 100, 102

Index

Roosevelt Corollary to the Monroe Doctrine, 87

Roosevelt/Truman policies, conservative opposition, 197–200

Rusk, Dean, characterizing Communist China, 201

San Francisco, founding Chinese institutions in, 72

Scott, Charles Ernest, 60

Second Great Awakening, 54–55

Service, John S., 184, 218, 266

Seward, William Henry, 71, 85, 93–95

Shanghai, Japanese attack, 158–159

Shaw, Samuel, 19, 28

Silk, American demand, 117

Silk Road, 8

Slavery. *See* Coolie trade

Smedley, Agnes, 149, 170, 181

Smith, Arthur H., 83–84

Snow, Edgar, 150–156, 164, 170, 178, 256; respect for Chinese Communists, 181–182; role in opening U.S.-China relations, 224–225

Snow, Helen Foster, 149

Soong family, 111, 134–135, 165, 170, 172–173, 191, 265

Soong Mayling, 170, 172, 192; tour of America, 175–179

Soviet Union: China's alliance, 115; as model for Communist Party of China (CPC), 130–131; view of Chinese as Communists, 185–186; and Cold War politics, 204–205; fractured relationship with China, 206, 219

Speer, William, 61–65, 71–74

Stiles, Ezra, interest in China, 25

Stilwell, "Vinegar" Joe, 178–180

Stimson, Henry, 137–140, 162

Strong, Anna Louise, 149, 181

Stuart, John Leighton, 136, 189–197, 265; attacked by Mao, 189, 195; years in America, 190, 195–197; as POW, 191

Sturgis, Russell, and Anglo-Chinese War, 34–35

Sullivan, Michael, 128–129

Summer Palace, destruction, 50

Sun Yatsen, 109–111, 115. *See also* Guomindang (GMD)

Taft, William Howard, 112

Taft, Helen, 117

Taiping Rebellion, 61–63

Taiwan: as "fictional" China, 204; Nixon's support, 221–222

Tea Act of 1773, 15–16

Tea trade, 16, 21–22

Thomson, James C., Jr., 196, 230

Tian'anmen Square tragedy, 236; impact on foreign trade, 241–242; political fallout, 244

Tobey, Mark, 121

Tongwen Guan, 92

Tongzhi Restoration, 92

Treaty of Beijing, 63

Treaty of Tianjin, 63

Treaty of Wangxia, 36–38

Treaty system, unfair to China, 49–51, 63, 107, 115

Twain, Mark, in defense of China, 107

Tyler, John, 32, 37

United China Relief, 164–165

United States. *See entries for America*

"The Unparalleled Invasion," 81–82

Updike, John, and peril literature, 250–251

Versailles Peace Conference, impact on U.S.-Chinese relations, 114–116

Vietnam War, depicted as war with China, 208–209. *See also* Asia: "hot wars"

Ward, Frederick Townshend, 62

Washington, George, knowledge of China, 26

Webster, Daniel, 32, 35, 42

Westward expansion, 40–43; and lure of Far East, 3, 40, 43–46; and Manifest Destiny, 42–43; and Whitney's vision of rail line, 44–45; Thomas Hart Benton's vision, 70–71

Whistler, James McNeill, 120

Whitney, Asa, 42–45

"Who lost China?" 6, 199

Wilbur, Ray Lyman, 123, 165–166

Williams, Robert F., 212–213

Wilson, Woodrow, and China policy, 112–115, 123, 190, 220

World Trade Organization, China admission, 245–246

World War I: U.S.-Chinese relations following, 114–116; and rise of Communist China, 130–131

World War II: Manchurian Incident as lead-up, 142; America's entry, 168

Worthy, William, defiance of travel ban to China, 210

Index

Wu Bingjian, 22, 28
Wu Tingfang, 84, 108, 150

Xi'an Incident, 158
Xi Jinping, 215, 247, 253–254
Xinhai Geming. See Republican Revolution
of 1911

Yanjing University, 136, 151, 164, 189,
190–191, 193, 196
Yankee clipper ships, 22
"Yellow face" actors, 177–178
"Yellow peril": and nineteenth-century
racism, 80–84; literature depicting,

81–82, 249–250; fears during Cold War,
206–208
You Can Get There from Here, 231
Young, John Russell, 97–98
Yuan Shikai, 111, 113–114
Yung Wing, 66–67, 92, 96, 124, 150

Zhang Deyi, 85
Zhang, Shuqi, 264
Zhou Enlai, 115, 131, 133, 150, 172, 175, 191,
193, 196, 226, 266; and Nixon's visit to China,
227; depicted in *Nixon in China*, 237–238
Zhuang Zedong, 225
Zongli Yamen, establishment of, 92